LIBERALISM AND CAPITALISM

LIBERALISM AND CAPITALISM

Edited by

**Ellen Frankel Paul, Fred D. Miller, Jr.,
and Jeffrey Paul**

 **CAMBRIDGE**
UNIVERSITY PRESS

PUBLISHED BY THE PRESS SYNDICATE OF THE UNIVERSITY OF CAMBRIDGE
The Pitt Building, Trumpington Street, Cambridge, United Kingdom

CAMBRIDGE UNIVERSITY PRESS
The Edinburgh Building, Cambridge CB2 8RU, UK
32 Avenue of the Americas, New York, NY 10013-2473, USA
477 Williamstown Road, Port Melbourne, VIC 3207, Australia
Ruiz de Alarcón 13, 28014 Madrid, Spain
Dock House, The Waterfront, Cape Town 8001, South Africa

http://www.cambridge.org

First published 2011

Printed in the United States of America

Typeface Palatino 10/12 pt.

A catalog record for this book is available from the British Library

Library of Congress Cataloging-in-Publication Data
Liberalism and Capitalism
edited by Ellen Frankel Paul, Fred D. Miller, Jr., and Jeffrey Paul.   p.   cm.
Includes bibliographical references and index.
ISBN 978-1-107-64026-9

1. Liberalism. 2. Capitalism.
I. Paul, Ellen Frankel. II. Miller, Fred Dycus, 1944- III. Paul, Jeffrey.

JC574.L5187 2011
320.51--dc22

The essays in this book have also been published,
without introduction and index, in the semiannual journal
Social Philosophy & Policy, Volume 28, Number 2,
which is available by subscription.

CONTENTS

INTRODUCTION

What are the core values of liberalism, and how can they best be promoted? Liberals in the classical tradition championed individual freedom, limited government, and a capitalist economic system with strong
rights to private property. Contemporary liberals, in contrast, embrace
more egalitarian values and allow for a far more prominent role for
government intervention in the market to reduce inequality, redistribute
wealth, and regulate economic activity. What accounts for these very
disparate liberal views of property rights and economic freedom? How
should we understand the transition from the classical view of liberalism
to its more egalitarian modern version? And what, ideally, should the
relationship be between the central values of liberalism and the economic
institutions of capitalism?

The eleven essays in this volume address these questions and examine
related issues. Some of them look at the shift from classical to modern
liberalism, analyzing the influence of transitional figures such as John
Stuart Mill, or focusing on the differences between the political philosophy of the American founding generation and the Progressive Movement
of the early twentieth century. Some essays consider the right to private
property, asking how it can best be justified, or tracing its historical development in U.S. constitutional law. Other essays explore the relationship
between government and its citizens in a liberal society: they seek to
determine the proper role of the state in regulating financial institutions,
providing access to medical care, or redistributing wealth. Still other
essays examine the influence of socialist ideals on contemporary liberals,
asking whether socialist values can be achieved under free-market institutions, or looking at the similarities between modern welfare liberalism
in the United States and social democracy in Europe.

The collection opens with three essays that explore the differences
between classical and modern liberalism. In "The Paradox of John Stuart
Mill," Alan Charles Kors looks at the role Mill plays as a transitional
figure between nineteenth-century liberalism, with its emphasis on the
creative power of free individuals unfettered by government or social
interventions, and twentieth-century liberalism, with its combination of
individual choice in matters of belief and lifestyle (on the one hand) and
collective control of the distribution of wealth through the welfare state
(on the other). Kors begins with a discussion of Mill's *On Liberty* (1859)
and *The Subjection of Women* (1869), which offer a utilitarian defense of
individual freedom, self-sovereignty, and voluntary association. Indeed,
although *On Liberty* is often read primarily as a defense of freedom of
belief and expression, Mill held that its arguments also applied to the

freedom to choose one's way of life, one's preferences, and one's use of one's time. As Kors notes, Mill appears to extend this freedom explicitly to the economic sphere when he argues that individuals should be free to carry their ideas into practice at their own cost, provided they do not directly harm others. Nonetheless, there is a separate strand of Mill's thought, put forward in his *Principles of Political Economy* (first published in 1848 and later revised through seven editions), which undermines the case for economic freedom and opens the door to governmental redistribution of wealth. Kors goes on to show how Mill's distinction in the *Principles* between the production and the distribution of wealth sets the stage for the modern welfare state. On Mill's view, the distribution of wealth is entirely a matter of convention: once wealth has been produced, a society is free to distribute it as it sees fit. Kors concludes with a brief discussion of Mill's posthumously published *Chapters on Socialism* (1879) and argues that while Mill rejected many of the socialists' central claims, he nonetheless favored an active and interventionist state that would use political power to improve the condition of workers.

In "Capitalism in the Classical and High Liberal Traditions," Samuel Freeman discusses the distinguishing features of two major liberal traditions and their respective positions regarding capitalism as an economic and social system. The first of these traditions, classical liberalism, evolved from the works of Adam Smith and the classical utilitarian economists; its major twentieth-century representatives include Friedrich Hayek and Milton Friedman. The second—which Freeman calls the high liberal tradition—developed from John Stuart Mill's works, and its major philosophical representatives in the twentieth century were John Dewey and, later, John Rawls. As Freeman notes, both traditions hold that legitimate political power is limited and is to be impartially exercised, only for the public good. Liberals of both traditions assign political priority to maintaining certain basic liberties and equality of opportunity. They advocate an essential role for markets in economic activity, and they recognize government's crucial role in correcting market breakdowns and providing public goods. While acknowledging these commonalities, Freeman's essay focuses on the differences between the two traditions, specifically with respect to economic freedom. Classical liberals regard economic liberties and rights of private property in productive resources to be nearly as important as basic liberties. They consider capitalist markets and the price system as essential not only to the allocation of productive resources, but also as the fundamental criterion for the just distribution of income, wealth, and economic powers. High liberals, by contrast, regard the economic liberties as subordinate to the exercise of personal and civil liberties. They are prepared to regulate and restrict economic liberties to achieve greater equality of opportunity, to reduce inequalities of economic power, and to promote a broad conception of the public good. Moreover, while high liberals endorse markets and the price system as essential to the allocation of productive resources, they do not regard markets as the fundamental criterion for assessing just distributions of income, wealth, and positions of responsibility within the social order. Freeman concludes his essay with some reflections on the role that dissimilar conceptions of persons and society play in grounding the different positions on economic justice that classical liberals and high liberals advocate.

Ronald J. Pestritto examines the transformation that took place in American liberalism during the Progressive era in his contribution to this volume, "Founding Liberalism, Progressive Liberalism, and the Rights of Property." He notes that the Progressive Movement of the early twentieth century represented a rejection of the eighteenth-century understanding of equality and natural rights embodied in the American Declaration of Independence. The Declaration's statement that "all men are created equal" meant that no individual could claim a natural right to rule another; rather, each individual had an equal right to preserve his own life and liberty, and to pursue his own happiness. In the view of the founding generation, the purpose of government was to secure these rights. Pestritto goes on to observe that the American founders understood property as essential to the pursuit of happiness, and thus held that government had an obligation to protect citizens' rights to the property they earned through their labor. In the remainder of the essay, Pestritto shows how the Progressives rejected this view of property rights in theory and in practice. Progressive theorists such as John Dewey and Woodrow Wilson maintained that the founding generation's view of rights and the role of government needed to be understood as a product of its historical context. In this way, the Progressives were able to argue that while strong protections for property rights might have been appropriate at the time of the American founding, they were no longer appropriate in the twentieth century, given the different circumstances and challenges faced by modern society. Pestritto concludes with a discussion of how Progressive political leaders, including Theodore Roosevelt, sought to employ the power of government to regulate the use of private property in ways that they believed would promote equality and improve the lives of ordinary working people.

The question of how to define and justify property rights within a liberal society is also the subject of the next two essays in this collection. In "The Property Equilibrium in a Liberal Social Order (or How to Correct Our Moral Vision)," Gerald Gaus notes that over the last four decades—following the publication of John Rawls's *A Theory of Justice* in 1971—political philosophers have put forward a variety of proposals seeking to show that philosophical reflection leads to the demonstrable truth of almost every conceivable view of the justice of property rights. Indeed, the method of rational reflection that Rawls developed has been used to justify unregulated capitalist markets (on the one hand) and the most extreme forms of egalitarianism (on the other). On Gaus's view, this trend represents an intrusion of ideology into the realm of political theory, as political philosophers devise elaborate arguments designed to show that their personal convictions concerning the proper organization of society are, in fact, supported by impartial reasoning. In practice, this leads to a politicization of private morality, as each individual theorist comes to believe that social institutions should be designed or altered to conform with his own moral intuitions or the dictates of his private conscience. As an alternative, Gaus seeks to use the tools of game theory to sketch a nonideological approach to the justification of social institutions—in particular, the institution of property. According to this approach, the primary aim of political philosophy is to reflect on whether our social rules of property are within what he calls the "optimal eligible set" of rules acceptable to all. If we follow this approach, Gaus argues, we will not seek to construct a system of morality from scratch; rather, we will seek to determine whether our existing rules and institutions fall within the optimal eligible set. That is, we will attempt to discover whether well-informed and good-willed individuals have reasons to endorse these rules and institutions. If we follow this approach, he concludes, we are likely to discover that more than one system of property rules may fall within the optimal eligible set.

In "Judicial Liberalism and Capitalism: Justice Field Reconsidered," Michael P. Zuckert explores a theory of judicial interpretation that is often thought to be especially friendly to the protection of property rights and economic liberties. This theory—known as substantive due process—holds that there are substantive (and not merely procedural) limits on what government may do under the due process clauses of the Fifth and Fourteenth Amendments of the U.S. Constitution. Zuckert proceeds by examining the judicial thought of one of this theory's strongest proponents, Justice Stephen J. Field, who served on the U.S. Supreme Court from 1863 to 1897. While critics of Field have contended that his jurisprudence was influenced by laissez-faire economic theory or by his sympathy for business interests, Zuckert sets out to show that it was in fact based on a philosophy of natural rights, which Field understood to be grounded in the Constitution. Field's belief in individual rights to liberty, property, and freedom of contract led him to embrace a strong presumption in favor of individual autonomy and freedom from governmental regulation. On his view, it was possible for the state to overcome this presumption, but to do so the state had the burden of demonstrating that it was exercising its power for legitimate ends, and that the means it employed were congruent with the achievement of those ends. In order to illustrate Field's judicial philosophy, Zuckert discusses a number of prominent Supreme Court cases concerning how government may regulate the use of private property. He argues that Field's opinions in these cases make it clear that he believed the state could legitimately take private property for genuinely public uses, could levy taxes on property for the support of government, and could limit uses of property that would violate the rights of others. At the same time, Field held that government action that went beyond these purposes (e.g., the regulation of prices) was illegitimate. Zuckert concludes that Field's judicial philosophy was not as unambiguously friendly to laissez-faire capitalism as some scholars have maintained, but that it was nonetheless far friendlier than many of the constitutional theories that have prevailed since Field's day.

The collection continues with four essays that consider the proper role of government in a liberal state. In "Liberty After Lehman Brothers," Loren E. Lomasky addresses the role of government in financial regulation, especially in the aftermath of the global financial crisis of 2008. He notes that theorists on both the left and the right have used the crisis to confirm their own long-held beliefs. Voices on the left have claimed that the crisis heralds the end of laissez-faire economic policy and that only careful governmental regulation of financial institutions can rein in the excesses of unchecked capitalism. Voices on the right have countered that existing regulations played a key role in provoking the crisis—pointing, for example, to the political and regulatory pressures that drove Fannie Mae and Freddie Mac to extend housing loans to less creditworthy borrowers. Lomasky believes that each of these explanations is too easy. In order to come to a better understanding, he discusses a series of paradoxes that help illuminate the causes of the 2008 crisis. The paradox of efficient markets states that if participants in the economy believe markets are efficient, they will assume that assets are priced accurately, rather than investing in research to assess the real value of the assets in which they invest; but as more and more participants forgo such research, markets become less efficient. The paradox of reduced risk states that if financial institutions believe they have reduced their level of risk (e.g., by diversifying their investments), they will conclude that it is safe to take on higher levels of debt; but as many interconnected institutions follow the same strategy, the level of risk in the marketplace increases dramatically. The paradox of hard-won knowledge states that as economists and regulators learn more about financial crises and how best to deal with them, they may become overconfident; if they assume that future crises will resemble those of the past, they may be slow to recognize and respond to novel circumstances. After discussing each of these paradoxes in detail, Lomasky concludes by setting out his own recommendations for preventing financial meltdowns. These include increasing capital reserve requirements for banks and financial firms and placing limits on the size of some financial institutions.

Daniel M. Hausman looks at the role of the state in the provision of medical care in his essay, "A Lockean Argument for Universal Access to Health Care." Although libertarian admirers of the political thought of John Locke typically oppose government involvement in health care provision, Hausman seeks to defend the counterintuitive claim that there is a good case to be made from a Lockean perspective for government action to guarantee access to health care. He begins by sketching what he takes to be the central values of the Lockean view, namely, the protection of life and property and the protection of individual freedom, understood in terms of independence and self-determination. While libertarian followers of Locke identify the protection of freedom with the protection of a right to be free from the interference of others, Hausman argues that the Lockean position is consistent with a broader role for government. On his interpretation of Locke's view, government may legitimately take action to secure any objective that is essential to citizen's independence and self-determination, provided that people are unable to secure the objective on their own, and provided that the government's action does not itself undermine the protection of life, property, and freedom. Hausman argues that government action to secure citizens' access to medical care satisfies each of these conditions. In the course of his essay, he compares his approach with the defense of universal health care proposed by Norman Daniels, which rests on a principle of fair equality of opportunity. Hausman points out a number of difficulties that Daniels's argument faces, and shows how the Lockean approach avoids these difficulties. Hausman concludes that a strong Lockean argument can be made in favor of the proposition that, just as government legitimately acts to protect citizens from crime and foreign invasion, it may also legitimately act to secure their access to basic health care.

In "Euvoluntary or Not, Exchange Is Just," Michael C. Munger explores the role of government in the regulation of commercial transactions and the redistribution of wealth. He begins by noting a feature of free-market exchange that many observers find troubling: namely, the fact that a series of voluntary exchanges that leave both parties better off can lead to large inequalities of wealth that critics of capitalism view as unjust. Faced with this fact, critics of the market may argue that seemingly voluntary transactions are not genuinely voluntary, since they take place between parties (e.g., employers and employees) who exercise sharply unequal bargaining power. Moreover, such critics may use this inequality to justify government intervention in the market to prevent the exploitation of the disadvantaged, and to redistribute the wealth created by market exchange. Munger contends that critics who embrace this sort of government intervention are relying on a mistaken conception of market exchange—and that allowing genuinely voluntary exchange actually tends to ameliorate the social injustices that critics find troubling. Munger introduces the term "euvoluntary exchange" to indicate exchanges characterized by an absence of both regret and coercion—that is, exchanges in which (1) both parties receive value that is at least as great as they anticipated prior to making the exchange, and (2) neither party is forced to exchange, either by the threat of violence or by the prospect of suffering some harm (e.g., starvation) if the exchange doesn't go through. He goes on to argue that

all euvoluntary exchanges should be permitted and that there is no justification for redistributive policies if disparities in wealth result only
from euvoluntary exchanges. In addition, he discusses a number of examples of transactions that are not euvoluntary, such as situations in which
merchants take advantage of desperate people by charging higher than
normal prices for essential supplies in the aftermath of a hurricane or
some other natural disaster. Even in these cases, Munger concludes,
exchanges should generally be permitted, because access to market
exchange may be the only means by which people in desperate circumstances can improve their position.

In "Rule Consequentialism Makes Sense After All," Tyler Cowen considers the merits of rule consequentialism as it relates to the justification of specific social policies and the justification of a liberal social
order in general. He notes that free-market advocates such as F. A.
Hayek and James Buchanan have linked their arguments for a free
society to the validity of a rule-based perspective. On their view, we
should look for rules that best define the scope of government rather
than evaluating each government policy on a case-by-case basis. As
Cowen observes, however, rule consequentialism is commonly held to
be vulnerable to the objection that it can be reduced to act consequentialism. The rule consequentialist holds that we should guide our conduct by those rules whose observance leads to the best consequences
overall; yet in specific situations we may be able to achieve a better
outcome by violating the rule. In such situations, the act consequentialist can object that if we really care about consequences, we should
follow rules only when doing so leads to the best consequences; thus,
rule consequentialism collapses into act consequentialism. But Cowen
suggests that this line of argument is less powerful than has been supposed, because it makes certain (implicit) assumptions that turn out to
be implausible. These assumptions have to do with the constraints under
which we make choices. The rule consequentialist seeks to choose a
policy today that will be applied in subsequent time periods by many
different agents, while the act consequentialist seeks to choose an action
for a single individual at one point in time. In the former case, the
focus is on a "bundle" of choices; in the latter, the focus is on a single
choice. Cowen argues that treating a bundle of choices as the relevant
variable is no less defensible than treating a single act as the relevant
variable. He concludes that rule consequentialism and other rule-based
approaches to policymaking are stronger than their critics would have
us believe.

The collection's final two essays examine the relationship between modern liberalism and socialism. In "Liberalism, Capitalism, and 'Socialist'
Principles," Richard J. Arneson asks whether free-market institutions are
compatible with the fulfillment of socialist ideals. He takes as his starting-
point an argument put forward by the political philosopher G. A. Cohen,

who held that the two are strongly incompatible. In order to illustrate the socialist principles he had in mind, Cohen offered the example of a group of friends organizing a camping trip. He imagined that for the duration of the trip, the members of the group treat their camping gear as common property; they approach the trip in a spirit of fellowship, dividing chores fairly and efficiently; and they commit themselves to ensuring that everyone enjoys the trip and is (roughly) equally fulfilled by the experience. Cohen argued that the camping trip model embodies principles of community and equal opportunity that are at once ethically attractive and incompatible with capitalism, and he added that if it is possible for a society to organize its economy according to this model, it ought to do so. In response, Arneson observes that Cohen failed to show that his socialist principles could not be promoted within a free-market economic system, using the familiar devices of taxation and redistribution (for instance) to advance equality of opportunity. More importantly, Arneson argues that Cohen's principles are, in fact, not attractive, and that they ought to be rejected. The socialist principle of community, for example, requires that those who are better off must work to improve the lot of those who are worse off, even if the latter are worse off through their own fault or choice. Arneson goes on to criticize Cohen's principle of equality of opportunity in detail and to reject the notion that equality of distribution (of opportunities or resources) is desirable in itself. Instead, Arneson concludes that our attitudes toward values like equality and freedom should depend on whether these values promote or hinder the advancement of people's welfare.

In "Are Modern American Liberals Socialists or Social Democrats?" N. Scott Arnold examines the extent to which contemporary liberals have embraced the values and ideals of socialism and social democracy. Arnold divides his essay into two main parts, with the first arguing that contemporary liberals are socialists, and the second arguing that they are also social democrats. The primary feature of a socialist system is collective ownership of the means of production, and although such collective ownership does not exist formally in the United States, Arnold maintains that the U.S. government has effectively taken control of the incidents of ownership (i.e., the bundle of rights and privileges that comprise ownership)—and has done so with the full support of modern American liberals. Though the ownership of property remains nominally in private hands, the state exercises extensive control over property in two ways: through its taxing and spending authority, the state has a kind of priority of ownership with respect to the income and wealth associated with private property; and, through its power to regulate, it is free to impose wide-ranging (and uncompensated) burdens on property owners. Arnold goes on to contend that modern American liberals, in striving to reduce levels of inequality in the U.S., have endorsed a set of institutions that, in effect, replicate the institutions of social democracy. These institutions are, at their core, forms of compulsory social insurance: they include unemployment insurance and workers' compensation (both with mandatory contributions by employers), Social Security, and the restructuring of the American health-care system with the stated aim of guaranteeing universal access. The foundation underlying all these institutions is the assumption—shared by American liberals and social democrats—that the market is not to be trusted and that it must be subordinated to politics so that it can serve the interests of society. Thus, Arnold concludes that contemporary American liberals have accepted the values of both socialism and social democracy, and in so doing have strayed from the original liberal ideals of the American founding generation.

Liberalism has a rich tradition as a political theory, from its classical version to its contemporary egalitarian and welfarist variants. The essays in this volume offer important insights into the nature of liberal values and the relationship between liberal government and capitalist economic institutions.

ACKNOWLEDGMENTS

The editors wish to acknowledge several individuals at the Social Philosophy and Policy Center, Bowling Green State University, who provided invaluable assistance in the preparation of this volume. They include Mary Dilsaver, Terrie Weaver, and Program Manager Ben Dyer.

The editors also extend special thanks to Administrative Editor Tamara Sharp, for attending to innumerable day-to-day details of the book's preparation, and to Managing Editors Harry Dolan and Pamela Phillips, for providing dedicated assistance throughout the editorial and production process.

CONTRIBUTORS

Alan Charles Kors is Henry Charles Lea Professor of European History at the University of Pennsylvania. He received his Ph.D. in European History from Harvard University. He has published several books and many articles on early-modern French intellectual history, and was editor-in-chief of the four-volume *Encyclopedia of the Enlightenment* (2002). A member of the National Council for the Humanities, he has received fellowships from the American Council for Learned Societies, the Smith-Richardson Foundation, and the Davis Center for Historical Studies at Princeton University. In 2003–2004, he was a Phi Beta Kappa Visiting Scholar, lecturing nationally on intellectual history and on academic freedom. In 2005, he received the National Humanities Medal.

Samuel Freeman is Avalon Professor of the Humanities and Professor of Philosophy and Law at the University of Pennsylvania. He is the author of two books, *Justice and the Social Contract* (2006) and *Rawls* (2007). He edited John Rawls's *Collected Papers* (1999) and his *Lectures on the History of Political Philosophy* (2007). In addition, he edited *The Cambridge Companion to Rawls* (2003) and (with R. J. Wallace and Rahul Kumar) *Reasons and Recognition: Essays on the Philosophy of T. M. Scanlon* (2011).

Ronald J. Pestritto is Charles and Lucia Shipley Chair in the American Constitution and Associate Professor of Politics at Hillsdale College, where he teaches political philosophy, American political thought, and American politics. He is Senior Fellow of the College's Kirby Center for Constitutional Studies and Citizenship and Senior Fellow of the Claremont Institute for the Study of Statesmanship and Political Philosophy. He has published seven books, including *Woodrow Wilson and the Roots of Modern Liberalism* (2005) and *American Progressivism* (2008). Among his other books are an edited collection of Wilson's speeches and writings entitled *Woodrow Wilson: The Essential Political Writings* (2005), a three-book series on American political thought, and *Founding the Criminal Law: Punishment and Political Thought in the Origins of America* (2000).

Gerald Gaus is James E. Rogers Professor of Philosophy at the University of Arizona, where he directs the program in Philosophy, Politics, Economics, and Law. Among his books are *On Philosophy, Politics, and Economics* (2008), *Justificatory Liberalism* (1996), and *Value and Justification* (1990). His most recent book is *The Order of Public Reason: A Theory of Freedom and Morality in a Diverse and Bounded World* (2010). Currently he and Julian Lamont are writing a book entitled *Economic Justice*, and with Fred

CONTRIBUTORS

D'Agostino he is editing the *Routledge Companion to Social and Political Philosophy.*

Michael P. Zuckert is Nancy R. Dreux Professor of Political Science at the University of Notre Dame. He has written extensively on the liberal tradition in political philosophy and American constitutionalism. He is the author of several books, including *The Natural Rights Republic* (1996), *Launching Liberalism: John Locke and the Liberal Tradition* (2002), and, most recently, *Natural Rights and American Constitutionalism* (2011).

Loren E. Lomasky is Cory Professor of Political Philosophy, Policy, and Law at the University of Virginia, where he directs the Philosophy, Politics, and Law program. He previously taught at Bowling Green State University and the University of Minnesota, Duluth, and has held visiting positions at Virginia Polytechnic Institute, Australian National University, the Australian Defence Force Academy, and the National University of Singapore. He is the author of *Persons, Rights, and the Moral Community* (1987), for which he was awarded the 1990 Matchette Prize. With Geoffrey Brennan he coauthored *Democracy and Decision: The Pure Theory of Electoral Preference* (1993) and coedited *Politics and Process: New Essays in Democratic Theory* (1989).

Daniel M. Hausman is Herbert A. Simon Professor of Philosophy at the University of Wisconsin–Madison and a member of the American Academy of Arts and Sciences. He is the author of *Capital Profits and Prices* (1981), *The Inexact and Separate Science of Economics* (1992), *Causal Asymmetries* (1998), and, with Michael McPherson, *Economic Analysis, Moral Philosophy, and Public Policy* (second edition, 2006). He has published more than 150 essays and reviews and is a cofounder, with Michael McPherson, of the journal *Economics and Philosophy*. His most recent research focuses on philosophical questions concerning generic health measurement, and he is currently completing a book on preferences, as they are understood in economics, philosophy, psychology, and everyday life.

Michael C. Munger is Professor of Political Science, Public Policy, and Economics at Duke University, where he served as chair of the Political Science Department for ten years. He directs Duke's Philosophy, Politics, and Economics program, working with Geoffrey Sayre-McCord at the University of North Carolina to run the joint program. He received his Ph.D. in Economics from Washington University in St. Louis in 1984.

Tyler Cowen is Holbert C. Harris Professor of Economics at George Mason University and is General Director of both the Mercatus Center and the James M. Buchanan Center for Political Economy. He is the author of numerous books, including, most recently, *The Age of the Infovore: Succeed-*

ing in the Information Economy (2010). In addition to his work in econom-
ics, he has also published in philosophy journals, including *Ethics* and
Philosophy and Public Affairs. He cowrites with Alex Tabarrok the blog
Marginal Revolution at www.marginalrevolution.com.

Richard J. Arneson is Distinguished Professor of Philosophy at the University of California, San Diego. He has published more than a hundred
essays on moral and political philosophy. Most of his work is on topics in
the theory of justice. He has recently published essays on Lockean libertarianism, on the justification of democracy, and on the interpretation and
defense of luck-egalitarian approaches to distributive justice.

N. Scott Arnold is Professor of Philosophy at the University of Alabama
at Birmingham, where he has taught since 1982. During 1991–1992, he
was a Title VIII Fellow at the Hoover Institution on War, Revolution, and
Peace, and he returned there as a Visiting Scholar in the summer of 1999.
He is the author of *Marx's Radical Critique of Capitalist Society* (1990) and
The Philosophy and Economics of Market Socialism (1994), and is the coeditor
(with Theodore M. Benditt and George Graham) of *Philosophy Then and
Now* (1998).

ACKNOWLEDGMENT

The editors gratefully acknowledge Liberty Fund, Inc., for holding the conference at which the original versions of many of these papers were presented and discussed.

THE PARADOX OF JOHN STUART MILL

By Alan Charles Kors

I. The "Mill Problem"

It is only the individuals or thinkers one loves who truly break one's heart. In the case of those thinkers, who has broken more hearts than John Stuart Mill? For defenders of individual rights—those who value the self-sovereignty of the individual in those actions that concern only the individual directly—*On Liberty* (1859) stands as a singular work, whatever its apparent and diversely perceived problems and flaws. For some, it fails to address the problems of social order sufficiently. For some, while it rightly limits governmental direction of individual lives, it gives too much power to social judgment and the coercion of public obloquy. For some, its final chapters, on "Applications," give too much power to the state—for example, the ability to tax rather than ban what the public deems vices. Most of these problems arise when readers seek to apply Mill as a blueprint or (worse yet as a category mistake) a constitution. Mill establishes two poles—first, an individual's freedom of choice about what is best for him or her in the domain of self-regarding beliefs and activities, and second, the molding and coercing of adult individuals by society itself—and he believes that it is in our individual and our communal interest to move, where possible, toward the former pole.

On Liberty is Mill's celebration of individuality, personal responsibility, freedom of speech and expression, human diversity in belief and in ways of life, and, indeed, the utility and, he stresses, the loveliness of self-defined lives. It is a work that occupies a remarkable place in the canon of the literature of liberty. In generation after generation, students of all ages fall in love with its author. Then they discover the other lives of Mill. The thinker one loves has had relationships with others. Between the Mill of individual liberty and of limits on power that allow a voluntary, uncoerced civilization in matters of belief, expression, association, and lifestyle, on the one hand, and the Mill of political economy, on the other, there falls the shadow. He has been living a double life. To put the matter directly and without metaphor, he is the critical transitional figure between the ideas of the liberalism of limited government and the values of the liberalism of the active public-welfare state.

II. The Satisfactions of *On Liberty*

Every sympathetic reader of *On Liberty* has experienced moments in the text or in discussions with others—Could public support of virtue be

doi:10.1017/S0265052510000191

dangerous? Do his "Applications" betray his principles? Is he consistent about the coercive dangers of public opinion?—that have raised doubts, large or small, about Mill's commitment to liberty taken in the sense that the reader first admired. These doubts, however, should not cloud the unparalleled defense of liberty one encounters there.

Mill carved out, in the endless debate between rights theorists and utilitarians, a strong and luminous position: individual rights were of ultimate utility to the human species. Where his mentor, Jeremy Bentham, notoriously declared "natural rights" to be "nonsense on stilts" in his *A Critical Examination of the Declaration of Rights*,[1] Mill found rights that were protected from state and social action to be indispensable to utilitarian theory itself. Absent those rights, the human species would suffer and stagnate. Mill indeed famously refused any advantage that might accrue to his argument for expansive individual liberty—if consistent with the preservation of society and with preventing direct harm to others—from claims of abstract natural rights. He would rest his case on utility.

Nonetheless, unlike Bentham (the most celebrated English utilitarian of the prior generation), Mill rejected the traditional utilitarian formula of "the greatest happiness of the greatest number," which Bentham had taken from the Milanese Enlightenment legal reformer Cesare Beccaria's *On Crimes and Punishments* (1764) and from the French Enlightenment philosopher Claude-Adrien Helvétius's *De l'Esprit* (1758). For Mill, short-term or even intermediate-term calculations of happiness were a wholly inadequate means of making moral judgments about human governance and about intervention in the life of the individual. Rather, he insisted, his own criterion of utility would be "utility in the largest sense, grounded on the permanent interests of man as a progressive being."[2]

In that "largest sense," for Mill, the present and, more importantly, the future needed individuals who had experienced self-sovereignty and responsibility. From that perspective, what mattered above all was not the positive things men accomplished in any particular frame of time, but, rather, "what manner of men" accomplished them, because only free individuals, responsible (absent *direct* harm to others) for their thoughts, expressions, choices, behaviors, and associations, could learn from trial and error and thus be agents of human adaptation and improvement.[3] Mill was concerned that "harm to others" could be taken too broadly, justifying a great amount of public intervention, so he propounded his doctrine narrowly: "The liberty of the individual must be thus far limited;

---

[1] This essay was first published in 1843, in a collection entitled *Anarchical Fallacies*. See Jeremy Bentham, *The Works of Jeremy Bentham*, ed. John Bowring (Edinburgh: William Tait, 1838–43), vol. II, *A Critical Examination of the Declaration of Rights*, "Preliminary Observations," art. II.

[2] John Stuart Mill, *On Liberty*, in Mill, *On Liberty with The Subjection of Women and Chapters on Socialism*, ed. Stefan Collini (Cambridge and New York: Cambridge University Press, 1989), 14.

[3] Ibid., 59–60.

he must not make himself a nuisance to other people. But if he refrains from molesting others in what concerns them, and merely acts according to his own inclination and judgment in things which concern himself, the same reasons which show that opinion should be free, prove also that he should be allowed, without molestation, to carry his opinions into practice at his own cost." [4] Later, Mill will ask society always to err on the side of self-sovereignty in deciding between direct and indirect harm: "But with regard to the merely contingent, or, as it may be called, constructive injury which a person causes to society, by conduct which neither violates any specific duty to the public, nor occasions perceptible hurt to any assignable individual except himself; the inconvenience is one which society can afford to bear, for the sake of the greater good of human freedom." [5]

For Mill, individual liberty and responsibility formed a *mode*—a manner, or form—of being human, and utility resided in that mode, not in any particular outcome. By analogy (mine, not Mill's), people might find a rightful outcome and satisfaction in frontier justice meted out to some miscreant. We preserve the more valuable form of justice, however—the civilized and civilizing mode of due process—in order to achieve a far greater good. Providing due process is a mode of administering justice that both elevates us and serves humanity deeply in the long run.

For Mill, such beneficial freedom ultimately was the unrestrained ability to act or abstain in all matters that did not affect others immediately and directly, however much Mill formally dissociated himself from any talk of theoretical right. In Mill's view, with respect to the part of conduct that does not directly harm others, a man's "independence is, *of right, absolute.*" [6] Over things affecting only himself directly, "the individual is sovereign." [7] Neither government nor society could appropriately deny such liberty to the individual. As Mill revealingly phrased it, certain individual interests "*ought to be considered as rights,*" a conclusion justified by long-term utility. [8] Individual self-government, individual choice, and individual responsibility for one's actions created better human beings, and better human beings, over time, created better societies. Paternalism might achieve its short-term goals, but it would kill the very spirit and dynamic that made for decent individuals and progressive societies. By analogy, to capture Mill's meaning, one well might achieve short-term happiness or avoidance of pain for one's children by means of frontal lobotomies, but their future intelligence, creativity, and self-fulfillment would be ruined. Thus, Mill offered a modal, long-term, utilitarian argument for individual rights in matters of belief, expression, association, and self-regarding behaviors.

[4] Ibid., 56–57.
[5] Ibid., 82.
[6] Ibid., 13 (emphasis added).
[7] Ibid.
[8] Ibid., 75 (emphasis added).

In *On Liberty*, Mill appreciated the necessity and value of the advance made by "democratic" theory and practice to restrict and overturn the despotic rule of the few over the many. Like the liberal French political theorist, historian, and political figure Alexis de Tocqueville, whose *Democracy in America* (1835–40) he read with admiration, Mill saw dangers in democratic governance that had been obscured by the positive struggle against tyrannies. Democracy was not self-government in the sense of each individual now governing his own life. Instead, it was the rule of all by those who democratically had assumed the agencies of power in society. This created an insidious danger, because individual or group despotism was generally visible to all, but democratic tyranny easily hid itself under the cloak of a people's "self-governance," even though there could be a vast discrepancy between the interests of the governors qua governors and the interests of the governed. Further, that cloak might allow for yet more tyranny to be exercised over an individual who sought to define himself and to live by his own voluntary choices.[9] In the midst of that danger, Mill called for a society of mutual forbearance in all matters that did not represent a direct threat to the lives, liberty, property, and peaceful enjoyment by others of the fruits of their labor. Men, in the long term, flourished by living in a society of voluntary choices, but they stagnated or regressed by making those choices, however wisely, for others. For Mill, "Mankind are greater gainers by suffering each other to live as seems good to themselves, than by compelling each to live as seems good to the rest."[10] Indeed, "The only freedom which deserves the name is that of pursuing our own good in our own way, so long as we do not attempt to deprive others of theirs, or impede their efforts to obtain it."[11]

Mill, in fact, worried that both the tyranny of public opinion and the tyranny of government might wage war on the enjoyment of property and the fruits of one's labor:

> We have only further to suppose a considerable diffusion of Socialist opinions, and it may become infamous in the eyes of the majority to possess more property than some very small amount, or any income not earned by manual labour. Opinions similar in principle to these, already prevail widely among the artisan class, and weigh oppressively on those who are amenable to the opinion chiefly of that class, namely, its own members. It is known that the bad workmen who form the majority of the operatives in many branches of industry, are decidedly of opinion that bad workmen ought to receive the same wages as good, and that no one ought to be allowed, through piece-

[9] Ibid., 5–9.
[10] Ibid., 16.
[11] Ibid.

work or otherwise, to earn by superior skill or industry more than others can without it. And they employ a moral police, which occasionally becomes a physical one, to deter skilful workmen from receiving, and employers from giving, a larger remuneration for a more useful service. If the public have any jurisdiction over private concerns, I cannot see that these people are in fault, or that any individual's particular public can be blamed for asserting the same authority over his individual conduct, which the general public asserts over people in general.[12]

Self-sovereignty, property, and enjoyment of the superior fruits of one's labor all depended upon private concerns remaining private and immune from public interference, suppositions that led Mill to his most celebrated principle for drawing the proper line between the individual's autonomy and the claims of social intervention:

[T]hat the sole end for which mankind are warranted, individually or collectively, in interfering with the liberty of action of any of their number is self-protection. That the only purpose for which power can be rightfully exercised over any member of a civilized community, against his will, is to prevent harm to others. His own good, either physical or moral, is not a sufficient warrant.[13]

Indeed, in Mill's judgment, when society does intervene in the voluntary choices of an individual, it almost invariably does so "wrongly."[14] Again, it is critical to a rightful judgment of Mill to understand that he is not attempting to provide a blueprint or utopian constitution in *On Liberty*, but, rather, defining the pole toward which he would have society move, however gradually, and with whatever compromises. When weighing alternatives, for Mill, we should move closer, whenever possible, to adherence to the harm principle as the only criterion for intervention and interference consistent with a limited government that permits the most dignity, peace, decency, moral freedom, responsibility, individual rights, safety, and security of rights of a civilized society. Intervention, in his view, not only was usually wrong in any particular case, but, above all, had the long-term effect of changing the manner of human beings we were—dulling, not improving, our moral senses.

For Mill, the best illustration of his central argument was seen in the protection of freedom of speech and expression.[15] Because of that, *On Liberty* is widely used and often read as primarily a work about that

[12] Ibid., 87–88.
[13] Ibid., 13.
[14] Ibid., 83–84.
[15] Ibid., 19–55.

particular freedom. In fact, of course, Mill meant his defense of inward and expressive belief to be the hardest case he had to prove in order to win the case for his general principles, since so many of his contemporaries were convinced that the freedom to attack belief in God or religion would undermine the very foundations of society. As Mill explicitly argued, every argument on behalf of freedom of belief and expression applied also to the freedom to choose one's way of life, one's preferences, one's use of one's time, and one's voluntary associations. Provided that individuals did not directly harm others and that they assumed themselves the full consequences of their own behaviors—"their own risk and peril"—society had no coercive claims upon them. In Mill's words, "the same reasons that show that opinion should be free, prove also that he [the individual] should be allowed, without molestation, to carry his opinions into practice at his own cost."[16]

It is noteworthy how appealing Mill has been to American courts, and how deeply Mill's harm principle and his defense of freedom of expression as an instance of that principle have penetrated American jurisprudence, most explicitly at the state level. (The spirit of Mill might inform federal justices, but they almost never cite him specifically, let alone dispositively.) In *Patricia E. Brophy v. New England Sinai Hospital, Inc.* (1986), the Supreme Court of Massachusetts upheld the right of a patient to refuse medical treatment precisely on the basis of *On Liberty*, citing Mill as if he were part of the foundation of American law: "The right of self-determination and individual autonomy has its roots deep in our history. John Stuart Mill stated the concept succinctly: '[T]he only purpose for which power can be rightfully exercised over any member of a civilised community, against his will, is to prevent harm to others. His own good, either physical or moral, is not a sufficient warrant. He cannot rightfully be compelled to do or forbear because it will be better for him to do so, because it will make him happier, because, in the opinion of others, to do so would be wise, or even right.' Mill, *On Liberty*." The court stated freely that its decision was based upon the "recognition of these fundamental principles of individual autonomy," which required a shift in emphasis "away from a paternalistic view of what is 'best' for a patient toward a reaffirmation that the basic question is what decision will comport with the will of the person involved."[17]

In *Armstrong v. The State of Montana* (1999), the Supreme Court of Montana struck down a statute limiting the performance of abortions to physicians and granted to all in Montana the right to choose the medical care

[16] Ibid., 56–57.
[17] *Patricia E. Brophy v. New England Sinai Hospital, Inc.*, 497 N.E.2d 626 (Mass. 1986). References to Mill in court decisions can be found by a simple Google search of "Mill + Court." The decision here is relatively brief, and the online version (http://homepages.udayton.edu/~ulrichlp/brophy.htm) does not have page numbers. A search for "Mill" within the document leads directly to the material cited.

of their choice, in this case (though the issue was decided more broadly) to choose to have an abortion performed by a certified physician-assistant. After citing federal and U.S. Supreme Court decisions, the court wrote of "modern legal notions" that governed the case, whose roots could be traced back to John Locke and the Founders, and that found expression in John Stuart Mill, the only author explicitly cited. In the court's words, "John Stuart Mill recognized this fundamental right of self-determination and personal autonomy as both a limitation on the power of the government and as a principle of preeminent deference to the individual." Correcting (with a *"sic"*) Mill's British spelling, it then quoted the full text of Mill's harm principle, "[T]he only purpose for which power can be rightfully exercised over any member of a civilised [sic] community, against his will, is to prevent harm to others," and so on to the end.[18]

In Mill's famous formula, stating the liberty of the individual with regard to free speech, "If all mankind minus one, were of one opinion, and only one person were of the contrary opinion, mankind would be no more justified in silencing that one person, than he, if he had the power, would be justified in silencing mankind." That sentiment, verbatim, also has found a place in American legal opinion. Thus, the Rhode Island Supreme Court, in *Cullen v. Auclair* (2002), ruled that statements based upon nondefamatory facts enjoyed the fullest protection. It cited the First and Fourteenth Amendments to the United States Constitution, and *On Liberty:* "This principle is eloquently illustrated by John Stuart Mill, who stated: 'If all mankind minus one, were of one opinion, and only one person were of the contrary opinion, mankind would be no more justified in silencing that one person, than he, if he had the power, would be justified in silencing mankind.' . . . Thus, such opinions are not actionable however dishonest the speaker may be in publishing that opinion."[19]

A central part of Mill's argument for freedom of expression was that we could not assume our own infallibility, and thus we could never be certain that an opinion was wholly false. Even if it were, Mill argued, society would lose greatly by its suppression, given the value to truth of the clash of opinions. In 2000, the Rhode Island Supreme Court, in *Beattie v. Fleet National Bank,* refused to allow a jury to "correct" a derogatory opinion and punish those who aided in the dissemination of it. The court granted summary judgment, quoting directly from *On Liberty:* "We decline to do so, however, because this type of communication constituted an opinion based upon disclosed, nondefamatory facts, mindful that, in such circum-

---

[18] *Armstrong v. The State of Montana,* 989 P.2d 365 (Mont. 1999). The online version of the decision does not have page numbers, but a search for "Mill" within the document leads directly to the material cited: http://fnweb1.isd.doa.state.mt.us/idmws/docContent. dll?Library=CISDOCSVR01^doaisd510&ID=003726845.

[19] *Cullen v. Auclair,* 809 A.2d 1107, 1110, p. 5 (R.I. 2002). The opinion is online at the website of the Rhode Island Supreme Court: http://www.courts.state.ri.us/supreme/pdf-files/01-588.pdf.

stances, '[w]e can never be sure that the opinion we are endeavoring to stifle is a false opinion; and even if we were sure, stifling it would be an evil still.' " The Rhode Island Supreme Court's conclusion has one footnote—Mill's *On Liberty*.[20]

Yale law professor Akhil Reed Amar analyzed Mill's view as indicative of a shift profoundly affecting American thought about government, law, and individual rights by the time of the Civil War, when fear of majoritarian tyranny at last overrode the understanding of liberty as majoritarian self-government, "as reflected in the publication in 1859 of John Stuart Mill's classic tract, *On Liberty*—on individual liberty."[21] In the opinion of some, U.S. Supreme Court decisions on privacy and personal choice have reflected more of Mill's thought than of American jurisprudence. Thus, Judge Henry J. Friendly and Judge A. Raymond Randolph, two distinguished American jurists, felt obliged to note that the authors of the Fourteenth Amendment (whose due process clause gradually led the Court to apply the First Amendment—prohibiting, among other things, laws that limited freedom of speech—to the states themselves) did not actually incorporate John Stuart Mill into the Constitution of the United States.[22]

Mill's influence is great, perhaps, not only because of the eloquence of his celebrations of individual liberty and autonomy, but because *On Liberty* can be appropriated both by casual rights theorists—individual sovereignty over one's life has a ring to it—and by casual utilitarians—Mill's stated goal is the long-term well-being of mankind as a species. What surely appears as a weakness to more philosophically minded moral and political theorists—a possible conflation of utility and rights—probably functions as a great source of Mill's enduring appeal.

For the philosophically ambivalent or skeptical, there seems to be something odd in a utilitarianism that can place no limits on what may be done to human beings if it increases future human happiness, raising the specter of Stalin's and Mao's use of the present, in theory, to secure the happiness of the future. One need not embrace the Golden Rule or Kant's celebrated categorical imperative—"Act only according to that maxim whereby you can at the same time will that it should become a universal law"—to have difficulty with that sort of utilitarianism. Equally, there seems to be something odd in a rights theory that ignores consequences,

---

[20] *Beattie v. Fleet National Bank*, 746 A.2d 717, p. 20 (R.I. 2000). The opinion is online at the website of the Rhode Island Supreme Court: http://www.courts.state.ri.us/supreme/pdf-files/98-338.pdf.

[21] Akhil Reed Amar, *The Bill of Rights* (New Haven, CT: Yale University Press, 1998).

[22] A. Raymond Randolph, "Before Roe v. Wade: Judge Friendly's Draft Abortion Opinion," *Harvard Journal of Law and Public Policy* 29, no. 3 (2006). Friendly's opinion of Mill and the Constitution was disclosed by Randolph (who had clerked for Friendly) in Friendly's unpublished papers, in the possession of Harvard Law School. Randolph's article was an extension of a talk that he had given to the Federalist Society in 2005: http://www.fed-soc.org/publications/pubID.368/pub_detail.asp.

that disregards human well-being as a criterion, that proclaims, in effect, *Let justice be done though the world perish*. That, also, appears to entail a coldness and detachment from ordinary human lives that few share.

The extremes of rights without utility and of utility without rights seem troubling to most of us, and few writers venture to either extreme without trying somehow to reassure us. Thus, in one defense of free enterprise and a voluntary society, philosopher and novelist Ayn Rand's *Atlas Shrugged*—a work enthusiastically received by a legion of American admirers (though much less well known abroad)—Rand pointedly, for whatever purposes, shows readers a world of suffering, want, and unhappiness in her portrait of the dystopia produced by "the looters." Nonetheless, John Galt, the hero of the work, speaking for Rand, declares "utilitarianism" to be the philosophy of "prostitutes" and rebukes all notions of altruistic obligations to the well-being of others. The freedom to craft one's own life, to pursue one's own goals, and to enjoy the fruits and satisfactions of one's own efforts—if one grants that same freedom to all others—arises from human nature and objective reality themselves. Utility plays no part in it. Nonetheless, Rand portrays an immoral world whose consequence is indeed a world of pain and deprivation.[23]

In another defense of free enterprise and a voluntary society, the eminent Austrian economist and political philosopher Ludwig von Mises, like Bentham before him, dismisses all talk of "rights" and individual autonomy as the stuff of "muddleheaded babblers" who may therefore argue interminably over whether all men are destined for freedom. There is only one compelling objection to slavery itself: "namely, that free labor is incomparably more productive than slave labor." For Mises, "Only free labor can accomplish what must be demanded of the modern industrial worker." "What we [classical liberals] maintain," he insisted, "is only that a system based on freedom for all workers warrants the greatest productivity of human labor and is therefore in the interest of all the inhabitants of the earth." If freedom were not the most productive system, in terms of the goods and services it calls forth, there would be no argument for it. Nonetheless, Mises reassuringly informs us, it would be impossible for slavery to be as productive as freedom.[24]

For Rand, Mises, and those who find one or the other compelling, there are no problems with each respective position. For Rand (and her admirers), the issue is an individual's rights, and it makes perfect sense that a world based on a false understanding of those rights would be dysfunctional and dystopian. One decides issues, however, on the basis of rights, and one concludes on behalf of a free and voluntary society. For Mises

---

[23] Ayn Rand, *Atlas Shrugged* (1957), 35th anniversary edition (New York: Signet Classic, 1996). For Galt on "the greatest good of the greatest number" as the moral standard of a "prostitute," see p. 943. For Rand on "rights," see pp. 972–73.

[24] Ludwig von Mises, *Liberalism: The Classical Tradition* (Indianapolis, IN: Liberty Fund, Inc., 2005), chap. 1, sec. 2.

(and his admirers), it is patently obvious that a world in which individuals were not free to work for their own well-being would be unproductive and immeasurably less satisfying in its outcomes. One decides issues, however, on the basis of utilitarian calculations of productivity, and one comes down on the side of a free and voluntary society. For the less consistent among us, it seems, at the very least, difficult both to dismiss consequentialist arguments about the effect of social organization upon the lives of our fellow creatures, and to dismiss the notion that there are no limits on what one human being may do to another—slavery, for goodness sake!—except in terms of productive efficiency.

Mill appears to resolve these tensions by embracing his modal justification of freedom and rights. For Mill, living under freedom and the recognition of rights is *a way of being human* that enhances our lives, now and in the future, in multiple ways. In his view, liberty and rights are indispensable to the progress of humanity, both in terms of "what manner of men" liberty produces and in terms of our future well-being. The species cannot know its future, but if it allows individual self-sovereignty, it has chosen the only path to innovation, to learning from experience, and to an exercise of intellectual and moral faculties that produces human beings capable of adaptation and progress. Mill argues, in a language that sounds neither utilitarian nor rights-based, but that can appeal to both camps (philosophers excluded), that the cultivation of individuality, limited only by "the rights and interests of others" in not being directly harmed, can make of human beings something different and higher than what we today might imagine: "Among the works of man," he writes, "which human life is rightly employed in perfecting and beautifying, the first in importance surely is man himself." If liberty prevails, the men and women of today's civilized world "assuredly are but starved specimens of what nature can and will produce."[25]

Mill offers us liberty, individualism, progress, human well-being, an end to tyranny, and both men and women free to develop in ways now unimaginable. Utility is there. Rights are there. Something ineffably beyond them both is there. One falls in love with Mill.

III. Utility, Justice, and Economic Freedom

Mill's *On the Subjection of Women* (1869) makes the confusion or symbiosis (take your choice) of his moral criteria all the more apparent. He offers a stream of utilitarian justifications of the legal and political emancipation of women: more competition and productivity in the workplace; the benefits from interaction that flow to all from the intellectual and professional emancipation of women; fewer unhappy women; better marriages; the full energies, available to society, of half of the human popu-

[25] Mill, *On Liberty*, 59–63.

lation. Mill does not stop there, though. There are high moral gains in and of themselves that would follow from the emancipation of women. He writes of "the morality of justice" that must replace the morality of submission or chivalry (*noblesse oblige* at the whim of the possessor of power). "Justice," he writes, must be "the primary virtue," based on "equality" and "cultivated sympathy."[26] He deplores "the peculiar injustice" of women's oppression and promotes "the dignity" of women if marriage were a contract between equals.[27] Even if society did not benefit as he anticipated it would, he notes, it would be "inconsistent with justice" to deny women "the equal moral right of all human beings to choose their occupation (short of injury to others) according to their own preferences, at their own risk."[28] Bridging (or obscuring) the usual distinction between justice per se and utility per se, Mill wants at times to argue simply that justice and utility are inseparable, both linked to our being higher, more civilized human beings: "The equality of married persons before the law is not only the sole mode in which that particular relation can be made consistent with justice to both sides, and conducive to the happiness of both, but it is the only means of rendering the daily life of mankind, in any high sense, a school of moral cultivation." It may take generations for society to realize it, Mill observes, but "the only school of genuine moral sentiment is society between equals."[29] Even when Mill is explicitly utilitarian in *The Subjection of Women*, the criterion is inextricably linked to the human heart. Ending the oppression of women would produce an "unspeakable gain in private happiness to the liberated half of the species," but the source of that happiness would be the fact that "after the primary necessities of food and raiment, freedom is the first and strongest want of human nature." The goal of emancipation is the enjoyment of "rational freedom" by women.[30] In short, the subordination of half of the species indeed is "now one of the chief hindrances to human improvement," but it is also "wrong in itself."[31] It reflects "the worse rather than the better parts of human nature."[32] It is a question of *both* "justice" and "expediency."[33]

The repercussion for economic policy of Mill's arguments for both "justice" and "expediency," for increase of bounty and satisfaction, on the one hand, and "rational freedom," on the other, is that all laws banning or "protecting" women from the workplace should be repealed, and that

[26] John Stuart Mill, *The Subjection of Women,* in Mill, *On Liberty with The Subjection of Women and Chapters on Socialism,* ed. Stefan Collini (Cambridge and New York: Cambridge University Press, 1989), 160.

[27] Ibid., 163–65.

[28] Ibid., 168. The "(short of injury to others)" is Mill's clarification, not mine.

[29] Ibid., 159.

[30] Ibid., 212.

[31] Ibid., 119.

[32] Ibid., 122.

[33] Ibid., 137.

the marketplace, not arbitrary laws and restrictions, should determine a
woman's opportunities and rewards. It is time to bring women into modern civilization, he argues, and the hallmark of civilization is that merit,
not birth or relationship to government, determines one's place.

The implications of this for Mill's view of economic freedom are dramatic and appear to commit him to an expansive view of a voluntary
marketplace freed from governmental interference. For Mill, the rise of
manufacturing, however pilloried, has produced inestimable improvements in human life, and that increase in the quality of our experience has
depended on merit, not on station. In his view, the principle of improvement in production and the principle of women's freedom are the same:
"Law and government do not undertake to prescribe by whom any social
or industrial operation shall or shall not be conducted, or what modes of
conducting them shall be lawful. These things are left to the unfettered
choice of individuals." Prior to the age of improvement and greater freedom, the prevailing belief had been that "the least possible should be left
to the choice of the individual agent," and that, in matters of economic
activity, the individual's role "should, as far as practicable, be laid down
for him by superior wisdom." The lessons of a millennium of human
experience, however, are now known, Mill believes, after every imagin-
able opposition to recognizing and applying that experience, and after
disastrous applications of precisely contrary theories. These lessons are,
first, "that things in which the individual is the person directly interested
never go right but as they are left to his own discretion"; and second, that
"regulation of [those things] by authority, except to protect the rights of
others, is sure to be mischievous," that is, harmful. Learning these lessons
is a prerequisite of any future economic progress.[34]

The fact is, of course, that not all processes of manufacturing and production are equally good, Mill notes, nor are all individuals equally qualified. It is the marketplace, however, not the government or law, that
should make the choices that follow from this. For too long, mankind
thought that regulation should sort things out, but, at last, "freedom of
individual choice is now known to be the only thing which procures the
adoption of the best processes." In Mill's example, no government or law
need decide that only strong men become blacksmiths: "Freedom and
competition suffice to make blacksmiths strong-armed men," and to convince the weak-armed that they will earn more in occupations to which
they are more suited.[35]

In short, generalizing from his grounds for the elimination of regulations that restrict the entry of women into the marketplace of labor and
production, Mill concludes that a competitive, voluntary economy is both
the most efficient and the most just means of production; that govern-

[34] Ibid., 134–35.
[35] Ibid.

mental regulation of individual economic choice and responsibility is a discredited model that blocks human progress and liberation; and that no legislator or government agent can know what is required by circumstances better than the individuals directly engaged and involved. The economic conclusions of *The Subjection of Women* would appear to be an invitation to an economic life free of governmental interference. At a yet deeper level, they would appear to mirror in the economic domain what Mill urged in the social and intellectual domain in *On Liberty:* that government and society should leave individuals to chart their own courses; to take responsibility for their own lives; to innovate; to learn from trial and error; and to become the independent beings whose very autonomy is the best guarantee of a richer and more successful human future. What classical liberal would not be in love with him? Yet what illicit flirtations are to come!

IV. Redistribution and "Expediency"

Mill's *Principles of Political Economy*, first published in 1848 and then revised, often substantially, through a seventh and final edition (which I utilize here), is assuredly not the work that sets hearts joyfully aflutter among classical liberals. Each new edition, from the second of 1849 to the final one published in 1871, offered extensive revisions, each more open to the notion of social problems created by industrialization that required governmental intervention. The final edition is not, to say the least, the "socialistic" work that some critics find there. Nor is it a fundamental repudiation of Mill's fears of governmental mischief and his celebration of individual liberty. It is, however, a work foundational to the emergence of at least a welfare state in the modern, not nineteenth-century, vision of "liberalism," and it views the relationship of individuals to society in ways that are often sharply distinct from those articulated in *On Liberty* and *The Subjection of Women*. To stay with the metaphor of infidelities and broken hearts, *The Principles of Political Economy* constitutes an ultimate betrayal of liberty according to followers of those classical liberals who reject the redistribution of wealth: Bastiat, Spencer, Mises (and his many disciples), among others. Mill does not invite illiberalism to live with him, nor even, perhaps, to spend a week or two with him, but he gives it a key to the home that classical liberals thought they shared with him. The modern liberals waited until he had passed on, and then they used that key, and they claimed simultaneously *On Liberty* (in the social sphere), *The Subjection of Women* (in the sphere of women's rights), and *The Principles of Political Economy* (in the sphere of economic policies and expedient government) as their own.

The Principles of Political Economy is about a myriad of things, large and small, but the heart of its contribution to the evolution of liberalism lies in one factor above all: the separation of production and distribution. Mill analyzes the laws of production as natural and independent of human volition, but he believes, empirically, that the distribution of wealth and the rules concerning property are in largest part man-made, arbitrary, and rightly subject to the political process. He warns readers that there is a point beyond which redistribution of wealth might, in effect, kill the goose that lays the golden eggs, sapping initiative and risk, but before society reaches that boundary, it may do with the fruits of production what it will. Further, he wishes to see both active redistribution of wealth and reconsiderations of the rules of property. In short, once capital and labor have produced wealth, society is free to redistribute it as it sees fit.

In his "Preliminary Remarks" to *The Principles of Political Economy,* Mill makes clear his distinction between the phenomena of "production" and "distribution." Production of wealth has "its necessary conditions," some purely physical, and "is evidently not an arbitrary thing." While political economy can trace the "secondary and derivative laws" of production that, tied to human nature, account for the diversities of circumstance of wealth in the world, it "assumes" the primary laws of production, referring for knowledge to "physical science or common experience."[36]

By contrast, the laws of distribution "are partly of human institution," and always will reflect "the statutes or usages" of a given society. While "governments or nations" cannot control how institutions will, in fact, work, they nonetheless "have the power of deciding what institutions shall exist," decisions that ultimately depend upon "the various modes of conduct which society may think fit to adopt."[37]

When Mill clarifies this point as he turns in the text from production to distribution, he makes the distinction yet more sharply. The laws of production, Mill asserts, "partake of the character of physical truths." Indeed, "There is nothing optional or arbitrary in them." Whatever men might wish, production will be determined "by the constitution of external things, and by the inherent properties of their own bodily and mental structure." Three times, Mill repeats that "whether they like it or not," these various laws of production obtain. "Opinions or wishes" do not and cannot determine outcomes here.[38]

In matters of "the Distribution of Wealth," however, things stand categorically otherwise: "That [i.e., distribution] is a matter of human institution solely." Mill may have intended this merely as an empirical inference, but it entailed a veritable invitation:

> The things once there, mankind, individually or collectively, can do
> with them as they like. They can place them at the disposal of whom-

---

[36] John Stuart Mill, *The Principles of Political Economy,* in *Collected Works of John Stuart Mill,* vols. II–III (Indianapolis, IN: Liberty Fund Inc., 2006), II, 21.
[37] Ibid.
[38] Ibid., 199.

ever they please, and on whatever terms. Further, in the social state, in every state except total solitude, any disposal whatever of those can only take place by the consent of society, or rather of those who dispose of its active force. Even what a person has produced by his individual toil, unaided by any one, he cannot keep, unless by the permission of society.[39]

For Mill, schemes of distribution have objective consequences, some knowable and some unknown, but that does not alter the wholly arbitrary nature of any particular scheme. For example, in terms of the state of current knowledge, the Communists' proposed system—an economy of equal distribution in which everyone works as hard as possible for the public good—might depend on an unobtainable public-spiritedness, but we do not know that: "To what extent, therefore, the energy of labour would be diminished by Communism, or whether in the long run it would be diminished at all, must be considered for the present an undecided question."[40]

Mill is, to say the very least, profoundly skeptical of almost all fundamental Communist and Socialist proposals for the redistribution of wealth, and he rejects various contemporaneous schemes for minimum wages, but these are all on the table, to be weighed solely in the light of what one believes would be their actual consequences. Mill is far more open to—indeed, at times, persuaded by—notions that wages could be raised by various means: by the education of the working classes toward voluntary limitation of population growth, by the sending of workers to the colonies, by the encouragement of emigration in general, and by the allocation of common land to poorer individuals.[41] There is still a Malthusian influence on Mill—a belief that gains in production never will keep up with population growth—which leads him to explore broad avenues of public intervention in economic life.

Mill also would prefer to have government enact some restrictions on the right of inheritance, noting that "I see nothing objectionable in fixing a limit to what any one may acquire by the mere favour of others." This would prevent wealth from "over-enriching a few" and make certain that wealth benefited more rather than fewer individuals.[42]

Although an ardent advocate of free trade and critic of protectionism, even here Mill sees an instance where "protecting duties [i.e., protectionist tariffs] can be defensible," namely, when they are "imposed temporarily . . . in hopes of naturalizing a foreign industry, in itself perfectly suitable to the circumstances of the country." Although individuals could,

[39] Ibid., 199–200.
[40] Ibid., 200–205.
[41] Ibid., 351–79.
[42] Ibid., 224–26.

in theory, attempt a new manufacture of such a sort "at their own risk," that would be an unreasonable expectation. "A protecting duty," therefore, might well be "the least inconvenient mode in which the nation can tax itself for the support of such an experiment."[43]

Mill's own agenda for government—its obvious role to him, in addition to security and justice—included protection of infants, lunatics, and imbeciles; coining money; prescribing standard measures and weights; maintaining and cleaning the streets and roads; building or improving harbors; conducting surveys for maps and charts; and building dykes and embankments. That was, relatively speaking, a modest list, but it was determined not by any sense of categorically appropriate and inappropriate activities to be undertaken by political power, but solely by the principle of utility—and *not* the long-term utility of *On Liberty*. Indeed, Mill immediately added, "Examples might be indefinitely multiplied without intruding on any disputed ground," and one should be certain to avoid "the ring-fence of any restrictive definition." It would be a dangerous error "to limit the interference of government by any universal rule," since the only operative principle is "general expediency." Whenever "the case of expediency is strong," the government has reason to interfere.[44]

For Mill, then, the distribution of wealth was separated from its production, which means that, in Mill's world, in principle, one might well live in a democratic capitalist society, with essentially voluntary and competitive modes of production, whose voters choose redistribution of wealth to suit what they deem "fit." Government, in that society, should not intrude for the sake of intrusion, but the principle of its action or inaction should be expediency alone. That, indeed, is the very world, of course, in which much of humanity currently finds itself. *The Principles of Political Economy* does not ask "what manner of men" such a society will produce.

V. CONCLUSION

In his posthumously published *Chapters on Socialism* (1879), Mill presented the Socialists' proposals for and criticisms of "the present order of society" fully and untendentiously. Indeed, he showed a strong sympathy toward their complaints both that the accident of birth determined almost everyone's position in life and that most of these positions were quite unfortunate.[45] He argued with the Socialists empirically, however, on some of their most essential claims. Wages were insufficient, he agreed, but they were not diminishing, and they were probably rising. Technological improvements had eased the influences of population growth that

[43] Ibid., III, 918–19.
[44] Ibid., 802–4.
[45] John Stuart Mill, *Chapters on Socialism*, in Mill, *On Liberty with The Subjection of Women and Chapters on Socialism*, ed. Stefan Collini (Cambridge and New York: Cambridge University Press, 1989), 228–48.

Malthus had feared and that the Socialists stressed. Economic competition was not a bad thing for workers, and was probably improving their lot, although the government needed to enact and enforce more effective laws against fraud. Profits and the distribution of capital in society were not unreasonable, given the wealth that was being tied up to create industry and jobs, the low rates of return that capital actually received, and the skill and superintendence that the owners of industry brought to their work. Capitalist society had expedients that might well prove to be in everyone's interest, from piece-work wages to profit sharing. Socialism was a profound risk as an economic system, and we had no experimental proof whatsoever of its possible success. The expansion of production depended upon vast accumulations of capital that Socialism most probably could never produce in a nation. It was extremely difficult to see how a motive for efficiency could exist under Socialism. Equality of remuneration would leave no incentives for effort. An end to economic competition would merely redirect ambition to the pursuit of power. The animating principle of too many Socialists was hatred, and if coupled with violence, that hatred posed the danger of a return to what Thomas Hobbes had described as the brutal state of nature. Mill was no friend of Socialism.[46]

Nonetheless, he simultaneously accepted the Socialists' view that the condition of the working class was, on the whole, wretched, that it was in the interest of all to alter the scheme of things in expedient ways, and (in his vastly influential *The Principles of Political Economy*) that it was wholly up to those who gained the reins of power to determine the distribution of wealth in society. Even if Socialism were "valuable as an ideal, and even as a prophecy of ultimate possibilities," Mill wrote, it could not work now, and private property probably had a long future ahead of it, even if provisional. What we could do now, he urged, even if just from prudence, was to reform our laws and customs concerning property, and, with proper remuneration, appropriate what was necessary for "the public good." Society must be made "to work in a manner more beneficial to that large portion of society which at present enjoys the least share of its direct benefits."[47] If that were expedient, then it followed from *The Principles of Political Economy* that achieving such an end was the proper and necessary role of government.

Mill had no vision of economic growth and progress that paralleled his sense in *On Liberty* of what free men and women would achieve in modal circumstances of individual liberty, individual responsibility, voluntary actions, sovereignty over self, and minimal coercion. The author who articulated the most compelling view of liberty ever penned could not extend that model to the economic sphere, and, ultimately, he encouraged precisely the formation of a political society that exercises more power

[46] Ibid., 248–74.
[47] Ibid., 275–79.

over individual lives than any force he feared in *On Liberty*. The paradox
of John Stuart Mill is a striking one, and it explains to a very large degree
the change in "liberalism" from the nineteenth century to the modern
world. He feared the tyranny of the majority—above all, its stultifying
effect upon the adaptive, self-reliant, and creative powers of free
individuals—but he was instrumental in delivering that tyranny to his
heirs.

History, University of Pennsylvania

CAPITALISM IN THE CLASSICAL AND HIGH LIBERAL TRADITIONS*

By Samuel Freeman

I. Essential Features of Liberalism

Liberalism holds that there are certain individual liberties that are of fundamental political significance. These liberties are fundamental or basic in that they are preconditions on the pursuit of other social values, such as achieving economic efficiency, promoting the general welfare, and moderating the degree of inequality in the distribution of income and wealth. None of these liberties are absolute, but the reasons for limiting their exercise are to protect other basic liberties and maintain essential background conditions for their effective exercise. For example, freedom of speech and expression can be limited when it imminently endangers others' safety or the freedom of their person, but not because the ideas expressed are found to be offensive by vast majorities of people. Liberal basic liberties are also inalienable: they cannot be given up voluntarily or permanently transferred to anyone else, though some liberties are forfeitable upon criminal conviction for serious crimes. No liberal government would enforce a contract in which a person sold himself into permanent servitude, or alienated his freedom to change religions, or legally bound himself to vote only as his employer insisted. An integral feature of a liberal constitution is the protection of the basic rights and liberties necessary to establish and maintain the equal civic status of citizens.

What liberties do liberals generally find to have this extraordinary status? Liberals now would all agree that among the basic liberties are freedom of thought, expression, and inquiry, freedom of conscience and of association, freedom and security of the person, and free choice of occupation. They also agree that the right to hold personal property is part of freedom of the person, since control over personal belongings and security of one's living space is necessary to individuals' independence and sense of self-respect. Finally, nearly all contemporary liberals accept that individuals have a basic right to live under a democratic government with universal franchise (though this was not seen as a basic liberty by

* For their helpful comments on a draft of this essay, I am grateful to David Reidy and other members of the philosophy department at the University of Tennessee; to Frederick Rauscher and other members of the philosophy department at Michigan State University; to Ellen Paul for her many helpful suggestions and editorial remarks on this essay; and to other contributors to this volume for their criticisms and comments.

doi:10.1017/S0265052510000208

classical liberals prior to the twentieth century). All citizens, then, should enjoy equal political rights and liberties, including the right to vote, hold office, and freely participate in political life.

Where liberals primarily disagree is on the nature and status of economic rights and liberties, including the extent of freedom of contract and rights to private property in land, raw materials, and other productive resources. Classical liberals generally hold that the economic liberties are to be regarded and guaranteed as among the basic liberties; or if they are not strictly basic liberties, then economic liberties resemble basic liberties in that they can only be restricted for special reasons.[1] Freedom of contract and rights of property are not absolute for classical liberals; for example, the inalienability of the basic liberties itself puts restrictions on freedom of contract and rights of property. Nor would classical liberals, or liberals generally, accept or see as legally enforceable individuals' attempts to permanently alienate their rights to equal opportunities to educate themselves and compete for open employment positions, or their right not to be discriminated against on grounds of race, religion, gender, or other classifications. One of the primary distinctions between classical liberalism and libertarianism is that libertarians regard freedom of coercively enforceable contracts as of such fundamental importance that it overrides the liberal restriction on the inalienability of basic liberties and also overrides equality of opportunity and equal rights to apply and compete for open positions.[2] For liberals, by contrast, one cannot alienate

---

[1] Following Joseph Schumpeter, I associate classical liberalism with the economic liberalism of the classical economists, starting with Adam Smith in the eighteenth century, and David Ricardo, Thomas Malthus, and other classical economists (including J. B. Say in France) in the nineteenth century (with the exclusion of John Stuart Mill, for reasons to be discussed). Classical liberalism in the nineteenth century was associated with the doctrine of laissez-faire, "the theory that the best way of promoting economic development and general welfare is to remove fetters from the private enterprise economy and to leave it alone." Joseph A. Schumpeter, *History of Economic Analysis* (Oxford: Oxford University Press, 1954), 395. Friedrich Hayek and Milton Friedman are major twentieth-century representatives of classical liberalism, along with James Buchanan and the "Virginia School" of public choice theory, Gary Becker and other members of the "Chicago School," Ludwig von Mises of the Austrian School of economics, David Gauthier among philosophers, and Richard Posner and Richard Epstein among legal scholars. While each of these thinkers may not strictly endorse each and every one of the features of liberalism I discuss that distinguish it from libertarianism, each does subscribe to a predominant majority of them. Some thinkers (Loren Lomasky perhaps) may not fit neatly into either category, and would reject my distinction between classical liberalism and libertarianism. For a more extensive discussion of the primary differences between liberalism and libertarianism, see my essay "Illiberal Libertarians: Why Libertarianism Is Not a Liberal View," *Philosophy and Public Affairs* 30, no. 2 (Spring 2001): 105–51.

[2] By "libertarianism" I mean primarily the doctrine argued for by Robert Nozick, and also accounts by Jan Narveson, Murray Rothbard, John Hospers, Eric Mack, and others (including perhaps Ayn Rand). There is also a school of thought known as "left-libertarianism." This position resembles libertarianism primarily in recognizing self-ownership and absolute freedom of contract. Otherwise, it bears little resemblance to traditional libertarianism, since it envisions qualified property rights along with extensive government redistribution to enforce egalitarian measures that (for example) neutralize the consequences of luck. See

the basic rights, liberties, and opportunities that define one's equal status as a person or citizen.

While classical liberals regard the economic liberties as having great importance, they do not really regard them as basic liberties in every respect. Classical liberals have generally recognized that freedom of economic contract and rights of property differ from basic liberties in that they can be restricted for reasons other than maintaining others' basic liberties and rights to equal opportunities. For example, classical liberals today accept that contracts for the purpose of fixing prices or putting restraints on trade and competition should not be enforceable; for in addition to foreclosing economic opportunities for others, such contracts are economically inefficient. Unregulated monopolies in certain resources are generally forbidden by classical liberals when they lead to economic inefficiencies. Also, contemporary classical liberals accept government's powers of eminent domain for public purposes (on the condition that compensation is provided for any government "taking"). And most can accept zoning restrictions of certain kinds, for example, noise restrictions or the exclusion of manufacturing and commercial development in residential neighborhoods.[3] Zoning restrictions do not protect any basic liberty or opportunity but are issued as a matter of convenience, or to maintain property values, or to keep out unwanted neighbors. And classical liberals recognize other restrictions on the economic liberties that they would not extend to the basic freedoms of expression, conscience, association, and other basic liberties.

This suggests that however much the economic liberties are revered by classical liberals, they are not really among the class of basic liberties that all liberals recognize. For while classical liberals reject restrictions on the basic liberties (except to protect the basic liberties), they generally allow for restrictions and regulations on economic liberties in order to procure and maintain the conditions necessary for free competitive markets and economic efficiency, as well as maintaining health and safety, and procuring other public goods.[4] The most enduring and (I believe) persuasive clas-

---

Peter Vallentyne and Hillel Steiner, eds., *Left-Libertarianism and Its Critics* (New York: Palgrave, 2000).

[3] Michael Munger suggests that many classical liberals incline toward relying on restrictive covenants and the law of nuisances rather than municipal zoning laws. Still, unlike libertarians, classical liberals are willing to use zoning and eminent domain powers when restrictive covenants are ineffective or not available.

[4] For example, Friedrich Hayek, in *The Constitution of Liberty* (Chicago: University of Chicago Press, 1960), discusses, among other legitimate government measures affecting economic liberty: the legitimacy of prohibitions on contracts in restraint of trade (ibid., 230); regulation or prohibition of certain monopolies (265); regulations governing techniques in production (224–25); safety regulations in building codes (225); and certain restrictions on land use (229). Regarding property, he writes: "[T]he recognition of the right of private property does not determine what exactly should be the content of this right *in order that the market mechanism will work as effectively and beneficially as possible*" (ibid., 229; emphasis added). Moreover, on freedom of economic contract, he writes: "The old formulae of laissez-

sical liberal justification of the economic liberties is cast in terms of the conditions required to establish and maintain economically efficient market allocations of resources and distributions of income and wealth. The enforcement of a scheme of private economic rights and liberties within a system of free competitive markets designed to achieve conditions of economic efficiency in both the allocation and the distribution of income and wealth is, as I understand it, the most fundamental feature of capitalism. It is also the primary feature of classical liberalism that distinguishes it from what I call the "high liberal tradition" (discussed in Section II below).

Karl Marx understood capitalism partly as a social and economic system, the predominant feature of which is the existence of two distinct and mutually exclusive economic classes with different functions and conflicting interests: the class of capitalists own and control the means of production; and the class of workers own no capital but own and control their labor power. The "petit bourgeoisie"—the class of shopkeepers, craftsmen, and other small businesspersons who own both their labor power and means of production—Marx found to be of no economic or historical significance. Since small businesses have always occupied a central position within the U.S. economy, and the United States is emblematic of contemporary capitalism, Marx's class-based definition of "capitalism" was never really adequate to describe capitalism or class conditions in the United States. While it may be true that during certain historical periods capitalism has been marked by class divisions and conflict, this seems incidental to what I will take to be central to a capitalist economy.

Capitalism (as Marx and the classical economists recognized) is not simply an economic system but also a social and political system. For essential to capitalism is the political specification and legal enforcement of a complicated system of extensive property and contract rights and duties that are all conditions of economic production, transfer, and consumption, as well as the political specification and enforcement of laws and regulations needed to maintain the fluidity of markets and competitive enterprise (laws restricting monopolies, price fixing, and other restraints on trade).

Rather than accepting Marx's class-based definition, I regard capitalism as an economic and social/political system which enforces a scheme of extensive private economic rights and liberties within a system of free markets, wherein these economic rights and liberties are specified and markets are designed to achieve conditions of maximal productive output and economic efficiency in both the allocation and distribution of income and wealth. Essential to this understanding of capitalism, then, is (1) a political system of extensive private property and contract rights, and

---

faire or non-intervention do not provide us with an adequate criterion for distinguishing between what is and what is not admissible in a free system. There is ample room for experimentation and improvement within that permanent *legal framework which makes it possible for a free society to operate most efficiently*" (ibid., 231; emphasis added).

other legal background conditions, (2) that are specified and adjusted to achieve efficient markets and the resulting maximization of productive output and, therewith, (3) maximal opportunities for consumption among those willing and able to pay for goods and services thereby produced. Finally, (4) the capitalist standard for the just distribution of income and wealth is fundamentally tied to market outcomes.

So defined, capitalism is not the only economic system that relies upon markets and private property in the means of production. Other alternatives will be discussed later (namely, property-owning democracy). But capitalism in this pure sense is the economic system that is defended by classical liberals, particularly the classical economists and their modern heirs. Thus, it should come as no surprise that capitalism, like the liberalism of the classical economists, has been closely associated with utilitarianism and attuned to utilitarian arguments, especially within the Anglo-American tradition.[5]

On this understanding, a system of robust private property rights and wide-ranging freedom of contract is not sufficient for capitalism. Capitalism also requires a system of free and efficient markets for the allocation of productive resources and the distribution of income and wealth. Liberals generally, including classical liberals, maintain that, when markets break down due to monopolistic concentration of market power, or when markets are incapable of adequately supplying goods or services that are important to individuals' independence and well-being, it is government's role to intervene and address such "externalities" or "neighborhood effects" by restoring competition and providing for these "public goods."[6] Thus, Adam Smith writes:

[5] Even major proponents of classical liberalism within the tradition of Austrian economics, such as Hayek or von Mises—while they may not put as much direct emphasis on economic efficiency and may emphasize instead the informational virtues of free markets (but why is this important if not for reasons of efficiency?)—should not find my characterization of capitalism at odds with their understanding. When Hayek rejects "utilitarianism," he in effect rejects rational planning and direct appeals to the principle of utility in regulating markets or assessing the distribution of income and wealth. Friedrich Hayek, *Law, Legislation, and Liberty, Volume II: The Mirage of Social Justice* (Chicago: University of Chicago Press, 1976), 22. Still, like David Hume, Hayek's arguments for the rules of justice and of capitalism are generally based in consequentialist considerations regarding their beneficial effects. As John Gray contends, Hayek ultimately relied upon indirect utilitarian arguments as the justification of his account of the rules of justice and capitalism. John Gray, *Hayek on Liberty* (Oxford: Basil Blackwell, 1984), 59–60.

Moreover, as Alan Kors points out in his essay in this volume, Ludwig von Mises's argument for economic freedom also relies upon instrumental appeals to utility and economic efficiency. Von Mises writes: "We liberals do not assert that God or Nature meant all men to be free . . . What we maintain is that only a system based on freedom for all workers warrants the greatest productivity of human labor and is therefore in the interest of all the inhabitants of the earth. . . . This is the fruit of free labor. It is able to create more wealth for everyone. . ." Ludwig von Mises, *Liberalism in the Classical Tradition* (Indianapolis, IN: Liberty Fund, 2005), chapter I, sec. 2.

[6] John Locke is generally regarded as the first great liberal. While Locke endorses each of the other features of liberalism I discuss, missing from his writings is a developed idea of

According to the system of natural liberty, the sovereign has only three duties to attend to . . . first [national defense]; secondly, the duty of protecting . . . every member of society from the injustice or oppression of every other member, or the duty of establishing an exact administration of justice; and, thirdly, the duty of erecting and maintaining certain publick works and certain publick institutions, which it can never be for the interest of any individual, or small number of individuals, to erect and maintain; because the profit could never repay the expence to any individual, or small number of individuals, though it may frequently do much more than repay it to a great society.[7]

Moreover, Smith writes, "The expence of defending the society . . . of the administration of justice . . . of maintaining good roads and communications," as well as "institutions for education and religious instruction, [are] likewise, no doubt, beneficial to the whole society, and may, therefore, without injustice, be defrayed by the general contribution of the whole society."[8]

Adam Smith's regard for "the administration of justice," "protecting . . . every member of society," and measures that are "beneficial to the whole society" underlines another significant feature of liberalism, namely, the *public nature of political power*. Political power is not conceived of as a private power to be exercised for the benefit of those who can afford it, or to benefit only members of certain religious, ethnic, or otherwise privileged groups. Rather, it is a public power that is held in trust by governments, to be impartially exercised, and, as John Locke says, "only for the public good."[9] The public nature of political power as impartially exercisable only for the public good is integral to the liberal idea of the rule of law, and is another feature of liberalism that distinguishes it from libertarianism. Libertarianism rejects the idea of the public good and regards political power as a private power, to be provided to people on the basis of private contracts and in proportion to their willingness and ability to pay for it.

---

the role of free markets in achieving economic efficiency. The idea was not sufficiently developed at the time he lived in the seventeenth century. Libertarians rely upon a Lockean account of natural property, but their account of absolute property rights is not Locke's view since, like liberals generally, he had no reservations about taxation and governmental regulation of property for important public purposes.

[7] Adam Smith, *An Inquiry into the Nature and Causes of the Wealth of Nations* (Indianapolis, IN: Liberty Fund, 1981), Book IV, chap. 9, pp. 687–88; see generally Book V, chap. 1, part III, pp. 723–816, "Of the Expence of Publick Works and Publick Institutions." Milton Friedman quotes approvingly and discusses the passage in the text, in Milton and Rose Friedman, *Free to Choose* (New York: Harcourt, Brace and Janovich, 1979), 19–25, adding a fourth duty of government, "to protect members of the community who cannot be regarded as 'responsible' individuals" (ibid., 24).

[8] Smith, *Wealth of Nations*, Book V, chap. 1, pp. 814–15.

[9] John Locke, *Second Treatise on Government*, sec. 3, ed. Peter Laslett (Cambridge: Cambridge University Press, 1988), p. 268.

I suggested that classical liberalism, like capitalism itself, has been closely associated with utilitarianism.[10] Utilitarianism provides an argument for each of the main features of classical liberalism, including its support for robust property and contract rights, conjoined with its emphasis on market efficiency and market distributions.[11] It should come as no surprise that nearly all the great classical liberal economists, including Adam Smith, David Ricardo, Thomas Malthus, John Stuart Mill, F. Y. Edgeworth, and Alfred Marshall, were utilitarians. Capitalism's association with utilitarianism also helps in understanding the evolution of laissez-faire capitalism into contemporary welfare-state capitalism. Utilitarians since David Hume have noted that a fixed sum of money causes greater utility for a poor person than for a rich person.[12] Most utilitarians conclude that we have good reason (other things being equal) to guarantee the most disadvantaged, or at least the disabled, a minimum income in order to raise them at least to the threshold of a minimally decent life. Though contemporary classical liberals often contest the extent of the welfare state and its limitations of economic freedoms, still they generally accept that it is the role of government to provide a "safety net" for persons who are incapable of providing for their own welfare. The disincentive to work that so-called "welfare" (or a negative income tax) can create must be taken into account, classical liberals insist, but they still generally have accepted government's duty to provide some kind of social minimum, at least in the form of "poor relief" to meet basic subsistence needs for those unable to provide for such needs themselves.[13]

[10] I do not claim that all classical liberals are utilitarians, but only that in the eighteenth and nineteenth centuries the two schemes of thought developed in tandem and mutually influenced one another. Of course, the idea of natural rights associated with John Locke played a significant role in the development of liberalism, and Adam Smith appealed to natural rights, in spite of his utilitarianism and Hume's rejection of natural rights. Still Smith, like Locke, endorsed a robust idea of the public or common good, and saw property rights as subject to requirements of the public good. The idea endorsed by contemporary libertarians, that property rights and economic liberties are absolute and are not to be regulated according to the public good, seems to be a nineteenth-century development. On my interpretation, libertarians' rejection of the idea of the public or common good, like their rejection of the public nature of political power, marks a significant departure from classical liberalism.

[11] Some contemporary welfarists (or "philosophical utilitarians" in T. M. Scanlon's sense) such as David Gauthier argue for capitalism and classical liberalism on Hobbesian contractarian grounds, but the argument is still driven mainly by considerations of economic efficiency. See David Gauthier, *Morals by Agreement* (Oxford: Oxford University Press, 1986).

[12] See David Hume, *An Enquiry Concerning the Principles of Morals*, 2d ed. (Oxford: Clarendon Press, 1970), sec. 3, "On Justice," pp. 193–94.

[13] On classical liberal support for "poor relief," see Hayek, *The Constitution of Liberty*, 285–86. He provides historical background in *Law, Legislation, and Liberty, Volume II*, 190 n. 8, quoting such classical liberals as N. W. Senior and Moritz Mohl (writing in 1848). It is noteworthy that Adam Smith accepted the English Poor Laws, which, as he says, date back at least to the Elizabethan era (i.e., to the Parliamentary Acts of 1597–98 and 1601). Smith objected to the requirement that each local government is responsible for raising funds to pay for the support of their own poor, since this requirement discouraged the free movement of labor—therewith providing an argument for the centralization of governments'

Classical liberals generally contend that redressing destitution is not a claim-right that individuals have, but a matter of charity,[14] grounded in the fact that provision of everyone's subsistence needs is a public good. Thus, Milton Friedman writes, it is because of the insufficiency of private charity due to "a neighborhood effect" that he endorses "governmental action to alleviate poverty; to set, as it were, a floor under the standard of life of every person in the community."[15] Friedrich Hayek writes that, in order to avoid "great discontent and violent reaction" among those whose capacity to earn a living ceases,

> The assurance of a certain minimum income for everyone, or a sort of floor below which no one need fall even when he is unable to provide for himself, appears not only to be a wholly legitimate protection against a risk common to all, but a necessary part of the Great Society.[16]

I have touched upon certain essential features of liberalism and shown how classical liberalism exhibits each of them. These features include equal basic and inalienable rights and liberties; freedom of occupation with equal opportunities to compete for open positions; free competitive markets; government's duty to respond to market breakdowns and provide public goods; a social minimum that is at least sufficient to meet the subsistence needs of those unable to provide for themselves; and the public fiduciary nature of political power. The libertarianism of Robert

---

duty to maintain disabled, incompetent, and destitute people. See Smith, *Wealth of Nations*, 152–57. The Poor Law Reforms of 1834 finally centralized poor relief, but—in part due to the influence of Bentham, Malthus, and Ricardo—made poor relief normally available only in the now infamous work houses. Mill approves of "public charity" on classical liberal grounds, namely, that private charity is not adequate, and that leaving the poor to private charity encourages them to commit crimes. See John Stuart Mill, *Principles of Political Economy* (Indianapolis, IN: Liberty Fund, 2006), Book V, chap. 11, sec. 13, pp. 960–62. Mill's departures from classical liberalism rest not in his views regarding poor relief, but in his conception of taxation (of estates especially), qualified property rights, remuneration of labor, and the organization of industry into workers' associations. See discussions in the text below.

On the continent, there is adequate philosophical precedent in central European liberalism for governmental provisions for the poor. Immanuel Kant in the eighteenth century saw it to be the duty of governments to "require the wealthy to provide the means of sustenance to those who are unable to provide the most necessary needs of nature for themselves." See Kant, *The Metaphysical Elements of Justice*, trans. John Ladd (Indianapolis, IN: Bobbs-Merrill, 1965), 93.

[14] See Hayek, *The Constitution of Liberty*, 292.

[15] Milton Friedman, *Capitalism and Freedom*, (Chicago: University of Chicago Press, 1962), 191. Friedman's proposal for a negative income tax to replace in-kind welfare benefits follows on pp. 191–95.

[16] Friedrich Hayek, *Law, Legislation, and Liberty, Volume III: The Political Order of a Free People* (Chicago: University of Chicago Press, 1979), 55. See also Hayek, *The Constitution of Liberty*, chapter 19, "Social Security." The problem with the modern welfare state, Hayek contends, is that "the doctrine of the safety net, to catch those who fall, has been made meaningless by the doctrine of fair shares for those of us who are quite able to stand" (ibid., 285, quoting *The Economist*).

Nozick and others rejects each of these essential features of liberalism; libertarianism's apparent resemblance with classical liberalism is misleading. What leads many to conflate libertarianism and classical liberalism is that both endorse similar (though not the same) robust conceptions of economic rights and liberties, and therewith endorse market capitalism as the appropriate mechanism for determining the just distribution of income, wealth, and economic powers and responsibilities.[17] It is this robust conception of property rights and economic liberties that distinguishes classical liberalism from the high liberal tradition and gives rise to their different conceptions of distributive justice. Classical liberalism's conception of property rights and economic liberties also explains the theory's more conservative estimate of what is required to guarantee equal opportunities and satisfy the social minimum; the more limited extent it assigns to government's role in regulating markets; its more restricted range of public goods; and its formal or legalistic conception of equality of opportunity. I discuss these differences within liberalism in the following sections.

II. THE HIGH LIBERAL TRADITION

Capitalism is essential to the classical liberal tradition. It is not essential to liberalism per se. For a primary feature of capitalism (as I use the term) is that the outcomes of free competitive market activity provide the fundamental basis for settling the distribution of income and wealth. Not all liberal conceptions endorse this important feature of capitalism.

By the "high liberal tradition" I mean the school of liberal thought that originates in the nineteenth century with the political and economic writings of John Stuart Mill; it includes T. H. Green and John Dewey in the late nineteenth and early twentieth centuries,[18] and its major representative in the second half of the twentieth century is John Rawls. Though Mill professes to be a utilitarian and Rawls a contractarian, there are close similarities in their conceptions of liberalism, democracy, and distributive justice. Rawls and Mill both affirm a principle of liberty that protects largely the same set of basic liberties, the primary exception being equal political liberties for all citizens.[19] Mill was an ardent defender of repre-

[17] Libertarians differ from classical liberals in that they do not recognize (among other things) government's authority to regulate contracts to maintain the fluidity of markets, or to restrict property rights for the public good, or to tax people to pay for public goods or poor relief.

[18] See T. H. Green, *Lectures on the Principles of Political Obligation* (Cambridge: Cambridge University Press, 1986). For a discussion of Green's "new liberalism," see David Brink, *Perfectionism and the Common Good: Themes in the Philosophy of T. H. Green* (Oxford: Oxford University Press, 2003), esp. pp. 77–88. For references to Dewey's works, see notes 24 and 72 below.

[19] Rawls's first principle of justice, the principle of equal basic liberties, states: "Each person is to have an equal right to the most extensive total system of equal basic liberties compatible with a similar system of liberty for all." John Rawls, *A Theory of Justice*, rev. ed. (Cambridge, MA: Harvard University Press, 1999), 266. In later work, Rawls substituted the

sentative democracy and a universal franchise for all citizens, female as
well as male; still he was prepared to allow for unequal voting rights,
with plural voting rights for those with greater education.[20] Rawls, by
contrast, argues that being respected by others as an equal person and
enjoying the status of an equal citizen is essential to a person's good and
sense of self-respect. Primarily for these reasons, he argues, citizens in a
democratic society ought to have equal rights to vote, hold office, and
freely express themselves in the political and public domains.[21]

While classical liberals rejected a universal franchise until well into the
early twentieth century, few classical liberals today would deny citizens
formal equality of political rights to vote and hold office. The category of
"passive citizens," which once included women, many free blacks, and
other citizens who did not meet property qualifications, is now limited to
children and others requiring legal guardians. Nonetheless, classical liberals generally do not accept efforts to neutralize the effects of wealth on
political campaigns and procedures in order to mitigate inequality of
political influence and promote political impartiality. High liberals, by
contrast, contend that the liberal principle of maintaining the equal status
of citizens requires that governments preserve the "fair value" (as Rawls
says) of the political liberties regardless of people's economic position in
society.[22] This is to be achieved primarily by the regulation of campaign
spending and political contributions and by public financing of campaigns, so that private wealth does not distort or unfairly influence the
democratic process. High liberals regard the dependence of legislators
and other political officials upon private contributions for their political
campaigns as a distortion of "public reason," since it tends to undermine
impartial judgment and gives to the economically more advantaged an
unfair influence in the political life of a democratic society. Classical liberals, including those who currently are a majority on the United States
Supreme Court, disagree; they generally see restrictions on political contributions and campaign spending, not as a requirement of political equal-

---

phrase "a fully adequate scheme" for "the most extensive total system." See John Rawls,
Political Liberalism (New York: Columbia University Press, 1993), 291. The basic liberties that
Mill and Rawls jointly recognize include liberty of conscience, freedom of thought and
expression, freedom of the person and of occupation (or as Mill says, "freedom of tastes and
pursuits"), and freedom of association. Rawls also includes among the equal basic liberties
political rights of participation, and the rights and liberties covered by the rule of law.

[20] As opposed to classical liberals and the political practice of the time which denied
voting rights to those who did not meet property qualifications (as well as to women), Mill
argued that those with more education, not with more property, are in a better position to
deliberate impartially and decide what measures best promote the public good (which Mill
understood in quasi-utilitarian terms). See John Stuart Mill, *On Representative Government*,
chap. VIII, "Of the Extension of the Suffrage," in Mill, *On Liberty and Other Essays*, ed. John
Gray (Oxford: Oxford University Press, 1991), 334–41. The only exception to a universal
franchise that he endorsed is the exclusion of recipients of poor relief. Ibid., 333.

[21] Rawls, *A Theory of Justice*, sec. 82.

[22] See Rawls, *A Theory of Justice*, 194–97; see also Ronald Dworkin, *Is Democracy Possible
Here?* (Princeton, NJ: Princeton University Press, 2009), 128–29.

ity, but as an unjustified restriction on freedom of political expression.[23] Money talks in classical liberal jurisprudence.

Again, the contrast here of classical liberalism with libertarianism is instructive. Notably, classical liberals do not regard campaign spending limitations as an unjust limitation on one's economic rights to spend one's money to buy whatever one pleases (within the limits set by basic rights and liberties). The classical liberal justification for not limiting private campaign contributions does not stem from their conception of the economic rights that attend capitalism. The liberal idea that political power is a public power to be impartially exercised for the good of all citizens implies a rejection of the idea that government or its officials have the power to auction off political decisions or that citizens should have a right to buy political protection or decisions, as though they were a private economic good. The right to make campaign contributions is regarded, not as an economic right to purchase political services, but as a political right of free speech and expression.

While classical and high liberals differ in their interpretations of political equality, their main differences stem from their positions on the nature and scope of economic rights and liberties. This will be the primary focus of the remainder of this essay. I will regard Mill and Rawls as the paradigmatic representatives of the high liberal tradition. John Dewey is an important representative during the first half of the twentieth century, but since he had less to say about institutional arrangements than Rawls and Mill, I will not focus on his "new liberalism" here.[24]

There are four significant common features of Mill's and Rawls's views regarding economic justice. I focus on these in the following discussion since they are primarily the features that distinguish the classical and high liberal traditions. First, both Mill and Rawls deny that property rights and economic liberties are among the rights and liberties that are protected by their principles of liberty. They both reject what Mill calls "absolute property" in favor of a more "qualified property" system, with greater regulation of economic contracts than laissez-faire traditionally allows.[25] Second, with respect to free markets, both distinguish between

---

[23] For example, recently the U.S. Supreme Court in a 5-4 decision struck down a long-standing prohibition on corporate and union payment for broadcasts of campaign-related materials supporting or opposing specific candidates, on the grounds that it restricted corporations' rights to free expression and political influence. See *Citizens United v. Federal Elections Committee*, 558 U.S. 50 (2010).

[24] Dewey's main works on liberalism and political philosophy are *Individualism: Old and New* (1930); *Liberalism and Social Action* (1935); and *Freedom and Culture* (1939). For an instructive account of Dewey's liberalism, see Alan Ryan, *John Dewey and the High Tide of American Liberalism* (New York: W. W. Norton, 1995), esp. chaps. 3 and 8.

[25] Mill, *Principles of Political Economy*, Book II, chap. i, sec. 3, p. 209. Jerry Gaus and Ellen Paul remind me that Mill's attitudes toward laissez-faire evolved through the several editions of *Principles*. Mill writes: "*Laisser-faire*, in short, should be the general practice: every departure from it, unless required by some great good, is a certain evil" (ibid., Book V, chap. xi, sec. 7, p. 945. But the next nine sections discuss "Large exceptions to laisser-faire,"

and emphasize the dual functions that markets play in allocating productive forces (on the one hand), and distributing income and wealth (on
the other). They argue that markets play their most crucial role in protecting freedom of occupation and choice of careers and in securing the
efficient allocation of productive resources, and they do not fundamentally tie the final distribution of income and wealth to markets and the
price system. Third, Mill and Rawls both endorse a conception of equality
of (social and economic) opportunity that goes well beyond the classical
liberal view of legal equality and careers open to talents. Finally, with
respect to control over the capital and productive resources and the distribution of income and wealth, both criticize capitalism for its tendency
to concentrate wealth and control over the means of production in the
hands of a relatively small class, and they advocate private property
market systems which, unlike capitalism, do not have this tendency. I
discuss each of the four ways that high liberalism differs from classical
liberalism and capitalism in the next several sections.

III. Private Property and Economic Liberties

Mill says that the economic liberties are not protected by the principle
of liberty. His reasons are not compelling. He says that trade is a "social
act" that is not "self-regarding" in the way that the basic liberties protected by his principle of liberty are supposed to be. Mill's distinction
between individuals' "self-regarding" conduct and their social or "other-
regarding" conduct with the potential for harm is, standing alone, hard to
sustain. Many kinds of speech and association protected by the purportedly self-regarding freedoms of thought, expression, association are "social"
and "other-regarding" insofar as their main purpose is to influence political and cultural opinion and conduct (e.g., political speech, political parties, the Chamber of Commerce). The real basis for Mill's distinction
between the "self-regarding" liberties that are protected by his principle
of liberty, and the economic liberties that are not, must lie elsewhere.
Though he says the principle of liberty is justified ultimately by the
principle of utility, his list of basic liberties and his exclusion of economic

---

including "Cases in which the consumer is an incompetent judge of the commodity." Here
Mill argues, among other things, for public support for elementary schools, making school-
ing free to children of the poor (ibid., 950). Moreover, in his discussion of "socialism," Mill
says that impoverished workers have no choice of whom to work for or on what terms, and
that freedom of contract is an absurdity, given the disparity of bargaining power that exists
between owners and wage workers. If all that Mill means above by "laisser-faire" is a
presumption in favor of markets in production, then Rawls accepts it in this limited sense.
Historically, however, the term implies much more than this, including minimizing government economic regulation and the endorsement of near-absolute freedom of contract and
nearly unqualified property rights in land and means of production, which Mill and Rawls
clearly reject.

liberties originates in considerations of "individuality" and an ideal of persons as "progressive beings" (discussed below in Section VII.)[26]

Rawls relies upon similar considerations to argue that the economic liberties are not among the basic liberties protected by his first principle of justice. He says that "the right to hold personal property" is among the basic liberties. But "the right to own certain kinds of property (e.g., the means of production) and freedom of contract as understood by the doctrine of laissez-faire, are not basic [liberties]; and so they are not protected by the priority of the first principle."[27] Instead, for Rawls the specification, scope, and extent of economic rights and liberties is decided by his second principle of justice (including the difference principle), which states:

> Social and economic inequalities are to satisfy two conditions: first, they are to attach to offices and positions open to all under conditions of fair equality of opportunity; and second, they are to be to the greatest benefit of the least advantaged members of society (the difference principle).[28]

Rawls's distinction between personal property and nonpersonal property, including means of production, might seem hard to maintain for economists. (For example, many people buy houses in which to reside for a limited time, always intending to sell them for a profit.) But Rawls's distinction is not made within economics or the social sciences, nor does it track the legal distinction between personal and real property. Rather, it is a distinction made within a theory of social and economic justice, and is defined relative to Rawls's principles of justice. "Personal property" for Rawls thus consists of institutional rights and responsibilities regarding possessions that enable persons to effectively exercise their basic liberties (freedom of conscience, expression, association, etc.), take advantage of fair equal opportunities, and achieve individual independence as they

---

[26] Thus, Mill says in *Principles of Political Economy*, Book V, chap. 11, sec. 3, p. 940, that in a democratic age, "There never was more necessity for surrounding individual independence of thought, speech and conduct, with the most powerful defenses, in order to maintain that originality of mind and individuality of character, which are the only source of any real progress."

[27] Rawls, *A Theory of Justice*, 53, 54. This inclusion of a right to hold personal property among the basic liberties in the first (1971) edition of *A Theory of Justice* (p. 61) led some critics to contend that a capitalist conception of robust property rights is protected by Rawls's first principle. They argued (on the assumption that a right to personal property must include nearly unqualified laissez-faire rights of use and transfer) that there is little space left for redistribution under Rawls's difference principle once Rawls assumes that a right to hold property is a basic liberty. In the 1999 revised edition of *A Theory of Justice* (p. 54), Rawls added the sentence quoted above in the text, which makes clear that this interpretation is a misunderstanding. Later, on the basis of his second principle of justice (discussed here), Rawls explicitly rejects laissez-faire conceptions of property, and contends that rights and other incidents of property are to be determined by the difference principle.

[28] John Rawls, *Justice as Fairness: A Restatement* (Cambridge, MA: Harvard University Press, 2001), 42–43.

pursue a plan of life that is chosen from the wide range of permissible ways of living. Rawls implies that, while ownership of one's residence and personal belongings is necessary for individual independence and privacy, laissez-faire rights of ownership of means of production and near-absolute freedom of economic contract are not necessary for these general purposes—however much certain individuals might want to enjoy these rights given their specific life-plans (to be wealthy, for example). If laissez-faire rights of property and contract are to be justified at all on Rawls's terms, it must be shown that a laissez-faire economic system satisfies the difference principle and is, compared with other alternatives, to the greatest benefit of the least advantaged. That is an empirical question, which Rawls, like Mill, does not think can be decided in laissez-faire's favor.

The bases for Rawls's and Mill's liberalism and accounts of economic justice reside in ideals of persons and their relations. These ideals provide the ultimate explanation for these theorists' refusals to include property rights and economic liberties among the basic rights and liberties as classical liberals do. This deeper explanation will be discussed in more detail in Section VII below. Here I will discuss the kinds of qualifications to property and economic liberties that Mill and Rawls endorse, and some intermediate reasons they provide.

Mill famously distinguishes between absolute and qualified property:

> The laws of property have never yet conformed to the principles on which the justification of private property rests. They have made property of things which never ought to be property and absolute property where only a qualified property ought to exist. They have not held the balance fairly between human beings, but have heaped impediments upon some, to give advantage to others; they have purposely fostered inequalities, and prevented all from starting fair in the race.[29]

For Mill, the justification of private property in productive resources lies, in the first instance, in its "expediency" in facilitating production. He condemns absolute property rights in land for their inefficiency. "In the case of land, no exclusive right should be permitted . . . which cannot be shown to be productive of positive good."[30] Thus, ownership of land that is cultivated "does not imply an exclusive right to it for purposes of access." And if land is not intended to be cultivated, "no good reason can be given for its being private property at all"; anyone permitted to own it "holds it by sufferance of the community":[31]

[29] Mill, *Principles of Political Economy*, Book II, chap. i, sec. 3, p. 207.
[30] Ibid., 231–32.
[31] Ibid., 232.

No man made the land. It is the original inheritance of the whole species. Its appropriation is wholly a question of general expediency. When private property in land is not expedient, it is unjust.[32]

With respect to bequests, Mill says that they are one of the attributes of property. An owner, for reasons of "expediency" and to encourage savings, should have the right to bequeath by will "his or her whole property, but not to lavish it enriching some one individual, beyond a certain maximum, which should be fixed sufficiently high to afford the means of comfortable independence:"

> I see nothing objectionable in fixing a limit to what anyone may acquire by the mere favour of others, without any exercise of his faculties, and in requiring that if he desires any further accession of fortune, he shall work for it.[33]

Rawls too would regulate bequests and limit rights of inheritance. Even if it were assumed that certain rights of gift and bequest are implicit in property, these rights do not include the absolute right to transfer all and everything owned to whomever the owner chooses.[34] It is true that rights of gift and bequest encourage individuals not to squander their economic resources, but to save and reinvest them. For this reason, instead of taxing estates, both Rawls and Mill favor a tax on inheritances, thereby limiting rights of individuals on the receiving end of gifts and bequests to a specified amount. Inheritance taxes have the socially desirable effects of encouraging owners to spread their wealth around to more people and to charitable and other beneficial institutions, as well as limiting the adverse consequences of large individual accumulations of wealth on the equitable distribution of social and political power.

Both Mill and Rawls reject "natural property" and "natural rights" to property in possessions. They endorse versions of a conventional "bundle of rights and interests" view, and contend that property is a social/legal institutional convention that can be designed in different ways, depending upon the specification of the "incidents of property" (including the many rights, powers, duties, and liabilities, to possess, use,

---

[32] Ibid., 230.

[33] Ibid., 223, 225.

[34] Rawls explicitly excludes rights of acquisition and bequest from the basic right to hold personal property (*Justice as Fairness*, 114). The nature and extent of these rights instead are to be settled by the difference principle. Regarding rights of bequest, he says: "An estate need not be subject to tax, nor need the total given by bequest be limited. Rather the principle of progressive taxation is applied at the receiver's end. . . . The aim is to encourage a wide and far more equal dispersion of real property and productive assets." Rawls adds that the aim is also "to prevent accumulations of wealth that are judged to be inimical to background justice, for example, to the fair value of the political liberties and to fair equality of opportunity." Rawls, *Justice as Fairness*, 160–61.

transfer, and dispose of things, both tangible and intangible). Rawls and Mill are both influenced by Hume's account of property as a social convention. Hume says that property is not a quality of objects or a natural relation of persons to things, but an "internal" or "moral" relation among members of a society that exists by "convention."[35] Rawls too regards property as a conventional institution, the incidents of which can be specified and designed in multiple ways. One of the primary tasks for an account of distributive justice is to set forth and justify a principle for the specification and regulation of the rights and duties of possession, use, transfer, and disposal of the tangible and intangible things we ordinarily call "property." For Mill, this role was ultimately to be served by the principle of utility—for Rawls, by his second principle of justice, primarily the difference principle. On either account—and this is perhaps a central feature of the high liberal tradition—the rights and other incidents of property (what might be called its "ontology") are relativized or adjusted to meet the requirements of antecedent principles of justice, as these principles are applied to different social and historical circumstances.

The "ontological relativity" that Mill and Rawls bestow on property is not peculiar to the high liberal tradition. Hume was, after all, a (nascent) classical liberal. Similarly, Friedrich Hayek and Milton Friedman both endorse the Humean institutional conception of property. Friedman writes:

> The notion of property . . . has become so much a part of us that we tend to take it for granted, and fail to recognize the extent to which just what constitutes property and what rights the ownership of property confers are complex social creations rather than self-evident propositions.[36]

Friedman says that among the essential roles of governments is "the definition of the meaning of property rights"—by which he means its legislative and judicial specification. With respect to distributive justice, Friedman affirms the classical liberal principle of market distributions, but qualifies it:

> The ethical principle that would directly justify the distribution of income in a free market society is "to each according to what he and the instruments he owns produces." The operation of even this principle implicitly depends on state action. *Property rights are matters of law and social conventions. . . . [Hence] The final distribution of income*

---

[35] David Hume, *Treatise on Human Nature* (Oxford: Oxford University Press, 1960), 527, 491.
[36] Friedman, *Capitalism and Freedom*, 26.

and wealth under the full operation of this principle may well depend markedly on the rules of property adopted.[37]

The implication is that we stand in need of some principle to specify the rules of property that underwrite the classical liberal precept, "To each according to what he and the instruments he owns produces." The ideas of ownership and property rights are but placeholders until this principle is specified and justified.

Like other classical liberals within the Anglo-American tradition since Hume and Adam Smith, for Friedman the ultimate grounds for robust property rights, economic freedoms, and market distributions depend, not on claims of natural property rights regarded as "self-evident propositions,"[38] but on considerations of economic efficiency and, ultimately, social utility. Insofar as claims of natural property rights are made, as in the work of Adam Smith, they too ultimately are conceived instrumentally, as the incidents of property that achieve efficiency and the public benefit.

IV. THE ALLOCATIVE FUNCTION VERSUS THE DISTRIBUTIVE FUNCTION OF MARKETS

The second important similarity between Mill and Rawls is their conception of the proper role of markets. This clarifies their attitudes toward capitalism and helps to explain why both reject capitalism as understood by classical liberals. Mill distinguishes between laws of economic production and laws of distribution. He contends that laws of production are of universal applicability, whereas laws of distribution are not and are guided by institutional arrangements that differ among societies. The laws of production, Mill writes, "partake of the character of physical truths," whereas "the Distribution of Wealth . . . is a matter of human institution solely. The things once there, mankind, individually or collectively, can do with them as they like."[39]

Similarly, Rawls distinguishes between the role of market prices in allocating productive resources and their role in the distribution of income and wealth. "The former [allocative function] is connected with their use to achieve economic efficiency, the latter [distributive function] with their determining the income to be received by individuals in return for what

---

[37] Ibid., 162 (emphasis added).

[38] Ibid., 26.

[39] Mill, *Principles of Political Economy*, Book II, chap. i, sec. 1, p. 199. See Alan Kors's discussion (elsewhere in this volume) of this aspect of Mill's position. Lionel Robbins, in his 1979–81 lectures *A History of Economic Thought*, ed. Stephen Medema and Warren Samuels (Princeton, NJ: Princeton University Press, 1998), 224, says: "I ran into my friend Friedrich Hayek in the summer, and he was saying that he thought that Mill had done great harm by his distinction between the laws of production and distribution."

they contribute." In using the market to allocate productive factors, "prices are indicators for drawing up an efficient schedule of economic activities":

> It does not follow however that there need be private persons who as owners of these assets receive the monetary equivalents of these evaluations.[40]

The general implication is the same point made by Mill, namely, that a society's use of markets to determine the distribution of wealth is separate and apart from its use of markets to allocate productive resources.[41] In general, the efficient allocation of productive resources does not require that the distribution of wealth that results be determined by market distributions that result from efficient production.

Liberals generally endorse free markets and the price system for at least two reasons. First, unlike planned economies, a market system is crucial to realizing the basic liberty of persons to freely choose their own careers and workplaces. Markets are, in this way, essential to realizing both freedom of the person and equality of opportunity to compete for open positions. Planned economies and traditional societies constrained by class customs restrict individuals' choices in these matters or give them none at all; a person's occupation and workplace are assigned either by someone in authority or by social class and custom—in the latter case, your profession and path in life is the same as your father's or mother's. The second reason liberals generally endorse markets is that the market allocations of productive resources and labor are believed to be more likely to result in an efficient allocation of these factors of production than is a nonmarket system. Markets thereby normally minimize economic waste.[42] There are other justifications which may be emphasized by classical liberals but are not endorsed by high liberals (for example, free markets are required by the basic liberty of freedom of economic contract, which is not recognized as a basic liberty by high liberals); but on these two grounds at least, liberals of both varieties can agree.

Significantly, both of these arguments—from freedom of occupation/equality of opportunity and from allocative efficiency—relate to production and the allocation of labor and resources for purposes of productive economic activity. In the absence of a particular conception of property, the arguments do not by themselves imply anything in particular about

---

[40] Rawls, *A Theory of Justice*, 273 (p. 241 of the 1999 revised edition). Rawls indicates that he draws on the work of J. E. Meade for this distinction.

[41] Rawls's more specific point here is that even a socialist society with public ownership of the means of production can use prices to allocate factors of production. This is what he calls "market socialism" or "liberal socialism."

[42] This is normally, but not always, the case, since markets often generate "irrational exuberance" causing speculative "bubbles" which eventually burst (e.g., the recent overbidding and oversupply in the housing market).

who has rights to the economic product that is the efficient outcome of the activities of freely associated producers and entrepreneurs. Assuming that the three traditional "factors of production"—land, labor, and capital—all contribute their share to the final product, the question is left open as to how the resulting income, profits, interest, and rent are to be distributed among those cooperating to produce them, or among members of society as a whole.[43] The answer to this question is determined largely by a society's specification of property rights in productive resources and the rights of workers and owners of capital to income from the product created by their respective contributions. As Friedman says, "Property rights are matters of law and social convention. . . . The final distribution of income and wealth . . . depend[s] markedly on the rules of property adopted."[44]

Here classical liberals have argued that economic agents—workers and those who own and control capital alike—should each receive the marginal value of the contribution that each makes to productive output. Drawing on marginal productivity theory, many classical liberals contend that each participant in a joint economic enterprise contributes his or her share of factors of production (labor, land and raw materials, or capital, both real and liquid) toward the final product. According to standard microeconomic theory, we can measure the economic value of each of the inputs to production by determining its marginal contribution to the final product. The *marginal product* of each factor that each participant owns and controls is then (it is said) what he or she can be said to "contribute" toward the final output. Since each participant is responsible for what he or she contributes, it follows that in accordance with the precept of justice "To each according to his or her contribution," economic agents *morally ought* to share in the distribution of income and wealth in a manner proportionate to the value of their marginal product.[45]

---

[43] Mill says of wealth and productive output: "The things once there, mankind, individually or collectively, can do with them as they like. They can place them at the disposal of whomever they please, and on whatever terms. Further, in the social state . . . any disposal whatever of those can only take place by the consent of society, or rather of those who dispose of its active force." Mill, *Principles of Political Economy*, Book II, chap. I, sec. 1, p. 199–200.

[44] Friedman, *Capitalism and Freedom*, 162. The following argument in the text relies on an argument in my essay "Equality of Resources, Market Luck, and the Justification of Market Distributions," *Boston University Law Review* 90, no. 2 (April 2010): 921–48.

[45] Robert Nozick relies on marginal productivity theory for a similar argument: "People transfer their holdings or labor in free markets. . . . If marginal productivity theory is reasonably adequate, people will be receiving, in these voluntary transfers of holdings, roughly *their* marginal products. Robert Nozick, *Anarchy, State, and Utopia* (New York: Basic Books, 1974), 187–88 (emphasis added); see also ibid., 301–2, 304–5. In Nozick's utopia, "[E]ach person receives his marginal contribution to the world" (ibid., 302). Similarly, David Gauthier maintains: "In the free exchanges of the market each may expect a return equal in value to her contribution. Thus the income each receives . . . is equal to the contribution she makes, or the marginal difference she adds to the value of the total product. See David Gauthier, *Morals by Agreement* (Oxford: Oxford University Press, 1986), 92–93. "The equation of income with marginal contribution ensures just this impartiality. . . . [E]ach benefits from, and only from, the contribution she makes." Ibid., 97.

This is a popular way of thinking among classical liberals and libertarians, and it appeals to a notion of fairness in the distribution of the products of economic cooperation. Classical liberals and libertarians argue that owners of capital should have a right to the entire profits, interest, and rent that result from their investment of capital—exclusive of others, whether they also contribute or not—because profits, interest, and rent measure the marginal product of their contribution.

What are we to make of this argument from fairness, that economic agents' share in the final product should be proportionate to their (marginal) contribution? There is a genuine naturalistic sense in which workers can be said to contribute their labor toward productive output, as well as a naturalistic sense in which land, raw materials, and real capital make a contribution. It is a natural fact, regardless of the form taken by social conventions and institutions, that nothing could be produced in the absence of labor (which includes knowledge), land, natural resources, and the instruments of production created by their combination. Under capitalism and other private property systems, owners of capital and other resources are also causal agents in the production process due to their ownership and control of means of production. But the sense in which owners of factors of production other than labor themselves make a "contribution" to productive output is different from the kind of contribution made by labor, land, and capital itself. The contribution of owners is notional when compared to the contribution made by the factors of production they own; it is a manner of speaking that is dependent upon the rights of ownership and control that owners enjoy by virtue of legal and other conventional arrangements.

By way of example to clarify the point, consider a slave economy. While it is clear that the slaves on a sugar plantation make a substantial contribution toward agricultural production, to say that the *owners* of the slaves also make their "contribution" of labor ("after all, they own it") is to use that word in a very different sense from the one we use when we say "workers contribute their labor." Owners of slaves "contribute" the labor of those persons they own in this notional sense; it is (to use Jeremy Bentham's term) a "legal fiction." This much seems obvious.

Generalizing, the same notional sense of "contribution" is at work when it is said that owners of land, real capital, liquid capital, and any other resources "contribute" to economic output. Their "contribution" may be causally necessary within the social context; production could not, under the circumstances, take place without it, due to conventional norms of property. But this contribution is not on a par with the natural contribution that labor itself makes, just as it is not on a par with the physical contribution that natural and artificial resources make to productive output. The contribution made by the owners of productive resources is not a natural fact of either kind. Unlike workers, owners, regarded purely in their capacity as owners, do not themselves actually produce anything.[46] Often they are not even aware of doing anything (for example, owners of shares of mutual funds). Theirs is a legal contribution effected by virtue of the legal rights and powers that owners of capital resources are recognized as having by other members of a society. Legal rights and powers are institutional facts made possible by peoples' beliefs and other attitudes, and by their social activities. Property exists by virtue of a background of social rules which are collectively accepted and generally recognized as authoritative by (most) members of society, and by virtue of people interacting according to these rules. It is by virtue of the institutional facts of private property that owners of capital are deemed to make a "contribution" to production. Their contribution is not a "brute fact"; it is, rather, a matter of peoples' attitudes and linguistic descriptions formed against a background of institutional facts (property, money, government, and the legal system) which themselves exist only by virtue of collective agreement, intentions, and activities.[47]

Here economists have said that the capitalist makes a substantial or natural contribution after all, for she contributes her "abstinence" or "waiting to consume." That is to say, owners of wealth and capital *could* consume what they possess, but do not, and instead invest their resources and undertake risks that most others are unwilling to take. By undergoing this sacrifice, owners benefit society by capital formation. Had someone not abstained from consumption and saved wealth and resources, there would be no capital for workers to labor on.

Mill himself relied on this so-called abstinence theory of interest when, in response to the socialist claim that labor is the source of all value, he argued that owners of capital have a right to a return on their investment too.[48] But even if we concede that owners may serve a valuable function and have a right to *some* return on investment, abstinence from consumption does not by itself imply that owners of capital should have complete rights to the monetary value of the *entire* marginal product of the resources they legally own. The mere fact that the capitalist *could* consume his capital instead cannot establish a right to the entire marginal product. After all, a professional thief could consume it too, but this fact surely does not entitle the thief to any return, either for refraining from theft of productive resources, or for abstaining from consuming resources already stolen and investing them instead. The reason the capitalist (as opposed to the thief) can be said to contribute her "abstinence" is precisely that the capitalist is legally entitled and normally has a *right* to consume what she

---

[46] Of course, owners often manage or otherwise work in their own firms (particularly in smaller businesses); but then they no longer act purely in their capacity as owners, but are contributing their labor to production.

[47] On the distinction between brute facts and institutional facts such as private property and money, and the constitution of institutional facts out of individuals' beliefs and other attitudes and their collective intentions and activities, see John Searle, *The Construction of Social Reality* (New York: Free Press, 1995), chaps. 2–3.

[48] Mill, *Principles of Political Economy*, Book II, chap. ii, sec. 1, pp. 215–16.

owns, but decides to invest instead. From this it does not follow, without further argument, that the capitalist should have a right to the entire marginal product that is created by the resources she owns.

A similar point applies to the claim that owners of capital assume risks that others do not, and that this assumption of risk is their contribution to productive output. What owners risk are their legal rights to the capital and natural resources they invest in, including the economic value of their initial investment. Normally, except in the case of perishables, productive resources and consumer goods will survive even if a venture fails and owners lose their capital and resources to someone else (through bankruptcy) or have to sell their goods and resources at a loss. It is not so much the real capital or natural resources that are put at risk; rather, it is entrepreneurs' legally recognized *property rights* that are put at risk, including their rights to the value of their initial investment. By itself, putting their rights at risk does not imply anything in particular about how much of the marginal product owners should be entitled to in return for assuming this risk, should their investment be successful. From the fact that they risk losing their rights to their entire investment, it does not follow that they should have a right to the entire value of the marginal product resulting from this contribution. They are surely due something, but more needs to be said to justify this conclusion.

The general point here is that the argument from marginal productivity theory for market distributions depends upon an ambiguity involved when we speak of someone's "contribution to" productive output. It is this ambiguity between the de facto and de jure sense of "contribution to" (or "worker's versus owner's responsibility for") the final product that is played upon by the argument for market distributions according to the marginal product of each party's "contribution."[49]

None of this is meant to deny that private property in productive resources often serves an important *function.* Economists will argue that without private ownership of productive resources, much of the productive surplus that is created by labor likely would be consumed if it were distributed to workers themselves, and would not then be saved and reinvested. By allowing for private property in productive resources, a society creates the strategic position of *owners,* which provides an effective way to both shepherd resources and save and reinvest the productive surplus. Allowing private ownership and control of productive resources creates a group of people who are willing to save their surplus income (profits, interest, and rent) and take risks on investments that lead to the development of new products and services. If we did not allow people some kind of market return on the risks they undertake with their wealth,

---

[49] Marx, in effect, remarks on this conflation of different senses of "contribution" in a well-known passage on the "Trinity Formula," in *Capital*, Book III. See *Karl Marx: Selected Writings,* ed. David McClellan (Oxford: Oxford University Press, 1977), 500.

they would not undertake these risks, and new innovations and other benefits of undertaking market risks would not be realized within a society.

If this argument is sound, then it supports some kind of market economy with private ownership of productive resources and some degree of market returns for their use (as opposed to a socialist system where the public owns the means of production and receives the return on their use). Still, the functional argument for private ownership just stated does not justify rewarding owners with the *entire* marginal product of the capital they contribute to production. Rather, the functional argument simply establishes the beneficial effects of private over public ownership, and implies nothing in particular about individuals' rights to income, the rate of taxation, or what the returns to ownership should be. Nor does the beneficial function served by private ownership even justify capitalism in the traditional sense argued for by classical liberals, for not all private-property market economies are capitalist.[50] I conclude, then, that whatever role marginal productivity theory plays in microeconomic explanations of the market price of labor and productive resources, that theory cannot be used to justify full market distributions of income and wealth going to the private persons who legally own productive resources. For once we go beyond the natural contribution made by workers' labor and productive resources, the idea of a particular person's "contribution" toward or "responsibility for" productive output cannot be specified independently of the legal institution of property. When it comes to productive resources other than labor, individuals' "contribution to" and "responsibility for" the social product are institutionally dependent, indefinable outside an institutional (and normally legal) context. Again, as Milton Friedman said (in endorsing the classical liberal precept of justice "To each according to his contribution"): "The final distribution of income and wealth under the full operation of this principle may well depend markedly on the rules of property adopted."[51]

There remains then the problem of justice that appeals to marginal productivity theory were supposed to resolve—namely, the problem of justifying market distributions of income and wealth that result from productive activity. Assuming that for any legal system that is in place we can specify the legal or de jure contribution that owners are convention-

---

[50] For example, a property-owning democracy, which Rawls contrasts with welfare-state capitalism, structures institutions to encourage workers' private ownership and control of their industries. See Rawls, *Justice as Fairness*, 135–40. Martin Weitzman advocates replacing the wage relationship with a system that ties workers' compensation to an index of a firm's performance, such as a share of revenue and profits. See Martin Weitzman, *The Share Economy* (Cambridge, MA: Harvard University Press, 1984). John Roemer advocates a model of profit-maximizing firms that distribute profits across society; all members of society are given an equal or fair share of corporate stock upon reaching maturity, with a right to dividends depending upon how their firms or mutual funds perform. See John Roemer, *A Future for Socialism* (Cambridge, MA: Harvard University Press, 1994).

[51] Friedman, *Capitalism and Freedom*, 162.

ally regarded as making toward production, this cannot morally justify
market distributions according to each party's legally recognized contributions. Since the contribution of capitalists is not a natural contribution
(in the way that the contribution of workers and productive resources
clearly is) but is instead an institutional artifact, the question arises, "Why
should owners receive the entire income or marginal product of the
resources they legally own in the form of profits, interest, and rent?" It
begs the question to say "They own it," since the very problem to be
addressed is the justice of existing property relations and what the rights
of return on ownership should be. Thus, the argument for market distributions of marginal product must depend upon something other than
marginal productivity theory. Ultimately, it depends upon some version
of a laissez-faire theory of property rights, such as a theory of natural
property, which contends that people legally should be entitled to complete rights to income generated by the use of economic resources they
own and control.[52] Some such argument is presupposed by the conten-
tion that individuals are due the full marginal product of resources they
own.

If this is correct, then it suggests that the question whether individuals
should be rewarded according to their contributions cannot be settled
independently of questions regarding the justice of the economic system
and system of property relations that is in place. The adage "To each
according to his or her contribution" is at best a secondary precept which
presupposes some more fundamental account of economic justice.

V. Equal Opportunity and Economic Liberty

The argument for equality within the liberal tradition is more an argument for social equality rather than political equality. When Alexis de
Tocqueville published *Democracy in America* in 1835, the majority of American citizens were regarded as "passive" and without the right to vote;
males who did not meet property qualifications were excluded from the
franchise, as were, of course, women and African Americans. What made
the United States democratic in de Tocqueville's sense was not so much
democratic government as it was the absence of an inherited class structure and legal barriers to positions and occupations. The idea of careers
open to talents, or "the natural liberty of exercising what industry they
please" (Adam Smith) regardless of birth or lineage or (most) religious
affiliations, was affirmed by classical liberals in the eighteenth century.[53]
Only much later was the idea to be extended to race and gender. One

[52] Thus, Robert Nozick devotes a substantial amount of space to discussing the state of
nature and a right of initial appropriation of "unowned" things, subject to a "Lockean
Proviso." See Nozick, *Anarchy, State, and Utopia*, 67–182.
[53] Smith, *Wealth of Nations*, 470.

argument for the equal opportunity to compete for open positions lies in the classical liberal view of economic liberties. Workers should be free to market their services, employers should be allowed to employ whomever they choose, and merchants and other businesses should be free to engage in the exchange of goods and services with whomever they please, without being burdened by the legal enactment of others' religious, social, or racial biases. Moreover, opening positions purely to talents and skills increases economic efficiency. The classical liberal ideal of equal opportunity played a major role in democratizing society by breaking down the barriers of inherited class privilege and legal discrimination according to social position, religion, wealth, and (eventually) race and gender.

Still, the classical liberal view of economic liberties did little directly to mitigate social (as opposed to legal) discrimination. Owners and employees still had the right in theory and in practice to refuse goods, services, and employment by virtue of their robust property and contract rights. Racial discrimination in hotels, restaurants, real estate sales, and many other areas of life was common in the United States, even in the absence of Jim Crow laws in the South and elsewhere which legally mandated it.[54] Segregation and racial discrimination by businesses were legally protected in most of the United States until the 1960s, even when not legally required. Of course, classical liberals do not endorse racial or other forms of discrimination. The vast majority reject it in theory as much as other liberals do. Classical liberals often contend that, because of freedom of contract, these sorts of problems will eventually sort themselves out. Businesses or entrepreneurs that discriminate on grounds not related to economic efficiency are at a disadvantage, since they are imposing higher costs on themselves. Free markets will tend to drive out of business those who discriminate on grounds other than economic efficiency.[55]

This is one of many examples where what is true in the economic theory of perfectly competitive markets is not true in fact of our social world of the "second best." Where there is widespread racial or ethnic bias, discrimination on these grounds is a precondition to economic success. Even where enlightened businesses might want to serve disfavored minorities, their trade would soon suffer due to ingrained social customs and prejudices. Until relatively recently in most parts of the South and in

---

[54] So-called Jim Crow laws arose in the South and elsewhere in the United States after the end of Reconstruction in the 1870s, and continued until the 1950s and 1960s. They mandated, among other restrictions, de jure segregation of most public facilities and accommodations, including schools, public restrooms, buses and trains, and restaurants and hotels. In 1954, the U.S. Supreme Court, in *Brown v. Board of Education*, declared segregation of public schools unconstitutional. This case was a milestone in the eventual elimination of Jim Crow laws by the Civil Rights Acts of 1957 and 1964 and the Voting Rights Act of 1965. See C. Vann Woodward's classic history, *The Strange Career of Jim Crow* (New York: Oxford University Press, 1955); and Michael J. Klarman; *From Jim Crow to Civil Rights: The Supreme Court and the Struggle for Racial Equality* (Oxford: Oxford University Press, 2004).

[55] See Friedman, *Capitalism and Freedom*, 109–10.

many other areas of the United States, the hotel or restaurant or business that freely served blacks would soon serve only blacks, since whites would cease doing business there (or worse). Only with the Civil Rights Act of 1964 in the United States, which banned racial discrimination by employers and "public accommodations," was this problem of social inequality addressed (to the extent that it could be addressed by law), and did things begin to change. All employers or businesses that do business with the public are now legally prohibited from discriminating among job applicants or customers "on the basis of race, color, religion, sex, or national origin." Economic contracts are no longer regarded as purely private transactions between willing parties, but are now recognized as having social consequences, sometimes serious, for others.

In response to such antidiscrimination measures and policies enacted by the Fair Employment Practices Commission (FEPC), Milton Friedman objected that measures such as the Civil Rights Act are serious violations of individuals' freedom. He wrote:

> There is a strong case for using government to prevent one person from imposing positive harm, which is to say, to prevent coercion. There is no case whatsoever for using government to avoid the negative kind of "harm." On the contrary, *such government intervention reduces freedom and limits voluntary cooperation.*
>
> FEPC legislation involves the acceptance of a principle that proponents would find abhorrent in almost every other application. If it is appropriate for the state to say that individuals may not discriminate in employment because of color or race or religion, then it is equally appropriate for the state ... to say that individuals must discriminate in employment on the basis of color, race or religion. The Hitler Nuremberg laws and the laws of the Southern states imposing special disabilities upon Negroes are both examples of laws similar in principle to FEPC.[56]

The laws are said to be similar in principle, and both are condemned, on the grounds that in both cases government's coercive powers are used in a way that "reduces freedom and limits voluntary cooperation." The political injustice done to the entrepreneur, restauranteur, or hotel owner who is legally required under the Civil Rights Act to fairly consider black job applicants or to serve Jews and Hispanics is then put on the same plane with the injustice done, not only to businesses and employers, but also blacks and Jews who are legally prohibited from entering employment positions or frequenting public places or businesses in the Jim Crow South and in Nazi Germany. In both cases, their freedom is limited and cooperative relations are no longer voluntary.

[56] Ibid., 113 (emphasis added).

There appears to be a conflation here between the reasons that underlie freedom of economic contract and those that underlie freedom of association in one's personal life. Freedom of association is among the most fundamental of the liberal basic liberties. It is a precondition of freedom of conscience that we be able to personally associate with others of like mind and conscientious convictions, and also a precondition for our realizing such great values as personal relations of love, friendship, and personal intimacy. For Friedman, economic contracts between strangers are to be regarded as if they were on a par with such private relations—both are forms of voluntary cooperation and, as such, freedom of contract should be given the same degree of protection as freedom of religious associations or of personal or intimate associative relations between friends or lovers. It is as if there would be no moral difference between my being legally required to sell goods to a black person that I offer for sale to the general public, and my being legally required to invite black guests over for dinner if I also choose to invite nonblacks.

One important difference between the liberal freedoms of association and contract is that contractual relations—unlike associative relations between friends, lovers, and members of private clubs, fraternities, or religious groups—are legally sanctioned and enforceable. We can enter into and break off friendships, intimate relationships, club memberships, and religious and other affiliations, and it is none of government's business. Government's lack of enforcement primarily distinguishes freedom of association from freedom of contract. Unlike freely associative relations, there is no right of exit from contractual relations without legal consequences; one either has to pay damages or restitution, or has to execute one's contractual obligations in cases of specific performance. Freely entered contracts thus have the imprimatur of government and are specifically designed to invoke the exercise of public political power.[57] There is no parallel to this in the case of freedom of association; instead, there is a presumption of a right of exit without legal consequences (unless, of course, one has made a contract explicitly invoking government's involvement, as in the case of civil marriages). For high liberals, it is in large part the exercise of public political power, to define and enforce legally recognizable contracts, that gives liberal governments the legitimate authority to specify certain terms and conditions that contractual relations must satisfy.

Of course, given liberals' endorsement of free-market relations, there has to be good reason for government to limit freedom of contract by

---

[57] This accords with the ruling by the U.S. Supreme Court in *Shelley v. Kraemer*, 334 U.S. 1 (1948), which held that private restrictive covenants barring blacks from ownership of real estate are unenforceable since they violate the equal protection clause of the Fourteenth Amendment to the U.S. Constitution. The Court said it is illegal for the government, including the judiciary, to enforce such covenants since the state then plays an integral role in a policy of racial discrimination in violation of the Fourteenth Amendment.

requiring (as in the case of FEPC legislation and the Civil Rights Act) that
merchants do business with certain customers they would rather avoid.
Friedman contends that there is not good reason. Continuing the argument above, he says that since both laws coercively restrict voluntary
cooperation, "Opponents of [the Hitler Nuremburg] laws who are in
favor of FEPC cannot argue that there is anything wrong with them in
principle"[58]—thus suggesting that there is no principled basis for limiting voluntary cooperation in one case but not the other. But for high
liberals, the basic reasons that the Nuremburg laws are unjust are not that
they limit voluntary cooperation. (As Friedman and other classical liberals recognize, there are often legitimate reasons for limiting voluntary
cooperation—for example, in cases of conspiracies to commit crimes, conspiracies in restraint of trade, bribery, and so on.) The main reasons why
Nuremburg, Jim Crow, and other racist laws are fundamentally unjust are
that (1) they publicly deny the equal moral and civic status of racial and
ethnic groups, and (2) they legally restrict group members' basic freedoms of occupation and choice of careers as well as (3) their rights to
equal opportunities to compete and take part in social and economic life.
These are the selfsame reasons and principles for which high liberals also
restrict freedom of economic contract (in the Civil Rights Act and elsewhere) in ways that many classical liberals will not countenance. Friedman is then mistaken; the principles that expose the obvious injustice of
the Nuremburg and Jim Crow laws are the selfsame principles that justify
compelling those who do business with the public not to engage in invid-
ious discrimination in their economic transactions.

A more robust conception of social and civic equality and equality of
opportunity is, then, the primary reason that high liberals restrict freedom of economic contract in ways that most classical liberals will not
countenance. John Stuart Mill's argument for the equality of women in
economic, political, and social life gives early expression to the high liberal position that civic equality and equality of opportunity are not simply to be regarded as formal requirements that forbid the legal exclusion
of women and other classes of individuals from taking advantage of
social, political, and economic opportunities.[59] Equality of opportunity is
a social requirement that is regarded as necessary to secure and maintain
the equal social and civic status of all citizens in the public domain and
in one another's eyes.

The public funding of educational opportunities is also explicable within
the high liberal tradition on similar grounds. Already, early classical liberals such as Adam Smith saw the benefits of publicly funded education
to a nation's efficient productive capacities.[60] Moreover, as Friedman notes,

[58] Friedman, *Capitalism and Freedom*, 113.
[59] See Mill, *The Subjection of Women*, in Mill, *On Liberty and Other Essays*.
[60] See Smith, *Wealth of Nations*, Book V, chap. 1, art. ii, on compulsory education: "For a
very small expence the public can facilitate, can encourage, and can even impose upon

education involves "neighborhood effects," the costs of which cannot be charged to those who benefit, and should thus be publicly assumed.[61] Thus, many classical liberals see general education of all children as among the public goods to be provided by government. Here again, for high liberals, classical liberals' primarily economic justification of equality of opportunity does not suffice or pinpoint the real reasons for a right to publicly funded education. As I will discuss in my concluding section, there is an ideal of persons and their relations as equals that underpins the high liberal view of the substantive requirements of equality of opportunity.

VI. DISTRIBUTIVE JUSTICE: INCOME, WEALTH, AND ECONOMIC POWERS

The idea of distributive justice does not find much favor among classical liberals or libertarians since (as Nozick said) it suggests that there is some pattern or end-state that must be met if the distribution of income and wealth is to be justified.[62] Here I use the term "distributive justice" more broadly than this, to refer to the standards that should be relied upon in society for assessing whether people have just entitlements to the income, wealth, and economic powers that they legally own, control, or exercise. So understood, capitalist market distributions against a background of robust private property rights specify the fundamental standard of distributive justice for classical liberals—on the assumption that economic agents have paid their proportionate share to maintain the institutions of justice and provide for public goods. Thus, the marginal productivity theory of just distributions discussed earlier says that the share of income that is owed to workers and owners of resources is to be determined by the market value of their respective contributions, which are construed as the (marginal) product created by their labor or property. This market distribution is a fundamental feature of capitalism as a social and economic system. For classical liberals, it stands as *the* fundamental principle of distributive justice. It may not be the only principle—people acquire rights to gifts and bequests, gambling winnings, abandoned property, and so on—but markets still provide the fundamental determining

---

almost the whole body of the people, the necessity of acquiring these most essential parts of education" (p. 785). Smith says that among the benefits to the state of educating "the inferior ranks of people" is that they are more disposed to work and be orderly and respectful of themselves, others, and their superiors, and less prone to disorder, superstition, and sedition (p. 788).

[61] "The education of my child contributes to your welfare by promoting a stable and democratic society." Friedman, *Capitalism and Freedom*, 86. Friedman argues for publicly issued vouchers to be used at privately run, for-profit or nonprofit schools (ibid., 89).

[62] Nozick, *Anarchy, State, and Utopia*, 149–50. Hayek more generally condemns the idea of "social justice." The title of the second volume of his *Law, Legislation, and Liberty* is *The Mirage of Social Justice*.

principle of distribution of the income resulting from productive economic activity itself.

Advocates of the high liberal tradition generally reject predominantly market-driven theories of just distributions. While they regard market transfers as an efficient instrument for distributing a substantial portion of the distributive shares that members of society are due, they reject (free and efficient) market distribution itself as the fundamental principle of economic justice in the distribution of income and wealth. Thus, Rawls contends that the fair distribution of income and wealth is to be determined by the "pure procedural" outcome of a "social process" wherein economic institutions and property are designed and specified according to Rawls's second principle of justice, including the difference principle.[63] Markets play an instrumental role in achieving this distribution, but they are not themselves the standard for determining just entitlements. Nor is the market the only procedural mechanism for realizing the fair distribution of income and wealth for high liberals. Rawls envisions income supplements (such as earned-income tax credits in the United States) as among the instrumental means of distribution of income required by distributive justice.[64] The ultimate standard for determining just distributions is the difference principle set against a background of institutions satisfying fair equality of opportunity. Distributive shares are fully just when economic institutions work, over time, to make the class of least advantaged workers in society better off in terms of their share of relevant primary social goods (income, wealth, and economic powers) than they would be in any other economic system that is compatible with the basic liberties protected by Rawls's first principle. (As I shall explain momentarily, this does not mean that the least advantaged are to have more income and wealth than in any alternative economy.)

I do not mean to say that all high liberals reject capitalism or the standard of market distributions altogether. Some do not, but rather contend that market distributions, while essential, are not sufficient for establishing just distributions. Thus, welfare-state capitalists might affirm market distributions as one among the fundamental principles of economic justice. But they deny the classical liberal position that the economic liberties and property rights are nearly coequal with the basic personal liberties. For example, Ronald Dworkin's position, "equality of resources," justifies

---

[63] Rawls's second principle of justice is set forth above in the second paragraph of Section III.

[64] Rawls, *A Theory of Justice*, sec. 43, see esp. pp. 242–45. On income supplements more generally, see Edmund Phelps, *Rewarding Work* (Cambridge, MA: Harvard University Press, 1997; 2d ed., 2007). Earned-income tax credits in the U.S. are means-tested income supplements paid primarily to low- and moderate-income workers with children (workers earning $48,278, or less if they have fewer than three children). In 2010, the EIC paid $3,050 for one child, $5,036 for two, and a maximum of $5,666. ($457 is paid to workers with no children earning less than $13,460, or $18,440 if married and filing jointly). See Publication 596 EIC at http://www.IRS.gov. Other countries, including Canada and the United Kingdom, have similar programs.

a form of welfare-state capitalism.[65] It says that once the consequences of arbitrary natural and social inequalities have been neutralized, entitlements to income and wealth are determined by our choices and how well we fare in market activity. Dworkin seeks to equalize starting positions in life and neutralize the effects of "brute luck," which include differences in natural talents, social position, and misfortunes for which people are not responsible. (Mill expresses a similar luck-equalizing position regarding remuneration of labor.)[66] Each person then has a duty to pay his or her fair share in taxes toward maintaining an economic system that meets this and other conditions. But Dworkin does not try to neutralize market luck (a form of "option luck") or otherwise put restrictions on the inequalities that free and efficient market activities and distributions may cause. He believes that, once individuals have paid their share toward public goods, social insurance, and other conditions necessary for maintaining justice, they should be entitled to whatever they gain by market activity. Dworkin's example shows that high liberalism does not necessarily imply a rejection of capitalism. Rather, what it implies is a rejection of unqualified capitalist market distributions, and of the reliance on (free and efficient) markets as the fundamental standard for the distribution of income and wealth.

The rejection of markets as the fundamental standard for just distributions of income and wealth is the most obvious respect in which high liberalism differs from the classical tradition. I want to focus, however, on a different characteristic of some (if not all) high liberal positions that suggests a more thorough rejection of capitalism as traditionally understood. This feature is implicit in Mill's and Rawls's (and John Dewey's) advocacy of institutions which enable workers' control of their work environment and ownership of productive resources. I shall approach this topic by noting a peculiar feature in Rawls's view. Rawls rejects welfare-state capitalism in favor of "property-owning democracy," a private-property market system which involves widespread private ownership of means of production. How can he do this consistent with the difference principle? Assuming, as classical liberals argue, that free-market capitalism is capable of producing greater economic output than any alternative economic system, how can Rawls avoid endorsing some form of welfare-state capitalism under the difference principle? For given efficient markets, increasing economic output, more reinvestment, and greater overall income and wealth, it seems that there will always be greater income and wealth created to redistribute to the less advantaged

---

[65] Ronald Dworkin's position on economic justice is set forth in his *Sovereign Virtue* (Cambridge, MA: Harvard University Press, 2000), esp. chaps. 1, 2, and 7–9; and also in his *Justice for Hedgehogs* (Cambridge, MA: Harvard University Press, 2011).

[66] Mill writes in *Principles of Political Economy*, Book II, chap. i, sec. 4, p. 210: "The proportioning of remuneration to work done, is really just, only in so far as the more or less of work is a matter of choice: when it depends on natural difference of strength or capacity, this principle of remuneration is itself an injustice: it is giving to those who have: assigning most to those who are already favored most by nature."

in a capitalist economy than in any alternative economic arrangement. Therefore, it would seem that the least advantaged should fare better under welfare-state capitalism than in any other economic system. How then can Rawls reject the capitalist welfare state?

The answer to this puzzle must be that Rawls's difference principle is the ultimate standard for distributing not only income and wealth, but also the primary social goods that Rawls calls "powers and positions of responsibility." By "powers" he means legal and other institutional powers of various kinds, primarily those powers required to make economic decisions, including powers of control over productive resources. What primarily distinguishes property-owning democracy from welfare-state capitalism, Rawls says, is that the former involves less inequality in primary social goods—income and wealth, and economic powers and positions—and greater worker ownership and control over productive resources and over their workplace conditions.[67]

Here again, Rawls's account resembles Mill's. In the third edition of his *Principles of Political Economy,* Mill revised his discussion "On the Probable Futurity of the Laboring Classes" (Book IV, chapter 7). In the revised version, he states that, as opposed to laissez-faire, his own position is based on "equality," and that the desirable form of production is "association without dependence." The wage relationship is undesirable, Mill says, since it makes workers "servants," dependent on capitalists for their subsistence and well-being. Moreover, it puts workers and owners of capital in conflict, and has a demoralizing effect on the working classes.[68] He optimistically predicts that eventually "the relations of masters and workpeople will be gradually superseded by partnership in one of two forms: in some cases, association of the labourers with the capitalists; in others, and perhaps finally in all, association of labourers among themselves."[69] Mill goes on to discuss these two arrangements in some detail: first, the share arrangement between owners and laborers where profits are divided among them; and second, "the association of the laborers themselves on terms of equality."[70] Either arrangement would give workers an interest in production and in the success of the firm, and would work to cure workers' indifference toward their work, and their hostility and conflict with owners. Mill's preferred arrangement is the second, which involves ownership and control of firms by workers themselves, where accumulations of capital "become in the end the joint property of all who participate in their productive employment. [This] would be the

---

[67] Rawls, *Justice as Fairness,* 135–40, 158–62, 176–78.

[68] Mill says that the wage relationship divides "the producers into two parties with hostile interests, the many who do the work being mere servants under the command of the one who supplies the funds, and having no interest of their own in the enterprise except to earn their wages with as little labour as possible." Mill, *Principles of Political Economy,* Book IV, chap. vii, sec. 4, p. 769.

[69] Ibid., 769.

[70] Ibid., 775.

nearest approach to social justice and the most beneficial ordering of industrial affairs for the universal good."[71]

These workers' "Associations" or "Co-operations" (as Mill calls them) are to take place within a framework of competitive markets for labor and productive resources. To be successful, he says, they must allow for incentives within the firm as well as worker-approved individual managers rather than collective management by workers themselves. Thus, unlike Marx and other socialists of his era, Mill affirmed a need for markets and competition among firms; he opposed a central and planned economy with public ownership; he endorsed some degree of inequality of income and wealth as necessary for incentives; and he opposed organized revolutionary activity by the working classes. But Mill still regarded it as essential to individual independence and the free development of "individuality" that employees not be subservient to their employers; that the wage relationship and the division between workers and capitalists be moderated if not dissolved; and that workers be given economic powers and ownership interests in their workplaces.[72]

Rawls refers to Mill's "Associations of workers" as one among several possible economic arrangements within property-owning democracy.[73] Rawls shares with Mill a rejection of capitalism and the endorsement of a private-propertied competitive market system where ownership and control of productive resources and wealth is widely distributed among workers and citizens generally. What is revealing about Rawls's claim that distributive justice requires a property-owning democracy rather than a capitalist welfare state is that it shows that his primary concern with distributive justice is not simply, or even primarily, the distribution of income and wealth—if that were his concern, then the capitalist welfare state probably could do the job better than other alternatives. Equally if not more important for Rawls is that workers be able to own a share of productive wealth and have some control over their own productive activities:

> What men want is meaningful work in free association with others, these associations regulating their relations to one another within a

---

[71] Ibid., 793–94.

[72] John Dewey also advocated arrangements that democratize work without socializing the means of production. He wrote: "Democracy is not in reality what it is in name until it is industrial as well as civil and political." John Dewey, "The Ethics of Democracy," in *John Dewey, The Early Works*, vol. I (Carbondale: Southern Illinois University, 1969), 246. Later in the same work, Dewey writes: "That the economic and industrial life is *in itself* ethical, that it is to be made contributory to the realization of personality through the formation of a higher and more complete unity among men . . . such is the meaning of the statement that democracy must become industrial." Ibid., 248. For a discussion of what he calls Dewey's "guild socialism," see Ryan, *John Dewey and the High Tide of American Liberalism*, 111–17 and 309–27.

[73] Rawls, *Justice as Fairness*, 176, 178.

framework of just basic institutions. To achieve this state of things, great wealth is not necessary.[74]

Having a share of economic powers while engaging in "meaningful work" is instrumental if not essential to fostering "perhaps the most important primary [social] good," the self-respect of free and equal democratic citizens.[75] This leads into my final topic, the conception of persons underlying the high liberal tradition.

VII. Conclusion: The Bases of the High Liberal Tradition

I have discussed the main differences between the classical and high liberal traditions. While they both endorse personal liberties as fundamentally important, the classical tradition also gives priority to robust if not unqualified rights of private property in productive resources and other economic liberties, regarding them as of nearly equal significance with other basic liberties. Consequently, the just distribution of income, wealth, and economic powers is for classical liberals largely determined by property rights and the exercise of the economic liberties within a framework of free and efficient markets. Property and economic liberties also largely determine the scope of the classical liberal requirement of equality of opportunity; it is regarded primarily in formal terms, as careers being legally open to talents with an absence of legal discrimination against disfavored groups. Finally, workers' private ownership and control of their means of production is regarded as hopelessly inefficient and hence undesirable. Moreover, the measures needed to put into place and maintain Mill's or Rawls's ideas of property-owning democracy would require the curtailing of many economic liberties and powers that classical liberals regard as fundamental.

What accounts for these differences between classical and high liberals regarding economic justice? Historically, utilitarianism has provided the main philosophical foundation for Anglo-American classical liberalism. Even among philosopher-economists who are part of (or influenced by) the Austrian tradition, such as von Mises and Hayek, a kind of indirect utilitarianism plays a significant role in the defense of their positions.[76] There are, of course, many philosophers who see themselves as classical liberals and nonetheless reject utilitarianism and welfarism generally in favor of a more Kantian or natural law grounding for their view. These views sometimes are hard to distinguish from libertarianism, and when

[74] Rawls, *A Theory of Justice,* rev. ed., 257.
[75] See ibid., 386–88, on the primary social good of self-respect; ibid., 477–78, on self-respect and equal citizenship; and Rawls, *Justice as Fairness,* 114, on property rights, personal independence, and self-respect.
[76] As discussed earlier in note 5.

they are, I would contend that they are not classical liberal views. But nothing rides on the honorific title "classical liberalism," or "liberalism." What is important are the central features of purportedly liberal views, and the justifications provided for them.

Here I will conclude with some remarks on the primary kind of argument that underwrites the high liberal tradition and the main features I have gone over that distinguish it from classical liberalism. Once again I shall rely on Mill and Rawls. In the work of both, there is to be found an ideal of persons and their essential good that underlies these theorists' conceptions of the distinctive features of high liberalism. For Mill, this is a kind of perfectionist ideal which he calls "individuality": "The free development of individuality is one of the leading essentials of well-being."[77] A person exercises individuality when he or she freely forms and lives according to a life-plan that consists of activities involving the free exercise and full development of the "higher faculties" of reason, understanding, creative imagination, feeling and emotions, and moral sentiments. Individuality, Mill says, includes both the self-development of one's "higher faculties" and self-government according to "the rigid rules of justice."[78] While Mill says that his principle of liberty is grounded not in natural right, but in utility, he famously qualifies this claim, saying that "it must be utility in the largest sense, grounded on the permanent interests of man as a progressive being."[79] Achieving individuality is primary among these "permanent interests" and is a large part of Mill's conception of utility.

It is helpful to understand not just Mill's principle of liberty, but, more generally, his account of political and economic justice and the rights of property, as grounded in this ideal of individuality which he incorporated into his utilitarianism. As the basic liberties protected by the principle of liberty are essential conditions of people realizing their individuality, so too this same ideal of a person's "permanent interests" justifies, for Mill, representative democracy, the social equality of women, and the "social-ist" revisions to capitalism (as Mill calls them) that he advocates as a necessary corrective to laissez-faire if a market economy is to prove superior to communism. The reason that absolute property and freedom of economic contract are not basic liberties for Mill is not that (in his words) "trade is a social act"; rather, these economic rights and liberties are not essential conditions for citizens generally to realize their individuality and exercise and develop their distinctly human capacities. Indeed, as Mill suggests in some places, the traditional conception of laissez-faire tends to undermine the possibility that many people will realize these

---

[77] Mill, *On Liberty*, 63 (chap. 3, sec. 2). Mill continues: "It [individuality] is not only a co-ordinate element with all that is designated by the terms civilization, instruction, education, culture, but is itself a necessary part and condition of all those things." Ibid.

[78] Ibid., 70 (chap. 3, sec. 9).

[79] Ibid., 15 (chap. 1, sec. 11).

great goods. Under those circumstances, "the great social evil exists of a non-labouring class" that is able to work but which subsists off the labor of others.[80] As a result, "the rich regard the poor as, by a kind of natural law, their servants and dependents," and the working classes are without "just pride," or a sense of self-respect; they "return as little in the shape of service as possible."[81] The principle well-being of the laboring classes is primarily dependent on their own mental cultivation and their taking care of their own destiny.[82] This can only occur under working conditions of "association without dependence."

Rawls makes it explicit that an ideal of the person and a person's essential good grounds his principle of equal basic liberties and provides the standards for specifying which liberties are basic and have priority over other social values. The ideal of "free and equal moral persons" who have fundamental interests in the realization of their "moral powers" of practical reasoning and social cooperation combines with an ideal of a "well-ordered society" that is grounded in relations of reciprocity and mutual respect which are acceptable to all its citizens. These ideals of persons and society underwrite Rawls's second principle of justice, including the difference principle. Like Mill, Rawls holds that classical liberal property rights and the enforcement of the traditional doctrine of laissez-faire are not conditions of free and equal persons' adequate development and full exercise of their moral powers and their achievement of their rational autonomy, "and so are not an essential social basis of self-respect."[83] Nor are laissez-faire property rights and relations generally acceptable terms of social cooperation among free and equal persons who desire to cooperate on grounds of reciprocity and mutual respect. Instead, laissez-faire undermines the likelihood that many citizens will ever achieve these essential goods.

One of the main contributions Rawls makes to liberal and democratic theory is the idea that the liberties and procedures historically associated with liberalism and with constitutional democracy should be conceived as grounded, not upon utilitarianism or an *a priori* conception of natural law and natural rights, but upon an ideal conception of persons and of society. The freedom and equality of persons are fundamental liberal values. Liberals have different interpretations of these values, and these are embedded in different ideals of persons and their social relations. Rawls's conception of the person and of society, and Mill's idea of persons' "permanent interests" in the free development of their individual-

---

[80] Mill, *Principles of Political Economy*, Book IV, chap. vii, sec. 1, p. 758: "I do not recognize as either just or salutary, a state of society in which there is any class which is not 'labouring'; any human being, exempt from bearing their share of the necessary labours of human life, except those unable to labour, or who have fairly earned rest by previous toil."

[81] Ibid., 767.

[82] Ibid., 763.

[83] Rawls, *Justice as Fairness*, 114.

ity, provide the foundations for these theorists' high liberal conceptions of fundamental liberties and social and economic justice. One or more alternative conceptions of persons and their social relations are implicitly relied upon by classical liberals too, to bolster their arguments for capitalism and market distributions. Many historical and contemporary classical liberals (such as David Gauthier, Richard Posner, et al.) see persons as rational utility-maximizers, who are willing to make trade-offs between all their desires and interests in pursuit of maximum individual utility. There are other classical liberals and libertarians who reject such welfarism and advocate laissez-faire capitalist freedoms and robust or absolute property rights on different grounds; they too rely, implicitly if not explicitly, upon a different conception of persons and their social relations than Rawls, Mill, and others in the high liberal tradition.[84] If there is any progress to be made in debates about the importance to liberalism of capitalism, robust private property rights, and the essential role of markets in establishing economic justice, it will require awareness and discussion of the different and conflicting ideals of persons and their social relations that liberals implicitly rely upon in the positions they advocate. At issue in these debates is not simply the nature of our economic and social relations, but ultimately the kinds of persons that we are and can come to be.

Philosophy and Law, University of Pennsylvania

[84] Thus, libertarians such as Nozick might regard persons in the first instance as self-owners with absolute rights in their persons as well as their possessions, and society as a free association of such owners whose relations are contractually specified. The question then becomes, what capacities and features of persons justify our seeing ourselves and our relations primarily in this way?

FOUNDING LIBERALISM, PROGRESSIVE LIBERALISM, AND THE RIGHTS OF PROPERTY

By Ronald J. Pestritto

I. Introduction

There may be no better indication in America of the growing opposition between capitalism and modern liberalism than the conscious and pervasive effort of today's liberals to connect themselves to America's Progressive Movement. As America's modern liberals have moved sharply away from the free-market foundations of classical liberalism, some of them, at least, seem to recognize that such a move necessitates their abandonment of the term "liberal" altogether. Few liberals (in the contemporary usage of that term) in national politics today proclaim themselves as such; instead, they claim the label "progressive." No doubt, in some cases, this is merely a tactical move: "liberal" is still a dirty word in the contemporary American lexicon due to the effects of the national political debate in the 1980s, and politicians on the Left are prudent to avoid being tarred with it. But there is something deeper than this at work; for many on the Left, self-identification as "progressive" goes well beyond finding a more palatable way of saying "liberal." When pressed about this in a debate during the 2008 Democratic primary campaign for the presidency, Hillary Clinton emphatically identified herself not just as a "progressive," but as a progressive who could best be understood by "going back to the Progressive Era at the beginning of the twentieth century."[1] What is arguably the most influential think-tank on the Left today, headed by John Podesta, a former aide to President Bill Clinton, is called the Center for American Progress; the title of Podesta's popular 2008 book is *The Power of Progress: How America's Progressives Can (Once Again) Save Our Economy, Our Climate, and Our Country.*[2] Considering these developments together with the national legislative agenda that has emerged from 2008 to 2010, it can be argued that modern liberalism has come home to its progressive roots.

What this development means is that the variant of liberalism that emerged over the course of the twentieth century does not have much to do with its eighteenth-century predecessor that was so influential on the founding of the United States. By invoking the American Progressive

---

[1] Democratic Presidential Debate, July 23, 2007, held at The Citadel in South Carolina.
[2] John Podesta, *The Power of Progress: How America's Progressives Can (Once Again) Save Our Economy, Our Climate, and Our Country* (New York: Crown Books, 2008).

doi:10.1017/S026505251000021X

Movement, modern liberals invoke the very movement which had as its chief characteristic an intellectual and political assault on the principles of eighteenth-century liberalism. Thus, in order to explore the relationship between liberalism and capitalism, liberalism and free markets, or liberalism and property rights, we must first determine which liberalism we are talking about.[3] The story of the move from classical, eighteenth-century liberalism in America to the liberalism of America in the twentieth century centers on the Progressive Era and the transformation undertaken there in our understanding of equality, liberty, and rights — property rights, in particular. This essay endeavors to contribute to the exploration of liberalism and capitalism by discussing how liberalism changed its premise about the rights of property as it became transformed by the intellectuals and politicians of the Progressive Movement.

The liberalism of the American founding was a liberalism of natural rights. The Progressives understood this, and it is why their major intellectual works begin, almost without exception, with a critique of natural rights and the theory of social compact. The topic of natural rights and the American founding is deep enough for a lengthy study of its own; since the purpose of this essay is to explore the Progressive departure from the early American idea of rights, I will wade into the theory of the founding only to the extent that it is necessary to understand the subsequent Progressive departure.

II. FOUNDING LIBERALISM

Progressives rightly identified the 1776 American Declaration of Independence as the preeminent statement of the new nation's governing philosophy, and they were especially troubled (as will be demonstrated below) by the transhistorical and limited account of the purpose of government contained in the Declaration. The Progressives identified the language of the Declaration with the social compact philosophy of John Locke's *Second Treatise of Government* (1689). Because the nature of Lockean liberalism is complex, we should be careful about unequivocally equating Locke's principles with the founders'; the actual significance of Locke's principles may be distinct from how those principles were understood by America's founding generation and applied in the statesmanship of the day. Nonetheless, there can be little doubt about the founders' adoption of the political teach-

---

[3] It is conceded that some scholars question the existence, or at least the degree, of a distinction between the old liberalism and the new liberalism, suggesting, in some cases, that certain inherent flaws present in the original liberalism are the cause of modern liberalism. For just one example, see Peter Augustine Lawler, "Natural Law, Our Constitution, and Our Democracy," in Ronald J. Pestritto and Thomas G. West, eds., *Modern America and the Legacy of the Founding* (Lanham, MD: Lexington Books, 2007), 207-37. The particulars of this debate lie beyond the scope of this essay, although by explicating the Progressive assault on the early American notion of property rights, the argument of the essay as a whole weighs against the assertions of Lawler and others.

ing of social compact theory:[4] the purpose of government, according to the Declaration, is the same for all men by virtue of their common nature, and does not change from one generation to the next. This purpose is to secure "certain unalienable rights," as the Declaration states—rights which all individuals possess in accord with "the Laws of Nature and of Nature's God." Natural rights are not conferred by government but by man's "Creator," and are thus not contingent upon whatever a particular society deems to be expedient at a given time. Government exists for the sake of protecting rights; without such a purpose, it becomes illegitimate, and the people rightly withdraw their consent.

This logic of the Declaration emerges out of its equality doctrine. Far from a command for government to use its power for the sake of bringing about an actual material equality, the Declaration's statement that "all men are created equal" was understood to mean that no man is the natural ruler of any other man. It was meant to counter the theory of divine right of kings or hereditary aristocracy. This meaning is evident not only from the Declaration itself, but also from the other public documents of the day, especially the many state declarations of rights. From those declarations, it is clear how the founding generation understood equality. For example, the Virginia Declaration of Rights—adopted just weeks before the Declaration of Independence—says that "all men are by nature equally free and independent." The Massachusetts Constitution of 1780, drafted by John Adams, says that "all men are born free and equal."[5] Equality for the founding generation pertained to equality of natural rights.

The Declaration's conception of natural rights is simply an extension of, or a consequence of, its equality doctrine. It is precisely because no other man is born my natural ruler that I may claim a right, by nature, to my life, liberty, and pursuit of happiness. Equality is a statement of fact in the Declaration—an observation about human nature—whereas the natural-rights statement derives a moral doctrine from that observation: because no one *is* naturally born my political superior, no one *ought* to interfere in the preservation of my life, my liberty, or my pursuit of happiness in whichever manner I choose. Because our natural equality of rights necessarily implies a duty on the part of others to respect those rights (without such a reciprocal duty, the assertion of rights becomes incoherent), this teaching of nature is also a "law" of nature, as seen in the Declaration.

The declarations of rights adopted by individual states are also useful in demonstrating that property was widely understood to be a funda-

---

[4] On this, see Peter C. Myers, "Locke on the Social Compact: An Overview," in Ronald J. Pestritto and Thomas G. West, eds., *The American Founding and the Social Compact* (Lanham, MD: Lexington Books, 2003), 1–35.

[5] For my understanding of how state declarations of rights help to illuminate the meaning of the Declaration of Independence, I have profited from Thomas G. West, "Jaffa vs. Mansfield: Does America Have a 'Constitutional' or 'Declaration of Independence' Soul?" *Perspectives on Political Science* 31 (Fall 2002): 235–46. See also Michael P. Zuckert, *The Natural Rights Republic* (Notre Dame, IN: University of Notre Dame Press, 1996), 17–20, 33–34.

mental natural right; private property rights are mentioned in *every* state declaration of rights. As Michael Zuckert has persuasively shown, Thomas Jefferson's employment of the "pursuit of happiness" language in the Declaration was not meant by him as a rejection of the right of property.[6] Rather, the understanding of the founding generation seems to have been that any legitimate government has an obligation to make its citizens secure in the title to the property they have earned through their labor. Without such an obligation on the part of government, individuals are not sufficiently free to pursue happiness in the manner that seems best to them. The point is not only to protect wealth already earned and held, but to allow individuals to pursue a living secure in the knowledge that whatever fruits come from their pursuit will also be protected. The natural right to property, with which we are all endowed equally, may therefore lead to an inequality in the amount and kinds of property we end up with. As James Madison explains in referring to the "rights of property" in *Federalist No. 10*, the equal protection of our unequal faculties of acquiring property will lead to unequal results. The job of a legitimate government is not to even out these results; indeed, one of the founders' greatest fears was that the power of government would be employed in such a mission at the behest of a majority faction. Rather, the job of government is to preserve the "different and unequal faculties of acquiring property." This job is called by Madison "the first object of government."[7] As we will see below, this formulation was at the heart of what Progressives found most objectionable about founding-era liberalism; they sought to undercut the recurrence to the "rights of property" as a defense against majority sentiment.

It should be acknowledged that some scholars have objected to understanding the American founding through the lens of eighteenth-century liberalism, and have downplayed the relevance of natural rights or social compact theory in early America.[8] Such arguments seem to defy the overwhelming evidence of the public documents of the founding era, as many other scholars have pointed out.[9] The relevant point for us is that the Progressives certainly did not downplay the role of natural-rights thinking in the American founding. Indeed, if eighteenth-century, natural-rights liberalism was not central to defining the original meaning of the

---

[6] Zuckert, *Natural Rights Republic*, 79–80.

[7] James Madison, *Federalist No. 10*, in *The Federalist*, ed. George W. Carey and James McClellan (Indianapolis, IN: Liberty Fund, 2001), 43.

[8] In addition to the "republican" school of interpretation, headlined by Gordon Wood's *Creation of the American Republic, 1776–1787* (Chapel Hill: University of North Carolina Press, 1969), see Barry Alan Shain, *The Myth of American Individualism* (Princeton, NJ: Princeton University Press, 1994); and John Phillip Reid, *Constitutional History of the American Revolutions: The Authority of Rights* (Madison: University of Wisconsin Press, 1986).

[9] Zuckert, *Natural Rights Republic*, 108–17, 246 n. 17. Paul A. Rahe, *Republics Ancient and Modern* (Chapel Hill: University of North Carolina Press, 1992), 555–60. Thomas G. West, "The Political Theory of the Declaration of Independence," in Pestritto and West, eds., *The American Founding and the Social Compact*, 98–111, 116–20.

American regime, one has to wonder why the Progressives would have wasted so much energy and ink in attacking that brand of liberalism. As I have mentioned, attacking the natural-rights liberalism of the founding was a signature characteristic of Progressive Era works.

III. The Progressive Interpretation of the Founding

For the Progressive intellectual John Dewey—arguably America's premier public philosopher for the first part of the twentieth century—identifying and understanding the natural-rights liberalism of the American founding was a critical part of understanding the crisis faced by progressive liberalism in Dewey's own day. In order to explain how liberalism faced a "crisis" in the twentieth century, Dewey employed a narrative of how liberalism had changed from the old to the new. His approach is curious, because his terminology implies that the changes in principle between eighteenth- and twentieth-century America are intra-family—they are, in other words, "developments" within liberalism itself, as opposed to a move from liberalism to something different. Yet Dewey's description of contemporary liberalism depicts it as the principled antithesis of the liberalism that dominated the American founding era.

For Dewey, America's original liberalism was Locke's liberalism, and his proof is the Declaration. "The outstanding points of Locke's version of liberalism," wrote Dewey, "are that governments are instituted to protect the rights that belong to individuals prior to political organization of social relations. These rights are those summed up a century later in the American Declaration of Independence." The prepolitical origin of these rights, Dewey went on to explain, gives primacy to the individual over the state. "The whole temper of this philosophy is individualistic in the sense in which individualism is opposed to organized social action. It held to the primacy of the individual over the state not only in time but in moral authority." Dewey also connected the dots in looking to the intellectual origins of the founders' natural-rights principles. He traced them not only to Locke, but to the older natural-law tradition; it was this connection to the broader tradition of natural law which made the founders' rights doctrine so inflexible, even in the face of strong majoritarian sentiment. The natural-law tradition, Dewey explained, "bequeathed to later social thought a rigid doctrine of natural rights." The natural-rights doctrine, in turn, "gave a directly practical import to the older semi-theological and semi-metaphysical conception of natural law as supreme over positive law." Dewey put the natural right to property squarely at the center of the American founding, and connected it directly to Locke's understanding. In fact, in his account of the Declaration, Dewey shifted seamlessly between it and the account of property rights from chapter 5 of Locke's *Second Treatise*. Dewey explained that "among the 'natural' rights especially emphasized by Locke is that of property, originating, according to him, in the fact that an individual has 'mixed' himself, through labor, with some natural hitherto unappropriated object." From this Lockean, natural right to property comes the natural "right of revolution," which is how Dewey tied Locke not just to the philosophy of the Declaration, but also to its immediate practical purpose.[10]

Woodrow Wilson, who, like Dewey, had done his graduate work at Johns Hopkins University, was a prolific Progressive academic before entering into public life, and he shared Dewey's assessment of the founding. Before one could talk about the Progressive conception of government, Wilson reasoned, one had to understand the flawed conception of government from which Progressivism aimed to rescue American politics. This is why, in the most comprehensive account that Wilson wrote of the principles of government—*The State* (1889)—Wilson devotes substantial portions of the very first chapter to the theory of social compact and natural rights.[11] From the point of view of Wilson, Dewey, and nearly every other Progressive intellectual, talking about American government necessitated talking first about social compact and natural rights. Wilson went on in subsequent works to trace the origins of American government to Jefferson's account of natural rights; this was a narrative that Wilson often repeated even in his political speeches. In one such speech from his 1912 presidential campaign, Wilson proclaimed that "the makers of our Federal Constitution read Montesquieu with true scientific enthusiasm. . . . Jefferson wrote of 'the laws of Nature,'—and then by way of afterthought,—'and of Nature's God.' And they constructed a government as they would have constructed an orrery [i.e., a mechanical model of the solar system]—to display the laws of nature."[12]

Frank J. Goodnow (1859–1939)—a more obscure, but influential Progressive—adopted the natural-rights account of the American founding to frame his broad view of what was happening in the America of his day. Goodnow was the founding president of the American Political Science Association, and was a very prominent and important academic who made his most effective contributions in the area of administrative law. With the vast discretion that Progressives wanted to grant to bureaucratic agencies, Goodnow pioneered the study of the kind of law that would be necessary to facilitate this delegation of power,[13] before he went on to become president of Johns Hopkins. In lectures reflecting on Progressive accomplishments, Goodnow explained how America had been born a child of eighteenth-century liberalism. "The end of the eighteenth cen-

---

[10] John Dewey, *Liberalism and Social Action* (1935; Amherst, NY: Prometheus Books, 2000), 15–16.

[11] Woodrow Wilson, *The State* (Boston: D. C. Heath and Co., 1889), sections 17, 18, 21, and 23.

[12] Woodrow Wilson, "What Is Progress?" in Ronald J. Pestritto and William J. Atto, eds., *American Progressivism* (Lanham, MD: Lexington Books, 2008), 50.

[13] See Frank Goodnow, *Comparative Administrative Law* (New York: G. P. Putnam's Sons, 1903); and Goodnow, *Politics and Administration* (New York: Macmillan, 1900).

tury," Goodnow said, "was marked by the formulation and general acceptance by thinking men in Europe of a political philosophy which laid
great emphasis on individual private rights. . . . The result was the adoption in this country of a doctrine of unadulterated individualism. Everyone had rights." In tying eighteenth-century philosophy to the origin of
the American regime, Goodnow's account is interesting because of his
emphasis on law and the courts. He recognized that the American understanding of rights originating in nature was distinct from the more pos-
itivistic English conception of rights, and that this distinction had profound
implications for the nature of the American judiciary. "The rights of men,"
Goodnow explained, "of which their liberty consisted, were, as natural
rights, regarded in a measure—and in no small measure—as independent
of the law." By this formulation, Goodnow meant that Americans understood their written Constitution as a manifestation of their natural rights,
and thus these rights inherent in the Constitution superseded the ordinary positive law. Goodnow reasoned that such a distinction between
fundamental rights and the positive law placed great power in the hands
of the judiciary, which was taken to be the safeguard of those fundamental rights.[14] This vision of the founding becomes crucial for Progressives,
especially those like Theodore Roosevelt who would regularly rail against
the judiciary precisely because it was employing the doctrine of natural
rights (property rights, in particular) as a weapon against Progressive
accomplishments in the arena of positive law.[15]

As clear as Progressives were about the origins of the American regime
in eighteenth-century liberalism, some of them were confused about
eighteenth-century liberalism itself. While they properly placed Locke at
the center of this older liberalism, some of them placed Jean-Jacques
Rousseau there as well, often using Rousseau's conception of the social
compact interchangeably with Locke's. It was because they conflated
Rousseau and Locke that Wilson, and especially Goodnow, considered
Rousseau to be an enemy of Progressivism, when in fact he was more of
a philosophic ally. Without going too far astray into a sustained discussion of social compact philosophy, it is important to note the critical
difference between Lockean and Rousseauian social compact theory if we
are to understand Progressivism and its case against the founding and
property rights. For Locke, property rights are natural and are thus a
trump card which the individual carries with him into civil society. Locke's
social compact has as one of its bedrock principles the necessity of protecting individual rights of property even against the will of a majority.[16]

[14] Frank Goodnow, "The American Conception of Liberty" (1916), in Pestritto and Atto,
eds., *American Progressivism*, 55–59.
[15] See, for example, Theodore Roosevelt, "The Right of the People to Rule" (1912), in
Pestritto and Atto, eds., *American Progressivism*, 251–60.
[16] John Locke, *Second Treatise of Government* (1689), ed. Peter Laslett (Cambridge: Cambridge University Press, 1960), chaps. 5, 9, esp. sections 26–28, 34, 123–24.

For Rousseau, at least in his *Second Discourse,* property rights are not natural at all; they are artificial, the invention of an "impostor" that mark the introduction of bourgeois society and the enslavement of man.[17] And while the status of rights in Rousseau's *Social Contract* is more ambiguous, a true social compact, for Rousseau, is liberated from its obligation to the artificial rights of property and is driven, instead, by a general will. Thus, in making their case against the preeminence of property rights, America's Progressives could have employed the Rousseau of the *Second Discourse,* as opposed to vilifying him. Wilson and Goodnow seem to have assumed the following: because social compact theory is bad (they knew from Locke that it was responsible for the natural-rights doctrine of private property), and because Rousseau wrote a book called *The Social Contract,* Rousseau (like Locke) must be an enemy of progress. In his account of social compact theory in *The State,* Wilson lumped Rousseau in with Richard Hooker, Thomas Hobbes, and Locke, using each interchangeably with the others,[18] in spite of the fact that Rousseau actually launched his own account of nature with a rejection of the accounts of these others.[19] Goodnow was similarly confused, laying the origins of the eighteenth century's radical individualism at Rousseau's feet, and casting Rousseau as an enemy of those who would favor the good of society as a whole over the prerogatives of the individual.[20]

In spite of the occasional confusion with respect to distinctions within eighteenth-century political philosophy (and it is important to note that Dewey is guilty of no such confusion), the essential Progressive understanding of eighteenth-century liberalism clearly identified it with Locke, and clearly connected Lockean natural rights with the American founding. This understanding was paradigmatic both for the original Progressives and those who would later take up the Progressive agenda. Franklin D. Roosevelt provides a pertinent illustration. Roosevelt consciously grounded his 1932 presidential campaign and New Deal in the ideas of the Progressive generation that had preceded him, and especially in Wilson's brand of Progressivism.[21] And like the Progressives, Roosevelt knew that in speaking of the origins of American government, he had to begin with the natural-rights doctrine of the Declaration. In his 1932 "Campaign Address on Progressive Government" (also known as the "Commonwealth Club Address"), even as Roosevelt argued for a new conception of

---

[17] Jean-Jacques Rousseau, *Second Discourse* (1755), in *The First and Second Discourses,* ed. Roger D. Masters, trans. Roger D. and Judith R. Masters (New York: St. Martin's Press, 1964), esp. 141–42. See also Rousseau, *On the Social Contract,* ed. Roger D. Masters, trans. Judith R. Masters (New York: St. Martin's Press, 1978), esp. 46, 62.

[18] Wilson, *The State,* section 18.

[19] Rousseau, *Second Discourse,* 102–3.

[20] Goodnow, "American Conception of Liberty," 55, 57.

[21] Franklin D. Roosevelt, "Campaign Address on Progressive Government," September 23, 1932, in Samuel I. Rosenman, ed., *Public Papers and Addresses of Franklin D. Roosevelt,* vol. 1 (New York: Random House, 1938), 749–50.

the rights of property that would justify his New Deal, he began by
identifying the old conception of these rights as the heart of the American
founding. "The Declaration of Independence," Roosevelt proclaimed, "discusses the problem of Government in terms of a contract."[22] In his 1944
Annual Message to Congress, where Roosevelt famously argued for a
second, economic "Bill of Rights" to go along with the original, he first
traced the old understanding of rights to those "inalienable political rights"
which had come from the Declaration.[23] And so we can see that the
launching of the new liberalism in America, by the Progressives and their
disciples, required a clear understanding of the essence of the old liberalism. Having identified the natural-rights doctrine at the heart of the old
liberalism, Progressives understood that that doctrine had to be undercut,
or at least redefined, in order for the new liberalism to take hold.

IV. The Progressive Rejection of Property Rights— In Principle

The primary weapon the Progressives employed against the principle
of natural rights—and against property rights in particular—was historical contingency. Locke had argued in the *Second Treatise* that the standard
for legitimate government is not to be found in history, but in nature—in
particular, in the law of nature.[24] The logic of this argument is premised
on the assumption that history is merely a record of human action, varying from epoch to epoch, sometimes witnessing events that are more just
and sometimes witnessing those that are less so. It seems reasonable to
conclude from Locke that one cannot derive a principle of what government *ought* to be from a mere record of what has been or what is; to do
so would be to embrace the idea that might makes right, and to deny
oneself an external standard of reference for judging the legitimacy of a
particular political regime.[25] This is why Locke's articulation of natural
rights was so congenial to the American colonists; nature was the ground
of appeal for them that transcended the conventional laws and practices
of the British regime in North America. The Progressives grasped this
central Lockean element of the founding, and saw it for what it was: a

---

[22] Ibid., 753.
[23] Franklin D. Roosevelt, "Annual Message to Congress," January 11, 1944, in Basil Rauch,
ed., *The Roosevelt Reader* (New York: Holt, Rinehart, 1957), 347.
[24] Locke, *Second Treatise*, section 6.
[25] Locke addresses the historical critique of his state-of-nature thesis in sections 101–18 of
the *Second Treatise*, although the argument I refer to here is based on the logic of the work
as a whole. The notion that justice can be found in the particulars of history reminds one of
Friedrich Nietzsche's devastating critique of such a notion as an "idolatry of the factual" in
Nietzsche, *On the Advantage and Disadvantage of History for Life*, trans. Peter Preuss (Indianapolis, IN: Hacket, 1980), 47—which is not to suggest that Nietzsche had much admiration
for Lockean natural-rights theory either.

permanent barrier to changing the aim and scope of government in accord with what they believed were new historical demands.

Dewey, Wilson, and other Progressives thus asserted historical contingency against the Declaration's talk of the permanent principles underlying man's individual rights of property. The preeminence of property rights may have been appropriate, Progressives argued, as a specific, time-bound response to the tyranny of King George III, but, they concluded, all government must be understood as a product of its historical context. The great sin of which the founding generation had been guilty was not its adherence to natural rights of property, but rather its belief that the natural-rights doctrine was meant to transcend the particular circumstances of that era. Such a conception of the founding provided a stark contrast to the one that Abraham Lincoln had offered in 1859, when he wrote of the Declaration and its principal author: "All honor to Jefferson—to the man who, in the concrete pressure of a struggle for national independence by a single people, had the coolness, forecast, and capacity to introduce into a merely revolutionary document, an abstract truth, applicable to all men and all times."[26]

As if speaking directly to Lincoln's ahistorical depiction of the founding, Dewey complained that the founders "lacked historic sense and interest" in explicating their natural-rights doctrine, and that they had a "disregard of history."[27] To this disregard of history, Dewey opposed a narrative of historical contingency. The natural-rights theory that undergirded the founders' conception of property rights had, Dewey argued, "blinded the eyes of liberals to the fact that their own special interpretations of liberty, individuality, and intelligence were themselves historically conditioned, and were relevant only to their own time. They put forward their ideas as immutable truths good at all times and places; they had no idea of historic relativity."[28] Instead of attacking the idea of property rights directly, Dewey placed them within the context of liberalism's development over time. It is in this way that liberalism can come to have a meaning in one era that is exactly opposite to its earlier meaning. The idea of liberty was not frozen in time, Dewey contended, but had instead a history of evolving significance. The history of liberalism was progressive—it told a story of the move from more primitive to more mature forms of liberty. Property rights were a characteristic of earlier liberalism.

[26] Abraham Lincoln, letter to Henry L. Pierce and others, April 6, 1859, in *Speeches and Writings, 1859–1865*, ed. Don E. Fehrenbacher (New York: Literary Classics of the United States, distributed by the Viking Press, 1989), 19.

[27] Dewey, *Liberalism and Social Action*, 40–41. Dewey's claim here seems to fly in the face of the deep reflection on history exhibited by most of the founding generation. To take *The Federalist* as only one example, the entire argument can be said to proceed from an understanding of the challenges popular government had faced since the time of ancient Greece, and it draws on the contributions made to the science of politics by thinkers from various points in history. See, for example, Alexander Hamilton, *Federalist No. 9*, in Carey and McClellan, eds., *The Federalist*, 37–38.

[28] Dewey, *Liberalism and Social Action*, 41.

Wilson, too, sought to explain away the property-rights origins of the American regime by casting them in historical perspective. He did so by interpreting the Declaration in such a way as to confine its ideas to the founding era. In a 1911 address ostensibly honoring Thomas Jefferson, he admonished his audience: "if you want to understand the real Declaration of Independence, do not repeat the preface."[29] By this he meant, of course, that one ought not look to that part of the Declaration which enshrines natural rights as the focal point of American government. If one were to take Wilson's advice, one would turn one's attention away from abstract notions like the rights of property and focus instead on the litany of grievances made against George III; one would conceive of the Declaration as a merely practical document, understood as a time-bound response to a set of specific (and now long past) historical circumstances. Since those circumstances are long gone, so too should be our conception of private property that was created to address them. Wilson thus claimed that "we are not bound to adhere to the doctrines held by the signers of the Declaration of Independence," and that every Fourth of July, instead of a celebration of the timeless principles of the Declaration, should instead "be a time for examining our standards, our purposes, for determining afresh what principles, what forms of power we think most likely to effect our safety and happiness."[30]

In order to see property rights through the lens of history—to see that their significance is contingent upon social circumstances—one must detach them from their mooring in nature. This was the goal of Wilson's account of the origin of political power in *The State*, which he offered as a "destructive dissolvent" to the social compact theory of Locke.[31] The problem with Locke was that his account of nature, upon which his entire standard of legitimate government rests, was purely speculative; the true foundation of government, Wilson countered, could only be uncovered by looking to the actual history of its development, not to conjecture or theory. Even while conceding that historical knowledge of the actual origins of government was imperfect, Wilson reasoned that even limited historical knowledge is far preferable to engaging in "a priori speculations" about the origins of government. In America, Progressives believed that a natural account of individual property rights was being employed to defy the wishes of popular majorities, and the only foundation for these rights was the philosophic musing of social compact theory—a theory which, according to Wilson, "simply has no historical foundation."[32]

---

[29] Woodrow Wilson, "An Address to the Jefferson Club of Los Angeles, May 12, 1911," in *The Papers of Woodrow Wilson*, 69 vols. (hereafter cited as *PWW*), ed. Arthur S. Link (Princeton, NJ: Princeton University Press, 1966–1993), 22:34.

[30] Woodrow Wilson, "The Author and Signers of the Declaration of Independence," in *PWW*, 17:251.

[31] Wilson, *The State*, 11.

[32] Ibid., 13–14.

Wilson's model for a form of government that looked for its principles to history, as opposed to nature, was England. As in Goodnow's account of the distinction between the American and English conceptions of rights (mentioned in Section III), Wilson worried about the American belief that permanent, abstract rights are enshrined in a written constitution that can be used to trump organic legislative development. Like Dewey, Wilson lamented the historical blindness of early liberals, and thought that America's written constitution exacerbated the inflexibility of early American notions of rights. The problem was made worse by the difficulty of the constitutional amendment process, which reinforced the idea that change and adaptation—what Wilson called organic development—were to be avoided. Too many Americans really looked at their constitution as a contract—as a permanent, definite creation not subject to organic development. "We have been too much dominated," Wilson worried, "by the theory that our government was an artificial structure resting upon contract only."[33] Wilson's fear was not only that the ahistorical conception of rights was inhibiting organic growth (and the new, enlarged role that Progressives had in mind for the national government), but that American government itself would ultimately burst and fall apart as a result. This fear can be traced back to Wilson's earliest days of thinking about government, as illustrated in the following 1876 entry to an early diary on the anniversary of American independence: "How much happier [America] would be now if she had England's form of government instead of the miserable delusion of a republic. A republic too founded upon the notion of abstract liberty! I venture to say that this country will never celebrate another centennial as a republic. The English form of government is the only true one."[34]

In contending for a more flexible, organic constitutionalism (in other words, the unwritten British constitution), Wilson argued that liberty and rights were concepts that could not be permanently defined. "Liberty fixed in unalterable law would be no liberty at all," he wrote. Liberty for the founding generation meant a doctrine of rights which protected the individual from tyranny in government, even when such a government might be fueled by a majority. But in his own day, Wilson reasoned, that founding-era conception of liberty was proving an impediment to liberty as it ought then to be understood. Liberty in contemporary times, Wilson explained, meant the liberty of majorities to use the power of government as they saw fit. Liberty thus had a history of evolving meaning, and the new meaning required an overturning of the old.[35] In his new conception of liberty as the right of majorities to rule unbounded by individual rights such as the right to property, Wilson sketched an idea that would later be taken up by Theodore Roosevelt when he crusaded against antimajoritar-

---

[33] Woodrow Wilson, "The Modern Democratic State," in *PWW*, 5:65–68.
[34] Woodrow Wilson, "From Wilson's Shorthand Diary," July 4, 1876, in *PWW*, 1:148–49.
[35] Woodrow Wilson, *Constitutional Government in the United States* (New York: Columbia University Press, 1908), 4.

ian judicial decisions. Too often, Roosevelt believed, Progressives had been successful in enacting parts of their legislative agenda—workers' compensation or labor regulation, for instance—only to see those successes turned into defeats when overturned by the courts.[36] Majority tyranny was no longer a problem that warranted concern, according to Roosevelt: "I have scant patience with this talk of the tyranny of the majority. . . . We are today suffering from the tyranny of minorities. . . . The only tyrannies from which men, women, and children are suffering in real life are the tyrannies of minorities."[37] This formulation demonstrates Roosevelt's belief that notions of liberty must be taken from "real life"—life which had changed drastically from the days of the founding— and not from abstract doctrines about the natural rights of the individual.

Goodnow, like Roosevelt, was quite direct in his 1911 criticism of the natural conception of rights. While acknowledging that the founders' system of government "was permeated by the theories of social compact and natural right," he contended that such theories were "worse than useless" because they "retard development":[38] the protections for individual liberty and property, in other words, inhibit the expansion of government. In contrast to this problem in America, Goodnow praised the conception of rights that was then becoming prevalent in Europe. There, he explained in 1916, "the rights which [an individual] possesses are, it is believed, conferred upon him, not by his Creator, but rather by the society to which he belongs. What they are is to be determined by the legislative authority in view of the needs of that society. Social expediency, rather than natural right, is thus to determine the sphere of individual freedom of action."[39] Property rights, under this model, could be adjusted to accommodate perceived social necessity. Indeed, as previously discussed, this is precisely the argument that Franklin Roosevelt would subsequently employ when drawing on Progressive principles in explicating his New Deal. When discussing the founding-era conception of fundamental rights, for example, in his "Campaign Address on Progressive Government," Roosevelt contended that "the task of statesmanship has always been the redefinition of these rights in terms of a changing and growing social order."[40]

V. The Progressive Rejection of Property Rights— In Practice

The Progressive critique of the principles underlying the original American understanding of rights paved the way for an attack on those rights

---

[36] Prominent examples of cases that particularly aggravated Progressives are *Lochner v. New York*, 198 U.S. 45 (1905), and *Hammer v. Dagenhart*, 247 U.S. 251 (1918).

[37] Theodore Roosevelt, "The Right of the People to Rule," 251–52.

[38] Frank J. Goodnow, *Social Reform and the Constitution* (New York: The Macmillan Company, 1911), 1, 3.

[39] Goodnow, "American Conception of Liberty," 57.

[40] Franklin D. Roosevelt, "Campaign Address on Progressive Government," 753.

in practice. Progressives called for significant changes both to political institutions and to national policy that were animated by their new conception of rights. Having argued that rights such as property should no longer be understood as grounded in nature, Progressives were liberated to seek changes to institutional arrangements that had originally been predicated on the old liberalism's privileging of natural rights. While it is impossible here to treat the numerous and varied ways in which the Progressive Movement affected the development of American political institutions, it is especially instructive to look at how Progressives conceived of the judiciary. The Progressive treatment of the judiciary is particularly relevant because it demonstrates how the meaning and relevance of property rights were transformed in the Progressive Era. As discussed in Section III, both Goodnow and Wilson saw it as a critical (but not felicitous) difference between America and England that fundamental rights in America were regarded as natural as opposed to conventional, and that they were thus distinct from and above the ordinary positive law. Such a construction, they knew, implied a role for the judiciary as the guardian of fundamental rights[41]—a role which could put it at odds with the organic development of legislation if such legislation was deemed a threat to the original meaning of rights.

   In Theodore Roosevelt's view, this is exactly what had happened, and he became the leading Progressive antagonist to a judiciary that he believed was upholding the old theory of natural property rights at the expense of Progressive majorities. Roosevelt was especially aghast at instances where state courts had overturned legislation achieved by Progressive majorities, and he lamented they had done so in the name of property rights or freedom of contract.[42] This led him to advocate, in his unsuccessful third-party campaign to recapture the presidency in 1912, what can best be described as popular referenda on judicial decisions—or, to put it in the language found in the Progressive Party platform of 1912: "That when an Act, passed under the police power of the State, is held unconstitutional under the State Constitution, by the courts, the people, after an ample interval for deliberation, shall have an opportunity to vote on the question whether they desire the Act to become law, notwithstanding such decision."[43] When judges defied the will of the people in the name of property rights, Roosevelt argued, this represented a corruption of democracy. "Democracy," he con-

---

[41] I am well aware that the founders did not see the judiciary as the exclusive guardian of fundamental rights, and that there is much debate on how the founders understood judicial review and the role of the courts in invalidating legislation. That debate is well beyond the scope of this essay, and probably beside the point. For us, what is relevant is that the Progressives understood the original conception of the judiciary in this way.

[42] See, for example, *Ives v. South Buffalo Railroad*, 201 N.Y. 271 (1911), where the New York Court of Appeals overturned the state's Workmen's Compensation Act of 1910.

[43] "Progressive Party Platform of 1912," in Pestritto and Atto, eds., *American Progressivism,* 276.

tended, "has a right to approach the sanctuary of the courts when a
special interest has corruptly found sanctuary there."[44] Roosevelt almost
always used the epithet "special interest" in cases where property rights
had been employed as protection against majority will. "Special interest" seems to have meant, for Roosevelt, any nonmajority entity asserting its natural property rights. It was the "special interests"—and their
property rights in particular—that stood in the way of Progressive social
legislation. The courts, Roosevelt complained, "have construed the 'due
process' clause[45] of the State Constitutions as if it prohibited the whole
people of a State from adopting methods of regulating the use of property so that human life, particularly the lives of the working men, shall
be safer, freer, and happier."[46] And whereas, under the old liberalism,
property rights had been grounded in human nature and were understood as an integral part of the range of rights inherent in human
personhood, Roosevelt conceived instead of "human rights" and "property rights" in opposition to one another. In calling for popular referenda on judicial decisions, he urged "that in such cases where the
courts construe the due process clause as if property rights, to the
exclusion of human rights, had a first mortgage on the Constitution,"
the people should be permitted to overturn the courts' adherence to
the rights of property.[47] Judges who struck down laws due to a judg-

---

[44] Theodore Roosevelt, "The Right of the People to Rule," 254.

[45] The Fifth Amendment to the U.S. Constitution stipulates that no person shall be "deprived
of life, liberty, or property, without due process of law." The Fourteenth Amendment applies
that exact language to the state governments, and most state constitutions have a similar
provision. Understood in the context of Roosevelt's complaint, the "due process" clause had
been employed by courts to protect the liberty interest of individuals against the exercise of
regulatory or "police" power by state governments. In the *Lochner* case, for example, where
the state legislature had enacted a law limiting the number of hours bakers could agree to
work, the U.S. Supreme Court reasoned that "the general right to make a contract in relation
to his business is part of the liberty of the individual protected by the Fourteenth Amendment of the Federal Constitution," and that "the right to purchase or to sell labor is part of
the liberty protected by this amendment unless there are circumstances which exclude the
right" (198 U.S. 45 [1905], at 53). The Court continued: "There is a limit to the valid exercise
of the police power by the State. There is no dispute concerning this general proposition.
Otherwise the Fourteenth Amendment would have no efficacy, and the legislatures of the
States would have unbounded power, and it would be enough to say that any piece of
legislation was enacted to conserve the morals, the health or the safety of the people; such
legislation would be valid no matter how absolutely without foundation the claim might be.
The claim of the police power would be a mere pretext—become another and delusive name
for the supreme sovereignty of the State to be exercised free from constitutional restraint"
(id. at 56). With respect to the regulation of bakers' hours, the Court concluded that "there
is, in our judgment, no reasonable foundation for holding this to be necessary or appropriate
as a health law to safeguard the public health or the health of the individuals who are
following the trade of a baker. If this statute be valid, and if, therefore, a proper case is made
out in which to deny the right of an individual, *sui juris*, as employer or employee, to make
contracts for the labor of the latter under the protection of the provisions of the Federal
Constitution, there would seem to be no length to which legislation of this nature might not
go" (id. at 58).

[46] Theodore Roosevelt, "The Right of the People to Rule," 254.

[47] Ibid.

ment that they contravened property rights were simply substituting a "political philosophy" for "the will of the majority."[48]

Roosevelt's strong reaction to courts that had employed the doctrine of property rights to thwart legislatures in "regulating the use of property" naturally raises the question of what kind of regulation he had in mind, and why it would have been considered as a threat to the rights of property. As had been the case in founding-era liberalism, Roosevelt recurred to the principle of equality. But equality for the founders, as outlined above, meant an equality of rights, and the equal protection of rights might often lead, as Madison explained, to an inequality of results or rewards, due to the "diversity in the faculties of men, from which the rights of property originate."[49] So equality and the protection of individual property rights were, for the founders, two sides of the same coin. Roosevelt, by contrast, spoke of an "equality of opportunity," and meant something very different, as became clear in his 1910 "New Nationalism" speech. Roosevelt's equality meant using the power of government to destroy the "special interests" or "special privilege"—defined, as I have explained, as those asserting property rights against the will of the majority. These "special interests" had used the "rules of the game" to benefit themselves and not society as a whole; "I stand," Roosevelt proclaimed, "for having those rules changed so as to work for a more substantial equality of opportunity *and of reward.*"[50] Unlike Madison, who accepted the fact that unequal rewards would result from the equal enforcement of individual property rights, Roosevelt seems to have called for the unequal

---

[48] Ibid., 257. Roosevelt here echoes the argument of Supreme Court Justice Oliver Wendell Holmes—whom Roosevelt had appointed to the Court—that the Constitution was not built on any political theory and that courts ought not use a theory of the Constitution to strike down legislation. See Holmes's dissent in *Lochner v. New York*, 198 U.S. 45 (1905), at 75–76. It should also be noted that Woodrow Wilson did not attack the judiciary in the way that Roosevelt did. In this respect, Wilson had more foresight than Roosevelt, for he foresaw the potential for the judiciary to be an agent of progress. There could well come a time, Wilson reasoned, when majority sentiment would lag behind the demands of progress, and that would be a time for judges to step up and take the lead. In any event, Wilson's defense of the judiciary should not be misconstrued; it came not from an attachment to the judiciary as a protector of individuals against Progressive majorities, but instead from a gratitude that the courts had often been willing to read the Constitution flexibly: "We can say without the least disparagement or even criticism of the Supreme Court of the United States that at its hands the Constitution has received an adaptation and an elaboration which would fill its framers of the simple days of 1787 with nothing less than amazement. The explicitly granted powers of the Constitution are what they always were; but the powers drawn from it by implication have grown and multiplied beyond all expectation, and each generation of statesmen looks to the Supreme Court to supply the interpretation which will serve the needs of the day" (Wilson, *Constitutional Government,* 157–58). Wilson, in other words, was able to see past the immediate sins of the Court during his own day, and to understand (correctly, as it turns out) that the Court was fundamentally a progressive institution—that it had helped the country to escape the bonds of its original constitutionalism, and would likely be a force for a similar kind of progressive change in the future.

[49] Madison, *Federalist No. 10,* 43.

[50] Theodore Roosevelt, "The New Nationalism" (1910), in Pestritto and Atto, eds., *American Progressivism,* 214–15 (emphasis added).

enforcement of rights (changing the "rules of the game," to use his language) so as to produce more equal results.

Roosevelt justified changing the "rules of the game"—that is, abandon-
ing the equal enforcement of natural property rights—because he sub-
scribed to the Progressive redefinition of rights themselves. One's right to
property did not come, as it had for the eighteenth-century liberalism that
influenced the founders, through an account of nature where individual
labor gave title to property. Rather, one had a "right" to property, in
Roosevelt's view, only insofar as it was socially beneficial for one to have
it. Title to property became contingent upon its serving a social purpose.
"We grudge no man a fortune which represents his own power and
sagacity," Roosevelt explained, "when exercised with entire regard to the
welfare of his fellows."[51] Property rights were no longer moored in nature,
to be used as a trump against social action, but were instead, as Goodnow
had urged they be, "conferred . . . by the society to which [an individual]
belongs," and determined by "social expendiency."[52] Roosevelt was explicit
about the contingency of property rights upon social utility, and about the
new scope of state power which would correspond with such a conception of rights:

> We grudge no man a fortune in civil life if it is honorably obtained
> *and well used.* It is not even enough that it should have been gained
> without doing damage to the community. *We should permit it* to be
> gained only so long as the gaining represents *benefit to the community.*
> This, I know, implies a policy of far more active governmental inter-
> ference with social and economic conditions in this country than we
> have yet had, but I think we have got to face the fact that such an
> increase in governmental control is now necessary.[53]

Roosevelt was conscious that his vision for equalizing rewards—the
"Square Deal," as he called it—was not compatible with the original
American conception of property rights, but was, instead, founded upon
a new theory. "We are face to face with the new conceptions of the relations of property to human welfare," he proclaimed. In justifying this
move from the old to the new, he once again employed the construction
of property rights in opposition to human rights, where property is not an
extension of the human person but serves instead to alienate man from
his own welfare. We had been brought to this point, Roosevelt concluded,
"because certain advocates of the rights of property as against the rights
of men have been pushing their claims too far."[54]

---

[51] Ibid., 217.
[52] Goodnow, "American Conception of Liberty," 57.
[53] Theodore Roosevelt, "The New Nationalism," 217 (emphasis added).
[54] Ibid., 220.

VI. Conclusion

This new conception of property rights undergirded a host of policies—advocated not only by Theodore Roosevelt but by Progressives generally—that fulfilled the call for "far more active governmental interference with social and economic conditions." Progressives sought not only to have the federal government supervise the manner in which private wealth was earned, but also to have the government redistribute private wealth in order to ensure that it would serve the common good. To this end, Progressives pursued a graduated income tax and a substantial inheritance tax, both of which were called for in the 1912 Progressive Party platform. Progressives also fought successfully for the ratification of the Sixteenth Amendment to the Constitution, which was written to overcome a Supreme Court decision denying to the federal government the power to tax certain forms of income.[55]

The dual aims of centralized regulation of economic activity and the redistribution of wealth comprised the heart of Theodore Roosevelt's "New Nationalism" campaign, the Progressive Party platform, and many other Progressive enterprises.[56] Progressive Era reforms thus helped to shape the future course of liberalism in the twentieth century. These reforms were grounded on a novel interpretation of the political theory of the American founding that was ultimately adopted, as Section III explains, by Franklin Roosevelt in his establishment of the New Deal order for American national government. This essay has endeavored to show how the Progressive reforms were built upon a rejection of the rights of property, both in principle and in practice.

The new liberalism in America was built, in other words, upon a Progressive transformation of the natural-rights principles that had served as a foundation for the old liberalism, and thus it seems fitting that new liberals have come to prefer the label "progressive."

Politics, Hillsdale College

---

[55] Specifically, in *Pollock v. Farmers' Loan and Trust Co.,* 157 U.S. 429 (1895), the Supreme Court had ruled that federal taxes on income derived from interest, dividends, and rents were "direct" taxes and thus were constitutionally required to be apportioned among the states on the basis of population. Taxes on wages were still considered to be indirect, and thus not subject to the apportionment requirement. *Pollock* thus made the question hinge on the source of income. In order to nullify this point, the Sixteenth Amendment declared that taxes on income, "from whatever source derived," could be levied by the federal government "without apportionment among the several States, and without regard to any census or enumeration."

[56] See, for example, the relevant works in the Social Gospel movement, which constituted the religious arm of Progressivism. Particularly revealing is Walter Rauschenbusch, *Christianizing the Social Order* (New York: The Macmillan Company, 1912), 419-29, where Rauschenbusch calls for the government to "resocialize property."

THE PROPERTY EQUILIBRIUM IN A LIBERAL SOCIAL ORDER (OR HOW TO CORRECT OUR MORAL VISION)*

By Gerald Gaus

I. The Ideological Din of Contemporary Liberal Theory

In the eyes of some, the ideological age of the late nineteenth and early twentieth centuries gave way in the later part of the twentieth century to a post-ideological age.[1] We have witnessed a widespread convergence on fundamental rights of the person, democratic governance, and the inelim- inable role of markets and private enterprise in securing economic pros- perity. The great ideological wars of the late nineteenth and early twentieth centuries between liberal capitalism, communism, and fascism—a world- wide clash of diametrically opposed forms of social, economic, and polit- ical life—were resolved by the victory of some broad, though thin, consensus on liberal capitalism.[2]

Ideology, however, was not destroyed, though it is, mercifully, gen- erally now much less deadly. Our chief ideological battleground today is "social" or "distributive" justice—which Bertrand de Jouvenel described as the "obsession of our time."[3] Certainly it is the obsession of con- temporary liberal political philosophy. The "welcome return" to "sub- stantive political philosophy" that John Rawls's *A Theory of Justice* was said to herald[4] has resulted in forty years of proposals seeking to show that philosophical reflection leads to the demonstrable truth of almost every and any conceivable view of the justice of markets and the dis- tribution of resources (or welfare, or opportunities). Select any view— from the justice of unregulated capitalist markets to the most extreme forms of egalitarianism—and one will find that some philosophers have

---

* Versions of this paper were delivered to the philosophy departments at the University of Richmond and Vanderbilt University, the government department at the London School of Economics, the University of Manchester Center for the Study of Political Thought, and the Institute for Humane Studies. My thanks to all participants for their questions, com- ments, and objections.

[1] Daniel Bell, *The End of Ideology: On the Exhaustion of Political Ideas in the Fifties*, rev. ed. (New York: The Free Press, 1962); Francis Fukuyama, *The End of History and the Last Man* (New York: The Free Press, 1992).

[2] As I have argued, given the prognoses for liberalism at the beginning of the twentieth century, and even nearly mid-way through it, this was indeed remarkable. See my "Liber- alism at the End of the Century," *Journal of Political Ideologies* 5 (2000): 179–99.

[3] Bertrand de Jouvenel, *Sovereignty* (Cambridge: Cambridge University Press, 1957), 139.

[4] Norman Daniels, "Introduction," in Daniels, ed., *Reading Rawls: Critical Studies of A Theory of Justice* (New York: Basic Books 1974), ix.

doi:10.1017/S0265052510000221

proclaimed that rational reflection uniquely leads to its justice,[5] though few convince many of their colleagues, much less what used to be called "the educated public." This is not merely a case of theoretical disorder, as one might expect during a Kuhnian revolutionary epoch in science, in which the dominant paradigm has broken down and no new one has replaced it.[6] It is, I believe, a sort of ideological (or, at best, utopian) thinking masquerading as philosophizing. Captivated by their personal moral visions of a better world, political philosophers construct elaborate arguments and frameworks to demonstrate that their own highly disputable convictions are the dictates of impartial reason (and that their colleagues down the hall advocate deep injustice).

If philosophical reflection on the relation between liberalism and capitalism is not simply to add to this ideological din, we must pause and think about political philosophy's range of competency. Political philosophers have their own moral and political convictions; the question is to what extent these are properly expressed in their political philosophy—their view of the just state, or the grounds and limits of the authority of the state. If a political philosopher is convinced by the moral case for Robert Nozick's historical entitlement theory, Joseph Raz's perfectionist morality, or Ronald Dworkin's egalitarianism,[7] does this mean that she must demand that a just or authoritative state be libertarian, or perfectionist, or egalitarian? If she is a committed libertarian, must she hold that a nonlibertarian state is unjust and nonauthoritative (or perhaps unjust and yet still authoritative)?[8] We might ask: Is the private conscience of the philosopher (or anyone else) authoritative over what public morality and the law must be?

My concern in this essay is to better understand the task of the political philosopher while analyzing the place of property rules in a liberal order. I begin by arguing that two dominant approaches to political philosophy (examined in Sections II and III) obscure the fundamental questions about the justification of property; if we succumb to their moral visions, the result will almost inevitably be a contribution to the ideological din surrounding property and justice. Sections IV and V then explore a third view, which is central to the thought of philosophers as diverse as T. H. Green, Kurt Baier, and F. A. Hayek. With this view, which stresses the

[5] For a litany of these incompatible truths about distributive justice, see my "On Justifying the Moral Rights of the Moderns: A Case of Old Wine in New Bottles," *Social Philosophy and Policy* 24, no. 1 (2007): 86ff.
[6] Thomas S. Kuhn, *The Structure of Scientific Revolutions*, 3d ed. (Chicago: University of Chicago Press, 1996).
[7] Robert Nozick, *Anarchy, State, and Utopia* (New York: Basic Books, 1974); Joseph Raz, *The Morality of Freedom* (Oxford: Clarendon Press, 1986); Ronald Dworkin, *Sovereign Virtue: The Theory and Practice of Equality* (Cambridge, MA: Harvard University Press, 2000).
[8] Another possibility, often advocated today, is that such a state would be unjust and without authority, but still could be "legitimate," in the sense that its use of coercive power may be nonwrongful. See Thomas Christiano, *The Constitution of Equality* (Oxford: Oxford University Press, 2008), 240ff.

social reality of moral rules, we finally begin to understand the moral status of private property in a liberal order—when it is part of the "true" moral order, and when it is subject to philosophical criticism and proposals for revision.

II. The Public Authority of Private Conscience

A. The Social Authority of Private Conscience thesis

Let us begin by exploring a view that, though I think it is ultimately mistaken, is nevertheless attractive. It commences with a real insight: when a person's action falls under social morality—that part of morality which concerns claims on others about what they must and must not do—it is no longer simply her business what she does, it becomes everyone's business.[9] We do not say that a person who violates the rules of morality is simply foolish or self-destructive: we accuse, reprove, and blame, we are indignant, and we may well punish.[10] We not only insist that what she does is our business, we insist that she must do as we demand. In a way, we claim authority over her, a standing to direct her action according to *our understanding* of the rules, and we hold her accountable for failing to obey.[11] Suppose you make a moral demand of another and she replies, "Well, that is what *you* think morality requires, but who are you to tell *me* what is morally required of *me*?" You are not apt to back down. When another denies your claim, at least sometimes you must reply that, having employed your reasoning as well as you can, your interpretation must not only hold for you, but for *her:* she must do as you demand of her. If you always refuse to uphold your moral demand in the face of disagreement, you are not advancing a moral *demand* at all, but simply offering an interpretation of morality for consideration by others (as one might offer a philosophical view at a philosophy conference). We thus seem to be committed to a rather startling thesis: Your own deliberations about the requirements of social morality justify you in claiming an authority to direct the lives of others as your interpretation dictates.

B. The priority of the moral to the political

Given the social authority of private conscience thesis, suppose we take the reasonable view that the state should conform to moral demands and requirements. You have reasoned as well as you can about the demands of social morality, and you have concluded, say, that resources should be

---

[9] See Kurt Baier, *The Moral Point of View,* abridged ed. (New York: Random House, 1965), xviii–xix.

[10] See Kurt Baier, *The Moral Point of View* (Ithaca, NY: Cornell University Press, 1958), 1.

[11] See further Stephen Darwall, *The Second-Person Standpoint: Morality, Respect, and Accountability* (Cambridge, MA: Harvard University Press, 2006).

distributed equally (or that only libertarian property rights are morally justified). Other reasonable moral agents disagree with you, but it seems that you cannot allow that to be a decisive objection. As Steven Wall, a contemporary political philosopher, says, "The model citizen believes that political justification should proceed from premises that are sound. Sound premises are not always uncontroversial."[12] Suppose that you have thought as hard as you can about the demands of morality, and have provided others with the best arguments you can devise upholding your interpretation. Just as one need not—indeed cannot always—withdraw a moral demand just because someone dissents, so you need not withdraw a demand for political action just because other, quite reasonable, people cannot grasp your moral justification. "[I]f people have sound political views and if they have good reasons for believing that they are sound, then they do not necessarily act wrongly if they impose them on others. The fact that some may reasonably reject their views does not in itself show that they should not enforce them."[13]

Thus, we appear to move seamlessly from the moral authority of private conscience over others to its political authority. You demand that the state institute the egalitarian (or libertarian) regime because you are convinced of its justice. At least this follows if we accept the thesis of the priority of the moral to the political. Once one has determined that one is justified in believing a conclusion about morality, this grounds a justified demand that political action accords with one's moral demands. We might distinguish two versions of this thesis:

The Sanctity of Conscience: An act of a political authority is morally acceptable to Alf only if it conforms to Alf's private conscience about the requirements of morality.

The Social Authority of Private Conscience: In addition to the Sanctity of Conscience, the fact that a political proposal conforms to Alf's private conscience is sufficient justification for him to morally demand that it be instituted by political authority.

The Sanctity of Conscience thesis claims that no act of political authority can be morally acceptable to Alf if it violates his private conscience—his own understanding of the requirements of morality. If a law seeks an egalitarian redistribution, but Alf believes that only strong libertarian property rights are morally justified, he must deny the moral authority of such a law. The Social Authority of Private Conscience thesis claims not only that moral conscience exercises a veto over the moral acceptability of

---

[12] Steven Wall, *Liberalism, Perfectionism, and Restraint* (Cambridge: Cambridge University Press, 1998), 35.
[13] Ibid., 101.

laws, but that Alf is always justified in morally demanding that the political authority enacts legislation required by his view of moral right and
wrong. Alf thus takes his moral judgment as legislative. This appears to
be antidemocratic. As a good democrat, Alf may insist that even if a piece
of legislation is morally required, he will not demand that the political
authority enact it unless it is also approved by the majority. But *why* is Alf
a "good democrat?" Either (1) Alf believes that the democratic requirement is also a moral requirement, or (2) he does not. If (1), then Alf's
commitment to democracy is simply part of his moral view (he is a good
democrat because it is the moral thing), and so his stance is, after all,
consistent with the Social Authority of Private Conscience thesis. His
commitment to democracy only poses a challenge to the Social Authority
of Private Conscience thesis if (2) is the case, but then we may wonder
why Alf allows a nonmoral political commitment to stop him from insisting on what morality requires. Does politics trump moral right and wrong?
Is not the democratic state wrong when it enacts what is immoral, or fails
to enact what morality demands?

C. *The sectarian nature of the view*

I have tried to convey how compelling, at least on first inspection, is
the private conscience's claim to public authority. Given two apparently compelling theses—the social authority of private conscience and
the priority of the moral to the political—it looks as if we are forced to
admit that a "model citizen" must insist that the enactments of political authority conform to his private conscience. Liberalism, however,
was founded precisely on the denial of the claim of sectarian belief to
authority over others. Although it is often claimed that liberalism arose
out of Martin Luther's doctrine of the priesthood of all believers—and
of course there is some truth in this—we must not forget that early
Protestants were as committed as Roman Catholics to uniformity of
religious belief and practice. If each was to interpret the Bible himself,
there was still the expectation that these readings would largely agree.
The priesthood of all believers was no excuse for idiosyncratic interpretations of scripture. And it was certainly no excuse for religious
toleration. Having interpreted scripture, one then rightly could demand
that others conform to one's convictions about God's will.[14] As religious pluralism took hold, sharply conflicting demands were pressed,
each based on a different interpretation of God's will and nature. Liberals such as John Locke insisted that such private conscience had no
public standing. The private judgment of each should rule his own life
in religious matters. In controversies between churches about whose

---

[14] I consider these matters in more detail in "Hobbes' Challenge to Public Reason Liberalism," in *Hobbes Today*, ed. S. A. Lloyd (Cambridge: Cambridge University Press, forthcoming).

doctrine is true, "both sides [are] equal; nor is there any judge . . . upon earth, by whose sentence [the truth] can be determined."[15]

It will immediately be replied that this tale is about religious conviction, not moral belief. In fundamental respects, however, moral and religious beliefs are remarkably similar. The libertarian holds that it is obvious that we are self-owners; the left-libertarian holds that the world is owned by mankind in common; the "liberal egalitarian" has a "single political vision" uniting liberty, equality, and community.[16] Each bases his political claims on a "seeming" or an "intuition"—what manifestly seems true to the proponent of the view. As Christopher Eberle's sophisticated work in political epistemology has shown, these seemings or controversial intuitions are epistemically very similar to "God Manifestation Beliefs"— beliefs about the world formed on the basis of perceptions of God's will and characteristics.[17] The proponents of the various seemings—both religious and moralistic—can seek to show how they make sense of other features of our world, how important they are to us, and how they are consistent with the rest of our experience. Yet to others who do not have this "moral vision," the conclusions are not justified, and the rejected principles do not help them make sense of their own world. As David Gauthier rightly stressed, claims to insight into non-natural moral properties and claims to religious insight are, in many ways, the same type of claim.[18]

III. The Politicalization of Morality

A. Moral judgment, private reason, and disagreement in the social contract tradition

The social contract tradition always recognized that moral judgment is an exercise of private reason and, consequently, that widespread and

[15] John Locke, "A Letter Concerning Toleration," in *The Works of John Locke in Nine Volumes*, 12th ed. (London: Rivington, 1824), vol. 5, 19.

[16] On the last, see Dworkin, *Sovereign Virtue*, 236.

[17] See Christopher J. Eberle, *Religious Conviction in Liberal Politics* (Cambridge: Cambridge University Press, 2002), esp. chap. 8.

[18] David Gauthier, "Why Contractarianism?" in *Contractarianism and Rational Choice*, ed. Peter Vallentyne (Cambridge: Cambridge University Press, 1991), 21ff. But, it will be pressed, we *argue* for our moral beliefs and political positions; moral argument is part of a public, shared discourse. Religious beliefs, though, also are supported by argument (that is why there are schools of theology), and some hold that sustained rational reflection is itself sufficient to arrive at truth about God—that is the very point of natural theology. And much moral argument is, contrary to the proclamations of some philosophers, itself not fully public and shared. Arguments for controversial moral conclusions invoke as premises seemings or intuitions that are quite rationally not shared by others, or propose interpretations of very abstract moral platitudes (e.g., "Don't harm others") that are not shared by others. Once these controversial seemings and interpretations are in play, there seems as little hope for progress in moral argument as there is in religious argument once the participants invoke different perceptions of the nature of God. To claim authority over the lives of others on the grounds of such seemings is quintessentially sectarian.

intractable disputes about the claims of morality are inevitable. "All laws, written and unwritten," Thomas Hobbes tells us,

> have need of interpretation. The unwritten law of nature, though it be easy to such as without partiality and passion make use of their natural reason, and therefore leaves the violators thereof without excuse; yet considering there be very few, perhaps none, that in some cases are not blinded by self-love, or some other passion, it is now become of all laws the most obscure, and has consequently the greatest need of able interpreters.[19]

Locke agrees: "though the Law of Nature be plain and intelligible to all rational Creatures; yet men being biassed by their Interest, as well as ignorant for want of studying it, are not apt to allow of it as a Law binding to them in the application of it to their particular Cases."[20] And to Immanuel Kant, the root of conflict in the state of nature is that "individual men, nations and states can never be certain they are secure against violence from one another because each will have the right to do what seems just and good to him, entirely independently of the opinion of others." Kant goes on to insist that justice is absent in the state of nature because each person relies on his own judgment, and thus "when there is a controversy concerning rights (*jus controversum*), no competent judge can be found to render a decision having the force of law."[21] For Hobbes, Locke, and Kant, a social order in which real justice obtains necessitates that individuals abandon reliance on their private judgments of equity and justice.

It is instructive to contrast the solutions of Hobbes and Locke to the conflict of private, sectarian reasoning about morality. To Hobbes the problem is endemic to all reasoning. The exercise of our rationality is fallible: "no one man's reason, nor the reason of any one number of men, makes the certainty."[22] Rational people aim at what Hobbes calls "right reason"—true rationality, which reveals the truth. However, because everyone's exercise of rationality is fallible, we often disagree about what is right reason; the private use of reason leads to disagreement and, thought Hobbes, conflict. Although in such controversies each person claims that the use of his own private reason is "right reason," these claims only exacerbate the conflict: "when men that think themselves wiser than all others clamour and demand right reason for judge, yet seek no more but

[19] Thomas Hobbes, *Leviathan*, ed. Edwin Curley (Indianapolis, IN: Hackett, 1994), 180 (chap. 26, sec. 20).
[20] John Locke, *Second Treatise of Government*, in *Two Treatises of Government*, ed. Peter Laslett (Cambridge: Cambridge University Press, 1960), sec. 124.
[21] Immanuel Kant, *Metaphysical Elements of Justice*, 2d ed., ed. and trans. John Ladd (Indianapolis, IN: Hackett, 1999), 116–19, 146.
[22] Hobbes, *Leviathan*, 23 (chap. 5, sec. 3).

that things should be determined by no other men's reason but their own, it is . . . intolerable in the society of men." Indeed, Hobbes insists that those who claim that their reason is obviously correct reason betray "their want of right reason by the claim they lay to it."[23] Someone who insists that *his* reason is right reason, and so *his* reason should determine the resolution of disputes, is not only a danger to society, but, because he sees "every passion" of his as an expression of "right reason," he is *irrational:* he demonstrates the lack of right reason by virtue of the claim he lays to it. On Hobbes's view, then, a stable and prosperous social life is only possible among individuals who acknowledge that their private judgment of the demands of reason cannot hold sway in their controversies with others; our very interest in a secure and peaceful social life instructs us to abandon reliance on our private judgment. Hobbes thus proposes that *all* disagreements in private reason—including disputes about religious doctrine and practice, as well as about equity and justice—are to be resolved by the sovereign, who is to serve as the sole voice of public reason.

Locke, in contrast, proposes to separate private disagreement about morality from private disagreement about religion. He writes: "I esteem it above all things necessary to distinguish exactly the business of civil government from that of religion, and to settle the just bounds that lie between the one and the other. If this be not done, there can be no end put to the controversies that will be always arising between those that have, or at least pretend to have, on the one side, a concernment for the interest of men's souls, and, on the other side, a care of the commonwealth."[24] As we have seen, Locke argues that private judgment should rule in religious matters. For the magistrate to seek to regulate such matters would be simply an exercise of private, not public, reason: "as the private judgment of any particular person, if erroneous, does not exempt him from the obligation of law, so the private judgment . . . of the magistrate, does not give him any new right of imposing laws upon his subjects, which neither was in the constitution of the government granted him, nor ever was in the power of the people to grant."[25] However—and here Locke largely concurs with Hobbes—except in the most extreme cases, "all private judgment of every particular Member [of the commonwealth]" must be excluded in determining the demands of morality.[26] It is the task of government to serve as the umpire and the voice of public reason about what morality requires. Once again the political order becomes the interpreter of the moral order regulating interpersonal actions.

---

[23] Ibid. See further David Gauthier, "Public Reason," in *Public Reason*, ed. Fred D'Agostino and Gerald F. Gaus (Brookeville, VT: Ashgate, 1988): 50ff; and R. E. Ewin, *Virtues and Rights: The Moral Philosophy of Thomas Hobbes* (Boulder, CO: Westview, 1991), chap. 2.

[24] Locke, "A Letter Concerning Toleration," 9–10.

[25] Ibid., 43.

[26] Locke, *Second Treatise,* sec. 88.

B. The over-politicalization of moral authority and the validation of ideological politics

The social contract tradition thus represents a wide-ranging rejection of all sectarian claims to public authority. For Locke, private judgment concerning religion is stripped of all public authority over others, being confined to voluntary religious associations. Claims based on private judgment about morality also are without authority (at least over those who disagree): private judgment is "excluded" from public authority, and the state becomes the judge of social morality. Because Hobbes sees no stable way to insulate religious disputes from moral and political ones, he puts everything within the ambit of public authority.

Hobbes, Locke, and Kant trace the problem of social disorder to conflicting claims of private conscience about morality, and all see the solution to be the establishment of the state as the final umpire with respect to the demands of justice.[27] When applied to democracy, the social contract solution would seem to confirm the characterization of the democratic state as the battleground of competing ideologies (or, perhaps more charitably, sectarian views about social and political morality). To be sure, no private advocate of an ideology (or controversial moral vision) has any claim to social authority unless and until her vision is ratified by the democratic umpire, but we can suppose that each citizen (or citizen-philosopher) presses her own controversial, private judgment about the demands of justice, hoping that it is selected by the umpire, and so may emerge as the view with bona fide social authority.

Note that the social contract tradition ends up denying, or at least severely weakening, the intuitive claims we examined in Section II, claims which seemed to make the private moral conscience authoritative over the political. The Social Authority of Private Conscience thesis is straightforwardly rejected: such claims to authority are the source of social disorder. We should not suppose that the social contract tradition is restricted to solving the disorder resulting from differing distinctively *political* views: the root of the problem is conflicting private judgment about all authoritative claims on others, including moral ones. The thesis that the moral is prior to the political *is*, if not abandoned, seriously compromised. Although for Hobbes, Locke, and Kant the principles of natural law, equity, or justice obtain prior to the advent of political association, the state's role as definitive interpreter implies that, except (in the case of Locke) for extreme violations of morality,[28] a "model citizen" must deny

---

[27] This is not to say that citizens must believe that the state is always correct about these matters. While Hobbes perhaps flirts with this view (and in some ways Rousseau did so as well), Locke and Kant are clear that the state can be wrong, and the citizen may conclude that it is. The core question is about the social authority of one's claims on others, not the truth of one's moral judgments.

[28] For Locke, if the majority becomes convinced "in their consciences, that their laws, and with them their estates, liberties, and lives are in danger, and perhaps their religion too,"

both the Sanctity of Conscience thesis and the Social Authority of Private Conscience thesis.[29] That is, the model citizen will not first form a judgment about the demands of authoritative social morality and then employ this judgment to determine the state's authority: it is not until the judge or umpire has ruled that a claim with public authority arises. The model citizen may have his opinion about the matter, but will not deem it to have authority until the umpire has spoken.

Surely this cannot be the correct solution to the problem of sectarian claims to moral authority—at least not for a society of free individuals. Admittedly, in some cases moral disputes end up in the political arena; but the state is not generally the arbiter of social morality. In some version or other, our initial theses (the Sanctity of Conscience and the Social Authority of Private Conscience) must be sound. Individuals quite properly employ their own judgment to make demands on their fellows, and very often there is no supposition that the state need confirm the demand. If I believe it is wrong to employ child labor, I will demand that those who do so cease (the Social Authority of Private Conscience), and I am apt to condemn the state if it fails to halt the practice. Moreover, I shall almost certainly deny the authority of any law that requires me to participate in the practice (the priority of morality to the political is invoked here). This, though, seems to drive us right back to the first view, under which the sectarian claims of private conscience claim public authority. We appear to confront a dilemma: sectarian authority or the effective moral superiority of political authority. In the next section, focusing on property rights, I explore a conception of social morality that is neither resolutely individualistic nor statist; and in Section V, I show how this conception resolves our dilemma.

IV. PUTTING THE SOCIAL BACK INTO SOCIAL MORALITY (AND PROPERTY)

A. Moral rules as social norms

The problem for the two views we have examined is essentially the same: they see nothing between the individual conscience and the authority of the state. Caught in this simple dichotomy, the first view grants authority to the private conscience. The second view (the social contract tradition) sees this as a threat to order, so when the demands of private

---

they may employ their private conscience and its authoritative claims to reject the government's claim to authority. See Locke, *Second Treatise*, secs. 208, 209, 225, and 230.

[29] To remind readers, the Sanctity of Conscience thesis holds that an act of a political authority is morally acceptable to Alf only if it conforms to Alf's private conscience about the requirements of morality, while The Social Authority of Private Conscience thesis adds that the private judgment of a person about morality gives her standing to demand that the state enact legislation that she deems morally required.

conscience conflict, it holds that the state's decision is definitive. After his review of the classical social contract theories of Hobbes, Locke, and Rousseau, T. H. Green concluded that "they look only to the supreme coercive power on the one side and to individuals, to whom natural rights are ascribed, on the other," and so "they leave out of sight the process by which men are clothed with rights and duties, and with senses of rights and duties, which are neither natural nor derived from the sovereign power." [30]

It is a mistake, then, to think of the state as an aggregation of individuals under a sovereign—equally so whether we suppose the individuals as such, or apart from what they derive from society, to possess natural rights [Locke], or suppose them to depend on the sovereign for the possession of rights [Hobbes]. A state presupposes other forms of community, with the rights that arise out of them, and only exists as sustaining, securing, and completing them. In order to make a state there must have been families of which the members recognized rights in each other (recognized in each other powers capable of direction by reference to a common good); there must further have been intercourse between families, or between tribes that have grown out of families, of which each in the same sense recognized rights in the other. . . . [31]

Green's insight is that between the individual's private conscience and the public authority of the state lies the authority of social practices, including the rules of social morality. In recent moral and political philosophy, the importance of social norms and rules in ordering the moral life of a society has been most consistently stressed by Kurt Baier and F. A. Hayek. Throughout his long career, Baier insisted that the morality of a society is a social fact or, as he sometimes put it, a sort of social order constituted by systems of mores or rules. [32] Hayek, too, consistently stressed that it is the evolved moral rules of a society that order the actions of its members by aligning their expectations. [33] Two of Hayek's claims are especially important for our purposes: (1) moral rules arise through an evolutionary process, and (2) they arise "endogenously."

[30] T. H. Green, *Lectures on the Principles of Political Obligation,* in Green, *Lectures on the Principles of Political Obligation and Other Writings,* ed. Paul Harris and John Morrow (Cambridge: Cambridge University Press, 1986), sec. 113.

[31] Ibid., sec. 134.

[32] See Kurt Baier, *The Rational and the Moral Order: The Social Roots of Reason and Morality* (LaSalle, IL: Open Court, 1995), 199ff.

[33] See my "The Evolution of Society and Mind: Hayek's System of Ideas," in *The Cambridge Companion to Hayek,* ed. Edward Feser (Cambridge: Cambridge University Press, 2006).

	Hawk	Dove
Hawk	z ⟍ z	0 ⟍ v
Dove	v ⟍ 0	$v/2$ ⟍ $v/2$

FIGURE 1. Generalized Hawk-Dove Game

This matching of the intentions and expectations that determine the actions of different individuals is the form in which order manifests itself in social life. . . . [The] . . . authoritarian connotation of the concept of order derives . . . from the belief that order can only be created by forces outside the systems (or "exogenously"). It does not apply to an equilibrium set up from within (or "endogenously"). . . .[34]

In their analyses of interpretive disagreements, Hobbes, Locke, and Kant all paid insufficient attention to our evolved ability to coordinate our actions on a common interpretation of norms. The tendency of our natural reason to produce divergent interpretations is countered by our tendency to converge on a common understanding of the norms that structure social life.

B. *Primitive property rights as correlated strategies*

To see how such convergence may evolve, let us start with a simple model of the development of property rights. Basic property rights can be modeled as conventions in correlated equilibrium about the mutual recognition of individual jurisdictions. In the most primitive case of all, the jurisdictions can be understood simply as territorial, as in the classic Hawk-Dove game given in figure 1.[35]

Suppose Hawks and Doves are types of individuals in the population. A Hawk always battles for a territory until either he is injured or his opponent retreats. A Dove engages in display battle: if he meets a Hawk, he quickly retreats without injury; if he meets another Dove, there is a .5 probability that he will retreat—in no case does he sustain injury. Let v be the value of the territory (and suppose it is positive), and w be the cost of

[34] F. A. Hayek, *Rules and Order* (Chicago: University of Chicago Press, 1973), 36. Compare Baier, *The Rational and the Moral Order*, 218.

[35] I am drawing here on Herbert Gintis's analysis in *The Bounds of Reason: Game Theory and the Unification of the Behavioral Sciences* (Princeton, NJ: Princeton University Press, 2009), 39–40, 201ff., and my presentation in *On Philosophy, Politics, and Economics* (Belmont, CA: Thomson-Wadsworth, 2008), 136–42. For the classic analysis, see John Maynard Smith, "The Evolution of Behavior," *Scientific American* 239 (1978): 176–92.

	Hawk	Dove
Hawk	-5 -5	0 10
Dove	10 0	5 5

FIGURE 2. A Specific Hawk-Dove Game

injury from fighting over a territory (and suppose that $w > v$); then let $z = (v - w)/2$. Figure 2 provides a specific set of payoffs.

Let us view this as an evolutionary game. Players do not change strategies, but play their strategy against whomever they meet. Table 1 gives the expected payoffs of three different strategies when they meet each other.

The expected payoff of a Hawk playing another Hawk is –5; the expected payoff of a Hawk meeting a Dove is 10; the expected payoff of a Dove meeting a Hawk is 0; and the expected payoff of a Dove meeting a Dove is 5. Though the players do not vary their strategies (and so they cannot make "moves" in the sense of traditional game theory), we can understand the population as "moving" in the sense that, if being a Hawk has a higher expected payoff than being a Dove, the population will move toward more Hawks and fewer Doves. In evolutionary terms, we can think of this as a *replicator dynamic* in which those strategies that tend to have higher average payoffs increase in the population and so displace lower-payoff strategies.[36] Thus, as the Hawks and Doves play each other repeatedly over long periods of time, the percentage of Hawks and Doves in the population from generation to generation will vary with how many points they gather in our Hawk/Dove game (points, let us say, indicate relative fitness). An *evolutionarily stable strategy* is one that cannot be invaded

[36] See Brian Skyrms, *Evolution of the Social Contract* (Cambridge: Cambridge University Press, 1996).

TABLE 1. *Expected Payoffs*

		Plays against		
		Hawk	Dove	Lockean
Player	Hawk	–5	10	$2\frac{1}{2}$
	Dove	0	5	$2\frac{1}{2}$
	Lockean	$-2\frac{1}{2}$	$7\frac{1}{2}$	5

by a mutant strategy.[37] It is immediately obvious that neither all-Hawk nor all-Dove is an evolutionarily stable strategy. For a population of all Hawks, the average expected payoff of the population is −5; since a mutant Dove would have a payoff of 0, he would outperform the population average and increase. For a population of all Doves, the average population payoff is 5; a mutant Hawk would receive a payoff of 10, thus again outperforming the average of the Dove population. In the case of figure 2, an evolutionarily stable equilibrium would be a mixed population evenly split between Doves and Hawks. At that mix, the average Hawk and average Dove payoffs are the same $(2\frac{1}{2})$, and thus neither population can grow at the expense of the other.[38]

Although this population mix is stable, it is an inefficient way to allocate property rights: our Hawks and Doves have arrived at a stable equilibrium, but this includes the cost of injury to warring Hawks.[39] (And remember that a population of peaceful Doves can always be invaded by Hawks.) Now suppose a new type of person arises, the Lockean. The Lockean acts aggressively to protect his territory, but is easily deterred from taking that of others. In short, the Lockean acts like a Hawk on his own territory and like a Dove on that of others. Suppose that our Lockean has half his encounters on his own territory, and half on that of others; the expected payoff of Lockeans interacting is 5; half the time a Lockean playing another Lockean will get 10, and half the time 0. Our Lockeans can invade pure Hawk or pure Dove populations, as well as our mixed population in equilibrium. Recall (table 1) that the average payoff of a Dove against a Dove is 5; but a Lockean playing a Dove will get 10 during the half of the time it is on its own territory ($10 \times \frac{1}{2} = 5$) and will receive the Dove payoff during

---

[37] According to one way of formalizing this, S is an evolutionarily stable strategy (ESS) if and only if, with respect to a mutant strategy S^* that might arise, either (1) the expected payoff of S against itself is higher than the expected payoff of the mutant S^* against S, or (2) while the expected payoff of S against itself is equal to the expected payoff of S^* against S, the expected payoff of S against S^* is higher than the expected payoff of S^* against itself. The idea is this. Suppose that we have an S population into which one or a few S^* types are introduced. Because of the predominance of S types, both S and S^* will play most of their games against S. According to the first rule, if S does better against itself than S^* does against S, S^* will not get a foothold in the population. Suppose instead that S^* does just as well against S as S does against itself. Then S^* will begin to grow in the population, until there are enough S^* types so that both S and S^* play against S^* reasonably often. According to the second rule, once this happens, if S does better against S^* than S^* does against itself, S will again grow at a more rapid rate. To say, then, that S is an ESS is to say that an invading strategy will, over time, do less well than will S. There are other ways of formulating the basic idea of an evolutionarily stable strategy, but that need not detain us here.

[38] In an evenly split Dove/Hawk population, a Dove will play half its games against other Doves, and in each game it receives 5 (so $\frac{1}{2} \times 5 = 2\frac{1}{2}$), while it plays the other half of the time against Hawks, for an average payoff of 0 ($\frac{1}{2} \times 0 = 0$); thus, a Dove's overall expected payoff against the entire population is $2\frac{1}{2}$. Hawks play Doves half of the time, and in each game receive 10 (so $\frac{1}{2} \times 10 = 5$); the other half of the time a Hawk plays against other Hawks, with an expected payoff each time of −5 (so $\frac{1}{2} \times -5 = -2\frac{1}{2}$); thus (5) + ($-2\frac{1}{2}$) = $2\frac{1}{2}$.

[39] See Gintis, *The Bounds of Reason*, 135.

the half the time it is on another's territory ($5 \times \frac{1}{2} = 2\frac{1}{2}$), for a total expected payoff of $7\frac{1}{2}$, thus outperforming the Dove. In a population of all Hawks, the average payoff is -5; the Lockean will also receive the -5 payoff during the half of the time it is on its own territory, but will receive the 0 payoff when it is off its territory, giving it a total expected payoff against Hawks of $-2\frac{1}{2}$, again outperforming the Hawk population. And the Lockean population cannot be invaded by either Hawks or Doves.[40] Lockeanism is an evolutionarily stable strategy, and an efficient equilibrium.[41]

Of course, the advantage of Lockeans depends on the costs and benefits of predation and defense; if preying on others is very easy and beneficial, Hawks may have an advantage. If preying is exceptionally difficult or yields small returns, Lockeans may have relatively little advantage over pure Doves. But societies filled with Hawks and Doves tend to reach inefficient equilibria over a wide range of values (concerning the variables in figure 1). If we add to our analysis competition between groups, societies of Lockeans overall have a distinct advantage. As Peter J. Richerson and Robert Boyd have demonstrated in an impressive body of work, cultural variation shows strong group selection processes.[42] Groups with fundamentally more efficient forms of organization tend to expand, and to be imitated by others. Within broad parameters, what Herbert Gintis calls the "property equilibrium"[43] is fundamental to social life, and over the long term, we can expect social convergence on some "Lockean" (in our broad sense) conception of property rights.

All this is fairly standard evolutionary game theory. Note, however, that we can redescribe "Hawks" as those who are assertive in their private judgments about the bounds of property rights, "Doves" as those who are deferential to the private judgments of others, and "Lockeans" as those who have achieved a common conception of the boundaries of property rights. Locke himself, perhaps, thought that the state of nature would be populated by Hawkish interpreters of the property convention:

[40] As table 1 shows, the expected payoff of Doves against Lockeans is $2\frac{1}{2}$ (half the time a Dove gets nothing, half the time 5); the expected payoff of Hawks against Lockeans is also $2\frac{1}{2}$ (-5 half the time for $-2\frac{1}{2}$, and 10 half the time for an average of 5, so $-2\frac{1}{2} + 5 = 2\frac{1}{2}$. Recall that the expected payoffs of Lockeans against themselves is 5, so they cannot be invaded. Lockeans can also invade the mixed population in equilibrium.

[41] It constitutes what Robert Aumann called a "correlated equilibrium," which is more efficient here than the Nash equilibrium characterizing our Hawk-Dove mixed population. Robert Aumann, "Subjectivity and Correlation in Randomized Strategies," *Journal of Mathematical Economics* 1 (1974): 67–69. See also Skyrms, *Evolution of the Social Contract*, chap. 4; my *On Philosophy, Politics, and Economics*, 140–41, Gintis, *The Bounds of Reason*, 135; and Robert Sugden, *The Economics of Rights, Co-operation, and Welfare* (Oxford: Basil Blackwell, 1986), chap. 4. For a sophisticated treatment, see Peter Vanderschraaf, *Learning and Coordination: Inductive Deliberation, Learning, and Convention* (New York: Routledge, 2001).

[42] See, for example, Peter J. Richerson and Robert Boyd, "The Evolution of Free Enterprise Values," in *Moral Markets: The Critical Role of Values in the Economy*, ed. Paul Zak (Princeton, NJ: Princeton University Press, 2008), 114.

[43] Gintis, *The Bounds of Reason*, 210ff.

each individual asserts, and employs force to defend, his own view of property rights with a strong bias toward self-interest.[44] If Locke was right about this—if the state of nature would be a world of interpretive Hawks—then indeed they would be apt to abandon all private judgment and abide by the umpire (the state) to avoid destructive war (–5). The first view we considered (Section II), upholding the sovereign social authority of private conscience, also seems Hawkish, though these Hawks seem more peaceful (perhaps it is supposed that they live among Dove-like deferential interpreters who will do as they are told!). Over the long term, however, successful and efficient social orders would heavily favor our correlated Lockean interpreters, who are often able to converge on a common understanding of the bounds of property norms. The ability to think like others—or, following Cristina Bicchieri's analysis, the tendency to share "scripts" about the detailed actions called for by rules—would be favored over Hawkish interpreters, and there is good reason to think that this ability has indeed evolved in all human cultures.[45]

C. Territory, resources, and jurisdictions

In the most primitive case, the property equilibrium divides territory.[46] We get closer to an adequate notion of property if we think of it as involving resources. Many of the fundamental conflicts among humans concern how those things that we can use to fulfill our needs, and that are required for production, are to be divided. However, while a focus on the division of resources rather than mere territoriality is a step toward a more adequate—a more human—conception of property, it is also easy to take a misstep here. Much current political philosophy, inspired by economic analysis, makes two claims about property rights:

(1) Property is about the division of resources.
(2) The property rights equilibrium is mutually beneficial.

From (1) and (2) it seems easy to infer:

(3) A property right in equilibrium over some resource must benefit others, and certainly must not be an overall cost.

---

[44] Recall that, according to Locke, "though the Law of Nature be plain and intelligible to all rational Creatures; yet men being biassed by their Interest, as well as ignorant for want of studying it, are not apt to allow of it as a Law binding to them in the application of it to their particular Cases" (*Second Treatise*, sec. 124).

[45] Cristina Bicchieri, *The Grammar of Society: The Nature and Dynamics of Norms* (Cambridge: Cambridge University Press, 2006). I explore the development of such norms in some depth in *The Order of Public Reason* (Cambridge: Cambridge University Press, 2011), chaps. 3 and 7. See also Daniel Friedman, *Morals and Markets: An Evolutionary Account of the Modern World* (New York: Palgrave Macmillan, 2008), 18.

[46] Gintis, *The Bounds of Reason*, 204-7.

In his original and insightful book *The Right to Exploit*, Gijs van Donselaar implicitly invokes this trinity of claims to argue against "parasitism," and thus against fixed property rights in resources. Natural resources, van Donselaar argues, are scarce, and so we compete for them; property rights divide these resources, and if the property system is to be mutually beneficial, this division must work to the maximal advantage of society. Consequently, if someone appropriates a natural resource but does not employ it in a way that improves the lot of others (and of course, more strongly, if he employs it in a way that worsens their lot), his claim to the scarce resource cannot be justified through appeal to a mutually beneficial property equilibrium. Compared to the world in which the unproductive appropriator did not exist, others are worse off: he denies the use of the scarce resource to others by claiming property over it, but does nothing with it. It turns out that doing *something* useful with it is not enough to avoid the charge of being an exploiter: one must use it in the most efficient manner. The entrepreneur's

> duty is not just to produce as efficiently as he can, but to produce at least as efficiently as any of his competitors would have done in his position (as far as that position is defined by control over resources). That implies that he may be required to produce more efficiently than he can. Where he fails to do so, he has no right to be in his position. Where he fails, his factor endowments ought to be adjusted.[47]

As interpreted by van Donselaar, our trinity of claims makes each individual the steward of external resources over which he has property rights, a stewardship that requires the most efficient use for its continuance. Fixed rights in resources license parasitism.[48]

Van Donselaar's case is grounded on efficiency: if the justification of property rights is a mutual benefit (qua efficiency), then only efficient users possess bona fide rights. As do most economists, van Donselaar equates two senses of efficiency or mutual benefit: (1) Pareto-superior changes that move us from distribution S_1 to a new distribution S_2, where in S_2 some have a higher level of preference satisfaction than in S_1, and no one has a lower level (no one is on a lower indifference curve in S_2 than in S_1 and at least one person is on a higher one); and (2) improvements in human welfare—at least one person's welfare is increased in the move from S_1 to S_2, and no one's is decreased. These, though, are quite distinct ideas, despite the unfortunate tendency of philosophers and economists

[47] Gijs van Donselaar, *The Right to Exploit: Parasitism, Scarcity, Basic Income* (Oxford: Oxford University Press, 2009), 54.
[48] A claim with which David Gauthier appears to concur in his endorsement on the back of van Donselaar's book. Gauthier advocated a weak requirement of efficient use as necessary for rightful possession in his *Morals by Agreement* (New York: Oxford University Press, 1986), 293.

alike to conflate them under the label "utility."[49] The notion of *welfare* concerns whether, according to some standard, the life of humans is bettered or worsened. Now certainly in some basic cases there is wide convergence on judgments about welfare—it is generally agreed that bodily integrity, food, and health (for example) are of crucial importance to life, and that their absence diminishes one's welfare. However, for "increase in welfare" to serve as a general standard for judging social improvements and property rights, we need to do more than simply identify this and that element of welfare (absence of physical harm, security of person, financial and workplace security, intellectual life and enlightenment, job skills, pleasure, riches, sex, religiosity, excitement, contentment, and so on); we must also be able to rank these elements or, more adequately, construct a trade-off rate such that x amount of intellectual activity is equivalent to, say, y amount of financial security. There are always those who believe they have constructed such interpersonally valid metrics, but a characteristic of modern societies is that such metrics are highly controversial among people of good will who are competent to make judgments about these matters.

Given the dispute about the welfare interpretation of "utility," we can appreciate the attraction of the other conception of "utility," as a mathematical representation of the degree to which a preference ordering is satisfied. This conception is often employed in modern welfare economics.[50] It seems enticing: letting people "prefer" whatever they wish and order their preferences in any way they like, the aim of social policy should be the efficient satisfaction of these preferences (or, if there is thought to be some interpersonal metric, their overall maximization). Now in some domains of analysis, in which we make simplifying assumptions about the types of preferences held by individuals, this may lead to enlightening results, but it is markedly unsuitable as a general criterion of acceptable rules and norms. A person's preferences can range over just about anything, from preferences for food, to doing one's Kantian duty, to having a world free of Catholics.[51] Since at least the late Middle Ages, Western European society has been characterized not only by a great diversity of preferences, but by a great diversity of preferences that some hold dearly that others decry. Imagine the preference orderings of Ayn Rand and G. A. Cohen. If we accept the crux of van Donselaar's argument in the foregoing quotation,[52] Ayn Rand's holding of property in resources

---

[49] See John Broome, *Ethics Out of Economics* (Oxford: Oxford University Press, 1991), chap. 2. See also my *Philosophy, Politics, and Economics*, 81–82.

[50] For the conception's application to social policy, see Louis Kaplow and Steven Shavell, *Fairness Versus Welfare* (Cambridge, MA: Harvard University Press, 2002).

[51] See further my *Philosophy, Politics, and Economics*, chap. 2.

[52] Van Donselaar's analysis is subtle; the possible counterfactuals he explores as to whether Alf would be better off if Betty did not exist, or did not claim a resource, are complex. See *The Right to Exploit*, 88ff.

would be contingent upon her use raising, or certainly not lowering, the preference satisfaction of G. A. Cohen.[53]

Once we understand preferences to be simply a ranking of options or states of affairs on the basis of one's values, ends, aims, and so on, the attraction of requiring that all uses of resources advance the preferences of all, or least do not set them back, evaporates. The use of my property is often important to me *because* it allows me to set back the satisfaction of your preferences. By opening my land to a Marxist summer camp, I set back the libertarian's key preferences: that is not simply a side-effect of my use of the land, it is the *point* of it. When a speaker uses the pulpit in a Catholic Church to denounce atheism, the point of the use of property is to set back atheistic preferences. The sense in which property rights are an efficient response to the problem of social life is much more general than the one van Donselaar (and, I think, Gauthier) has in mind. Property rights divide the social world into different jurisdictions. Over some questions Q, my choices constitute the definitive social choice; over other questions R, your choices are definitive for all. If we can coordinate on the boundaries of Q and R, we can go about our business without the destructive Hawk-Hawk interactions. By dividing social life into different jurisdictions, in which each person's values, ends, and goals hold sway, the mutual respect of these jurisdictions allows us to live together in partly cooperative, partly competitive arrangements with a minimum of conflict about whose values are to hold sway where. This, indeed, is the quintessential liberal response to the fact that our aims and values so often differ, and indeed conflict: the social recognition of spheres in which one's ends hold sway, and one may act on the basis of one's own values and interests.[54] This is the sense in which property rights are the foundation of a social order among people who fundamentally disagree in their aims and values, as opposed to a social order premised on the devotion of all to a collective project, be it the glory of Calvin's God, the spirit of the nation, or a fully egalitarian society. In a liberal order, each individual has a sphere in which her personal interests, religious convictions, or personal moral visions hold sway, and others respect those spheres and thus do not seek to impose their interests, convictions, and visions within them. A property rights equilibrium is a socially efficient solution to the problem of individuals living together in that mix of competition and cooperation that we call modern society— which helps explain why all contemporary social orders have tended to gravitate to the liberal solution.

[53] It would at least have to be the case that he would be better off given Rand's existence and her appropriation than he would have been in a world without her. Van Donselaar, *The Right to Exploit,* chap. 2.

[54] I have developed this case in some detail in "Recognized Rights as Devices of Public Reason," *Philosophical Perspectives: Ethics* 23 (2009): 111–36.

D. From convention to a moral equilibrium

I have argued thus far that a "Lockean" property rights equilibrium, in the sense of a set of shared or joint individual strategies dividing society into various jurisdictions, is a critical part of an efficient solution to the problem of social order given differences in aims and interests. However, as David Schwab and Elinor Ostrom argue, there are compelling reasons to conclude that mere shared strategies are insufficient to sustain free-market transactions.[55] If we suppose that individuals are solely devoted to their own private ends, the development of market exchange—which depends on trust—is difficult to explain. As Hobbes so effectively showed, individuals who are solely devoted to their private ends will be sorely tempted to renege on "covenants": if the other party performs first and so gives the second party what she wants, there seems to be no incentive for the second party to perform her part of the bargain.[56] Rather than exchanging, she will be tempted to snatch the goods and flee.[57] Given sufficiently narrow, self-interested utility functions, she may often do better by snatching: she gets the good without paying for it.

To some extent, reputational knowledge can mitigate this problem: if the person is known as a snatcher rather than an exchanger, exchangers will boycott her, thus giving her an incentive not to snatch in order to avoid future boycotts. However, the ability of reputational knowledge to constrain snatching behavior is surprisingly limited. Peter Vanderschraaf, employing dynamic game analysis, has shown how sensitive this reputational solution is to accurate common knowledge. In his model, Vanderschraaf takes account of the effects of false as well as true gossip: once we model information as gossip (true and false) and allow snatchers to adopt slightly more sophisticated strategies (such as only snatching half the time rather than always), Vanderschraaf shows that the snatchers can fare better than the exchangers "in a community that must rely upon private information or 'gossip' only to spread information."[58] In a world of such imperfect information, Vanderschraaf concludes that "Rationality alone does not explain reciprocal cooperation."[59]

Natalie Henrich's ethnographic research among the Chaldeans also supports the limits of cooperation through reputation. The Chaldeans are a non-Arabic, Christian ethnic group with a population of approximately 100,000 that has emigrated from Iraq to the Detroit metropolitan area.

[55] David Schwab and Elinor Ostrom, "The Vital Role of Norms and Rules in Maintaining Open Public and Private Economies," in Zak, ed., Moral Markets, 204–27.
[56] Hobbes actually thinks that a person has some reason to perform second, but this is usually too weak to outweigh her selfish passions. See Hobbes, Leviathan, chap. 14.
[57] On the game of snatch, see Schwab and Ostrom, "The Vital Role of Norms and Rules in Maintaining Open Public and Private Economies," 205ff.
[58] Peter Vanderschraaf, "Covenants and Reputations." Synthese 157 (2007): 184.
[59] Ibid., 185.

Henrich's research indicates that intragroup cooperation is to a large extent sustained though reputational knowledge. As one subject reported:

> Everyone knows which families are good or bad, and you just do business with people who come from good families—I go by family name. If I don't know someone, I call people and ask about his family. People just mention who they are and [if they have a good reputation], they get credit.[60]

Because the Chaldeans have social networks in which almost everyone is heavily enmeshed (family businesses, clubs, organizations, and churches), and because they have "a fondness for gossip," only a few calls are required to get information about the reputation of any potential participant in a business deal.[61] The costs of a bad reputation are quite severe. "Among Chaldeans, a person with a bad reputation is less likely to be given credit, to be hired, to be desired as a business partner, or to be lent money. People will also not want to date or marry a person with a bad reputation and if they do so people will gossip about them."[62] The Chaldeans, then, are a case of a reasonably large group in which cooperation is to a large extent sustained by knowledge of reputations. Henrich and Henrich's analysis however, also displays a number of pathologies and inefficiencies of social cooperation sustained through reputational knowledge. For example, individuals spend a great deal of time establishing reputations; because it is important that a person establish a generalized reputation as a cooperator, there is a significant incentive to ratchet up one's reputation in public arenas with a show of cooperative behavior even with noncooperators; conflict arises because of competition among individuals within groups, and between groups, to claim credit for accomplishments to bolster reputations; individuals exploit opportunities to gain reputations without contributing; to have a reputation as a cooperator is not simply about one's past tendencies to engage in certain well-defined cooperator behavior, but is closer to having a reputation as a good group member, who conforms to the group's customs and norms; and those who are members of families with good reputations are treated as having good reputations, while those in families with historically bad reputations are treated as having bad reputations, even if they have no such individual history. Chaldean cooperation is focused on other Chaldeans: there is considerable distrust of out-group members. Chaldeans prefer to do business with co-ethnics, even at significant costs to themselves.[63] All these are significant costs to social

---

[60] Natalie Henrich and Joseph Henrich, *Why Humans Cooperate: A Cultural and Evolutionary Explanation* (Oxford: Oxford University Press, 2007), 123.
[61] Ibid.
[62] Ibid., 124.
[63] Ibid., 193–96.

cooperation through reputational knowledge. Overall, it is unclear to what extent such reputational knowledge actually can sustain cooperation within large groups without intense social networks conveying reliable information.[64]

A large body of work indicates that extended market societies are only possible when the property equilibrium evolves into a moral equilibrium: individuals come to conceive of property and exchange rules as morally authoritative.[65] Participants largely refrain from cheating and exploiting others, not primarily because they are worried about their reputations, but because they believe it is wrong to violate rules that *are generally followed by others.* This last phrase is important: people tend to follow rules that are generally followed—they tend to ignore normative exhortations to follow rules when the exhortations are not backed up by actual general conformity.[66] A striking feature of market economies is a strong acceptance of a norm that requires that strangers be treated fairly. In a now-classic cross-cultural study, Joseph Henrich and Natalie Smith found that participants in market societies (the United States, Indonesia, and Israel) were much more likely to treat anonymous strangers fairly than were those in two small-scale societies—the Machiguenga of the Peruvian Amazon and the Mapuche of Southern Chile.[67] Henrich and Smith concluded:

> In order to exist, modern, industrial, urban centers must have developed norms (behaviors and expectations) to deal effectively with

[64] See Robert Boyd and Peter J. Richerson, "The Evolution of Indirect Reciprocity," *Social Networks* 11 (1989): 213–36.

[65] See, for example, Richerson and Boyd, "The Evolution of Free Enterprise Values"; Schwab and Ostrom, "The Vital Role of Norms and Rules in Maintaining Open Public and Private Economies"; and Friedman, *Morals and Markets,* esp. chap. 3.

[66] See here Cristina Bicchieri and Erte Xiao, "Do the Right Thing: But Only If Others Do So," *Journal of Behavioral Decision Making* (2008), published online in Wiley InterScience (www.interscience.wiley.com), doi: 10.1002/bdm.621. In their experimental work on public-goods games among the Machiguenga and the Mapuche, Joseph Henrich and Natalie Smith also found that "the primary indicator of what a subject will do is what the subject thinks the rest of the group will do." Henrich and Smith, "Comparative Evidence from Machiguenga, Mapuche, and American Populations," in *Foundations of Human Sociality: Economic Experiments and Ethnographic Evidence from Fifteen Small-Scale Societies,* ed. J. Henrich, R. Boyd, S. Bowles, et al. (Oxford: Oxford University Press, 2004), 125–67. See also Richerson and Boyd, "The Evolution of Free Enterprise Values," 114–15.

[67] These results are partly based on the "ultimatum game," which involves two subjects, Proposer and Responder, who have X amount of some good (say, money) to distribute between them. In the simplest version of the game, Proposer makes the first move, and gives an offer of the form: "I will take n percent of X, leaving you with $100 - n$ percent," where n is not greater than 100 percent. If Responder accepts, each gets what Proposer offers; if Responder rejects, each receives nothing. If both parties were narrowly self-interested, Proposer would suggest, say 90:10 splits, and Responder would accept. In fact, in market societies, 60:40 splits tend to be the norm, though Henrich and Smith did find some differences among market societies: the outcomes of the experiments in the market societies of Israel and Indonesia show more low offers, and the Israeli data shows a lower mean offer. Henrich and Smith question the importance of means and modes in analyzing the results of ultimatum games. Heinrich and Smith, "Comparative Experimental Evidence from Machiguenga, Mapuche, and American Populations," 133–34.

anonymous transactions, and allow people to cooperate in a wide variety of contexts. Market societies are filled with opportunities to "cheat," such that, if most people took advantage of these loopholes, our systems would rapidly crumble. We think that these systems persist because people share sets of re-enforcing norms about how to behave in different contexts, what is "fair" in different contexts, and what to punish. . . . The point is, large-scale, market-based societies could not function without well-coordinated norms for dealing with anonymous, one-shot, monetary interactions. However, there is no reason to expect other societies, where anonymous monetary trans-actions are recent and rare, to share such norms.[68]

The Machiguenga, for example, "have little or no expectation of favorable treatment from anonymous persons, no sense of group fairness, and thus no reason to punish." [69] Thus, the Machiguenga have not developed norms about cutting into waiting lines, a basic rule of fairness that unites market societies such as Chile, the United States, and India.[70] As the market order expands, groups adopt its norms of fairness.[71]

V. The Basic Conditions for a Moral Equilibrium

A. The optimal eligible set

If the property equilibrium is to be a genuine moral equilibrium, it must be the case that the population can endorse the property norms as authoritative, so that an individual does not defect on them whenever he can "snatch rather than exchange" without being observed. As with almost all equilibrium solutions, this certainly does not mean that the norm must be judged "the best" by everyone. An equilibrium describes a set of actions that satisfies everyone's utility function—now understood in an extended sense to include devotion to norms as well as private ends[72]—to the extent that each person ranks acting on the equilibrium as better than unilateral defection. When the property rights equilibrium is also a moral equilibrium, each person, drawing on her set of values and ends, affirms that the property norm is authoritative for her. That the norm requires

---

[68] Henrich and Smith, "Comparative Evidence from Machiguenga, Mapuche, and American Populations," 162–63.

[69] Ibid., 159.

[70] Ibid., 163–64; R. Shweder, M. Mahapatra, and J. Miller, "Culture in Moral Development," in *The Emergence of Morality in Young Children*, ed. Jerome Kagan and Sharon Lamb (Chicago: University of Chicago Press, 1987), 47ff.

[71] This may be happening with the Machiguenga. See Henrich and Smith, "Comparative Evidence from Machiguenga, Mapuche, and American Populations," 141.

[72] See Schwab and Ostrom, "The Vital Role of Norms and Rules in Maintaining Open Public and Private Economies," 126ff. I analyze these sorts of extended utility functions in some depth in *Philosophy, Politics, and Economics*, chap. 2.

exchanging rather than snatching, or requires that one treat strangers fairly in market transactions, is itself a strong reason to do so, and one would normally see oneself as having done wrong, and as properly liable to blame and rebuke, for failing to conform to it.

To help make the point more precise, suppose that each person has a well-informed and coherent "extended utility function," which includes not only her private ends, but her values, normative intuitions, and so on.[73] For a property norm to be in universal moral equilibrium in a society, it must be such that each person, consulting her extended utility function, endorses the property norm as authoritative—a moral norm that she has reason to follow if others do so as well. Now suppose that, consulting her own extended utility function, each person i proposes a property right rule p_i, which she believes is the rule that best satisfies her extended utility function. (This is basically what philosophers do when they argue for their preferred theory of property rights and distributive justice.) Assume further that each individual has made a proposal, and so we have a set of all proposals $\{p_1 \ldots p_n\}$. If there is any proposal in $\{p_1 \ldots p_n\}$ that some well-informed person cannot accept as authoritative—if *that* were the property right convention, she would defect rather than comply when she could do so unobserved—it must be excluded from the set of acceptable property norms. It could not serve as a possible moral equilibrium. Let us also exclude any norm that is Pareto-dominated by another in the set: if, for everyone, p_x is ranked better than p_y, then we exclude p_y from the final set. The set of remaining norms is *the optimal eligible set of property norms*: any norm in the set is preferred to the absence of a moral equilibrium, and none is dominated by any other.

B. Testing our moral property rights

As Baier stressed, the place to begin our moral thinking is with our existing social rules. Moral philosophy does not construct a system of morality *de novo*; a society's morality is a social fact that structures the actual interactions of its members. As we have seen, it is only when social norms are a social fact—when others are generally conforming to them— that a person tends to act on them. Mere moral exhortation is seldom effective in generating moral behavior. Given this, when we are confronted by an existing social norm the primary question for moral philosophy must be whether that norm is within the optimal eligible set. If our current property rights are within the optimal eligible set, they provide a bona fide moral equilibrium, and they can perform the social tasks that a property rights regime must perform, because they are seen by all

---

[73] I am simplifying here, of course. The set of persons must be further constrained, at least to those who are capable of forming extended utility functions, and so internalizing moral norms.

as morally authoritative. The existence of an actual social rule that is
generally followed by a society is entirely different from a fanciful construction of what rule would be fairer, or nicer, or better: only an existing
rule can provide a moral structure for human society. If our existing
property rules are within the optimal eligible set, we are fortunate enough
to live in a moral order.

If we understand a rule of a true morality as one that is within the
optimal eligible set, then we must agree with Baier that "[t]here is no a
priori reason to assume that there is only one true morality. There are
many moralities, and of these a large number may happen to pass the test
which moralities must pass in order to be called true. It would, therefore,
be better to speak of 'a true morality' or of 'true moralities' than 'true
morality'."[74] If our existing property practice is within the optimal eligible set, each person has sufficient reason to affirm it as an authoritative
moral norm: consulting only her own reasons ("extended utility function"), she sees that given that others are complying, she too has sufficient
reason not only to comply, but to endorse the norm as authoritative. In
that sense, each person freely complies: she freely accepts the norm as
authoritative over her.

Reconsider now one of our troublesome theses (from Section II.B
above). According to the Social Authority of Private Conscience thesis,
each person consults her own private conscience and makes authoritative moral claims on others. This seems to be precisely the type of
sectarian claim to authority that the liberal tradition has decried (see
Section II.C). Now when a moral rule is within the optimal eligible set,
each person has reason both to demand that others comply (it is, say,
essential to the practice of property) and to accept this demand as
authoritative over her, because the moral rule is in equilibrium. It might
seem to some that if all endorse the moral equilibrium, there would be
no reason why one must *demand* that others comply—all would freely
do so. As Richerson and Boyd observe, though, "we are imperfect and
often reluctant, though often very effective cooperators."[75] We need
authoritative moral rules because we are a complex combination of
selfish and moral creatures: the moral system, we might say, has developed on top of an earlier selfish set of motivations.[76] In less psychological terms, we are often tempted to put aside our normative
commitments and cheat, even when we accept that this violates a norm
we have good reason to endorse and internalize. Thus, others must
have authority to insist that we live up to our normative commitments,

---

[74] Baier, *The Moral Point of View* (unabridged edition), 181. See also Baier, *The Rational and the Moral Order*, 199. Peter Strawson agrees: "There is no reason why a system of moral demands characteristic of one community should, or even could, be found in every other. Strawson, "Social Morality and Individual Ideal," *Philosophy* 36 (2001): 11.

[75] Richerson and Boyd, "The Evolution of Free Enterprise Values," 114.

[76] See ibid. See also Friedman, *Morals and Markets*, chap. 1.

but if the norms are really in moral equilibrium, they are not making mere sectarian demands on us.

C. The priority of morality to politics

Recall our other troublesome thesis, the priority of morality to politics; consider for now simply the Sanctity of Conscience interpretation. This interpretation states that an act of a political authority is morally acceptable to Alf only if it conforms to Alf's private conscience about the requirements of morality. The thesis allows Alf to deny authority to any political act that violates his understanding of a moral norm. As we saw in Section III, the social contract tradition can be interpreted as something close to a renunciation of this thesis. I hope it is now clear that, insofar as the relevant moral norm is based on a moral equilibrium, it is not problematic, and indeed is essential to a liberal social order. That the political must be constrained by the moral is fundamental to any free society: the political must operate within the area of the morally acceptable. When citizens conclude that the state has legislated, or enacted policy, that violates our bona fide moral equilibrium, citizens are right to deny the legislation's authority. States are useful but precarious devices: unless those who operate them are constrained by moral norms, their use of coercion allows them to make almost any outcome a social (though not a moral) equilibrium.[77]

Hobbes and Kant, and to a lesser degree Locke, thought that this was a recipe for social chaos; individuals would always use their private reason to interpret rules differently, and thus morality itself would become a source of conflict. Now, to be sure, sometimes we do disagree about morality (see below), but the driving force of social life is our ability to share very similar understandings of what is required of us. Just how we share these similar "scripts" is fundamental to understanding normative behavior,[78] but we certainly do; we are generally excellent at knowing what the moral rules require and at detecting cheaters.[79] The phenomenon of moral disagreement is real and must be dealt with, but it occurs around the periphery of

---

[77] On this important point, see Schwab and Ostrom, "The Vital Role of Norms and Rules in Maintaining Open Public and Private Economies"; Robert Boyd and Peter J. Richerson, *The Origin and Evolution of Cultures* (New York: Oxford University Press, 2005), chap. 9.

[78] For a sophisticated account, see Bicchieri, *The Grammar of Society*, chap. 2.

[79] For an overview of the psychological findings about these competencies, see K. I. Manktelow and D. Over, "Deontic Reasoning," in *Perspectives on Thinking and Reasoning: Essays in Honor of Peter Wason,* ed. Stephen E. Newstead and Jonathan St. B. T. Evans (East Sussex, UK: Lawrence Erlbaum Associates, 1995), 91–114. See also Schwab and Ostrom, "The Vital Role of Norms and Rules in Maintaining Open Public and Private Economies," 217; Denise Dellarosa Cummins, "Evidence for the Innateness of Deontic Reasoning," *Mind and Language* 11 (June 1996): 160–90; and Paul L. Harris and María Núñez, "Children's Understanding of Permission Rules," *Child Development* 67 (August 1996): 1572–91. For an accessible overview, see Friedman, *Morals and Markets,* 19ff.

great agreement. When the rules are in moral equilibrium, our private judgments have strong tendencies toward convergence.

D. Moral disequilibrium and disagreement: The role of the state

Of course, our moral rules may not be in equilibrium. That is, we may be outside the optimal eligible set, in which case aspects of our current social morality may be oppressive: we demand of some that they comply with rules they do not have sufficient reasons to endorse as normatively authoritative. Because the property equilibrium is so essential to social life, rules in moral disequilibrium may nevertheless exhibit considerable social stability. It is generally in our interests to comply with an unjust property system—especially one that is coercively enforced—rather than have no property system at all. Here concern with distributional issues is certainly appropriate: if some receive little private benefit from the system of property, we may well be skeptical that it can serve as a possible moral equilibrium. Fairness is crucial to our understanding of market and property relations. We must ask: What types of property rules are such that all individuals have normative reason to grant their authority? In our eagerness to give a definitive answer to this question, though, we must not forget that authoritative property rules are a tremendous social good, and that well-informed individuals would certainly not reject the authority of all rules except those which give them their preferred outcome. The range of possible moral equilibria is almost sure to be extensive, and our own social rules of property, imperfect as they are to philosophers, may well be within it.

Certainly a critical role of politics is to address oppression and deep unfairness when they occur. The great power of the political order is that it can move us from moral disequilibrium to a moral equilibrium (a property rule within the optimal eligible set). The great danger, as I said, is that it can effectively move us to *any* social equilibrium: it can move us from moral equilibrium into moral *dis*equilibrium by using its coercive power to impose norms that some people have no good reason to endorse (or, we may say, norms that are not endorsed by their "extended utility function"). Just how we can use the state to move us toward, rather than away from, moral equilibrium, is the core question of liberal constitutionalism.

And, of course, the social contract theorists were right that sometimes we disagree about the moral rules. Often too—perhaps especially in the case of property rights, which must adjust to rapid technological and social changes—our moral equilibrium only provides a core understanding, which must be developed and expanded via the state. Patent protections, copyright laws, and property rights in financial instruments are obvious examples; we cannot wait for the evolution of social conventions.

We come back to T. H. Green, who properly conceived of the state as the protector, sustainer, *and* developer of the social system of rights.[80]

VI. Conclusion: Toward a Non-Ideological Political Philosophy

It may seem that, after all, this analysis does not really restrict the scope of ideological political philosophy—or, we might say, the political philosophy of utopian vision. On the account I have offered, the task of political philosophy is, first and foremost, to reflect on whether our moral rules (say, of property) are within the optimal eligible set: Is our society oppressive, or do everyone's normative reasons converge on endorsing the rules? Here, of course, there is great room for disagreement. But a non-ideological political philosophy is not to be confused with a bland political philosophy in which we all agree. The crucial point is that the proper perspective is not the sectarian perspective of a philosopher with elite access to the moral truth, but an analysis of what rules are objects of moral convergence by well-informed and good-willed individuals. If we do conclude that our rules are outside the optimal eligible set, then the philosopher may again don his beloved legislative hat, proposing rules that he believes would pass the justificatory test. There is, though, no supposition that the rule endorsed by the philosopher's personal vision is even in the optimal eligible set, and if it should be, it is almost certainly simply one of many rules in the set.

The scope of political philosophy, and even applied public policy advice, remains wide. But I believe it will be both a more modest, and a less ideologically strident, political philosophy. We will not insist that justice demands that our own, often rather idiosyncratic, theories be adopted. And we will not make a profession of criticizing pervasive "everyday" attitudes, such as the supposedly silly conviction of people that they have claims to their pretax incomes.[81] Many philosophers chafe under the actual moral rules of their society and are convinced that they can do better, and so construct complex and controversial "theories of justice" that, amazingly, they see as uniquely correct. Only by appreciating that morality is a social device, and not simply a report of their private intuitions and elaborate constructions, can philosophers become part of the solution, rather than the ideological pollution.

Philosophy, University of Arizona

---

[80] By far the most sophisticated contemporary statement of this view is Rex Martin's *A System of Rights* (Oxford: Clarendon Press, 1993).

[81] This "everyday libertarian" view of ownership—that when the government taxes me it takes away *my* property—is criticized by Liam Murphy and Thomas Nagel as a "myth." See Murphy and Nagel, *The Myth of Ownership: Taxes and Justice* (New York: Oxford University Press, 2002), 32–33.

JUDICIAL LIBERALISM AND CAPITALISM: JUSTICE FIELD RECONSIDERED

By Michael P. Zuckert

I. Introduction

Long long ago (in the late nineteenth century through the New Deal era) in a legal galaxy far far away, there was a form of judicial liberalism particularly friendly to capitalism, a form sometimes known as Lochnerism or substantive due process jurisprudence—that is, a jurisprudence that found substantive (not merely procedural) limitations on what governments may permissibly do under the due process clauses of the Fifth and Fourteenth Amendments of the U.S Constitution.[1] In the 1930s, Lochnerism was replaced by another form of judicial liberalism, much less friendly to capitalism and the claims of property in general, but more systematically solicitous for civil liberties like freedom of speech and the equal rights of minority groups. The story of the New Deal "court crisis" and the shift in judicial doctrine and behavior is familiar enough that it can be quickly retold. The New Deal brought an unprecedented amount of congressional legislation regulating both the industrial economy (as in the National Industrial Recovery Act of 1933) and the agricultural economy (as in the Agricultural Adjustment Act of 1933). The Supreme Court, acting on its conceptions of the constitutional division of powers in the federal system and of the inherent protections afforded liberty and property under the due process clauses, struck down much of this legislation as unconstitutional. These bold judicial acts led to a strong backlash from the political branches, culminating in the so-called court-packing proposal by President Franklin D. Roosevelt in 1937. This plan called for the addition of an additional justice to the Supreme Court for every sitting justice over the age of seventy. It was publically presented as a measure to alleviate the burdens on an aging Court, but it was transparently an effort to allow the president to appoint more-sympathetic judges. Whether the court-packing plan was the cause or not is a highly debated issue to this day, but soon after Roosevelt proposed it, the Court made its famous "switch in time that saved nine" as the size of the Court, and began upholding New Deal legislation.

---

[1] The due process clause of the Fourteenth Amendment reads: "nor shall any state deprive any person of life, liberty, or property without due process of law." The Fifth Amendment version: "No person . . . shall be deprived of life, liberty, or property without due process of law."

doi:10.1017/S0265052510000233

For a long while, both on and in most circles off the Supreme Court, the story of the shift from Lochnerism to "Warren Courtism" was told as a tale of unalloyed progress. A reactionary, selfish, foolish, narrow-minded, runaway (choose your adjective) Court was replaced by one that was enlightened, judicially modest, humane, law-abiding, equality-protecting, and/or creative (again, choose your adjective). More recently, however, a revisionism about Lochnerism has been underway, and I intend in this essay to join in that effort.

My focus will be Justice Stephen J. Field (1816–1899), a man who was no longer on the Court when the infamous *Lochner* case was decided in 1905,[2] but who articulated the broad case for the property-sensitive jurisprudence of the substantive due process era. My aim in the essay is twofold: first, to reinterpret Justice Field's judicial philosophy in light of the many earlier accounts of it; and second, having established, I hope, a more adequate account of his judicial liberalism, to assess it in terms of whether it is justified under the U.S. Constitution. Along the way, I will attempt to assess its relationship to capitalism.

After a brief introduction to Justice Field (in Section II), I will sketch the shifting assessments of Field and the *Lochner* era, from the early, generally highly critical ones to the more recent set of revisionist views that set *Lochner* more firmly than had been done into the context of traditional American jurisprudence (Section III). With that context in place, I will turn (in Sections IV–VI) to Field's judicial activity in order to develop an alternative, more rights-based revisionist understanding of the substantive due process approach to the Constitution. I will first look to Field's important pre–Fourteenth Amendment decisions, which are exceedingly revealing of his judicial philosophy, given that they antedate the presence in the Constitution of a due process clause binding on the states. I then look to his post–Fourteenth Amendment decisions, focusing on two of the most significant ones, the *Slaughterhouse Cases* (1873) and *Munn v. Illinois* (1877), in both of which Field was in dissent. In a concluding section (Section VII), I consider explicitly the relationship between Field's jurisprudence and capitalism.

II. Justice Field

When he retired in 1897, Justice Field was the longest serving justice on the Supreme Court up to that time (a position from which he would later be supplanted by William O. Douglas). Field had been Abraham Lincoln's

---

[2] *Lochner v. New York*, 198 U.S. 45 (1905). The *Lochner* case overturned a New York law setting maximum working hours for bakers as a violation of "liberty of contract," a protected right under the Fourteenth Amendment's due process clause. The most thorough account of *Lochner* is Paul Kens, *Lochner v. New York: Economic Regulation on Trial* (Lawrence: University Press of Kansas, 1998). For a survey of current perspectives on *Lochner*, see the dedicated issue of the *New York University Journal of Law and Liberty* 1, no. 1 (2005).

fourth Supreme Court appointment, named to the newly created tenth seat in 1863.[3] Congress created the extra seat in response to the reorganization of the judicial circuit on the West Coast. It was understood that it would go to a citizen of the relatively new state of California, which Republican leaders were eager to keep loyal to the Union. At the time of the creation of the extra seat, Field was widely expected to be the appointee.[4] He was then chief justice of the California Supreme Court and, though a Democrat, was known as pro-North and antislavery.

Field's career spanned the period when the great issues of the Civil War dominated, through the era of Reconstruction, and on into the "Gilded Age" when industrialization and related social processes associated with capitalism dominated the political and legal landscape. The American people can never claim not to have gotten their money's worth out of him. As the justice assigned to the Pacific Coast, Field had to make the long trip west every year in order to ride circuit. On the Supreme Court itself, he authored over 550 Opinions of the Court and nearly eighty dissenting opinions. Although he is not remembered as a "great dissenter," some of his most important opinions were written in dissent, as we shall see. In his long and prolific career on the Court, he became its intellectual leader, as John Marshall had been before him and as, say, William Brennan would be after him. Field's greatest fame, as well as his genuine claim to importance on the Court, lay in the part he played in developing a theory of rights protection that eventually led to the reigning substantive due process approach of the so-called *Lochner* era.

III. CLASSICAL JUDICIAL LIBERALISM:
ORTHODOXY AND REVISIONISM

Undoubtedly the classic critique of Lochnerism was Justice Oliver Wendell Holmes's dissent in the *Lochner* case itself: "This case is decided upon an economic theory which a large part of the country does not entertain." The economic theory alluded to had nothing to do with the Constitution the Supreme Court was seemingly invoking: "The Fourteenth Amendment does not enact Mr. Herbert Spencer's Social Statics," Holmes wrote.[5] On his view, the justices who supported the substantive due process doctrine were neither interpreting the Constitution nor allowing the democratic branches to speak the will of the people. They were acting on the basis of their own conception of good public policy, a

---

[3] The number of justices serving on the United States Supreme Court has varied over time. The Judiciary Act of 1789 set the number at six justices, but the Court was expanded in 1807 (to seven), 1837 (to nine), and 1863 (to ten). The Judiciary Act of 1869 set the number of justices at nine, where it remains to this day.

[4] Carl Brent Swisher, *Stephen J. Field: Craftsman of the Law* (Chicago: University of Chicago Press, 1969), 116.

[5] 198 U.S. at 75 (Holmes, J., dissenting).

conception based on the controversial economic theory of laissez-faire capitalism. Holmes's point is not so much that this is a bad theory (although he arguably thought it was), but rather that acting on the basis of any economic theory whatsoever is inappropriate for the courts.[6]

Holmes's notion that the justices favoring Lochnerism were acting on the basis of extra-constitutional economic theories has been supplemented in various ways by later justices and scholars. Those of a legal-realist turn of mind surmised that Field's role in laying the ground for Lochnerism was less the result of a commitment to a philosophy of laissez-faire, and more a matter of whom he knew, whom he admired, and whom he wished to please, for Field had been a great friend of railroad men and industrialists like Leland Stanford and Collis Huntington.[7] Others saw Field's actions much as Holmes had: political scientist Robert McCloskey thought that Field was obsessed with laissez-faire economics;[8] Field's biographer Carl Brent Swisher agreed with Holmes that Field was pre-eminently committed to laissez-faire, but traced this commitment to Adam Smith, not Herbert Spencer. In addition to Field's commitment to free markets, Swisher saw in Field a strong belief in natural rights and natural law as exemplified by the Declaration of Independence.[9] McCloskey saw the presence of less traditional doctrines. Instead of a Lockean or a Jeffersonian, Justice Field was, on McCloskey's view, far more a creature of his own epoch. Thus, McCloskey's Field displays an attachment to the tenets of social Darwinism that places him squarely in the temper of his times.[10] Legal historian Howard Jay Graham pointed to a more political motive for Field's judicial work: fear of class conflict.[11] Although the factors these scholars point to are many and diverse, they share the feature that they are, one and all, nonconstitutional doctrines. Implicit in their varied portrayals of Field's classical judicial liberalism is the imputation that it has little or nothing to do with the Constitution itself. All the critics so far mentioned are in agreement that Field and the Court he led made a significant mistake in entering the realm of Lochnerism.[12]

The arguments of the Progressive and New Deal era critics of laissez-faire constitutionalism are familiar and need no extensive elaboration

[6] For a thorough discussion of Holmes's charges against the Court's majority, see Ellen Frankel Paul, "Freedom of Contract and the 'Political Economy' of *Lochner v. New York*," *New York University Journal of Law and Liberty* 1, no. 1 (2005): 515–69.

[7] Swisher, *Stephen J. Field*, 426.

[8] Robert McCloskey, *The American Supreme Court* (Chicago: University of Chicago Press, 1960), 101–35; Robert McCloskey, *American Conservatism in the Age of Enterprise, 1865–1910* (Cambridge, MA: Harvard University Press, 1951). See also Sidney Fine, *Laissez-Faire and the General Welfare State* (Ann Arbor: University of Michigan Press, 1956).

[9] Swisher, *Stephen J. Field*, 424–27.

[10] McCloskey, *American Conservatism*, 75, 103.

[11] Howard Jay Graham, *Everyman's Constitution* (Madison: State Historical Society of Wisconsin, 1968), 124–28.

[12] For a further survey of the literature upholding the "standard view," see Howard Gillman, *The Constitution Besieged: The Rise and Demise of Lochner Era Police Powers Jurisprudence* (Durham, NC: Duke University Press, 1993), 207–8 n 8.

here. Revisionist scholars, however, are both less well-known and more complex in their understanding and assessment of the *Lochner* era and its aftermath. They are revisionist in that they promulgate a different version of Lochnerism, a version far more sympathetic in many ways to those who promoted this approach to the Constitution. One such scholar, Michael Les Benedict, gives a good brief description of the revisionist positions: "the traditional view [was] that judges imposed laissez faire on the Constitution to protect the interests of big business. . . . [The revisionists], in contrast, see laissez-faire constitutionalism as the natural outgrowth of widely held constitutional doctrines, the origins of which lay in hostility to special interests rather than in protection of them." [13] The revisionists find the jurisprudence of laissez-faire constitutionalism to be far more (and far more legitimate) than the personal or class interests, biases, and theories of the justices of the period. Nonetheless, they also maintain (almost as much as Progressives do) that it was well that the Court ultimately jettisoned laissez-faire doctrines and moved on to post-classical judicial liberalism.

Since the mid-1970s, a substantial number of revisionist scholars have written on the *Lochner* era, but I will focus on only two of them: Charles McCurdy and Howard Gillman. These two are the most thorough, and, at the same time, they promote fruitfully different interpretations of classical judicial liberalism.[14] All the revisionist scholars share the basic idea that the doctrine that Field and others developed had much support in constitutional text and tradition, and that the doctrine was by no means invented by judges bent on imposing their favorite economic theory on the nation, or on insulating their business friends and allies from governmental regulation.[15] Where they differ is on the identification of the precedents and principles most relevant to the mature substantive due process doctrine.

McCurdy's 1975 essay "Justice Field and the Jurisprudence of Government-Business Relations" attempts a comprehensive account of Field's constitutional approach to issues of political economy. McCurdy

[13] Michael Les Benedict, *The Blessings of Liberty* (Lexington, MA: D. C. Heath, 1996), 246.

[14] For important revisionist statements apart from those on which I focus below, see John V. Orth, *Due Process of Law: A Brief History* (Lawrence: University Press of Kansas, 2003), 51–72, 85–102; John Semonche, *Charting the Future: The Supreme Court Responds to a Changing Society, 1890–1920* (Westport, CT: Greenwood Press, 1978); Michael J. Phillips, *The Lochner Court, Myth and Reality: Substantive Due Process from the 1890s to the 1930s* (Westport, CT: Praeger, 2000); James W. Ely, Jr., "The Oxymoron Reconsidered: Myth and Reality in the Origin of Substantive Due Process," *Constitutional Commentary* 16 (1999); James W. Ely, Jr., *The Guardian of Every Other Right: A Constitutional History of Property Rights* (Oxford: Oxford University Press, 1992); Michael Les Benedict, "Laissez-Faire and Liberty," *Law and History Review* 3 (Fall 1983): 295–331.

[15] It should be added that there were scholars of a classical liberal persuasion who always had a more favorable view of the *Lochner* era courts. Among these are the authors in the *New York University Journal of Law and Liberty* special issue on *Lochner*, cited in note 2 above, and Bernard H. Siegan, *Economic Liberties and the Constitution* (Rutgers, NJ: Transaction Publishers, 2005).

locates the "fundamental theorem" of Field's jurisprudence in the "Jacksonian, radical anti-slavery precept that under 'the Declaration [of Independence] of 1776' each individual had a natural right 'to pursue the ordinary vocations of life without other restraint than such as effects all others and to enjoy with them the fruits of his labor'." [16] That "free labor" doctrine had a long and honorable pedigree within the American political tradition, even if it had not been developed quite in the manner that Field would develop it. The doctrine had received heightened prominence in the era leading up to the Civil War, when antislavery forces appealed to it in their opposition to "the peculiar institution." [17]

Building on the free labor doctrine, McCurdy attempts to reveal the inner logic of Field's position. It is not a logic of favoring business at every turn. Rather, Field was attempting to articulate a clear line between private and public, a line that would govern both what government could constitutionally do *for business*, and what it could do *to business*. Once he had defined this line, Field could be stringent in denying governmental power to aid or subsidize business enterprise, just as he could be supportive of governmental efforts to regulate business or even to set prices. McCurdy attempts to show, then, that Field's approach was one of constitutional principle (not economic theory or personal predilection) and that Field achieved a doctrine of remarkable consistency and logical coherence. Moreover, as Benedict suggested, it was a doctrine intended to prevent governmental underwriting of special interests, and to empower governmental action for the common good—all propositions contrary to the received Progressive interpretation.

The other major revisionist voice to be considered here is that of Howard Gillman, whose book *The Constitution Besieged: The Rise of Lochner Era Police Powers Jurisprudence* appeared in 1993. Gillman's focus was not on Justice Field, but rather, as his title suggests, on the entire experience of Lochnerism, or what I am calling classical judicial liberalism. Nonetheless, no other justice receives nearly as much attention from Gillman as Field does. Although Gillman traces Lochner era police power jurisprudence back to Jacksonian times, he presents Field as the justice who was particularly energetic in driving the Supreme Court to accept the doctrine and to apply it actively. Thus, Gillman presents Field as the one who, in the *Slaughterhouse Cases* (1873), was willing to accept the implications of the Fourteenth Amendment—that the Jacksonian standards governing the use of the police power could now be applied by the U.S. Supreme Court against the states, thereby overturning, even revolutionizing, the

---

[16] Charles W. McCurdy, "Justice Field and the Jurisprudence of Government-Business Relations: Some Parameters of Laissez-Faire Constitutionalism, 1863–1897," *Journal of American History* 61, no. 4 (1975): 973. (McCurdy is here quoting Justice Field in his *Slaughterhouse* dissent.)

[17] Eric Foner, *Free Soil, Free Labor, Free Men: The Ideology of the Republican Party before the Civil War* (Oxford: Oxford University Press, 1975).

traditional federal system.[18] Moreover, Gillman identifies Field as the one who applied these standards by refusing to settle for state claims that legislation served the valid police-power aims of safety, health, welfare, or morality. On Field's view, courts should not take the word of the state but should investigate on their own whether a given piece of legislation accomplished (or even really aimed to accomplish) what was claimed for it.[19] Gillman agrees, in other words, that Field was particularly important as an architect of the new judicial liberalism, and I think it fair to conclude that he sees Field as a particularly able articulator of the tenets of that position.

An important part of Gillman's revisionism (as with that of McCurdy and others) is to skewer the myth that the Supreme Court in the *Lochner* era struck down all or nearly all legislation aiming to regulate economic activity or hostile in any way to business. "There were many circumstances," Gillman tells us, "in which judges allowed legislatures to interfere with market liberties, including relations between employers and employees. Judges certainly believed in liberty of contract, but their commitment to it was far from absolute: it may even be fair to say that using liberty of contract to trump legislation was the exception, and not the rule."[20] Citing McCurdy, Gillman insists that Field was no exception to this rule: "Field ... was more than willing to uphold statutes that prohibited certain businesses considered detrimental to the public welfare, prescribed standards of fitness for lawyers and doctors, required railroad corporations to erect cattle guards and eliminate grade crossings at their own expense, and regulated working hours or compelled hazardous businesses to compensate workers injured on the job."[21] Gillman concludes that "Field shared much of the Court's (forgotten) willingness to uphold legislative interventions in market relations."[22]

Neither Gillman nor McCurdy wishes to deny, of course, that there was some basis for the view that Field and the Court he led did take an active role in overseeing state legislative activity, and often acted to arrest "legislative interventions in market relations." But that activity was far less frequent and pervasive than the standard myth held, and the standard explanations for it are too blunt to explain the actual pattern of behavior that can be observed. Field and the so-called laissez-faire Court did not act to impede all such legislative interference, but only to impede legislative acts that denied "equality before the law."[23] In effect, Gillman reinterprets substantive due process as a form of substantive equal pro-

[18] Gillman, *The Constitution Besieged,* 166.
[19] Ibid., 75.
[20] Ibid., 6. For a more precise and quantitative argument to the same effect, see Phillips, *The Lochner Court, Myth and Reality;* see also Semonche, *Charting the Future.*
[21] Gillman, *The Constitution Besieged,* 7.
[22] Ibid.
[23] Ibid., 66.

tection. It guarded not against interferences with liberty (or property) per se, but against arbitrary interferences, interferences in which some group or class used the legislative process to gain benefits for itself at the expense of the community. Gillman, like McCurdy, thus concludes that Field was not, as the standard version has it, a protector of special interests. He was instead an enemy of special interests, of those who would use legislation to extract special benefits for themselves at the expense of others.[24] Gillman captures his overall understanding of Field and of classical judicial liberalism in a quotation from an 1883 opinion written by Field. Under the Fourteenth Amendment, Field wrote:

> [States] can now, as then, legislate to promote health, good order and peace, to develop their resources, enlarge their industries, and advance their property. It [i.e., the Fourteenth Amendment] only inhibits discriminating and partial enactments, favoring some to the impairment of the rights of others. The principal, if not the sole, purpose of its prohibitions is to prevent any arbitrary invasion by state authority of the rights of person and property, and to secure to everyone the right to pursue his happiness unrestrained, except by just, equal, and impartial laws.[25]

The revisionists thus mean to rehabilitate Field and his fellow justices, but only up to a point. They are not lobbying for a revival of classical judicial liberalism; indeed, they see its passing as appropriate and good. Both McCurdy and Gillman see it as a historically bound position. McCurdy goes so far as to say that the *Lochner* decision itself was not an embodiment of Field's constitutional vision, but was decided by a group of justices who had moved on to a whole new set of concerns, approaching them with new and different judicial tools.[26] "Field's 'immortal truths', if viable at all, provided solutions only for the policy issues of the 1870s."[27] By the early years of the twentieth century, "questions involving labor-management strife or governmental control of 'ordinary trades'" rose to the surface—questions on which Field's rigorous attempt to separate public and private had little purchase.[28] Similarly, Gillman sees the continued evolution of American capitalism as rendering Field's type of judicial liberalism outdated and counterproductive. Field and his fellows were committed to "a constitutional ideology of state neutrality" that resisted state intervention on behalf of any special or partial interests. But the evolution of capitalism led to a situation where state inaction left some

[24] Ibid., 199.
[25] Ibid., 70. Gillman is here quoting Field's opinion in *Butcher's Union v. Crescent City*, 111 US 746, 750–59 (1883). On the significance of this case, see Paul, "Freedom of Contract," 561–67.
[26] McCurdy, "Justice Field," 1005. See also Paul, "Freedom of Contract," 561.
[27] McCurdy, "Justice Field," 1005.
[28] Ibid.

groups vulnerable to "the coercive effects of the market," in the face of which state intervention on behalf of the vulnerable no longer represented the kind of special-interest intervention contrary to the public good that Field and his peers thought it was. The old formulas and approaches no longer corresponded to the political and economic realities. Classical judicial liberalism may have been legitimate and justified when first introduced in the Jacksonian era, but by the time of the New Deal it had more than outlived its usefulness.[29]

My study of Justice Field takes as its point of departure the somewhat different explanatory emphases among the leading revisionists: can a fresh look at Field's jurisprudence give us a more unified and perhaps philosophically deeper grasp of classical judicial liberalism? I am equally concerned with the question of whether the revisionists are right to see judicial liberalism as a well-rid-of relic of an earlier phase of capitalist development. Is there anything to be said for the continuing validity—constitutional and philosophical—of the Field approach, and even for a revival of it as a living constitutional doctrine?

IV. Rights Protection Before the Fourteenth Amendment: The Test Oath Cases

Justice Field is best known for decisions made under the Fourteenth Amendment, but, ironically perhaps, the best ingress to his classical judicial liberalism may lie in two cases decided in 1866, well before the Fourteenth Amendment was ratified and became part of the Constitution. Even in his most famous Fourteenth Amendment opinion, Field provides a genuine basis for thinking that the Amendment is not itself at the root of his decisions. In his 1873 *Slaughterhouse Cases* dissent, after stating the facts of the case, Field revealingly commented: "No one will deny the abstract justice which lies in the position of the plaintiffs in error; and I shall endeavor to show that the position has *some support* in the fundamental law of the country."[30] First, Field affirms the "abstract justice" of his position, and then he finds "some support" for that position in the Constitution.

The two pre–Fourteenth Amendment cases to which I've referred, *Cummings v. Missouri* (1866) and *Ex Parte Garland* (1866), involved test oaths prescribed by the state of Missouri and the U.S. Congress, respectively, oaths that had to be taken before Cummings could take up his old position as a priest and Garland his position as an attorney practicing before federal courts.[31] The oaths were instituted during and in the immediate aftermath of the Civil War and required the subject to swear that he had

---

[29] Gillman, *The Constitution Besieged*, 200.
[30] *Slaughterhouse Cases*, 83 U.S. 36 (1873), at 86–87 (Field, J., dissenting; emphasis added).
[31] *Cummings v. Missouri*, 71 U.S. 277 (1866); *Ex Parte Garland*, 71 U.S. 333 (1866).

never participated in the rebellion in a long list of specified ways. In the case of the Missouri oath, any individual unable to so swear was prohibited by the Missouri constitution from holding "any office of honor, trust, or profit under its authority, or of being an officer, councilman, director, or trustee, or other manager of any corporation, public or private, now existing or hereafter established by its authority, or of acting as a professor or teacher in any educational institution, or in any common or other school, or of holding any real estate or other property, in trust for the use of any church, religious society, or congregation." Moreover, persons not taking the oath were forbidden from serving as "an attorney or counselor-at-law . . . [or] a bishop, priest, deacon, minister, elder or other clergyman, of any religious persuasion, sect, or denomination." [32] The Missouri oath prohibited so much that Field commented that it was "for its severity, without any precedent that we can discover." [33] One of Field's biographers summed up the effect of the Missouri oath as follows:

> Its result . . . was to give loyal citizens of Missouri almost a monopoly of the remunerative and influential positions in the state, while excluding from these positions persons who had been to the least conceivable minimum disloyal, and who were probably almost as numerous as those by whom they were being excluded.[34]

The oath that was the subject of the *Garland* case was less draconian, for it forbade those who could not take the oath only from holding any office in the government of the United States or from being a member of the federal bar.

Both cases were decided by the same five judge majority against the oaths. Field wrote the majority opinion both times. Justice Samuel Miller wrote a dissent for the four-person minority in an opinion applying to both cases, but attached to the *Garland* case. Justice Miller opened his opinion with an oblique reference to Field's observation on the "severity" of the oath requirement:

> It may be hoped that the exceptional circumstances which give present importance to these cases will soon pass away, and that those who make the laws, both state and national, will find in the conduct of the persons affected by the legislation just declared to be void, sufficient reason to repeal, or essentially modify it.[35]

The dissenters, in other words, agreed with Field in hoping that the harsh and punitive laws could give way to more conciliatory actions. Nonethe-

---

[32] *Cummings v. Missouri*, 71 U.S. 277 at 317.
[33] Id. at 318.
[34] Swisher, *Stephen J. Field*, 141.
[35] *Ex Parte Garland*, 71 US 333 at 382 (Miller, J., dissenting).

less, Miller chided Field and the others in the majority for letting their judgments about justice and good policy interfere with their proper judicial role:

> It is at all times the exercise of an extremely delicate power for this Court to declare that the Congress of the nation or the legislative body of a state, has assumed an authority not belonging to it, and by violating the Constitution, has rendered void its attempt at legislation. . . . [T]he incompatibility of the act with the Constitution should be so clear as to leave little reason for doubt, before we pronounce it to be invalid.[36]

The incompatibility with the Constitution was not that clear to Miller and thus he dissented, suggesting while doing so that Field had tested the law by policy and abstract justice rather than the Constitution. The constitutional issues in the two cases varied slightly, but the core issue in both, as Miller understood it, was whether the incapacities that were consequent on failing to take the prescribed oaths amounted to punishment or not. That was the crucial issue, for Field had made his explicit case against the test oaths not on the basis of abstract justice but on the basis of the constitutional clauses prohibiting bills of attainder and ex post facto laws. As Miller pointed out, both clauses could be appealed to if and only if the result of not taking the oath was rightly considered a punishment, for the ex post facto clause had been held (in a long string of cases) to apply only to criminal prosecutions, and the bill of attainder clause forbade certain sorts of nonjudicially imposed punishments. Miller had a relatively easy time showing that various features of the oath and the results of failing to swear to it looked nothing like ordinary criminal law or the kinds of punishment forbidden by the bill of attainder clause.[37] Thus, Field's biographer Paul Kens observed that "even people who agreed with the outcome of the *Test Oath Cases* would have difficulty denying that Field stretched the Constitution to get there. . . . He employed considerable imagination in defining ex post facto, bill of attainder, and punishment."[38]

Miller thought that the oaths were not a punishment at all, but were the exercise of a very ordinary state power to set the qualifications for individuals practicing certain professions. Thus, it is nothing extraordinary for governmental bodies to set qualifications for those attempting to practice law.[39] It may be more unusual for state authorities to regulate the qualifications of the clergy, but, as Miller noted, nothing in the Constitu-

[36] Id.
[37] Id. at 386–95.
[38] Paul Kens, *Justice Stephen Field: Shaping Liberty from the Gold Rush to the Gilded Age* (Lawrence: University Press of Kansas, 1997), 117.
[39] *Ex Parte Garland*, 71 U.S. 333 at 385 (Miller, J., dissenting).

tion prohibited the states from doing so: the First Amendment's religion clauses applied only to the U.S. government.[40]

Miller made an impressive argument, but his approach to these two cases fails to respond to the core of Field's argument. Contrary to what Miller implied, Field accepted the responsibility to ground his decision in the Constitution: "The Court cannot decide the case upon the justice or hardship of these provisions. Its duty is to determine whether they are in conflict with the Constitution of the United States."[41] Miller correctly identifies the particular constitutional clauses to which Field appeals, but he fails to grasp how Field arrived there. Contrary to his laissez-faire image, Field conceded at the outset of his *Cummings* opinion that "among the rights reserved to the states is the right of each state to determine the qualifications for office, and the conditions upon which its citizens may exercise their various callings and professions within its jurisdiction."[42] Field saw, in other words, that the oath could be viewed as Miller viewed it, as prescribing a qualification for a "calling within its jurisdiction," but Field quite self-consciously rejected that interpretation of it.

Field concedes that states may set qualifications for offices and callings, but, he insists, "it by no means follows that, under the form of creating a qualification or attaching a condition, the states can in effect inflict a punishment for a past act."[43] Some purported efforts to set qualifications may in fact not do that, but instead do something else—for example, serve as a punishment. Presumably, they may do other things as well, such as set up barriers factually unrelated to the qualifications for a calling or office, in order to benefit a favored group in the community by granting it a monopoly of access to the profession or office. For example, a law establishing that only graduates of the local state university may practice law or medicine in a given jurisdiction might well be an effort to favor certain groups in the community and disfavor others.

Field does not conclude that alleged efforts to set qualifications that in fact do something else are ipso facto invalid. There is the further question of "whether there is any inhibition in the Constitution of the United States against their enforcement."[44] Field thus outlines a three-step process. The court must determine, *first*, if the law does set a qualification. This is largely a matter of classification, the performance of which requires a court to apply a general standard to determine what counts as a qualification for a given profession, calling, or office. This clearly requires the court to enter upon substantive judgments that may involve the court in holding its own judgment about qualifications up against the judgment of the legislators, or, as in this case, the framers of the Constitution. If the

[40] Id. at 397.
[41] *Cummings v. Missouri,* 71 U.S. 277 at 318.
[42] Id. at 319.
[43] Id.
[44] Id. at 322.

court concludes that the provision in question indeed sets a valid qualification, then that, presumably, is the end of the inquiry.

The *second* stage of the process occurs when the court finds the provision to go beyond (or fall short of) setting a qualification. Then the court
must ask: If this provision is not actually establishing a qualification,
what is it doing? In *Cummings*, Field concluded that the provision was
serving as a means of inflicting punishment. That sets the stage for the
third and final inquiry: Does anything in the U.S. Constitution bar the
state from imposing that punishment in that way?

We might look briefly at Field's handling of all three inquiries, for the
structure of thought underlying his inquiries came to play a central role
in the judicial liberalism he articulated. Field first establishes that the test
oath is not in fact a regulation setting qualifications for the various professions covered by it. He begins by announcing a general principle:
"Qualifications relate to the fitness or capacity of the party for a particular
pursuit or profession." Qualifications may include "any natural endowment or any acquirement which fits a person for a place, office, or employment, or enables him to sustain any character with success." [45] Field has,
on the face of it, a capacious notion of what counts as a qualification. He
goes into very little detail in delineating what sorts of considerations are
legitimate in setting qualifications, but he develops at some length the
case for judging that the provisions of the test oath do not establish valid
qualifications for the priesthood:

> There can be no connection between the fact that Mr. Cummings
> entered or left the State of Missouri to avoid enrollment or draft in
> the military service of the United States and his fitness to teach the
> doctrines or administer the sacraments of his church; nor can a fact
> of this kind or the expression of words of sympathy with some
> persons drawn into the Rebellion constitute any evidence of the unfit-
> ness of the attorney or counselor to practice his profession, or of the
> professor to teach the ordinary branches of education, or of the want
> of business knowledge or business capacity in the manager of a
> corporation, or in any director or trustee. [46]

These observations led Justice Field to the conclusion that "the oath
could not, therefore, have been required as a means of ascertaining whether
parties were qualified or not for their respective callings or the trusts with
which they were charged." [47] It might be objected that Field is deploying
a rather narrow notion of qualification. Might it not be a relevant qualification for a teacher of the young in Missouri that he be loyal to the

[45] Id. (Field is quoting Webster's dictionary).
[46] Id. at 319–20.
[47] Id. at 320.

government and the Union and that he not be likely to teach his impressionable young charges subversive doctrines like the rightfulness of secession and the injustice of the Union cause? Might not similar considerations relate to the priesthood, a calling that stands in high prestige in the community and whose members often exert great influence on the minds of those to whom they minister? And is it not the case that many (though perhaps not all) of the acts and words held to be disqualifying from these professions would be evidence of a frame of mind likely to lead to behavior in the profession that is, in the broad sense, inappropriate, and even disqualifying?

Given the extremity and blunderbuss quality of the oath in the *Cummings* case, Field did not have to face these more subtle issues. His opinion leaves some room for a more refined oath, but other than affirming the rightfulness of asking subjects to swear present and future loyalty, he does not make clear what (if anything) of past behavior may be taken to be disqualifying.

Field, having established that the oath as written did not set legitimate qualifications for the various callings it regulated, proceeded to ask what the oath was. He concluded, of course, that it was a punishment. The oath "was required in order to reach the person not the calling. It was exacted, not from any notion that the several acts designated indicated unfitness for the callings, but because it was thought that the several acts deserved punishment, and that for many of them there was no way to inflict punishment except by depriving the parties who had committed them, of some of the rights and privileges of the citizen."[48]

If the disabilities imposed on those who did not take the oath were indeed punishments, then it would not be difficult to show that they indeed run afoul of various constitutional prohibitions. For example, if being unable to serve as a clergyman or an attorney is a punishment, then Cummings and Garland were being punished for acts that were not crimes when they performed them. Or, alternatively, they were being punished with penalties not affixed to the crimes at the time committed. That is to say, the test oath amounts to a prohibited ex post facto law.

The test oath cases, then, clearly hinged on the finding that the results of not taking the oath were punitive, a finding that depended in part on the prior finding that the oath was not a valid means of establishing qualifications for the professions involved. Field knew in advance that his conclusion that the inability to practice law or serve as a priest was a punishment would be challenged. The state of Missouri had argued that "to punish one is to deprive him of life, liberty, or property, and that to take from him anything less than these is no punishment at all."[49] Field thought that definition too narrow by far, and in order to establish that

[48] Id.
[49] Id.

point he had recourse to "the theory upon which our political institutions rest." [50] He found that theory in the Declaration of Independence, which holds that

> all men have certain inalienable rights—that among these are life, liberty, and the pursuit of happiness; and that in pursuit of happiness all avocations, all honors, all positions are alike open to every one, and that in the protection of these rights all are equal before the law.[51]

As Charles McCurdy points out, Field appeals to the "free labor" ideology of the Jacksonians and the antislavery movement as inferences from "the theory upon which our political institutions rest." As Howard Gillman points out, Field emphasizes that in legislation touching these matters, "all are equal before the law," that is, there must be no legislating of special privilege for some at the expense of others. What both scholars miss, or at least deemphasize, is the dependence of both these themes on Field's more general affirmation of "certain inalienable rights."

From the basic rights follow the free labor commitments of the Jacksonians: "in pursuit of happiness all avocations, all honors, all positions are alike open to every one." Field understands the pursuit of happiness as a comprehensive right to follow a self-chosen path in life, consistent with the agent's views of what may lead to happiness. Since all are equal possessors of the right to the pursuit of happiness, all possess equally the right to pursue "avocations, honors, and positions." There is no room in a society built on inalienable rights for professions passed on as heritable goods, excluding others from their pursuit, or for exclusions based on qualifications unrelated to the talent and ability required to perform the tasks of the position. The law is to protect these basic rights, including the right to opportunity to pursue vocations and positions. Field accepts the implication that protection of rights involves setting limitations on activities arguably related to the rights. Thus, he concedes that the state may set qualifications for the practice of professions. For example, the state may require demonstration of knowledge of the law and competence in its practice, as well as "good character," as a condition for being an attorney. But it must do so in a way that recognizes that "all are equal before the law." It must not single out individuals or groups for special burdens or benefits in its regulating activities aimed at protecting the inalienable rights.

---

[50] Id. at 321.

[51] Id. at 321–22. On the Declaration of Independence as a ground for protecting liberty, see Paul, "Freedom of Contract," 562–63. I differ from her in maintaining that Field (not Justice Bradley) first made this appeal, and that it was central to all that Field did in the area of economic rights. I also differ in the way I trace out the links between Field's constitutional doctrines and the natural rights philosophy of the Declaration.

Thus, the jurisprudential emphases that McCurdy and Gillman identified as components of Field's thought are subsumed under and derivative from Field's more fundamental commitment to rights. Field does not explain at length whether the right to pursue vocations (i.e., the free labor right) is best understood as a means to other rights—for example, as a means to the right to life, or as a part of the right in itself. I am inclined to the view that if pressed he would identify it as both. He would almost certainly agree that this right is a means to the other rights; in a civil society marked by division of labor and private property, the right to labor where and how one chooses would be in service to one's rights to life and the pursuit of happiness. But the direct link that Field draws between the right to pursue happiness and the right to pursue vocations and positions suggests that he regards the connection as more intimate than a means-end relation. If human beings have a comprehensive right to pursue happiness in ways of their own choosing, then the right to pursue occupations would be a part of that right, and not just a means to it.

Justice Holmes and other critics accused Field and the other *Lochner*-era judges of appealing to airy nothings like natural law and natural rights, which were actually covers for their pet economic theories or policy preferences. These critics pressed for a jurisprudence that did not appeal to natural-law sources, but to positive law only. Field agrees with Holmes and the positivists that laws that violate the precepts of natural political morality are not ipso facto invalid. He insists that there must be a constitutional basis for finding a law invalid. However, Field freely appeals to natural political morality as part of his explication of the Constitution. Thus, in *Cummings* and *Garland,* he adumbrates a novel theory of what constitutes punishment en route to finding the test oaths to be violations of constitutional prohibitions in Article I, sections 9 and 10. Justice Miller, notably failing to follow Field in appealing to natural rights, reads the constitutional clauses in question in a much more traditional manner.

Field appeals to natural political morality in his judicial reasoning, but unlike some of our contemporary legal theorists he does not countenance appeals to the judge's personal view of moral right; rather, he appeals to "the theory upon which our political institutions rest," the Lockean theory of natural rights to which the founding generation was committed. Field looks to extra-textual material in order to aid in interpreting the text of the Constitution, but this is not material chosen on the basis of his personal judgment. He sees the need to appeal beyond the text in order to understand the text; but like the positivists, he recognizes that as a judge he must be guided by the law given to him, rather than creating the law.[52]

---

[52] Two obvious issues arise. First, Holmes and present-day allies like Robert Bork might say that this appeal to "the theory upon which our political institutions rest" is little different from an appeal to Field's pet policy preferences or "values." The "theory" of our institutions is not, after all, so clearly set out as to guide and discipline a judge. To notice but one indication of this, the literature on John Locke, the articulator of the theory on which the

Field uses his appeal to the theory of inalienable rights, and not an appeal to an economic theory, in order to ground his analysis of the test oaths as indirect and partially concealed punishments. First, he implicitly rejects the theory put forth by counsel for Missouri that punishment involves the deprivation by the state of "life, liberty, or property" understood narrowly and literally. Thus, to execute, to imprison, or to fine or seize property would count as deprivations of rights (or objects of rights), but nothing else would. Field deploys a more capacious notion of rights. In the notorious words of a much later case, he sees the basic rights as containing "penumbras and emanations" such that the concept of "deprivations" of rights encompasses far more than the state of Missouri contends. He says, for example, that property includes "those estates which one may acquire in professions."[53]

Being inalienable, the basic natural rights have a continued existence in civil society as "civil rights." These rights include far more than freedom from imprisonment or loss of title to one's property, but in this context Field does not explore very far what counts as a civil right. He does say that "the deprivation of any rights, civil or political, previously enjoyed, may be a punishment."[54] He seems to have in mind a strong doctrine of vested rights, but it is not clear what he regards as the vehicle of investiture—perhaps it is no more than the previous enjoyment of some liberty or property.

The deprivation of any of these rights "may be a punishment." "Disqualification from office may be a punishment, as in cases of conviction upon impeachment."[55] He supplies other such examples. The most striking part of what he says, however, is his claim that deprivation of a previously enjoyed right "may be a punishment." Not all such deprivations are punishments. What distinguishes a punishment from other deprivations is delineated by Field as follows: "Any deprivation or suspension of any of these rights for past conduct is punishment, and can be in no otherwise defined."[56] In the *Cummings* case, Cummings is being deprived of his right to pursue his profession on the basis of past conduct—his actions or words in sympathy with the rebel cause. The inquiry does not stop here, however, for Field is not saying that all punishment (i.e., deprivation of a right, based on past conduct) is illegitimate. There are estab-

---

Declaration of Independence rests, is not only voluminous but highly contentious. Hardly any two of the large crew of Locke scholars agree on what Locke means, much less on what "the theory" of our institutions is. A second and related issue concerns the stance of a judge who no longer shares the theory on which our institutions rest. Field appeals to the theory of rights because it is the background theory of the Constitution, but there can be little doubt that he also believed it to be the true theory of political right. But what if he or some other judge believed otherwise? Should they, can they, appeal to the theory of rights as Field did?
[53] *Cummings v. Missouri*, 71 U.S. 277 at 320.
[54] Id.
[55] Id.
[56] Id. at 322.

lished rules delineating what sorts of past conduct are relevant and what sorts of processes may be involved to effect deprivations of rights. When, as here, the past conduct was not illegal when committed, the deprivation is illegitimate according to natural principles of political morality, which are also recognized in the Constitution's ex post facto clause.

Field says little about prohibitions or regulations of future conduct, other than to concede that rights may be regulated (for the sake of broad or overall rights protection) and that these regulations must occur in such a way as to recognize each individual's equality before the law. Although he does not speak of it here, Field has in mind the doctrine that the state, under its "police power," may regulate or even "deprive" individuals of rights. A regulation establishing demonstrated medical knowledge as a prerequisite for the right to practice medicine would be an exercise of the police power, and presumably a valid one, even though it prevented some members of the community from pursuing that profession.[57]

Field's *Cummings* opinion is an important source for understanding his overall jurisprudence of liberty and rights. It is a doctrine based not on personal preference or economic theory but on the political philosophy underlying American institutions. It may support capitalism with its emphasis on the individual's right to freely pursue a calling of his own choice (within some limits), thereby establishing a more or less free labor market. But while creating a free labor market, and thus contributing to the economic efficiency of the market in general, may have been a consequence of the affirmation of the right to freedom of vocation, it was not the purpose of that affirmation. Field's is a liberalism very much grounded on rights understood as natural and inalienable and not as consequential implications from market values.

As valuable as *Cummings* is for explaining some of the grounds of Field's position, it is also very limited, for it is bound to the specific factual situation posed by the test oath. Field thus explores only a small piece of the police power as it applies to the power to set qualifications for callings and to punish. The larger questions about the police power in relation to inalienable rights (e.g., the larger questions involving the relation of government and economy) are barely touched on. For a fuller understanding, we must look to two more of Field's classic opinions—his dissents in the *Slaughterhouse Cases* (1873) and in *Munn v. Illinois* (1877).

V. THE *SLAUGHTERHOUSE* CASES

Field's *Slaughterhouse* dissent is almost certainly his best-known opinion, for in the first case under the new Fourteenth Amendment he lays down an interpretation of the text that loses out in that case, but goes on to influence the way the Supreme Court treats the amendment in the not

---

[57] *Dent v. West Virginia*, 129 U.S. 114 (1881).

too distant future—and, arguably, for many years to follow. The dissent is also an impressive achievement, both as constitutional interpretation and as a statement of political/constitutional principle.

A much better known case than *Cummings* or *Garland, Slaughterhouse* probably requires less background explanation. The basic character of the case is this: in an attempt to regulate sanitary conditions in the area of New Orleans, the Louisiana legislature passed regulations establishing where and by whom the slaughtering of animals in the surrounding counties could take place. The regulatory scheme had two main parts: Slaughtering was prohibited everywhere except in a designated area, and one corporation was given exclusive right to establish a slaughterhouse in that area. The law provided that other butchers could use the slaughterhouse facilities, but they could do so only if they paid a fee to the owners of the slaughterhouse.

The legal issue raised by the case was whether this regulatory scheme ran afoul in any way of the relatively new post–Civil War amendments. The Court's five-member majority, speaking through Justice Miller (Field's nemesis from *Cummings* and *Garland*), held that the scheme did not. Field, speaking for a four-member minority, held that it did. The case was complicated in part because there was no settled law on the new amendments, and in part because it mixed, as cases in American constitutional law so often do, considerations of federalism with substantive considerations. The most central constitutional issue concerned the Fourteenth Amendment's first section, particularly the clause that read "No state shall make or enforce any law which shall abridge the privileges or immunities of citizens of the United States": Miller held that the law did not abridge these privileges and immunities; Field held that it did. The disagreement between them occurred along two dimensions, only one of which is of particular interest to us here. The part of the debate that has attracted the most attention over the years concerns the textual issue of the meaning of the privileges and immunities clause. Miller, noticing that the opening sentence of the amendment defined two kinds of citizenship that each citizen holds, U.S. and state, proceeded to read the amendment as assuming two sets of privileges and immunities, corresponding to the two kinds of citizenship. The amendment protected only the privileges and immunities attached to U.S. citizenship, which, according to the majority in the case, were relatively few and did not include the basic rights of citizenship, which remained attached to state citizenship in the American federal system.[58]

Field deemphasized the dual citizenship in the amendment and insisted on the subordinate nature of state citizenship; according to the amendment, individuals were citizens first of the United States and, secondarily and derivatively, "of the state wherein they reside." The four justices in

[58] *Slaughterhouse Cases,* 83 U.S. 36 at 73–79.

the minority concluded from this that the basic privileges and immunities attach to U.S. citizenship, not to state citizenship.[59] Although many constitutional scholars believe that Field had the better of the argument, on the immediate issue of the privileges and immunities clause the Miller view has so far prevailed, and that clause has remained almost a dead letter in the Constitution.[60]

The Court majority upheld the Louisiana law in part because they gave such a narrow reading to the privileges and immunities clause (for federalism reasons), but also because they thought the Louisiana law would be valid even if the Constitution had established a unitary system and the privileges and immunities clause applied within that unit. This is the part of the case of most immediate interest here. Justice Miller, even before he turns to the constitutional issues raised by the Fourteenth Amendment, pronounces this law valid as an exercise of the state's police power and not a violation of citizen rights. The regulation of slaughtering is a well-known instance of valid police-power regulation, and the grant of exclusive rights to the slaughterhouse corporation is a reasonable and perfectly valid means of regulating slaughtering. None can claim a deprivation of rights, since the statute guarantees all butchers the right to use the corporation's facilities upon payment of a reasonable fee. Thus, although the Court did not address the issue quite so directly, it is rather clear that Miller would have held the law to be valid even if he had found that the privileges and immunities clause protected basic rights of citizens.[61]

As I noted earlier, Field orders his dissenting opinion in a way that highlights his dependence on considerations of abstract principle as prior to constitutional text. He writes: "No one will deny the abstract justice which lies in the position of the plaintiffs in error; and I shall endeavor to show that the position has some support in the fundamental law of the country." Field refuses to rest his decision on abstract justice alone, but he suggests here that he knowingly exploits ambiguities in the constitutional text of the privileges and immunities clause in order to read the text in the way most congruent with abstract justice.[62]

In a forceful affirmation of the police power (to which we shall return in a moment), Field upholds all the parts of the Louisiana legislation except that part that grants to the corporation the exclusive right to erect

---

[59] Id. at 94–101.

[60] See, e.g. Michael Kent Curtis, *No State Shall Abridge: The Fourteenth Amendment and the Bill of Rights* (Durham, NC: Duke University Press, 1986); and William Wiecek, *Liberty Under Law: The Supreme Court in American Life* (Baltimore, MD: Johns Hopkins University Press, 1988), 98.

[61] *Slaughterhouse Cases*, 83 U.S. 36 at 60–66.

[62] For the presentation of a theory of constitutional interpretation that explains Field's style of reasoning, see Michael P. Zuckert, "Epistemology and Hermeneutics in the Constitutional Jurisprudence of John Marshall," in Thomas C. Shevory, ed., *John Marshall's Achievement: Law, Politics, and Constitutional Interpretations* (New York: Greenwood Press, 1989), 193–216.

and maintain a slaughterhouse and the consequent requirement that all other butchers pay the corporation a fee in order to practice their calling. What Field calls a legally imposed monopoly is the target of his judicial artillery. Thus far, Gillman is correct to emphasize Field's concern for "equality before the law." [63] Field makes clear, however, that the ground of his affirmation of "equality before the law" (or, to put it otherwise, his rejection of legally established privilege) is to be found in "the immortal document which proclaimed the independence of the country." That document "declared as self-evident truths that the Creator had endowed all men with certain inalienable rights, and that among these are life, liberty, and the pursuit of happiness; and that to secure these rights governments are instituted among men." [64] These are rights "which are the gift of the Creator, which the law does not confer, but [since the adoption of the Fourteenth Amendment] only recognizes." [65] Field's hostility to legally imposed "exclusive privilege" derives from his affirmation of the basic natural rights outlined in the Declaration of Independence. "All monopolies in any human trade or manufacture are an invasion of these privileges [protected by the Fourteenth Amendment] for they encroach upon the liberty of citizens to acquire property and pursue happiness." [66] The natural rights come first, and they both guide Field in his reading of the positive law of the Constitution and provide the basis for his inference of secondary principles of natural justice such as the illegitimacy of exclusive privilege. A prohibition of state-granted privilege or monopoly stands in *Slaughterhouse* as a limitation on state action, just as the idea of ex post facto punishment did in *Cummings*.

Field is never too precise in deriving his anti-privilege principle from the basic natural rights. He is not, for example, very careful in identifying which basic right is the basis for his inference; indeed, at different points, he identifies each of the three basic rights (life, liberty, and the pursuit of happiness) as a ground for his principle of equality before the law.[67] The right to labor as one chooses and the right to the fruits of one's labor are not implausibly seen as implications of all three rights, including the right to pursue happiness. Field quotes Adam Smith (sounding very much like John Locke) to make his basic point: "The property which every man has in his own labor, as it is the original foundation of all other property, so it is the most sacred and inalienable." [68]

The illegitimacy of laws that are not "just, equal, and impartial" follows from the logic of natural rights and the construal of government as a social contract. All men are equal in their possession of inherent rights. The rights

---

[63] Gillman, *The Constitution Besieged*, 66.
[64] *Slaughterhouse Cases*, 83 U.S. 36 at 105 (Field, J., dissenting).
[65] Id. at 193–216.
[66] Ibid. at 101.
[67] Id. at 101, 110.
[68] Id. at 110n.

both express the character of human beings as owners of their own labor (i.e., of themselves and their actions) and stand as the means to the satisfaction of the most basic right of all, the right to life. Government must be conceived to derive its legitimate authority from the rights-possessors over whom it would exercise coercive power, but the power it may rightly exercise must be such as the citizens could conceivably have delegated to it. Citizens seek from government security in their rights, which requires surrendering some of the liberty they would otherwise possess in exchange for the establishment of laws backed by force that protect them in their remaining rights. They cannot be thought to create government for the sake of granting governmentally imposed privileges to some citizens at their own expense. Most especially, they cannot be conceived to have empowered government to strip them of rights and liberties that are then to be vested exclusively in others. It is emphatically not the case that government is to have no power to restrict liberties or property, but the restrictions must be for the benefit of all and thus must impinge, mutatis mutandis, equally on all. Thus, Field is clear that certain actions or professions could be prohibited outright if deemed to be dangerous to individuals or to society at large. Certain individuals could be licensed to follow certain professions, and others prohibited from doing so, if the qualifications required for licensing are appropriately related to the competent and safe practice of the profession. Such was the situation Field addressed in *Cummings*. What is not acceptable is what happened in Louisiana, where some were arbitrarily allowed to follow their profession, and others, equally qualified, were forbidden to do so except upon paying a fee to the privileged.

It is thus no accident that almost the first thing in Field's opinion is a paean to the police power. This power, he says, "undoubtedly extends to all regulations affecting the health, good order, morals, peace, and safety of society, and is exercised on a great variety of subjects, and in almost numberless ways." Far from being a pro-laissez-faire judicial activist eager to negate exercises of state power, Field affirms that "all sorts of restrictions and burdens are imposed under [the police power], and when these are not in conflict with any constitutional prohibitions, or fundamental principles, they cannot be successfully assailed in a judicial tribunal."[69] Field believes that he differs from the Court majority not in a lesser willingness to affirm exercises of the police power, but in recognizing that purported uses of that power may be "pretence" only: "under the pretence of prescribing a police regulation the state cannot be permitted to encroach upon any of the just rights of the citizen, which the Constitution intended to secure against abridgement."[70]

The serious question for Field, then, is how one distinguishes the legitimate exercise of the police power from the pretence. He begins with a

---

[69] Id. at 87.
[70] Id.

strong affirmation of the background principle of the system: the basic
natural rights that translate into a rebuttable presumption in favor of
liberty. When basic liberties (for example, the liberty to pursue a calling)
are at stake, Field acts on the maxim that courts must consider whether
the legislation is restricting liberty for a valid police-power purpose. Field
has two ways of so judging. First, as in *Cummings*, he can ask whether the
legislation actually matches, as a proper means, the valid police power
purpose alleged to justify the legislation. Thus, Field does not for a moment
question the right of states to set qualification for callings, but he does
challenge their right to set qualifications unrelated to the proper conduct
of the calling. When the state sets unrelated qualifications, it is doing
something other than it alleges. In judging the congruence between the
state's means and its declared ends, Field seems to deploy something like
what we now call intermediate scrutiny. He does not subject regulations
to a kind of test that is nearly always fatal, as his extensive record of
upholding legislation demonstrates. However, he seeks a level of review
more stringent than Miller, writing for the majority, required. Field acts as
if he believes that the category of "pretence" is a real one, and that it is the
job of the Court to ensure that legislatures stick to their legitimate
tasks. Paul Kens thus concluded that "perhaps" the "most important"
element of Field's "police power jurisprudence" was his "insistence
that the power to determine whether a statute fell within the boundaries of the police powers or violated an individual right rested with
the courts, not the legislature."[71] But applying the congruence test
required courts to substitute their judgment of suitable means (at least
some of the time) for the legislative judgment, thus threatening always
to turn the courts into the "super legislatures" they were often accused
of being. This problem lay behind Field's effort to shift as much of the
burden of judging state legislation onto the kind of test he applied in
Slaughterhouse. There Field proceeds in a somewhat different manner.
He applies what we might call an adverbial test to the legislation ("adverbial" because it concerns how something is done). The state may regulate economic activity in the name of a whole array of public goods,
but whatever regulations it imposes must not single out classes of persons for treatment arbitrarily different from what others receive. This
too is a test of means, but not for congruence with alleged police-
power purposes; rather, it is a test of whether the means is itself forbidden. Certain means are in themselves forbidden, such as the granting
of exclusive privileges to some at the expense of others, or the use of
bills of attainder. The first kind of test one might call a test for congruence; the second, a test for adverbial nonarbitrariness; it is a test not
of what may be done, but of how it may be done. It is this second kind
of test on which Gillman focused.

---

[71] Kens, *Justice Stephen Field*, 253.

Field clearly allows a large role for principles of natural justice, but at the same time, he always insists that natural justice is not enough; there must be constitutional warrant for constitutional decisions. With the adoption of the Fourteenth Amendment, read as Field reads it, the gap between natural principles of justice and the constitutional text narrowed considerably. All fundamental principles of justice are incorporated in the amendment, as parts of the privileges and immunities of citizens of the United States. Had the Fourteenth Amendment been in place at the time of the test oath cases, Field would have been able to treat them much more directly, for as alleged attempts to set qualifications for the pursuit of ordinarily lawful callings, they went well beyond the limits warranted by the legitimate police power of licensing. Field would have seen these oaths as abridgements of privileges and immunities and would not have had to stretch for the ex post facto and bill of attainder grounds he relied on. Recall that Field's biographer Kens argued that in relying on these clauses he "stretched the Constitution."[72] With respect to *Cummings*, I do not believe that conclusion is justified; *Garland* is a harder case, but the difficulty there concerns the greater plausibility of seeing the oath as a qualification for office.[73]

It should be apparent why Field initially favored the privileges and immunities clause over the due process clause. The former accomplished more purely what Field believed the Fourteenth Amendment was meant to accomplish—making the fundamental natural rights binding against the states. The due process clause, with its protection of life, liberty, and property, could also be read to accomplish the same thing, as Justice Bradley did in his *Slaughterhouse* dissent, but it did so in a much more ambiguous way, for it forbade deprivation of the objects of the basic rights only if not done with "due process of law." To transform the phrase "due process of law" into a substantive restraint on legislative action was to counter the process language of the clause and open the Court to the charge that it was indeed stretching the Constitution.[74]

VI. *MUNN V. ILLINOIS*: RATE SETTING

The limitation of Gillman's approach is quite visible in the 1877 case of *Munn v. Illinois*, where Field again wrote a stunning dissenting opinion. This case much better fits McCurdy's emphasis on Field's effort to draw a more or less impenetrable line between public and private matters as a

---

[72] Ibid., 117.

[73] For discussion of Field's initial desire to distinguish the two cases, upholding *Garland* and striking down *Cummings*, see Michael A. Ross, *Justice of Shattered Dreams: Samuel Freeman Miller and the Supreme Court during the Civil War Era* (Baton Rouge: Louisiana State University Press, 2003), 133–34.

[74] On the paradoxes of appealing to the due *process* clause for *substantive* limitations, see Ely, "The Oxymoron Reconsidered."

way of distinguishing licit from illicit exercises of the police power. (Interestingly, in his brief treatment of *Munn*, Gillman treats the case in the terms of public and private, more or less adopting McCurdy's way of understanding Field.)[75]

Field's approach in *Slaughterhouse*—emphasizing the exclusive privileges granted by law—had little traction in *Munn*, for what distinguishes the latter case in Field's mind is the complete absence of legally granted privilege. In *Munn*, the Illinois legislature—pursuant to provisions of the Illinois Constitution declaring all grain storage facilities "to be public warehouses" and requiring the Illinois General Assembly to pass laws "for the protection of producers, shippers, and receivers of grain and produce"—had set maximum rates that could be charged in these facilities for the storage of grain.[76] These laws were part of the broader Granger movement of the late nineteenth century, aimed at protecting the interests (mainly) of farmers by curbing perceived abuses and hardships imposed by railroads, owners of grain elevators, and others involved in the now mostly national commerce in agricultural products.

The legislative rate-setting in *Munn* was completely different from the legislative scheme in *Slaughterhouse,* for here the laws applied uniformly to all engaged in the commercial storage of grain. There was no question of different classes of owners being treated differently. The absence of the equal protection dimension in *Munn* may have accounted for the fall-off in support Field had for his dissent in the case. In *Slaughterhouse*, Field spoke for a four-member minority; in *Munn*, he had only one other justice with him, that one (Justice Strong) ironically having been in the *Slaughterhouse* majority. But Field lost two of the justices who had been with him in *Slaughterhouse*, Bradley and Swayne, both of whom had joined his *Slaughterhouse* opinion and had also written their own strong dissents. Both had emphasized the exclusive privilege aspect of the Louisiana law, and we might at least presume that the absence of that feature in *Munn* led to their joining the majority in the latter case.

The question posed in *Munn* was whether the price-setting scheme was a violation of the due process clause of the Fourteenth Amendment (the privileges and immunities clause having been taken off the table by *Slaughterhouse* and some successor decisions). Three different answers to the chief question posed can be discerned in *Munn* and in the earlier version of the case as decided by the Illinois Supreme Court. The Illinois court decided there was no violation of the due process clause because "so long as the owner was not deprived of the title and possession of his property," there was no deprivation within the meaning of the clause.[77] Chief Justice Waite, speaking for the U.S. Supreme Court majority, upholds the law but

---

[75] Gillman, *The Constitution Besieged*, 68–69.
[76] *Munn v. Illinois*, 94 U.S. 113 (1877), at 114–15.
[77] Id. at 139.

not on such broad grounds as the Illinois court took. Instead, he takes a broader view of protections afforded by the due process clause: It is "a guaranty against any encroachment upon an acknowledged right of citizenship by the legislatures of the states."[78] He does not understand the term "deprive" in so narrow a way as the Illinois court did.[79] Thus, he denies that "statutes regulating the use, or even the price of the use, of private property necessarily [deprive] an owner of his property without due process of law." Unlike the Illinois court, he affirms that "under some circumstances, but not under all," such regulations "may" work such a deprivation.[80] Put otherwise, the due process clause does protect against some regulations and particularly against price settings. Waite and Field are thus closer to each other than either is to the Illinois court. Field agrees with Waite that not all regulations, not even all price-setting regulations, are unconstitutional, but he has a much more stringent doctrine on when such regulations are valid.

The differences between Waite and Field are two. First, Field sets price setting off more firmly from other legislative acts relating to property than Waite does, and second, he has a tighter notion of what will constitutionally justify legislative price setting. Waite accepts the same large narrative about rights and governmental power that Field does. Individuals possess prepolitical rights, but "when one becomes a member of society, he necessarily parts with some rights and privileges which, as an individual not affected by his relations to others, he might retain." On Waite's view, limitations do remain on what government may rightly do: "This [parting with some rights] does not confer power upon the whole people to control rights which are purely and exclusively private,"[81] but, he also insists, "it does authorize the establishment of laws requiring each citizen to so conduct himself, and use his own property, as not unnecessarily to injure another."[82] The police powers include the right to regulate all sorts of uses of private property, including the right to fix maximum rates for services provided.[83]

The standard that governs valid regulations, including price-setting regulations, is whether property is being "used in a manner to make it of public consequence, and affect the community at large. When, therefore, one devotes his property to a use in which the public has an interest, he, in effect, grants to the public an interest in that use, and must submit to be controlled by the public for the common good to the extent of the interest he has thus created. He may withdraw his grant by discontinuing the use; but so long as he maintains the use, he must submit to the

[78] Id. at 124.
[79] Id. at 123.
[80] Id. at 125.
[81] Id. at 124.
[82] Id.
[83] Id. at 125.

control."[84] This is the doctrine of "clothed with a public interest" made famous by *Munn* and excoriated vehemently by Field.

It is a strange doctrine and requires some explication. Perhaps its most striking feature is its effort to construe regulations of the uses of property as voluntary submission to legislative conditions, or as voluntary waiving of the private (immune) character of the property use in question. It is clearly an attempt to sidestep the question of whether any such regulations amount to deprivations. The "clothed with a public interest" doctrine provides an alternative path to legitimizing legislative power, one that does not require the Illinois Supreme Court's narrow reading of "deprive" to mean only stripping of title and possession. In principle, according to Waite, legislative acts that leave title and possession can nonetheless work deprivations, and by implication could violate the due process prohibition.

The fiction of a voluntary granting to the public of "an interest in that use" of property may have almost the same effect as the Illinois court's narrow notion of "deprivation," however. Waite's fiction depends on a deep equivocation in the use of the word "interest." The key sentence is this: "When . . . one devotes his property to a use in which the public has an interest, he, in effect, grants to the public an interest in that use. . . ." The first use of interest is equivalent, in effect, to "concern" or even "attention"; the second use is equivalent to "a legal share in something."[85] If the legislature takes action, that is prima facie and perhaps irrebuttable evidence that the public has an "interest," that is, a concern about that use of property, a concern which automatically(?) triggers the conclusion that the owner has granted to the public an "interest," that is, a legal share in the property which then justifies the legislation. The Court's doctrine would thus amount to the position that the existence of the legislation would be its own justification. If this is a fair reading, then Field's general response would seem justified: "The principle upon which the opinion of the majority proceeds is, on my judgment, subversive of the rights of private property."[86] Although Waite sets his opinion within a doctrinal context in which there may be some regulations that violate the due process clause, his path to determining that the Illinois law is not such a violation seems to shut the door he had opened. The "clothed with a public interest" doctrine, in other words, does not appear well-crafted for the purposes it was developed to serve.

Field develops an alternative doctrine, one that retains a strong commitment to the police power and the permissibility of the regulation of property, but one which also retains some power to protect property rights. Field agrees with Waite and the others in the majority on the

---

[84] Id. at 126.
[85] Black's Law Dictionary.
[86] *Munn v. Illinois*, 94 U.S. 113 at 136 (Field, J., dissenting).

general story about rights and governmental power. Government may regulate property in a large number of ways; "indeed," Field says, "there is no end of regulations with respect to the use of property which may not be legitimately prescribed, having for their object the peace, good order, safety, and health of the community." [87] The police power "embraces an almost infinite variety of subjects." [88]

As wide-ranging as the police power is, Field nonetheless makes the case that regulation of price is special and normally not legitimate. He does so in the context of a comprehensive review of the kinds of actions governments may, under appropriate circumstances, take with regard to property. The state has the power "to take ... property for public uses, upon just compensation being made there for." The state may go so far as to extinguish title and seize possession upon the two conditions of a (genuine) public purpose and just compensation.[89]

The state may also take some but not all of an individual's property in the form of "taxation for the support of government." [90] Field does not specify the limitations on the taxing power, but he no doubt would endorse the standard one, that taxes be laid by representatives of the property owners. The state may also "regulate the use and possession of his property, so far as may be necessary for the protection of the rights of others, and to secure to them the equal use and enjoyment of their property." [91] All property use is to be limited by the rights of others, and Field is generous in recognizing state authority to operate in service of these rights. Taking, taxation, and regulation—these are the three legitimate uses of state powers relative to property: "The power of the state over the property of the citizen does not extend beyond such limits." [92]

What lies on the other side of these limits is price and rate setting. Certain kinds of police-power regulations of the grain storage business are perfectly acceptable, such as the setting of standards for weights and measures to prevent fraud and promote honest dealings. But price setting is special. First, Field makes clear that "the prices which the owner [of a grain warehouse] shall receive for its uses" are part of the property right protected by the due process clause.[93] While other aspects of the property right (for example, the right to use property as the owner wills to use it) may readily impinge on the rights of others, the prices at which an owner makes his property or services available do not. Thus, an automobile manufacturer may reasonably be required

---

[87] Id. at 146.
[88] Id. at 145.
[89] Id. For an excellent presentation of Field on takings, see McCurdy, "Justice Field," 974–76.
[90] *Munn v. Illinois*, 94 U.S. 113 at 145 (Field, J., dissenting).
[91] Id.
[92] Id.
[93] Id. at 142.

under the police power to equip his automobiles with safe brakes, for
unsafe brakes threaten public safety. There is no comparable police-
power purpose to be served by a regulation of the price at which the
manufacturer sells his product. Consumers are free not to purchase the
good or service if the price is too great, and thus they have the power
to act on their own to respond to prices. To set the price is to impinge
on labor, liberty, and property with no police-power justification. As a
matter of standard practice, then, the state's power does not extend to
setting prices (or wages). They are specially protected by the due process clause.

This is not to say, however, that Field thinks all price setting is unconstitutional. In fact, he accepts a great deal of it, but he rejects the
grounds for it and the legitimacy of it in this instance, as put forward
by the various actors in this case. Thus, he rejects the efforts of the
framers of the Illinois Constitution to render price setting legitimate by
declaring grain storage facilities public institutions. Declaring them public "does not make them so," Field remarks, ". . . One might as well
attempt to change the nature of colors, by giving them a new designa-
tion."[94] The nature of the grain elevators is what it is, and no legal
"redescription" can change that. Field also rejects the Illinois Supreme
Court's ultra-narrow definition of the character of the rights protected
by the due process clause.[95] And he rejects Waite's approach to the
"clothed with a public interest" doctrine as not much different in practice from the Illinois Constitution.[96]

Field accepts the idea that the public may possess or acquire "an
interest" in an enterprise or a property, but not merely through its
being a matter of public concern or even public impact.[97] There is a
sense in which Field's argument mimics that of Waite; there are cases
where, in effect, the owner of a property "implies an assent to the
regulation of its use and the compensation for it." This occurs when
the enterprise depends upon "some special privilege granted by the
State or municipality." If such a privilege is involved, then "no one,"
least of all Field, "has ever contended that the State had not a right to
prescribe the conditions upon which such privilege should be enjoyed."
"It matters not how limited the privilege conferred," the result is the
same—the openness to state control. This is the paradigm case McCurdy
has in mind when he speaks of Field's effort to draw a bright and
shining line between public and private, with the former subject even
to price and rate setting and the latter not. To accept a governmental
privilege is to be removed from the category of the purely private. The

[94] Id. at 138.
[95] Id. at 142.
[96] Id. at 139–40.
[97] Id. at 140.

owners of the grain warehouses in *Munn* had no such privileges and thus were not vulnerable to price setting.[98]

The public-private distinction is important to Field, but we must note the particular context in which it is important, and we must notice also the way in which Field's version of the natural rights philosophy lies behind this aspect of his jurisprudence, just as it lay behind his commitments to free labor and the rule of equal, uniform law, and his rejection of exclusive privileges.

VII. Conclusion: Field's Judicial Liberalism and Capitalism

The story of the influence Field's brand of judicial liberalism came to have on the U.S. Supreme Court is a large one, but not one to be told in this essay. My aim here has been to develop a coherent and relatively comprehensive account of what is arguably the best-developed version of judicial liberalism friendly to laissez-faire and capitalism that was ever embraced by a justice on the Court.[99]

What might one conclude, then, about Field's judicial liberalism and capitalism? First, I remain firmly in the camp of the revisionists. Field's approach to legal questions of political economy was shaped by a political philosophy of rights, understood by him to be incorporated in the Constitution, and not shaped by a theory of economics, or by sympathies with corporations or property owners. The account here differs from earlier revisionist accounts in emphasizing Field's rights commitments as deeper and more general than the specific but important themes previously emphasized by revisionists.

It does not follow that because Field's judicial liberalism did not derive from an economic theory and was not tailored to serve business and corporate interests, it has no implications or impact on capitalism. In fact, one might note significant connections, some positive, some negative. First, Field's emphasis on rights of liberty, free labor, property, and contract is tremendously supportive of markets and capitalist interests. His jurisprudence contains a strong presumption in favor of the autonomy of private activity and freedom from governmental control; this presump-

---

[98] Id. at 190. Field also recognizes a category of property "dedicated to public use," which is amenable to rate-setting. He mentions "land for a park or a street." He does not analyze this category any further, however. (Id. at 150.)

[99] It might well be denied that Field was the most friendly justice to laissez-faire policy who has been on the Court. To take just one prominent example, it should be apparent from our discussion of Field's approach to issues of political economy that he might well not have sided with the majority in *Lochner*. In that case, the New York legislature attempted to limit the maximum hours that bakers could work, as a health measure. Field always accepted health as a valid police-power aim, and while he would have shared the majority's desire to be sure that the health claim was not a mere pretense, enough evidence was amassed in Justice Harlan's dissent that there was a genuine health issue involved that Field might well have joined his opinion upholding the law.

tion can certainly be overcome, but to do so, the state always has a burden of showing a valid police-power end, congruence between ends and means, and conformity to what I have called adverbial requirements. One thing not to be found among the legitimate police-power ends is redistribution for the sake of ensuring greater equality of income or wealth. Any scheme that has redistributive effects will have to be justified in some other manner.

Field not only carved out judicial doctrines and tests highly protective of property and liberty rights, but he regularly attached those rights to the deepest well-springs of American political morality. Thus, he insisted on the relation between the protected rights and the "pursuit of happiness" as proclaimed in the Declaration of Independence. That is to say, he worked hard to establish, against alternative versions of American public philosophy (as articulated by, say, Justice Miller), that individual liberty, not popular sovereignty and democratic decision, was the highest good in the American pantheon of goods. In all of these ways, Justice Field's judicial liberalism supported capitalism, free markets, and economic activity aimed at profit.

Not all parts of his jurisprudence were so supportive, however. As all revisionist accounts of Field (and of the Lochnerist Courts) have emphasized, Field had a robust vision of the police power and never had any qualms about upholding legislative restrictions of free economic activity when police-power ends were genuinely being sought. As McCurdy has emphasized, Field's attempt to distinguish public from private set limits on the power of eminent domain, limits which often served to protect property by insisting on valid public purposes. But that same insistence stood in the way of his approving many exercises of eminent domain that arguably might have aided economic development. It also stood in the way of public subsidies for private economic activity, which also arguably would have been pro-capitalist. And when enterprises received subsidies or privileges, he was strong in insisting that this opened them up to great measures of governmental control, including the setting of rates and prices. He warned those who sought public subsidy and other aid that it was a bargain with the devil. He was by no means one-sidedly favorable to business interests.

But was Field's judicial liberalism constitutionally justifiable? Is it a doctrine that is justifiable as a matter of political morality and worthy of revival? These are both large questions, and I will close in an assertive and sketchy way. On the whole, I believe that Field's judicial liberalism was constitutionally justifiable. My own analysis of the drafting and logic of the post–Civil War amendments leads me to the conclusion that the Fourteenth Amendment does indeed mean to constitutionalize the natural-rights position as expressed in the Declaration of Independence. Field was much closer to being correct in his reading of the Fourteenth Amendment than Justice Miller. However, this is not to say that Field was perfectly correct. His reading of the privileges and immunities clause in *Slaughterhouse* is incorrect and misses the pro-federalism dimension of the amendment. Relatedly, he misunderstands the nature of federalism in a series of cases where he joined the Court's majority in restricting congressional legislation under the amendment, cases that I have not discussed here, but which are important for a complete assessment of his judicial liberalism.[100]

So far as the natural rights philosophy championed by Field is sound, so is his judicial liberalism. Of course, the soundness of the natural rights philosophy is a most contested question, and I do not presume to attempt to settle it here.[101] The revival of Field's judicial liberalism would have many advantages. It would overcome the now long-lived disjunction between the way the Court treats rights that touch property and the economy, and the way it treats rights embodied in other parts of the Bill of Rights. Such a revival would, at the same time, provide a firmer grounding and better guidance to the courts and the country in trying to think about the rights that courts do recognize. For example, the debate over the right to abortion, as initially articulated in *Roe v. Wade* (1973) and then rearticulated in *Planned Parenthood v. Casey* (1992), would be greatly aided by the kind of structured thinking about rights provided by Field's judicial liberalism.[102]

This is not to say that Field's doctrine is perfectly adequate either. Perhaps the chief weakness is the obverse of the strength I have been emphasizing. His theory is a theory of rights and not a theory of economics. The priority of rights over economics is visible in his *Munn* dissent when he refuses to attribute any significance to the fact that the grain elevator operators were quite openly fixing prices. According to Field, if the government is not involved, there can be no such thing as a monopoly, and owners have a right to set prices even by colluding with each other to get more than a competitive market would bear. He is not concerned with the operation of markets per se. But he always conceded that the use of property was rightly limited by the requirement that such use not harm the rights of others. What is important about free markets is that they serve to coordinate private property rights with the common

[100] I am referring especially to cases related to race, such as *U.S. v. Cruikshank*, 92 U.S. 542 (1876), and the *Civil Rights Cases*, 109 U.S. 3 (1883). The basis for the claims about the proper meaning of the Fourteenth Amendment expressed in the text are my essays "Congressional Power under the Fourteenth Amendment," *Constitutional Commentary* 3 (Winter 1986): 123–56; and "Completing the Constitution: The Fourteenth Amendment and Constitutional Rights," *Publius* 22, no. 2 (1992): 69–91.

[101] For my thoughts on the matter, see my *Natural Rights and the New Constitutionalism* (Princeton, NJ: Princeton University Press, 1994), chap. 9; and *Launching Liberalism* (Lawrence: University Press of Kansas, 2002).

[102] *Roe v. Wade*, 410 U.S. 113 (1973); *Planned Parenthood v. Casey*, 505 U.S. 833 (1992). See my "Casey at the Bat: Taking Another Swing at *Planned Parenthood v. Casey*" in Christopher Wolfe, ed., *That Eminent Tribunal: Judicial Supremacy and the Constitution* (Princeton, NJ: Princeton University Press, 2004), 37–58.

good in a way that noncompetitive markets do not. On his own terms, Field ought to be open to the possibility of market failures that would justify intervention for the sake of keeping markets free. Perhaps he is correct to resist price setting as generally illegitimate, but he should be open to antitrust or anticollusion regulation to a degree he was not in practice. Nonetheless, it seems to me that an addendum of this sort can be readily made to his jurisprudence to make it more serviceable and more consistent with his own principles.

Political Science, University of Notre Dame

LIBERTY AFTER LEHMAN BROTHERS

By Loren E. Lomasky

I. Introduction

Like a motor that stutters, deceptively jerks back to life, and then entirely seizes up, the engine of world finance was thrust into crisis by events of the weekend of September 13, 2008. The New York Federal Reserve Bank had called a meeting of potential suitors to see if troubled Lehman Brothers might be reclaimed in its eleventh hour by an arranged marriage to some fiscally more robust firm. On this occasion, however, potential rescuers were less ardent than they had been six months previously when JPMorgan Chase swept in to snatch Bear Stearns from the financial abyss. They had been chastened by the intervening cascade of discouraging news in housing markets and throughout the financial industry. Nor would the Fed sweeten the dowry enough to persuade the reluctant to commit. Lehman Brothers would be allowed to sink or swim on its own. And sink it quickly did; when the new business week dawned, Lehman Brothers filed for bankruptcy.

Perhaps government officials would not have been so keen to subject the company to the disciplinary forces of the market if it had comprehended how severe and broad the reaction to the fall of Lehman would be. This had been a firm with creditors among the world's financial elite, and these counterparties were interlocked with innumerable other firms in a web of delicate trust relationships. Once doubt arose concerning who could pay and who could not, the rational course for each firm was to build up its own cash balances by selling marketable assets and by calling in loans. What was individually rational, however, proved to be collectively disabling. Firms that had been solvent just the day before found themselves unable to meet demands they had not expected. Like one domino striking the next and that the one after, contagion spread beyond all accustomed bounds. First Bear Stearns, then Lehman: who would be next? Answers came discouragingly quickly: insurance giant AIG, quasi-governmental mortgage leviathans Fannie Mae and Freddie Mac. Iceland's banking industry went into receivership, taking most of the country with it. The pathology of finance bled profusely into other sectors. Legendary titans of American industry Chrysler and General Motors sought bankruptcy protection, and numerous other American, British, and European firms were put on financial life-support by panicking governments. GDP everywhere plummeted as unemployment soared. Was it to be Great Depression II?

doi:10.1017/S0265052510000245

The cautious answer is: Not yet. Indeed, as I write a year after Lehman sank beneath the waves, a majority of the pundits seem to be emerging from their foxholes and offering some hope that, although no robust recovery is to be expected anytime soon, the worst may be behind us. There are still more bankruptcies to weather, more firestorms to be put out by harried public officials, more broken balance sheets to be painstakingly mended. Yet even while crisis-management mode remains very much the order of the day, this may also be an apt time to step back from the day-to-day tremors and perturbations and to consider what enduring lessons are to be learned from the Crunch of 2008.[1] Not since the 1930s has there been an occasion to think so intensely about the adequacy of accustomed modes of economic interaction. Like hangings, financial panics wonderfully concentrate the mind. The technology to contain bank failures, we had been told, was well established; global markets for financial instruments had promoted a spreading of risk that fortified not only the various players in the investments industry but also the system as a whole. Yet over a few days in September these assurances were shown to be hollow. The Great Machine was not the reliably self-correcting mechanism its savants and caretakers had advertised. How was it to be brought back into good repair?

Early responses were variations on: *Round up the usual suspects!* To what should have been no one's surprise, the word from the Continent, especially Paris, was that Anglo-Saxon market fundamentalism had been discredited once and for all in favor of the more prudent and humane *dirigisme* of the technocratic planners. Before the corpse of Lehman Brothers was cold, French president Nicolas Sarkozy was heard to declare, "Self-regulation as a way of solving all problems is finished. Laissez faire is finished. The all-powerful market that always knows best is finished."[2] Government had meekly stepped aside so as to allow the unfettered market its dizzying rise and yet more dizzying collapse. The indicated remedy was a reversal of the preceding two decades' abdication of responsibility to rampaging capitalism and a move to place business firmly under regulatory wraps. In one way or another, this verdict was seconded by numerous other politicians, business moguls such as George Soros, and Nobel prize-winning economists Paul Krugman and Joseph Stiglitz.

A very different tune was heard from the right. What had brought on the debacle? Government! How are future crises to be avoided? Less governmental intrusiveness! Should deregulation be reversed? No, it needs

---

[1] A word about nomenclature: The events of 2008 remain too recent for a consensus on terminology to have emerged. My preference is "Crunch." "Crash" overemphasizes the fall of asset prices as opposed to the sheer breaking down of markets and is too much an echo of 1929. "Recession" is too mild and "Depression" too tendentious. "Panic" might be acceptable but suggests something more temporary and subjective than what transpired after the fall of Lehman Brothers.

[2] Nicolas Sarkozy, quoted at http/www.csreurope.org/news.php?type=&action=show_news&news_id=1727.

to be accelerated! Libertarian and conservative critics pointed to political pressures on Fannie Mae and Freddie Mac to extend housing loans to a wider, less financially capable range of borrowers. Special scorn was held out for the 1977 Community Reinvestment Act which, in the words of the Federal Reserve, "intended to encourage depository institutions to help meet the credit needs of the communities in which they operate, including low- and moderate-income neighborhoods, consistent with safe and sound operations."[3] The problem was, of course, that the imperative to provide mortgages to those previously deemed not creditworthy was blatantly in tension with the "safe and sound operations" qualifier. Congressional representatives were solicitous of low-income constituents, President George W. Bush pushed his model of the "ownership society," and an already excited real estate market was set on a course to explosion.[4]

The great virtue of these "explanations" is that they afford one the comfort of preserving ideological convictions unchanged—no new thoughts required. Indeed, the Crunch can be displayed as decisively confirming prior warnings that, take your pick, buccaneer capitalism/ubiquitous government is brewing the apocalypse.

To be sure, rational individuals do not summarily abandon what they take to be well-attested theories when confronted with an anomalous instance or two. However, it is also a part of rationality to reflect critically on one's beliefs in the hope of securing yet better ones. When ideologies ossify, they render themselves impervious to the significance of new data. With regard to the Crunch of 2008, there is ample reason to believe that the instant analyses from both the left and the right are, at a minimum, incomplete. Broadsides against so-called laissez-faire capitalism conveniently fail to observe that institutional failures were less a matter of market deregulation than misregulation. Traditional commercial banks, for which overseers are thick on the ground, suffered worse breakdowns than did the more lightly regulated hedge fund industry. Nor does quantity of regulation translate into quality of regulation. Short-term interest rates are closely controlled by the Federal Reserve (and other central banks), yet one of the most frequently cited factors alleged to have generated the Crunch is an easy money policy pursued too long and too lavishly by the Fed. As quasi-governmental agencies, Fannie Mae and Freddie Mac are subject to scrutiny by their political controllers, yet their failures were no less catastrophic than those of the great investment banks. And although not directly contributive to the Crunch, the fecklessness of piling up new boards of governmental supervisors is underscored by the massive Bernie Madoff fraud, the most ruinous Ponzi scheme ever perpetrated by a private party. It simmered for more than a decade under

[3] The Federal Reserve Board, "Community Reinvestment Act," http://www.federalreserve.gov/dcca/cra/.
[4] See, for example, Stan J. Leibowitz, "Anatomy of a Train Wreck," *National Review* 60 (October 20, 2008).

what should have been but emphatically was not the watchful eye of the Securities and Exchange Commission. Foresight is devoutly to be wished, but it can never be as acute or reliable as hindsight. It is fatuous to suggest that the events of 2008 can be attributed to a scarcity of bureaucrats.

No less fatuous, however, are complaints from the other side of the political spectrum that the Crunch was primarily or simply a governmental failure. The unsatisfactoriness of this response should be especially troubling to friends of free markets, among whom I count myself. Yes, it's true that policies pursued by Congress, the various regulatory authorities, and semigovernmental entities introduced distortions into real estate (and other) markets, but state actions *always* introduce perturbations into perfect free-market models. It isn't a surprise when opportunists or wide-eyed idealists grasp the levers of political control in order to serve their various ends; what would be truly surprising is if they ceased to do so.[5] No doubt rent-seeking and the like impose costs, but they do not typically drive the economy off the cliff. These costs tend to be less than they might otherwise be because prudent actors anticipate their direction and take intelligent measures to counteract them. Sometimes they do so by opposing politicking with counter-politicking—the dance of dueling lobbyists— but they also do so through voluntary exchange. The primary virtue of the market is not that it works efficiently on frictionless surfaces but rather that it tends to respond effectively to exogenous disturbances: those generated by governmental action just as much as acts of God. Entrepreneurs make money by seizing opportunities that dubious governmental undertakings create. In 2008, however, friction won. It does seem that market participants en masse lost their heads. To be sure, some financial institutions were under pressure from their political masters to write mortgages of dubious creditworthiness, but that does not explain why other investors not under such pressure then snapped these up, yet others decided that these were assets fit for securitization, rating agencies evaluated as AAA what soon proved to be toxic treacle, and final purchasers leveraged themselves to dizzying heights in order to expand their share of the action. That is not how the textbooks—I mean the textbooks written before the demise of Lehman Brothers—tell us that rational profit-maximizers are motivated to behave. Yet they did so, at costs now well into the trillions of dollars and rising. Because that is the case, it especially behooves friends of markets to reevaluate our creed. Did we miss something that now needs to be added to the standard textbook presentation? Or if not absent, were there some aspects of capitalistic exchange that were under- or over-emphasized? Those who saw it all coming and took appropriate measures, thus generating proud records of predictive success and personal fortunes, need not review the events of 2008. I, alas, am

---

[5] The obverse diagnosis lays the blame for the Crunch on the "greed" of speculators. When haven't the money men been in it for the money?

not among them.[6] This essay is a first reflection on the legacy of Lehman Brothers. What are the implications of the Crunch for the political economy and philosophy of liberalism?

II. Two Metaphors

Two metaphors dominate the theory of voluntary interchange among independent actors each acting with exclusive concern for his own self-interest. The first is that of the *invisible hand*. Although assuming its canonical form in the work of Adam Smith, it appears only once in *The Wealth of Nations* (1776) and once in his other great book, *The Theory of Moral Sentiments* (1759). Counting occurrences, however, radically understates the impact of the controlling idea. Smith's system of political economy over and over again provides instances of individuals' self-regarding behavior which, when pursued within the context of a "system of natural liberty," generates results that benefit not only the party in question but also other members of the social entity. Private interest is midwife to the common good. Smith's invisible hand should not be interpreted theologically or mystically. Rather, it is a reliable mechanism via which benign outcomes spontaneously emerge as the unintended consequence of the activities of the various actors. Central controlling authority is not required, and indeed is inconsistent with the optimal working of the invisible hand.

Smith is not the first important social theorist who advances an invisible-hand model. He is preceded by Bernard Mandeville, who contends in *The Fable of the Bees* (1714) that private vices generate public benefit (while private virtue would enfeeble the hive). Their accounts differ in important respects, especially with regard to the underlying moral philosophies, but the implications for political economy are very similar. The twentieth century's great theorist of the grip of the invisible hand was Friedrich Hayek, 1974 Nobel laureate for economics, who simultaneously punctured the pretensions of central planners to achieve an effective top-down ordering of the economic realm and demonstrated the power of spontaneous orders to facilitate coordination. It is only a slight exaggeration to say that the invisible hand is the dominant motif of all free-market theorizing since Smith.

The other commanding metaphor is the *prisoner's dilemma*. As with the invisible hand, it refers to a scenario featuring interaction among independent self-interested agents. Unlike invisible-hand cases, results are

---

[6] Nor was Alan Greenspan. Critics have pilloried his rueful admission to Congress in October 2008 that "[t]hose of us who have looked to the self-interest of lending institutions to protect shareholder's equity—myself especially—are in a state of shocked disbelief" (http://oversight.house.gov/documents/20081023100438.pdf). Without wishing either to affirm or to deny Greenspan's considerable culpability for the Crunch and its aftermath, I find the candor of this declaration refreshing. It marks a greater personal integrity than that possessed by certain previously effusive admirers-turned-critics.

baleful. The strategy that each party adopts leaves it worse off than would have been the case had all parties followed the contrary strategy. What makes the prisoner's dilemma appear strikingly paradoxical is that by each acting rationally in his own self-interest, they are collectively worse off than had each acted against self-interest. Uncoordinated activity here leads to disaster, but the prospects for the affected parties to escape this result are dismal because each has an incentive to defect from the strategy that would evade it.

The label "prisoner's dilemma" goes back only to the mid-twentieth century, but the concept has long been known to political philosophers. Most famously, it is the structure that governs the behavior of denizens of Thomas Hobbes's state of nature, whose lives, consequently, are solitary, poor, nasty, brutish, and short. For Hobbes, the moral is undeniable, and he develops it in *Leviathan* (1651) with unequaled brusqueness: in order to survive, the parties must contract away their primal freedom. Uncoordinated choice is the problem to which the state is the solution. The Hobbesian interactive scenario is anticipated as far back as Book II of Plato's *Republic* in a thought-experiment advanced by the character Glaucon.[7] For Plato, as with Hobbes, the way out of the trap is a directive central authority.

Two controlling metaphors and two diametrically opposed equilibria: the Pareto-superior invisible hand and the Pareto-inferior prisoner's dilemma. Which is the one to be credited? The consensus among theorists is that *both* obtain. The traditional liberal synthesis holds that central direction is required to break out of the prisoner's dilemma–like state of nature, but then, under the discipline of the minimal (or in later incarnations, not-so-minimal) state, independent agents suitably constrained by the rule of law will reap the rewards of the invisible hand. Anarchists demur, arguing that the invisible hand itself is sufficient to undo the grip of the prisoner's dilemma, perhaps through sequences of iterated games. For the anarchist, then, it's invisible hand all the way down. The paradigmatic model of traditional socialism is similarly monistic, but with centralized authority taking the place of individual self-directedness on all levels. Market socialism/social democracy attempts to carve out niches somewhere in between.

There exist vast literatures on prisoner's dilemma strategies, the alleged impossibility of socialist planning, the feasability of rational anarchism, and related concerns. For purposes of this essay, I am going to assume that some version of the liberal synthesis is correct. If my assumption is mistaken, if either unbridled anarchism or thoroughgoing socialism is capable of bringing about tolerable levels of peaceful coexistence and prosperity, then that is how political life should be. My view is that

---

[7] It can be argued that Plato also anticipates invisible-hand dynamics in the *Republic*'s account of the "city of pigs."

neither theory nor practice renders either of the monisms plausible, but that will not be argued here. Liberalism is a more delicate structure than either of its rivals because it acknowledges that the uncoordinated activity of diverse parties is sometimes to be welcomed but sometimes to be combated. The trick is to work out which is which.[8]

As a first approximation, it can be agreed that, all else equal, it is good that individuals be unimpeded in exercising their liberty in accord with their own conceptions of the good. Those who disagree, either on grounds of paternalism or as friends of virtue in its constant vigilance to root out vice, may have a point, but, again, it is beyond the ambit of this essay.

The first approximation is sorely in need of a second. Individuals are self-directed agents of their own ends in invisible-hand scenarios, but so too are they in prisoner's dilemmas. The difference is that in the former they bear the lion's share of the costs of their own goal-directed actions, while in the latter they impose costs on nonconsenting others. Moreover, those costs exceed *in toto* for each agent the benefit she secures from her own choice. That is the sense in which prisoner's dilemmas are negative-sum games. What the centralized authority of the Sovereign does in Hobbes's telling of the story is to thwart individuals' pursuit of their own advantage—a negative—but to secure for them liberation from external costs imposed by the choices of others—a decisive positive.

Only in the most stylized examples of invisible-hand interactions (e.g., two-party exchange without externalities) is it strictly true that individuals fully bear the costs of the benefits they secure for themselves. To take the most obvious example, markets with open entry allow competition that can and does drive less-capable parties to the wall. The rise of the automobile spelled doom for buggy-whip manufacturers. (The recent humbling of General Motors can be viewed as a tardy sacrifice to the god of the buggy whip.) To constrain the liberty of actors with the proviso that they not impose external costs on any nonconsenting party would be intolerably demanding in a world with non-zero transactions costs. A functional system of private property rights will, however, go a long way toward countenancing only those exchanges that generate benefits in excess of the external costs thereby imposed and—this is crucial if the structure is to be deemed both reasonably efficient and just—will tend over time to spread benefits and costs in such a way that almost all persons will enjoy an ex ante expectation of thereby being rendered better off than if such exchanges were blocked. Conversely, activities that generate excessive external costs—and, most especially, those tending to set off cascades of costs—are to be restrained. This is a tolerably simple set of dicta for political institutions, but of course it is not as simple as one that

---

[8] For all the brilliance and rigor of his political logic, Hobbes ultimately places himself outside the perimeter of what is recognizably liberal in virtue of allowing the necessity of avoiding prisoner's dilemmas to occupy nearly all the political space there is.

recognizes only one variable, e.g., "The government is best that governs least." To the contrary, sometimes less government is better than more— and sometimes it isn't.[9]

I propose instead a normative structure with two parameters. The first of these is the *Personal Choice variable:* more scope for self-directed choice is better than less. The second is the *External Cost variable:* less imposition of unconsented costs on others is better than more. A moment's consideration reveals these variables to be in permanent tension. The greater the scope of permitted choice, the greater the likelihood of interfering with the designs of others. Which of the variables captures our conception of personal liberty? Both do. As the scope of permissible choice expands or contracts, liberty waxes and wanes. Similarly, the greater one's liability to bear unconsented costs, the less free one is to live according to one's own lights rather than those foisted on one by others.

Hobbes's state of nature is a condition in which individuals have a right to all things, notoriously even to the bodies of others.[10] Rights so understood are not claims that impose duties of forbearance on others but rather naked choice that constrains no one. In the state of nature so conceived, the personal-choice parameter is maximized. This is, Hobbes claims, a condition of perfect liberty. He would be correct if liberty were only a function of the scope of personal choice, but it is not. At any rate, it is not the liberty that we have reason to care about. The other extreme might be a traditional society in which external interference is absent but the only option open to each person is to adopt the same social role as that formerly held by one's same-sex parent. This too falls short of full-bore freedom. The indicated moral is that there is an irreducible duality to liberty. Therefore, there is an irreducible complexity to social life: the two parameters are in permanent conflict, and all reasonable principles of permissibility will incorporate strategies for trading off one against the other.

This is vague. To render the structure operational, it is necessary to answer the question: How much does a gain in choice of magnitude M_1 outweigh costs of magnitude M_2? I do not believe that there exists a programmatic metric to resolve such conflicts. Rather, particular applications of the structure require case-by-case estimation of the gravity of the personal-choice interest at stake and the severity of associated external costs. For example, one central chapter of the history of liberty in the West involves the growth of a strong consensus that the choice of a preferred mode of religious expression is a very weighty interest, one to be secured even when it causes acute psychic externalities. Assessment of the weight of a choice to smoke cigarettes has taken an opposed trajectory, being routinely trumped in public

---

[9] Similarly, Ronald Reagan's statement in his First Inaugural Address that "government is not the solution to our problem; government is the problem" is approximately 88 percent correct. That's a splendid result for a practicing politician, but it isn't adequate as the foundation for political philosophy.

[10] Hobbes, *Leviathan,* chap. 14.

practice by even minimal external impositions. Is there an alternative possible world in which the ordering would have been reversed: great attentiveness to the external costs of religious belief and little to those of burning tobacco? That seems entirely plausible. Indeed, there are corners of the world in which, for better or worse, it is actual.

Where the weight of either variable is taken to be very great, the discourse of liberalism often speaks in terms of *rights*. Rights appear on both sides of the choice/cost calculus. If you have a right to open a McDonald's franchise next door to my sandwich shop, then the fact that your choice to do so will be exceedingly costly to me does not afford me standing to block your enterprise. I may, however, bar you from crossing through my establishment on the way to yours even though the cost to me of your trespass is slight and the inconvenience to you of having to detour is substantial.[11]

If I were a *natural rights theorist*, I would not speak in this way. Rather, I would reverse the order of implication. According to a natural rights account, it is not the costliness to others of a particular kind of activity that renders such behavior a rights violation. Rather, what makes the imposition of a cost a matter of considerable gravity is the fact that it constitutes violation of a (natural) right. The metaphysical foundation of natural rights discourse is obscure, especially within theories that eschew theological underpinnings.[12] This is a theoretical burden natural rights proponents deem worth bearing because the alternative of (merely) conventional rights is judged to be too frail a barrier against predation: what the state giveth it also taketh away. The concern is legitimate, and I sympathize to some extent with a tactic of natural-rights-as-Noble-Lie. One problem with it, though, is that it makes rights more mysterious than they need be, more mysterious than if they are understood as derivative from the two parameters. A second problem is that it casts doubt on the legitimacy of an *evolutionary technology of rights*. Illustrating that point is the burden of the following section.

III. THE EVOLUTION OF CONVENTIONAL RIGHTS

Rights can be conventional without being *merely* conventional. They will not be shallow constructions if they are solidly grounded on the two

[11] It is, however, too great a stretch to conclude that all real rights are *absolute*, inviolable come what may. If to flee from an assassin, you run across my private property—even property displaying a large *No Trespassing* sign—you have not acted improperly (although you may subsequently owe compensation for damages inflicted). Rights can be robust without being infinitely stringent. I address these issues in "Compensation and the Bounds of Rights," in *Compensatory Justice: Nomos XXXIII* (New York: New York University Press, 1991), 13–44.

[12] John Locke in *Second Treatise of Government* explicitly grounds rights in Divine provenance; Thomas Jefferson in the Declaration of Independence is slightly more coy. Robert Nozick in *Anarchy, State, and Utopia* (New York: Basic Books, 1974) is content to leave unspecified the status of the so-called Lockean rights he invokes.

parameters. I offer three examples of unarguably conventional practices that are now woven almost everywhere into the economic fabric of free societies.

A. Personal bankruptcy protection

In virtue of a voluntary undertaking, negligence, or plain bad luck, a person can find herself mired in debt from which she is unable to extricate herself. Failure to make good on the debt constitutes a nonconsensual imposition of costs on the creditor. He has been deprived of property that is rightfully his. Several responses suggest themselves. First, the failure to repay can be adjudged a *crime*, on a par with assault and theft. Given that conception, the indicated response is *punishment*. Sending debtors to prison or shipping them off to labor in Van Diemen's Land is adequate expressively as a response to the perceived wrongness inherent in trampling on the property rights of others.

More responsive to the harm done to the injured party would be to transform the claim on unavailable financial assets into a claim on the labor of the transgressor. Such bondage need not be perpetual, but it might be. John Locke in the *Second Treatise* advances an argument like this for the propriety of slavery. A somewhat gentler remedy than making the debtor the personal property of the creditor is to give the latter a lien of indeterminate duration on any assets that may subsequently be acquired by the debtor. If the amount owed is large enough, and if the debt compounds at the going rate of interest, the obligation may very well not be discharged prior to death. This approach is maximally responsive to people's concern not to be victimized by external cost impositions, but, especially in the slavery variant, it comes down quite hard on the offending party's choice interest.

Compared with either of the preceding options, personal bankruptcy protection is markedly less "natural." Rather, it is a convention through which individuals can be absolved of indebtedness and then make a fresh start unencumbered by the residue of prior obligation. Because of our familiarity with the bankruptcy convention, the extent to which it distorts what would otherwise be the rights and obligations of the concerned parties may not be readily observable. In a world without the bankruptcy convention, a creditor's right to full repayment may be *violated*, but that right does not thereby *cease to exist*. However, in a world with bankruptcy protection, an individual possessing a strong right to repayment may, through no fault of his own, not only lose the repayment but also lose the right to be repaid. This is a moral phenomenon curious enough to deserve some comment. In terms of the model sketched in the preceding section, overwhelming indebtedness sets the interest of the creditor in not bearing unconsented costs against the unencumbered choice interest of the debtor. There is no necessity written in the stars that the conflict be addressed after the fashion of contemporary bankruptcy law. From an *a priori* theoretical point of view, both the punishment approach and the bondage approach are at least as plausible. It has, however, been judged over the course of the history of responses to indebtedness[13] that an available but not-too-available mechanism for relieving obligations strikes a better overall liberty balance between the parameters than do alternatives. Of course, it is an imperfect mechanism. Like other forms of insurance, it generates moral hazard. Probably it raises the cost of funds to debtors. These defects, however, are outweighed by the liberation brought to incautious or unlucky debtors. And because potential creditors know that one possible outcome of making a loan is default, they can rationally appraise the likelihood of being repaid in full, and can price accordingly, thereby self-insuring against what they take to be excessive risk.[14] Alternatively, they can purchase credit default swaps on the open market. (More on this later.) Bankruptcy law is something of a kludge, but it is one that works.

B. Limited liability corporations

Nothing is more clearly an artifice than the status of corporations as legal persons standing at a remove from their stockholders. Between Adam Smith's time and ours, the corporation has emerged as the dominant form of economic organization. Factors spurring this transformation are clear. When individuals pool their resources as partners in an enterprise, their joint and several personal liability is, this side of the bankruptcy court, unlimited. Therefore, they have reason to be cautious in such undertakings. Prudent investors will carefully vet potential business partners and agree to share risk only with those known to be of sterling probity and impeccable financial credentials.[15] This means that firms will tend to be small. In the wake of the Industrial Revolution, however, it transpired that a growing number of initiatives that people wanted to pursue in order to improve the material conditions of their own lives (and those of their transactors) required enterprises of larger scale than had ever previously existed. Invention of the limited liability corporation prompted vastly increased capital investment, which in turn afforded individuals enhanced means to pursue their old ends and develop some new ones. For would-be entrepreneurs and their transactors, the personal-choice variable is significantly enhanced. It was not only advances in industrial technology that spurred the nineteenth century's revolutionary trajectory of production; innovations in financial technology were hardly less crucial.

---

[13] Including its ancient history. The Hebrew scriptures' institution of a sabbatical year in which (some) debts are canceled is an early variation on the bankruptcy theme.

[14] This capacity holds to a lesser extent in the case of tort damage.

[15] Corporations similarly have a prudential interest in avoiding liability for debts incurred by their shareholders. I am grateful to David Ciepley for making me aware of this symmetry.

Corporate ascendancy was not, however, pure gain from the perspective of liberty, for it lessened the capacity of parties on whom external costs had been imposed to recover full damages. To put it another way, when a partnership turns into a limited liability corporation, all those who either voluntarily or inadvertently transact with it are placed at greater risk. Their possibilities for recovering costs imposed on them have been lessened. For example, holders of General Motors bonds will do less well than they would have done if the debts of the company passed through as claims on the personal funds of its owners. In that case, though, there would have been no General Motors. It is because we deem ourselves to be benefited on balance by the corporate form that we welcome its presence in market arrangements. Things could have been otherwise. Once they were.

C. Intellectual property

Intellectual property rights that impose duties of non-trespass on others are intensely troubling to traditional natural rights theories. There are two reasons why this is so. First, the sort of thing that an intellectual property right encompasses may seem metaphysically occult. It is not a concrete object that can be held in one's hands like an apple, walked across like a field, weighed, transported, or chopped to little bits. The property right is to an abstract object, what philosophers call a *type* rather than a *token*. Scarcity does not work in the same way for types as it does for tokens. If I appropriate your apple, then you have one apple fewer. If, however, I build a widget of a type over which you hold a patent, then my having this particular widget does not mean that the quantity of widgets you own has diminished. If there is no particular thing of yours, no spatiotemporally individuated entity against which I trespass, then in what sense can I be said to have intruded on any property that is yours?

Even more troubling is the time-delimited status of intellectual property rights. Suppose that the term of patent duration in this jurisdiction is twenty years from the date of filing. This means that the mere passage of time can render something—assuming that abstract types are indeed something—to which one had a strong, enforceable property right an item that instead is the property of no one. Ownership of concrete property does not work that way. In the Lockean paradigm, one mixes one's labor with an object and renders it one's own—period. Unless it is abandoned, one's tenure over it is indefinite. And if it is abandoned, then some other person is at liberty to claim it, thereby having exclusionary rights against all other people in the world. Intellectual property is altogether different. The extent of the term of protection is a matter of arbitrary fiat. It could have been shorter, could have been longer, could have been zero, could have been infinite. And once the term of the right expires, the abstract object is owned by no one.

The critic of intellectual property errs in confusing what is *conventional* with what is *arbitrary*. A system of patents under which they last twenty-one years rather than twenty would have been in virtually every respect as manageable as what in fact obtains (although the attractiveness of round numbers should not be underestimated). However, patent durations of either twenty days or twenty decades would undermine the purpose of the intellectual property system. That purpose is, law-and-economics scholars contend, wealth maximization. Although in a broad sense that may be right, it is too undiscriminating a rendering. There are at least two routes to increasing wealth. One is to enhance the choice capacity of individuals to engage in activities they value, and the other is to discourage impositions of external costs. As has been noted previously, these often run at cross purposes. Limited-term protections of intellectual property represent a balancing between these two parameters such that a tolerably good result is achieved. (Only in the economists' fantasies is it a social optimum.) In the absence of intellectual property rights, non-innovators could free-ride on the efforts of those who innovate, thereby depriving them of what would otherwise have been the fruits of their labors. The result would be less innovation, rendering everyone worse off with regard to their capacity to better their lives by making effective choices. However, if intellectual property rights were of indefinite duration, then the liberty of non-innovators would be permanently trammeled. (We are all of us, even the most prolific artists or inventors, non-innovators with regard to the vast preponderance of goods we enjoy.) Limited-term intellectual property rights split the difference. It is, of course, legitimate to call into question how well they do so. Perhaps the conventions we now have are not the very best conventions we could have; perhaps they are not even nearly good enough. What is much less defensible, however, is to suppose that the purity of the free market is sullied by the existence of rights that are thoroughly conventional. These conventions are themselves grounded on interests that are not matters of artifice: the interest in directing one's life in accord with one's own lights, and the interest in not being forced to bear costs externally imposed.

The aim of rehearsing these familiar stories about the development of personal bankruptcy protection, limited liability corporations, and intellectual property rights is to underscore the fact that there is no such invariant species as the "free market." At one time, markets lacked these practices, just as they lacked antitrust legislation, regulatory oversight commissions, lenders of last resort, and dozens of other time-bound bits of institutional apparatus.[16] Individuals transact with willing others in a variety of institutional contexts that evolve in response to changing technologies of production and distribution. The great classical theorists of liberalism were writing about an economic world radically different from

---

[16] To forestall possible confusion, this is not to be taken as an endorsement of all or any of these constructs.

our own. John Locke knew nothing of Chapter 11 bankruptcy, nor Adam
Smith of the World Trade Organization's TRIPS agreement.[17] That does
not render works in the liberal canon less relevant. Although most of their
specific policy proposals are now obsolete,[18] the underlying theory of
what it is for human beings to live well among others continues to speak
to the contemporary condition. Indeed, the record of adaptability of the
liberal conception to new vistas (as contrasted, for example, with the
progressively more pronounced sclerosis of socialism) shows that it possesses greater universality than might have seemed to be the case in its
infancy. But although the reasons that free markets are desirable remain
essentially unchanged, what constitutes the conditions of a free market,
one suitably responsive to the two parameters, does not remain fixed. The
Industrial Revolution gave cause for reconsideration. So too does the
Crunch of 2008.

IV. The Lessons of the Crunch of 2008

In the days after Lehman Brothers hauled up the white flag, the entire
world of finance took on the likeness of a paradigmatic prisoner's dilemma.
Chastened by the demise of Lehman (and the earlier close escape of Bear
Stearns), each firm saw its interest as shoring up its balance sheet. That
meant calling in loans, unloading vendable assets, and conserving cash.
By doing so, each was worsening the liquidity of all the others. The spiral
threatened to descend to an equilibrium in which the quantity of lenders'
assets and the economy's money supply were drastically lower than pre-
Lehman Brothers. When and how it would have bottomed out we will
never know, because the central banks of the United States, Europe, and
other key economic players rushed to restore liquidity to the system. That
we didn't find out is almost surely a fortunate thing.

Note that the hypothesis entertained by each bank that its counterparties were dangerously likely to be overstretched was not false. That is
because it became self-fulfilling. If, however, they had acted instead on
the assumption that the others were solvent and capable of meeting their
obligations, that too would have been largely self-fulfilling. Those market
participants that were truly insolvent could have been dealt with via an
orderly liquidation process (or at least as orderly as the process can be in
times of financial stress). Others, no longer bogged down by weaker
hangers-on, would have gotten back to doing the business of business.
The resultant equilibrium then would have been achieved at a higher

---

[17] TRIPS is the Agreement on Trade-Related Aspects of Intellectual Property Rights, signed
in April 1994.
[18] Some are not. For better or worse—mostly worse—the need to make and remake Adam
Smith's case for free trade across national borders is perennial.

level of wealth than if each distrusted all the others. This disparity is the defining structural feature of a prisoner's dilemma.

The most important lesson of 2008, then, is that sometimes financial markets are aptly self-regulating, but sometimes they are not. The term of art for the latter condition is "systemic failure." Roughly, what this means is that each party, in pursuing its own interest (in the aftermath of September 2008, shoring up vulnerable balance sheets), thereby imposes external costs on others to whom it is tied by the web of relationships that constitute twenty-first-century finance. Each is acting in keeping with individual rationality, but the result is collective disaster. In this as in other prisoner's dilemmas, when a strategy of defection becomes dominant, there can be a long way to fall.

In principle, the rush for liquidity could have been addressed through voluntary arrangements among the participants. Because they understood that each had an interest in the maintenance of an unconstricted flow of credit, they could have agreed, conditional on the like performance by others, to keep their cash drawers open to those with whom they had a history of transacting. Something like this occurred during the Panic of 1907, when J. P. Morgan assembled in his Madison Avenue mansion the aristocracy of Wall Street and forged with them a pact to restore liquidity to besieged financial institutions.[19] It is beyond expectation, however, that any similar rescue operation by market participants could be effected a century further on. Not only is there no single commanding figure comparable to Morgan, but there also no longer exists a tidy coterie of individuals or institutions that constitute the U.S. banking industry. Not only has finance gone global, it has spawned a wide array of near-banks, quasi-banks and bank-substitutes generically known as the shadow banking industry. What they have in common is that they intermediate between borrowers and suppliers of funds. Their operations are too multifarious, occasional, and impersonal to provide the basis for an agreement such that each could have justified confidence that all others would comply. Even if, beyond all expectation, the potential parties to a pact could be identified and then signed up, the means to monitor their performance would be inadequate. Should this be described as a "market failure"? A less misleading locution is "market limitation." The picture of fully informed parties seamlessly transacting among themselves in a world of zero transaction costs and self-enforcing bargains is and always has been a fairy tale. It becomes dangerous when taken to be either a depiction of or a normative standard for actual markets.

The trades of butchers, brewers, and bakers would be grossly impeded, if not altogether scuttled, in the absence of (i) generally recognized prop-

---

[19] See Ron Chernow, *The House of Morgan: An American Banking Dynasty and the Rise of Modern Finance* (New York: Grove Press, 1990). Milton Friedman and Anna Schwartz also recount this episode in their magisterial *A Monetary History of the United States* (Princeton, NJ: Princeton University Press, 1963).

erty rights, (ii) transactions that are mostly peaceful and undisputed, and
(iii) a reliably authoritative enforcement mechanism that can be brought
to bear when parties find themselves unable to resolve their own differences. No less are these primary structures of a liberal order required for
the business of buying and selling money. Bank stability, however, requires
further background conditions.

To the best of my knowledge, there exists no history of brewer panics.
If one batch of beer is bad, the issue gets resolved between its maker and
purchasers. At the extreme, the brewer loses custom and goes out of
business. This is not bad news to other venders. To the contrary, the
externalities are positive. They have gained a welcome opportunity to
pick up additional custom. Once they do, thirsts are quenched and stability is restored. However, banks (and near-banks) are interconnected in
webs where the assets of some are the liabilities of others. Failure by one
firm, or even rumor of its fiscal unsteadiness, redounds to the harm of
others in the network. Minor slips cascade into major panics. This is, then,
the opposite of the dynamic in which the misfortune of one competitor is
the good fortune of another. Rather, everyone is made worse off.[20]

The peculiar character of the money business has been familiar since
the first bank panic.[21] In some respects, the events of 2008 repeated the
pattern of earlier busts: highly leveraged speculators extend themselves
in a bull market; eventually the bubble bursts; they and those who have
lent to them come a cropper. In other respects, however, 2008 is distinctive
and so provides a basis for learning new variations on old tricks. The
particular wrinkles of Lehman Brothers and its aftermath can be expressed
as the product of three paradoxes:

A. The paradox of efficient markets

Suppose one believes that markets are efficient in the sense that prices
reflect all the knowledge that is available to participants. It then follows
that investment in research to determine whether pricing is fair is largely
wasted. At most, it will supply at the margin a tiny increment to the
knowledge that the thousands or millions of other market participants
have already incorporated into the valuing of the asset under review. A
rational agent will, then, choose to free-ride on the cognitive undertakings of others. The greater the confidence in the overall efficiency of the
market, the greater the incentive to take a free ride. At the extreme,

[20] I hereby follow the usual philosophical convention in which "everyone" means *those
parties the writer is choosing to take into account so as to advance a particular theoretical point.* To
set that useful convention aside for the moment, I acknowledge that when banks fail, short
sellers, investors rich with cash who have been sitting on the sidelines, Marxist revolution-
aries, and misanthropes may thereby be advantaged.
[21] The story is informatively and entertainingly told in Niall Ferguson, *The Ascent of
Money: A Financial History of the World* (New York: Penguin, 2008).

everyone is free-riding on everyone else, and no one is actually monitoring the condition of the underlying assets. Well before that stage is reached, however, serious informational distortions will have been introduced.

To believe in the informational efficiency of markets requires bold and sustained leaps of faith. The global stock market crash of October 19, 1987 ("Black Monday"), Long Term Capital Management's sudden and dramatic demise in 1998, and the turn of the millennium's dot-com bust certainly gave the appearance of an excess of excitement over efficiency. Theories, though, especially when purveyed at a high level of mathematical abstraction by acclaimed savants, are as hard to kill as Rasputin. Nothing better sustained the efficient-markets hypothesis than the extraordinary string of profits that the financial industry accrued during Lehman Brothers' final decade. Looking is good but leaping is better. Or in the words of Citigroup CEO Charles Prince that perhaps best expressed the period's sentiments, "As long as the music is playing, you've got to get up and dance."[22]

The proposition that markets are efficient tends to be self-refuting. The more it is believed, the less accurate it becomes. The more skeptical market players are of its truth, the more effort they will invest in monitoring their potential investments, the overall effect of which is to enhance efficiency. That will then create conditions under which those who subscribe to the efficient-markets proposition will do better than the skeptics. And the merry-go-round takes another spin.

B. The paradox of reduced risk

Over the period that roughly coincided with the term of Alan Greenspan as Fed chairman and the early days of his successor, Ben Bernanke, it appeared to many investors that markets were safer than they had ever been before.[23] The recent slaying of the dragon of inflation had put to rest one chief concern of investors,[24] and wondrous growth in the formal theory of risk assessment had eased another. As far as the eye could see, interest rates were low and gently dropping. Moreover, many of the innovations of the period were explicitly addressed to making risk easier to hedge. For example, credit default swaps allow those holders of securities who are reluctant to bear the risk of default to insure against that eventuality with those who are willing, for a price, to assume the risk. Collateralized debt obligations allow those who are in the business of making loans (mortgages especially, but also credit card debt and other

---

[22] Charles Prince, cited in http://dealbook.blogs.nytimes.com/2007/07/10/citi-chief-on-buyout-loans-were-still-dancing/.

[23] Greenspan was appointed Fed chairman by Ronald Reagan in 1987 and was succeeded in 2006 by Bernanke.

[24] See Robert J. Samuelson, *The Great Inflation and Its Aftermath: The Past and Future of American Affluence* (New York: Random House, 2008).

assets) to pass along the contract to other parties. They, in turn, package it into products of differing degrees ("tranches") of riskiness and then sell them on to yet other parties whose situations are consistent with assuming that particular degree of chanciness. Firms that possess tools to scientifically assess their assets at risk, and then hedge against those risks deemed significant, are less likely to fall victim to the vagaries of the economy.

The single most important component of risk-reduction via diversification was the increasing globalization of world finance. It is risky to be a lender whose exposure is predominantly in one locale. An economic downturn specific to that region could generate defaults that swamp the capital standing behind those assets. It is much less likely that holdings spread out nationally and internationally will simultaneously undergo distress. Rather, peaks and crests will tend to balance each other out. Common knowledge during the Greenspan years was that housing markets may be locally vulnerable but do not undergo collapse on a national level. Most conspicuous among those affirming that homily was Greenspan himself.[25] Americans became enthusiastic buyers of foreign financial assets, and foreign concerns with even greater enthusiasm snapped up products of the vibrant American market—including those securitizing mortgages of less-than-prime quality.

If assets had become less risky than the equivalent products of ten or twenty years earlier, then the capital levels necessary safely to secure those assets had become lower. Especially in an environment in which interest rates were low, the path to significant profits led through increased leverage. In the aftermath of the collapse of Lehman Brothers, innumerable sermons have been preached on the lunacy of 30-to-1 or 50-to-1 debt-to-capital ratios. However, if it is known—or rather, "known"—that risk has been put to rest, then what is irrational is to bear the cost of additional equity when debt is more remunerative. From the perspective of each participant, the enhanced safety of the market provides reason to accept bets that would be rejected as too dangerous in a less well-managed environment. However, each firm's counterparties—and the counterparties of the counterparties—are thereby rendered more vulnerable to its losses. This is, then, another aspect of externalizing costs.

It can be objected that the costs are not externalized in the relevant sense but rather voluntarily assumed by those who choose to make loans to or purchase credit default swaps from inadequately capitalized firms. In a formal sense, that is correct. However, if all parties believe that overall risk levels are lower and then act on the basis of that belief, they will systemically undermine the conditions that generated the belief in the first place. In an era of breakneck financial innovation in which new and untested products are constantly being marketed, it will be especially

---

[25] Alan Greenspan, cited in http://realtytimes.com/rtpages/20041021_bubbleburst.htm.

difficult to judge the financial soundness of the firms with which one deals (whereby I mean both ultimate solvency and current liquidity). Given the prevalence of the hypothesis of efficient markets, the general belief will be that these products are fairly priced. Observe also that in a densely interconnected financial services web, the status of one's transactors is in large measure a function of the status of those with whom they are dealing, and so on until it comes around full circle. I am unsure whether in theory this problem is mathematically resolvable, but in fast-moving markets where billions of dollars may be lost to those who tarry (or, to use Prince's expression, who sit out the dance in order to catch their breath), relevant externalities are largely unsuspected.

The paradox, then, is that the more markets are believed to be safe, the riskier they become. This perhaps helps explain one of the most baffling components of the Crunch of 2008: the utter failure of ratings agencies such as Standard and Poor's, Moody's, and Fitch accurately to judge the likelihood of default of the new financial instruments being peddled by the vanguard of the finance industry. There has been much remarking in the literature about the prima facie conflict of interest posed by rating agencies who are paid by the issuers of the securities to which they attest soundness. In retrospect, that does indeed seem to be a curious way to police the players. It does not explain, however, why the structure worked reasonably well until just before 2008 and then was overwhelmed by a hemorrhage of AAA defaults. Nor does it explain why purchasers of securities did not seem to be much chastened by the potential conflict. The paradox of reduced risk suggests that raters had developed an understanding of the overall environment in which finance was conducted that led them systematically to underestimate the likelihood of any particular security going belly-up. Probably this fed on itself; if one enormous collateralized bundle is deemed safe, then others put together more or less on the same model will be judged similarly. This was largely uncharted territory that the credit rating agencies were entering, and so both they and those who relied on their evaluations might be supposed to have had reason to be vastly more cautious. However, the paradox of efficient markets had led them to believe that they could accurately assess the value of an instrument by observing its pricing,[26] and the paradox of reduced risk reinforced the efficiency supposition.

C. The paradox of hard-won knowledge

It can hardly be denied that the science of economics and the practice of financial intermediation have grown by leaps and bounds since the days of J. P. Morgan (the person, not the eponymous institution). No episode was

[26] "How many financial analysts does it take to screw in a lightbulb?" Answer: "None. The market has already done it."

of greater instructive value than the experience of the Great Depression. The moves made by all the key players in the catastrophe both inside and outside of government have been minutely examined by numerous scholars, not least Milton Friedman and Anna Schwartz in their *Monetary History of the United States*.[27] Although much controversy still obtains concerning causes and responses to the Depression, macroeconomists have since World War II increasingly gained confidence that they know how recessions can be stopped in their tracks before they pose significant threats to the integrity of the financial system as a whole. Central bankers need only lubricate the wheels of a creaking economy with an infusion of money to ensure that landings are smooth and that growth quickly resumes. The further lesson of the "Great Moderation" is that they can do so without thereby engendering any inflationary eruptions.[28] In a November 2002 tribute to Milton Friedman on his ninetieth birthday, Ben Bernanke concluded with this confession that is also a boast:

> Let me end my talk by abusing slightly my status as an official representative of the Federal Reserve. I would like to say to Milton and Anna: Regarding the Great Depression. You're right, we did it. We're very sorry. But thanks to you, we won't do it again.[29]

A few months later in his presidential address to the American Economics Association, Robert Lucas observed:

> Macroeconomics was born as a distinct field in the 1940s, as a part of the intellectual response to the Great Depression. The term then referred to the body of knowledge and expertise that we hoped would prevent the recurrence of that economic disaster. My thesis in this lecture is that macroeconomics in this original sense has succeeded: Its central problem of depression-prevention has been solved, for all practical purposes, and has in fact been solved for many decades.[30]

If the best and the brightest representatives of the profession concur in pronouncing that the problem of macroeconomic instability has been

---

[27] See note 19.
[28] "Great Moderation" refers to the two decades between the conquering of double-digit inflation in the mid-1980s and the demise of Lehman Brothers. According to the *New York Times*, the expression originates in a paper by Harvard economist James Stock and is given widespread currency in a 2004 speech by Ben Bernanke. See "Origins of 'The Great Moderation'," http://www.nytimes.com/2008/01/23/business/23leonside.html.
[29] The speech is available at http://www.federalreserve.gov/BOARDDOCS/SPEECHES/2002/20021108/default.htm. "Anna" refers to Anna Schwartz, coauthor with Friedman of *A Monetary History of the United States*.
[30] Robert E. Lucas, Jr., "Macroeconomic Priorities" (January 10, 2003), available at http://home.uchicago.edu/~sogrodow/homepage/paddress03.pdf.

solved once and for all, it would take an unusually brave or foolhardy person to demur.

Knowing how to avoid the awful mistakes of the past is indeed a wonderful achievement. It may, however, lead one to suppose that new challenges will be resolvable by just those means that have worked in the past. This is a reliable inference when addressing inorganic phenomena: the astronomical regularities that generate prediction of the next lunar eclipse will be exactly like those that predicted the last one. However, when the phenomenon in question involves human institutions and expectations, the possibility that some seemingly negligible variance will profoundly affect outcomes is not to be dismissed. The paradox of hard-won knowledge is that by coming to understand what had previously been mysterious, one is thereby rendered more prone to believe that one understands what in fact still is mysterious.

I believe that this paradox played itself out in the United States during the early years of the new century. The dot-com collapse and, especially, the attacks of September 11, 2001, had put crimps in the long economic expansion. The Federal Reserve acted to keep interest rates very low, even though the United States was running an enormous trade deficit, federal fiscal policy was also generating large and growing deficits, and a few people were starting to use the word "bubble" in the context of real estate and stock markets. Chairman Greenspan and his successor both held that so long as inflation remained thoroughly in check, there was no justification for raising interest rates. They had also learned (or "learned") that when markets are not distorted by intrusive government policies, they can be relied on to be self-correcting. That did not, of course, mean that the regulators themselves could relinquish the levers of monetary policy and hoist golf clubs instead, for they had absorbed the greatest lesson of all: it is the special function of the central bank to lean against both inflation on the one side and deflation on the other. (The Japanese "lost decade" of the 1990s underscored the importance of the latter.) Therefore, the regulators would keep all their constituencies happy for as long as they could by leaving the money faucet open. If inflation indicators began to nudge upwards, they would have adequate lead time to stanch the flow before it became worrying. And should economic growth measures turn lethargic, a well-timed further monetary infusion would restore them to vitality. This was the hard-won knowledge of postwar macroeconomic practice.

When you believe that you already know how to do something, it is irrational to invest resources in relearning how to invent the wheel. However, if the next great economic disruption coming along is significantly unlike recent recessionary episodes, then tried and tested habits may prove unavailing. And if the global economy were to seize up to an extent that it had not done since the 1930s, but the dynamics of the current crisis proved to be crucially different from those of the Great Depression, then a little knowledge could indeed prove to be a dangerous thing. The after-math of Lehman Brothers showed that neither the Federal Reserve nor the Treasury was prepared for what had befallen. Apparently they had not taken advantage of the previous months' intimations to run simulations of a steep decline in housing prices, massively increased foreclosure rates, and ensuing stresses on lenders and their counterparties. Had they been a bit less confident in their own expertise, they might have done so. They would, then, have avoided the clumsy lurching about of a Troubled Asset Relief Program (TARP) that first told the country that it would restore the banking system by buying up and sequestering toxic assets and then admitted that it didn't know how to do that and so would instead directly provide capital to reeling institutions. Most of all, they would have brought to the weekend of September 13, 2008, a clearer idea of the likely conse-quences of a Lehman Brothers default.[31]

The Crunch of 2008, then, was of the genus of other busts that had gone before, but it was also specifically distinct. The vaunted efficiency of post-millennium markets, their capacity to spread and absorb risk, and the scientific progress of their overseers combined to engender a unique degree of false confidence. When the storm was brewing—a perfect storm—regulators were ill-equipped to spot it on the horizon while it was still of a size smaller than a man's fist. When it assumed more ominous propor-tions, they were clumsy in their initial measures to blunt its force. Lehman Brothers was neither the first nor the last ship to capsize, but it was central to the catastrophe.[32]

---

[31] Best of all, as numerous post-Lehman critics aver, would have been a campaign several years earlier to put a foot firmly down on the brake of monetary expansion, thereby popping the real estate bubble before it expanded to dangerous proportions. Simultaneously, author-ities should have imposed legislative or regulatory barriers to lax lending practices. See, for example, John B. Taylor's critique of Fed policy, *Getting Off Track* (Stanford, CA: Hoover Institution Press, 2009). Alan Greenspan responds to Taylor and other critics in "The Crisis," Brookings Institute paper, April 15, 2010, available at http://www.brookings.edu/~/media/Files/Programs/ES/BPEA/2010_spring_bpea_papers/spring2010_greenspan.pdf. Taylor takes another bite of the apple in "Getting Back on Track: Macroeconomic Policy Lessons from the Financial Crisis," *Federal Reserve Bank of St. Louis Review* 92 (May/June 2010): 165-76.

In the glare of hindsight, these reflections are incontestable. Was there ever a realistic chance that they might have been taken up? It is difficult enough for the Fed to step up interest rates when the Consumer Price Index is beginning to climb; powerful political interests are more attached to easy money than to low inflation. In a period of stable consumer prices, the howls that would confront the (unelected and so democratically sus-pect) monetary authorities would be unendurable. At least that would have been so prior to Lehman; we now possess new hard-won knowledge. As for tightening up mortgage lend-ing, it had been for many years the settled policy of both political parties, whether in Congress or the White House, to encourage greater rates of home ownership. (Recall George W. Bush's abortive "ownership society.") Holders of risky mortgages vote too.

[32] Suggestions in this section that the causes of the Crunch were largely endogenous to the workings of the financial system were anticipated by the work of the mid-twentieth-century economist Hyman Minsky. See his "The Financial Instability Hypothesis," Jerome Levy Eco-nomics Institute of Bard College, Working Paper 74 (May 1992), available at http://papers.ssrn.com/sol3/papers.cfm?abstract_id=161024. On Minsky's relevance to the Crunch, see Janet

V. Regulation After Lehman Brothers

Analysts will, no doubt, contend for many decades concerning the causes and therapeutic regimens applied to the Crunch of 2008. Debates about the Great Depression and the New Deal still bubble, and contemporary events cast them in a new light. (For example, reruns of the John Maynard Keynes/Milton Friedman clash sometimes are declared to have a different winner.) With greater insight will come greater clarity concerning appropriate policy measures. I believe, however, that the Crunch has confirmed the proposition that financial markets are susceptible to prisoner's dilemma configurations of an especially virulent form.[33] To believe that these will invariably prove to be self-correcting at tolerable cost requires a leap of faith less supportable now than it was pre-Lehman Brothers. Tamping down the imposition of external costs is one of the twin directives of liberal institutions; liberty consists not only in an entitlement to choose one's path in accord with one's own lights but also to be protected from fallout from others' activities. The indicated conclusion is that liberty after Lehman Brothers will best be served by new institutional structures designed to prevent financial meltdowns from occurring and to halt contagions before they spread. Some of these structures will be created by market participants themselves. Others will have a governmental provenance. One sort of change concerns rules[34] to be impersonally enforced on the various parties. The other concerns grants of heightened discretionary powers. I take these up in turn.

Yellen, "A Minsky Meltdown: Lessons for Central Bankers," *FRBSF Economic Letter*, Number 2009-15 (May 1, 2009), http://www.frbsf.org/publications/economics/letter/2009/el2009-15.html#5; and "Minsky's Moment," *The Economist* (April 2, 2009), http://www.economist.com/businessfinance/displaystory.cfm?story_id=13415233. My understanding of Minsky is that he offers a model alleged to apply to all business cycles. The intended application of the analysis of the preceding section is more modest, expressly limited to the Crunch of 2008.

[33] It is a proposition affirmed by Adam Smith in *The Wealth of Nations*, Book II, chap. 2, "Of Money Considered as a Particular Branch of the General Stock of the Society":

> To restrain private people, it may be said, from receiving in payment the promissory notes of a banker, for any sum whether great or small, when they themselves are willing to receive them, or to restrain a banker from issuing such notes, when all his neighbours are willing to accept of them, is a manifest violation of that natural liberty which it is the proper business of law not to infringe, but to support. Such regulations may, no doubt, be considered as in some respects a violation of natural liberty. But those exertions of the natural liberty of a few individuals, which might endanger the security of the whole society, are, and ought to be, restrained by the laws of all governments, of the most free as well as of the most despotical. The obligation of building party walls, in order to prevent the communication of fire, is a violation of natural liberty exactly of the same kind with the regulations of the banking trade which are here proposed.

[34] I do not distinguish here between *legislation* and *regulation*, although these would have to be separated in a more sophisticated normative account.

A. Rules of the game

An obvious flaw in the pre–Lehman Brothers system was seriously inadequate capital requirements for banks and quasi-banks. The Basel international conventions on capital adequacy[35] proved to be inadequate protection against default risk, and national strictures did not plug their gaps. In retrospect, it is easy to see why capital cushions were likely to prove too slim. It is costly for banks to carry inert reserves. Insofar as they seek to secure impressive profits and to ring up returns that are at least no worse than those of their competitors, they will angle to skirt capital requirements and to increase leverage. Financial institutions' own Value at Risk (VaR) models were probably not deliberately designed to present an unduly rosy picture of overall exposure, but it is perhaps asking too much of executives that they be very skeptical of profit engines that are decked out in state-of-the-art mathematical sophistication. We have learned post–Lehman Brothers that reserve requirements need to be raised.

Raised how far? This is not a question appropriate for philosophers to hazard an answer—at least not this philosopher. Capital adequacy standards should, though, be at a level substantial enough to shift costs away from external parties who will be caught up in the backwash of bank failures and place them instead on those banks and their clients.[36] Banks will, of course, point out that increasing equity and meeting higher reserve requirements impose significant burdens, and they will be correct. The central guiding principle in allocating risk here and elsewhere is that the onus should lie on those who are directly participating in the business of financial intermediation and securing its benefits, rather than on the public at large. If that makes the life of bankers less interesting—as in the saying "May you live in interesting times"—so be it.

Second, Lehman Brothers has taught us that if it walks like a bank and quacks like a bank, then whether or not it is technically a bank, it needs to be regulated as if it were one. This should have been apparent at the time that relics of the New Deal such as Glass-Steagall[37] were sent into retirement. There were too many players in the finance market of a heft and concomitant dangerousness to subject some to minute agency scrutiny and others to a much less restrictive regulatory regime. Again, I beg off from stipulating the extent to which oversight ought to be applied and who the regulating party or parties should be. I content myself instead

---

[35] See http://www.bis.org/publ/bcbsca.htm.

[36] An aptly countercyclical way to do this might be to encourage financial institutions to issue during good times special debt securities that automatically convert to equity when specified emergency situations arise. See Raghuram G. Rajan, "The Credit Crisis and Cycle-Proof Regulation," *Federal Reserve Bank of St. Louis Review* 91 (September 2009): 397–402.

[37] Glass-Steagall is the 1933 act that, among other things, separated ordinary commercial banks from investment banks. After an extended period of whittling away, it was repealed in 1999. Again to forestall misinterpretation, I am not claiming that the repeal was unjustified.

with citing Aristotle's dictum that like cases are to be treated alike. In the 1990s and beyond, Aristotle was too little heeded.

Third, there ought to be more transparent advance indication of just which parties are deemed "too big to fail." Part of the problem that beset governmental functionaries in the pre–Lehman Brothers period is that they were uncertain in their own minds who was to be protected against ultimate collapse and who could be allowed to go to the wall. The only given was that depositors in federally insured financial institutions would not be allowed to lose their funds.[38] Beyond that, ad hoc ruled. If relatively little Bear Stearns was shepherded to a soft landing (albeit one exquisitely painful to shareholders), then could it not be inferred that larger entities such as Lehman Brothers would secure a like solicitude? In the event, it could not. Were nominally private corporations Fannie Mae and Freddie Mac really governmental agencies in drag? The answer was not completely revealed until they were hastily put into receivership. It seemed clear that the Federal Reserve's mandate to be lender of last resort applied to member banks but not to insurance companies such as AIG. However, through its credit default swap business, AIG was deeply implicated in every avenue of global banking. Were it to be allowed to fail, the repercussions would be incalculable, and so it was spared Lehman's fate.

It is asking too much to demand complete precision in distinguishing those parties that are too big to fail from those that are dispensable. Nor is the locution quite right; the operative variable is "too interconnected to fail." Size matters only to the extent that it indicates the number and thickness of tendrils growing through the financial network. However, it is not too much to ask of regulators that they distinguish with some reasonable degree of specificity those firms to which they will lend, in whole or in part, the full faith and credit of the United States (and who, therefore, will be subject to more stringent precautionary rules) from those which, when seas get rough, will be allowed to founder. Such advance notice will not only inform the decisions of investors; it will inform the regulators themselves so that their own perceived uncertainty does not add a further toxin to distressed markets.

Fourth and most speculative, there may be sufficient grounds to block the formation through merger or internal growth of unduly massive financial concerns. If magnitude makes their possible failure too grave a risk to be prudently borne, then they may justifiably be cut down to size. A variation on the size test as such is that those firms that are deemed to be too interconnected to be allowed to fail will be subject to special constraints such as higher reserve standards or additional disclosure requirements. Conversely, their smaller and more nimble brethren will be allowed

---

[38] Even here, there was some residual uncertainty as to the extent of the protection. Prior to 2008, the maximum insured amount per account per bank was $100,000. When rumblings of bank reserve shortfalls were heard, it was then raised to $250,000.

to bear greater, perhaps unlimited levels of risk, but with the proviso that if and when they fail, they truly fail. I say that this is speculative because it is not clear that regulators have adequate means to determine in advance for which firms failure is tolerable and for which it is not. Perhaps even more important, there is serious doubt that governmental bureaus can precommit to keeping their hands off of failing enterprises when all those who stand to lose considerable sums are wheedling for relief. Nonetheless, some mechanism seems necessary to avoid a repetition of 2008's massive socialization of the losses of the financial industry. One prong of the strategy will be to extend public insurance only to those entities that agree to operate conservatively. Against complaints that this will bring back the stodginess of banking during the Glass-Steagall era, the response must be that we have been well reminded that stodginess is not the worst vice that bankers can display. The second prong is to allow innovative entrepreneurship and conspicuous risk-bearing among players who internalize cost externalities.

Some will argue that any such regulatory gap between central and peripheral market participants is inefficient. The reason that firms become very large, they will say, is that there exist economies of scale that favor giant banks over smaller ones; otherwise they would not be induced to grow. What this argument fails to account for are the probability-weighted costs of bailouts. If the reason that the cost of funds to megaliths such as Citigroup is smaller than it is to pygmy banks is that suppliers are confident that they will be protected in the event of a severe downturn, then risk has been socialized to the public at large. Not only is this inefficient, it is inequitable. In a first best world, all players in the financial market fully bear the cost of their own profit-seeking activities. However, in a world of second best, a prohibition of unlimited growth can be justified.

There are dangers attached to all these measures. Some dangers are "merely economic," but others raise deep concerns of justice. In attempting to shield third parties from impositions of external costs, the regulatory regime may erect roadblocks to entrepreneurial innovations which, if left unimpeded, would allow individuals to pursue their ends more effectively. The problem is endemic; the two parameters of liberalism are in tension, and there exists no algorithm for arriving at the optimal trade-off. I confess that with regard to financial regulation the difficulties are greater than usual. Given the extraordinary sums at stake, rent-seeking by interested parties is likely to tip resolutions away from what an impartial spectator would commend. And because the scale on which twenty-first-century regulation must be pursued is largely global, political frictions are exacerbated. Only someone exceedingly optimistic will predict that governing authorities are likely to hit on measures that are optimal or nearly so. The more pertinent question, however, is: Do we have a reasonable expectation of improving on the status quo pre–Lehman Brothers? There, I think, we do indeed have some reason for optimism. It would be quite extraordinary if we have altogether failed to learn some-thing from the events of 2008, and it would be thoroughly depressing if that knowledge cannot be put to some good use. I concede, though, that in the political realm the extraordinary and the depressing do have a tendency to go hand-in-hand.

B. Discretionary authority

I turn now to the exercise of regulatory powers. Perhaps the single clearest lesson of the collapse of Lehman Brothers is that it should not have been allowed to happen. Governmental officials could have arranged a financial cocoon for the firm, but chose not to do so. Perhaps their concern was the aggravated moral hazard that piling a Lehman Brothers rescue on that of Bear Stearns would generate. The worry is not in itself inappropriate, but the very worst time to indulge it is just as the sky is beginning to fall. Either much earlier or much later would have been preferable. I cannot supply figures for how much a rescue of Lehman Brothers would have cost in September 2008, and I am prepared to con-cede that the sum would have been considerable. However, that amount is dwarfed by those that subsequently were expended to address the Crunch that ensued. If Ben Bernanke and Treasury Secretary Hank Paulson supposed that they were being prudent, they were very much mistaken.[39]

A further lesson of Lehman Brothers is that timeliness is next to god-liness. By waiting until the world of finance was in freefall, American (and not only American) officials exacerbated what had to be. This is not to maintain that as late as September 2008, a clean escape could have been made; almost certainly that is not the case.[40] However, what turned into a catastrophe might instead have been merely a disaster. (Or is it the reverse?) The moral is that decisive action is much to be preferred to indecisive waffling. At least that is the case when it is the *right* decisive action. If not (if, for example, the action undertaken is to preempt possible employment of weapons of mass destruction when in fact there exist no such weapons), then the cost calculus is quite otherwise. These are prob-lems that analysts will almost never get wrong—provided they are allowed to address them in the light of hindsight. I am not without sympathy for those who are not afforded this luxury.[41] However, no one is forced to be a cabinet secretary or governor of the Federal Reserve. Their job is to get things right, or at least not to get them terribly wrong. That did not

---

[39] A contrary view was offered on the one year anniversary in Joe Nocera, "Lehman Had to Die So Global Finance Could Live," *New York Times*, September 11, 2009, http://www.nytimes.com/2009/09/12/business/12nocera.html.

[40] A similar verdict is offered by Kenneth Rogoff, "The Confidence Game," http://www.project-syndicate.org/print_commentary/rogoff59/English/.

[41] I am a tenured professor of philosophy. In my discipline, the scope of hindsight is centuries if not millennia.

happen in 1929, and it did not happen in 2008. Few things can be more important for the prosperity and freedom of citizens than that comparable errors not recur anytime soon.

Lovers of liberty must always be made uneasy by writs permitting to their governors scope for discretion. "A government of laws and not men" is the preferred dictum. I heartily concur. However, it is too much of a good thing to infer that the optimal mix is 100 percent rule of law, 0 percent discretion. I do not see how, in a world of imperfect knowledge in which the future resembles the past only imperfectly, all exercise of state powers can be ordained in advance in accord with general and universal laws. But if discretion cannot be avoided, then its worst excesses can be countered by a regime of transparency and accountability. Perhaps if the Bush administration had not been in lame duck mode in the autumn of 2008, it would have been more vigilant in spotting little fires before they became conflagrations. This is speculation, but it may account for some of the fiddling that went on while the contemporary version of Rome was burning. Of no less explanatory value is the paradox of hard-won knowledge. Because authorities believed that they knew what to do and how to do it, they failed to put in the intensive thought that might have led them to safer ground.

These sorts of reflections are of value, but it is limited value. The sad truth is that we are much better at plotting strategy for the last war than the next one.[42] Just as authorities were fully primed to prevent a recurrence of 1929, the next time around they will be vigilant to head off another 2008. So too will be private parties. Even if no elevated reserve levels are mandated, counterparties are liable to insist on enhanced security prior to transacting. Similarly, they will demand and be willing to pay for greater transparency. Does this mean that new governmental measures are unnecessary? That is to take a step too far. They may be valuable simply to assure market participants that those with whom they deal (and those with whom these parties in turn deal, and so on) have taken what are generally agreed to be prudent measures. The costs of making private contracts are decreased by the parties' confidence that, if something breaks down, enforcement will be forthcoming from the ruling authorities. Similarly, the costs of bringing about greater financial stability will be minimized by governmental assurances that counterparties have behaved prudently.

That we can learn something from the collapse of Lehman Brothers does not mean that we will learn all and only the right lessons. In the next and concluding section, I turn to possible educational failures.[43]

---

[42] The Maginot Line was an excellent strategy for holding back the Kaiser's troops. It worked decidedly less well against the Wehrmacht.

[43] As final revisions of this essay were being prepared, the Dodd-Frank Wall Street Reform and Consumer Protection Act of 2010 made its passage through Congress and to the pen of the president. I would be claiming more for myself than is justified if I professed to under-

VI. Conclusion

The single most dangerous reflection on the Crunch of 2008 takes the form, "The bankers got their bailout, so why shouldn't the builders/distressed homeowners/auto manufacturers etc. get theirs?" The second most dangerous is from Rahm Emanuel, President Obama's chief of staff: "You never want a serious crisis to go to waste." Combined, they wedge open the Treasury's gates. Of course, so did the original bank bailouts. I have contended that, although clumsily handled, these bailouts represented the least bad alternative at the time. It is, however, a serious error to conflate bank rescue with the various spending packages that followed Lehman Brothers' demise.

The reason for infusing the banks with capital was not a humanitarian concern for harried bankers; no group on earth has a weaker claim on grounds of distributive justice for relief. Rather, it was to prevent further pain from engulfing those who rely on access to credit. Directly or indirectly, that includes almost everyone. Although on one level it would have been supremely gratifying to see the proximate causes of financial distress go down in flames, consumed in the ashes of their own cupidity,[44] spite is a dubious basis for policy. The realistic alternative is to shore up battered institutions until they can stand on their own. Policy authorities did not do this smoothly, they did not do it in a manner that inspired confidence, and they certainly did not do it in a timely fashion. However, before everything fell apart, the financial landscape was refashioned so as to avoid a second Great Depression. Perhaps not even two cheers are merited, but an honest appraisal should acknowledge that as bad as the aftermath of Lehman Brothers was, it could have been worse.

Other bailouts are more questionable. Clasping a bankrupt General Motors to the federal bosom was economically unjustifiable, although for a newly elected Obama administration it may have been politically irresistible. To be sure, when an ordinary industrial firm chalks up a steady stream of losses, it does externalize costs over the whole economic landscape. General Motors' slow dying negatively impacted its many suppliers, dealerships, employees, and the municipalities dependent on them. However, if it goes into liquidation, its productive assets do not suddenly disappear. Rather, they are available to be put in the hands of those who are better able to generate value from them. Plants, skilled workers, and technology will be reallocated. In the process some will lose out, but others—Ford, Toyota, possibly holders of senior debt and U.S. taxpayers—

---

stand the text of this legislation (available at http://thomas.loc.gov/cgi-bin/query/z?c111:H.R.4173:), let alone to pronounce on the likelihood that it will improve the financial environment. At any rate, a thoroughly globalized financial industry does not take all its cues from the United States.

[44] This is meant metaphorically. There are many Americans who would endorse it literally. I'm not sure that I couldn't be talked into becoming one of them.

will be gainers. Unlike bank meltdowns, this destruction is genuinely creative. I admit that this is a conceptually difficult point. Losers from a General Motors liquidation are clearly identifiable, especially by themselves and the politicians for whom they vote. Gainers, however, are dispersed and largely anonymous. This is the stuff of a Principles of Economics course, but most Americans weren't A students in their econ class.

State ownership inevitably conduces to state management and then to state micromanagement. Is it really the task of the White House to decide when to sack the CEO and with whom to replace him? Or to determine salary levels and bonuses of executives who work for companies in which the government has a stake? The politically indicated answer is yes. A central precept of foundational liberal theory is state neutrality concerning citizens' (rights-respecting) activities, but ownership precludes neutrality. What the government chooses not to prohibit, it thereby chooses to allow. Many of these determinations will benefit some citizens at the expense of others. The political constellation of forces rather than narrow economic rationality will determine how they work themselves out. Other decisions engage the passions: for example, "obscene" AIG bonuses paid out only a few weeks after the firm's rescue.[45] It is unrealistic to suppose that policymakers will be able simultaneously to heed the legitimate concerns of their constituents (not to mention heeding some concerns that are a good deal less than legitimate) while prudently managing enterprises that have fallen into their lap. This is true of banking as much as it is of automobile manufacturing, but entry into the latter field was chosen, not forced. The next choice should be to exit as deftly and as soon as possible.

Once the banks were cosseted, governments of the United States, the United Kingdom, and, to a more limited extent, Europe turned to stimulus packages. Debates over their efficacy go back generations, and this is not the place to attempt an independent assessment. It is undeniable that the pace of economic transactions slowed dramatically in the wake of Lehman Brothers and that governmental purchases and transfers counteracted the slowdown to some extent. It is also undeniable that the national deficits of these countries will be massively greater a decade from now than they are today. (In fairness, it should be noted that deep recession would have bloated deficits even in the absence of explicit stimulus.) Addressing deficits will involve some level of higher taxation, inflation, or both. (In theory, it could occasion spending decreases, but that would be to let the crisis go to waste. Expanded health care coverage, green energy, and educational subsidies may or may not be justified in their own right, but they are not compatible with a decrease on the expenditure side of the budget.) Financing a larger deficit means higher

---

[45] See Andrew Samwick, "AIG Bonuses: Some Perspective," http://www.capitalgains andgames.com/blog/andrew-samwick/817/aig-bonuses-some-perspective/.

interest rates, crowding out of some private borrowers, and concomitantly reduced rates of growth. Programs created or expanded in the name of temporary stimulus create constituencies that will be loath to relinquish their largesse. Even if the gravity of the emergency did indeed justify passage of stimulus measures, one of the hardest to learn lessons of Lehman Brothers will be how to reverse the expansion. Democracies are simply not very adept at destimulating.

The task for liberals/libertarians in the post–Lehman Brothers environment is to continue to remind those who can be persuaded to listen that invisible hands really do direct market relations, and that interference with their workings is generally counterproductive. For example, as unemployment rates jump and then remain discouragingly high, protectionist impulses predictably rear their head. Adam Smith was aware that those who succumb to the blandishments of beggar-thy-neighbor also beggar themselves. That seems, however, to be a message impossible to impart once and for all. Programs such as paying people large subsidies to junk functional vehicles and purchase new ones that are more fuel efficient ("Cash for Clunkers") need to be described as what they are: silly. Nothing new here.

I am sure that some of those who read this essay will conclude that there is nothing new, period. Verities are as they were in the mid-1930s when Hayek debated Keynes. I respectfully disagree. Liberal enthusiasm for invisible-hand interactions should not blind one to the fact that this is not the universal form taken by interaction, not even in markets. Prisoner's dilemmas are real, and they are lethal. They can be engendered (or, conversely, overcome) by innovations in law, technology, or common practice. An enthusiasm for liberty that shows itself oblivious to the imposition of external costs is an enthusiasm that is, at best, incomplete. A more adequate understanding will recognize the need from time to time to develop new institutional structures, both private and governmental, to secure better trade-offs between the two parameters. Liberalism requires not only a creed but wisdom. If Dr. Johnson is correct in claiming that the prospect of hanging concentrates the mind wonderfully, then perhaps the near-death experience of September 2008 will indeed have left us a bit wiser.

Philosophy, University of Virginia

A LOCKEAN ARGUMENT FOR UNIVERSAL ACCESS TO HEALTH CARE*

By Daniel M. Hausman

I. Introduction

One important and heated contemporary debate concerns what role government should play in guaranteeing or providing access to health care. Given the general skepticism about government action that characterizes many libertarians and classical liberals, one might think that they should be firmly opposed to government involvement. Yet I shall argue that there is a good argument to be made from a classical liberal and, more specifically, Lockean perspective for government action to guarantee access to health care. Indeed, I shall suggest that this argument is in some regards more robust than the well-known argument in defense of universal health care spelled out by Norman Daniels.

According to John Locke, the chief end of civil society and of government is the protection of property, where property includes property in oneself.[1] So the protection of property includes protection of lives and protection of persons from assault. It is puzzling why Locke folds personal security into the protection of property, especially since Locke maintains that most property arises as an unforeseen consequence of the consent people have given to the use of money. The answers to this puzzle that seem most faithful to Locke lie in the instrumental importance of property to self-determination and to life itself and in the instrumental importance of the security of property to social prosperity. In Locke's era, property set one free to make one's own choices. Without property, one's choice set was restricted and, in addition, one would be at the beck and call of another. As Adam Smith wrote of a North American "artificer" who chooses to become a planter,

> He feels that an artificer is the servant of his customers, from whom he derives his subsistence; but that a planter who cultivates his own

* Portions of this paper were delivered at a conference in December 2008 in honor of the publication of Norman Daniels's book *Just Health* (Cambridge: Cambridge University Press, 2007). I am indebted to participants at that conference, particularly Norman Daniels. J. Paul Kelleher commented on the paper on that occasion, and he also offered helpful criticisms of a subsequent draft of this essay. I am also indebted to Allen Buchanan, Norman Fost, and Robert Streiffer for comments on earlier versions of this essay. The final version profited from detailed criticisms by Ellen Frankel Paul and by other contributors to this volume.

[1] John Locke, *Second Treatise of Government* (1690), in John Locke, *Two Treatises of Government*, ed. Peter Laslett (Cambridge: Cambridge University Press, 1960), secs. 85, 138, 222.

doi:10.1017/S0265052510000257

land, and derives his necessary subsistence from the labour of his own family, is really a master, and independent of all the world.[2]

Although Locke is an emphatic defender of private property, he obviously did not defend industrial or post-industrial capitalism, which he could not have foreseen. He envisions an economy dominated by agriculture, where the most important nonhuman property is land. Unlike contemporary liberals who emphasize neutrality and who see the main or even sole goal of the state to be the protection of freedom, Locke repeatedly endorses the promotion of welfare as an objective of government. For example, he writes, "The end of Government is the good of Mankind. . . ."[3] That objective is, however, constrained by a prohibition on the taking of property.[4] Exactly what Locke means by "the good of Mankind" is not entirely clear. Presumably, he has in mind happiness, health, and prosperity, not merely the protection of rights.

The prohibition on the state taking people's property is, in turn, tempered by a surprisingly sweeping defense of taxation. In principle, Locke opens the way to big government when he writes:

> 'Tis true, Governments cannot be supported without great Charge, and 'tis fit every one who enjoys his share of the Protection, should pay out of his Estate his proportion for the maintenance of it. But still it must be with his own Consent, *i.e.* the Consent of the Majority, giving it either by themselves, or their Representatives chosen by them.[5]

Locke did not intend to defend an expansive welfare state, which, like advanced capitalism, he could scarcely have envisioned, but he does think that the government should promote welfare and that taxation is justified if a majority approves. Since he is obviously also very concerned to protect property rights and to limit government, it is not surprising that there are different interpretations of Locke and different versions of liberalism.

If one fast-forwards three centuries to post-industrial societies, questions about the role of the government look rather different than they did to Locke. As Smith and Marx emphasized, the extension of the market brings individuals into intricate, anonymous relations with multitudes of other people spread across the globe. Although in many ways mutually beneficial, these relations are not uniformly so. Negative externalities have

---

[2] Adam Smith, *An Inquiry into the Nature and Causes of the Wealth of Nations* (1776; Oxford: Oxford University Press, 1976), Book III, chapter 1.

[3] Locke, *Second Treatise*, sec. 229.

[4] "*Thirdly, The Supream Power cannot take* from any Man any part of his *Property* without his own consent." Ibid., sec. 138 (emphasis in the original).

[5] Ibid., sec. 140.

grown apace with the expansion of markets. In addition, huge enterprises concentrate the benefits and the drawbacks of market relations and private ownership of the means of production. Many of those who have experienced the downside of the development of the market have demanded that the government intervene both to regulate the market and to provide goods and services that the market fails to provide in what they deem to be an adequate way. These interferences have been controversial both politically and philosophically, and they have created opportunities for corruption, rent-seeking, and bureaucratic bloat.

II. Sketch of a Lockean Argument for Government Action to Secure Public Health and Ensure Access to Health Care

Locke can be interpreted in different ways, and the guidance he provides concerning what government should do and when government should intervene in markets depends on how he is interpreted. Locke prohibits taking property without consent and emphasizes that property is central to self-preservation. But he also allows a majority vote to constitute consent, and he thinks government should promote welfare.

For the purposes of this essay, I shall suppose that the core political values of what I shall call "a Lockean" are (a) the protection of life and property, and (b) the protection of freedom, understood as independence and self-determination.[6] As I have already mentioned, Locke is concerned about welfare as well, and one could remain faithful to the text of the *Second Treatise* and nonetheless define a different and more welfarist Lockean. Equality of moral standing and rights is also obviously important to Locke,[7] but I shall take equality as governing the interpretation and implementation of the core values of life, property, and freedom, rather than as a separate value. I make no claim to have provided the one true interpretation of Locke.

Many twentieth- and twenty-first-century followers of Locke identify the protection of freedom with the protection of individual rights to be free of interference from others, and they regard the proper role of government to be limited to the protection of these individual rights. But Locke himself specified a broader role for government, and even if one restricts government action to the protection of life, property, and freedom, other things besides the protection of rights serves these ends. On

---

[6] As contemporary critics of Locke (especially among feminists) have noted, the extent to which any human being can be independent and self-determining is narrowly limited by the reality of human dependence in childhood, sickness, and old age, and by more-general human needs for emotional support and cultural definition. See, for example, Eva Feder Kittay, *Love's Labor: Essays on Women, Equality, and Dependency* (New York: Routledge, 1999). Emphasizing dependency grounds rather different arguments for health-care provision, which I will not explore in this essay.

[7] Locke himself speaks of "that equal right, that every man hath, to his natural freedom, without being subjected to the will or authority of any other man," *Second Treatise*, sec. 54.

my interpretation of a version of liberalism that is faithful to Locke, government action to secure any objective is justified if and only if it satisfies three conditions:

(1) The objective of the government action is crucial to independence and self-determination;
(2) People cannot secure for themselves the objective of the government action; and
(3) Government action to secure the objective does not itself undermine the protection of life, property, and freedom.

If there are other things that government can do besides protecting rights that meet these conditions, then government will have an obligation to do those things, too. These cursory remarks stipulate my starting place.

Many of those who reject liberalism also value life, property, and freedom (along with equality and welfare), but nonliberals may interpret freedom and equality differently, and they typically place less weight on freedom and more weight on welfare and equality. Nonliberals may have other core values, such as solidarity, salvation, or national glory. For the purposes of this essay, the reader can take the preoccupation with protecting life, property, and freedom (in the sense of independence and self-determination) as a stipulative definition of a "Lockean."

The question I hope to answer in this essay is whether in affluent countries such as the United States, there is a Lockean case for government action to secure public health and to ensure that everyone has effective access to basic medical care. Those who have embraced Locke's liberalism have usually opposed government intervention in the market provision of goods and services (other than public safety and self-defense), and for good reasons. But health is so important to self-preservation and freedom, and both public health measures and medical care (unlike other necessities such as food and shelter) are so difficult for individuals to provide for themselves, that just as a liberal defends government protection of public safety, so a liberal might defend the public protection of health. The public protection of health arguably satisfies the three justifying conditions specified above and thus, like the protection of individual rights, would be a legitimate function of government.

Medical care or public health measures are, of course, no more synonymous with health than policing is synonymous with public safety, and some aspects of health care (like some aspects of personal security) should be conceptualized and treated in the same way as consumption goods such as food, clothing, or books, which individuals can provide for themselves. In fact, it is only relatively recently that medicine has become sufficiently effective that health care matters to the health of a population. Medical care still, on average, makes less difference to people's health than housing, nutrition, education, and social status, but its efficacy is growing and the cases in which it saves people from death or severe morbidity are every day more numerous. On the interpretation of Locke stipulated above, there is a case for government action to ensure that people get health care if the three justifying conditions are met.

If government should ensure that people get basic health care, it does not follow that government should *provide* health care, because providing health care is not necessarily the best way of ensuring that people get it, and because government provision of health care might conflict with other core values or might otherwise make people worse off. Yet if "the preservation of Property" is "the end of Government, and that for which Men enter into Society,"[8] and if property includes our lives and bodies, then it seems that Government should be deeply concerned about the preservation of our bodies and hence (assuming the efficacy of health care) concerned with basic health care.

My goal is to explore this sketchy argument for *universal effective access to basic health care* and determine whether it is sound. I shall not attempt to clarify what health care counts as "basic," other than to note that whether health care is basic or not depends on its efficacy, its expense (and other factors that interfere with individual provision), and the extent to which it affects life and independence. One might say that "basic" health care is care that is known to be crucial to life and normal functioning and not so expensive that making sure that everyone has it will seriously diminish people's freedom. Clearly, what counts as basic medical care will be a contentious matter and will vary depending on the wealth of a society and changes in technology. An appendectomy will clearly count as basic medical care in the United States, while most cosmetic surgery is not basic. But there is a great deal in between.

By "universal effective access" to a particular set of health care services, I shall mean the state of affairs in which all residents are normally able to get these services without severe difficulty or hardship. Universal effective access does not require state provision, but it cannot in fact be secured without a good deal of government involvement. The high cost of many treatments and the unpredictability of needs for them make it impossible for individual savings to provide universal access.[9] Voluntary private insurance fails to provide universal access, because it is beyond many people's means, and severe adverse selection problems[10] cause market

---

[8] Locke, *Second Treatise*, sec. 138. Of course, I am not reading "the preservation of Property" merely as protection from predation; but as I argued at the beginning of this essay, there are ample textual grounds for a broader interpretation.

[9] Simple appendectomies cost on average more than $15,000 in the United States.

[10] There is adverse selection, because health insurance is a better investment for those who have reason to think they will need medical care. So insurance premiums must be increased, which makes health insurance an increasingly bad investment for those who are in good health. To combat problems of adverse selection, insurance companies refuse to cover preexisting conditions, which holds down the cost of health insurance while at the same time making health insurance effectively unavailable for those who need it most. The

failures. How much government involvement is required depends in part on the set of health care services to which access should be universal, and, as we shall see, the Lockean defender of universal effective access will have a different conception of which services everyone should be able to access than other proponents of universal access. Although I will be concerned with what health care services people should have access to, this essay will not be concerned with problems of implementing universal access.

A Lockean liberal must be concerned about the fact that when the government guarantees universal access, regardless of how this is implemented, government agencies or the insurance companies the government subsidizes will have to make choices about which drugs and procedures are covered and which are not. Though such choices are often described as rationing, what is being rationed is not medical care, but insurance coverage. Individuals are still free, if they have the means, to seek other treatments and purchase other drugs. From the perspective of those who cherish freedom, it would unquestionably be better for individual choices not to be so heavily influenced by bureaucrats in insurance companies or government agencies, but there is no way to secure individual choice without at the same time depriving people of the financial wherewithal to make meaningful choices. The best one can do is to endorse policies that require that individuals pay for their own inexpensive routine care, perhaps with the addition of vouchers or subsidies for those who are indigent, while at the same time insuring everyone against more expensive conditions.[11]

I shall develop the Lockean case for government provision of public health measures and basic health care by comparing it to Norman Daniels's semi-Rawlsian and largely egalitarian defense of a state guarantee of universal access to health care. Since Daniels rests the case for universal access to health care on a principle requiring fair equality of opportunity, one might question whether Daniels could be a useful foil for a Lockean account of health care provision. Rawls's and Daniels's egalitarian concern with disparities in economic advantage, life prospects, and the range of choices available to individuals is foreign to Locke and to most classical liberals. Yet there are affinities. Although they are not Lockeans, Rawls

discussion in this paragraph marks a crucial point of disagreement with Loren Lomasky's otherwise complementary discussion in "Medical Progress and National Health Care," *Philosophy and Public Affairs* 10 (1981): 65–88.

[11] Making such a system work is very difficult. An approximation can be found in Singapore, in which two-thirds of the funding for health care comes from private funds, and government-sponsored health insurance covers only "catastrophic" expenses. But to make this work requires incursions on individual freedom in the form of mandatory health savings, regulation of health-care provision and costs, and significant subsidies. See John Tucci, "The Singapore Health System—Achieving Positive Health Outcomes with Low Expenditure," *Towers Watson Healthcare Market Review,* http://www.watsonwyatt.com/europe/pubs/healthcare/render2.asp?ID=13850.

and Daniels are both liberals, and opportunity is an interpretation of
freedom (though obviously not the same thing as self-determination). In
any case, I hope to show that the comparison between Daniels's case and
a Lockean case is instructive. The Lockean case for universal access to
health care has significant advantages over Daniels's case, but it faces
some of the same objections, as well as problems of its own.

III. Daniels's Case for Universal Access to Health Care

Over the past four decades, Norman Daniels has developed a comprehensive liberal-egalitarian (and definitely not Lockean) view of what justice requires with respect to health care and, more generally, with respect
to the protection and improvement of health. His view is philosophically
sophisticated and practically applicable, and on my reading of the literature, no alternative account comes close to matching its comprehensive-
ness. In his 2007 book *Just Health*, Daniels incorporates his views on
health care into a larger theory of justice with respect to health, but his
account of what justice requires with respect to health care is essentially
unchanged from the account he defended in his 1985 book *Just Health
Care*.[12]

Daniels endorses the "biostatistical" view of health defended by Christopher Boorse,[13] which takes health to consist in the statistically normal
functioning of the parts and processes that make up human bodies and
minds. Diminished health prevents people from doing some things and
pursuing certain life-plans. Daniels maintains that because diminished
health in this sense limits opportunity, it raises questions of justice. (A
Lockean will instead point to the consequences of diminished health for
freedom, property, and life itself.) The principle of justice Daniels invokes
to govern the provision of health care and public health measures is a
reinterpretation of John Rawls's fair equality of opportunity principle.[14]
In Daniels's egalitarian view, the same range of life-plans should be available to those whose talents and motivation are the same. Just as justice (as
embodied in fair equality of opportunity) requires the elimination of
social barriers that limit opportunities, so it requires protecting and restoring health, subject to feasibility constraints, resource limitations, and com-

[12] Norman Daniels, *Just Health* (Cambridge: Cambridge University Press, 2007); Norman
Daniels, *Just Health Care* (Cambridge: Cambridge University Press, 1985).
[13] See Christopher Boorse, "Health as a Theoretical Concept," *Philosophy of Science* 44
(1977): 542–73; and Boorse, "A Rebuttal on Health," in James Humber and Robert Almeder,
eds., *What Is Disease?* (Totowa, NJ: Humana Press, 1997), 1–134. Jerome Wakefield defends
a very similar account in "The Concept of Mental Disorder: On the Boundary between
Biological Facts and Social Values," *American Psychologist* 47 (1992): 373–88; Wakefield, "Disorder as Harmful Dysfunction: A Conceptual Critique of DSM-III-R's Definition of Mental
Disorder," *Psychological Review* 99 (1992): 232–47; and Wakefield, "The Concept of Mental
Disorder: Diagnostic Implications of the Harmful Dysfunction Analysis," *World Psychiatry* 6
(2007): 149–56.
[14] John Rawls, *A Theory of Justice* (Cambridge, MA: Harvard University Press, 1971).

peting moral considerations. Daniels says little about the claims of those who cannot be restored to normal functioning, just as the Lockean will say little about the claims of those whose life expectancy and independence cannot be protected or enhanced by health care.

Daniels maintains that, other things being equal, justice with respect to health requires that everyone possess their "fair share" of the normal opportunity range, and that a necessary condition to secure to everyone their fair share of the normal opportunity range is providing universal access to health care. As Daniels is well aware, other factors (such as education, nutrition, housing, stress, and lifestyle) have a greater overall influence on health than does health care, and he does not clarify why fair equality of opportunity should lead a Rawlsian liberal to single out health care. Presumably, the explanation turns on the urgency of health care and the inability of individuals to provide for their own health care.

Although a Lockean, as I have characterized her, would not make Daniels's argument, there are some affinities between the two, and it is worth looking more carefully at the philosophical premises of Daniels's argument. In *A Theory of Justice* (1971), Rawls formulates two principles of justice to govern the basic structure of society:

> First, each person is to have an equal right to the most extensive basic liberty compatible with a similar liberty for others.[15]
>
> Second: social and economic inequalities are to be arranged so that they are both (a) to the greatest benefit of the least advantaged and (b) attached to offices and positions open to all under conditions of fair equality of opportunity.[16]

Advantage is measured in terms of social primary goods: rights and liberties, opportunities and powers, income and wealth, and the social bases of self-respect. The least advantaged is the least advantaged "representative agent" or social class. Provided that the institutions of a society satisfy the principles of justice, the specific distribution among individuals is a matter of pure procedural justice. Satisfying the first principle (which is closer to Locke's views than the second, but will not be under discussion in this essay) is lexically prior to satisfying the second principle, and part (b) of the second principle—that is, fair equality of opportunity—is supposed to be lexically prior to part (a), the so-called difference principle. In *A Theory of Justice*, Rawls idealizes and supposes that all citizens are in full health over their lifetime. Thirty years later, in his last restatement of the theory in *Justice as Fairness* (2001), Rawls remarks that

---

[15] Ibid., 60.
[16] Ibid., 83.

provision for medical care . . . is to meet the needs and requirements of citizens as free and equal. Such care falls under the general means necessary to underwrite fair equality of opportunity and our capacity to take advantage of our basic rights and liberties, and thus to be normal and fully cooperating members of society over a complete life.[17]

Notice that Rawls suggests that medical care helps to make the equality called for by his first principle of justice substantial rather than merely formal. Although the interpretation of equality goes well beyond the equality of status and rights that Locke endorses, these remarks suggest a liberal conception of health care as enabling individuals to enjoy the rights and liberties that justice promotes and protects.

Rawls formulates what he calls "fair equality of opportunity" as an improvement over mere "formal equality of opportunity." The latter rules out formal barriers to "positions and offices" but leaves in place informal barriers rooted in status, wealth, education, social contacts, race, gender, religious affiliation, and so forth. Fair equality of opportunity aims to eliminate such social barriers. Given the full-health idealization in *A Theory of Justice*, eliminating such social barriers implies that those whose talents and motivation are the same have the same expectations of employment and status. Talents and motivation include all nonpathological traits of a person that are relevant to employment and status.[18] I shall use the word "talents" to include not only skills and abilities, but also character traits such as ambition, perseverance, effort, and willingness to take risks.

Fair equality of opportunity is only a fragment of a theory of distributive justice, which may demand very little. Without any specification of what constitutes a "talent," of when talents are "equal," or of how talents ought to influence the probability of achieving a position, fair equality of opportunity may require a good deal less than what Rawls and Daniels intend.[19] Furthermore, from Rawls's and Daniels's egalitarian perspective, even if we clarify the nature of a talent, the criteria that determine which talents count as "the same," and how talents should matter, the rewards and status attached to social positions may be unjust. Fair equality of opportunity by itself places no limits on disparities between the opportunities of individuals whose talents differ or between the outcomes of those whose talents and opportunities are equal.[20]

---

[17] John Rawls, *Justice as Fairness: A Restatement*, ed. Erin Kelly (Cambridge, MA: Harvard University Press, 2001), 174.

[18] Daniels is ambivalent about special sensitivities to workplace toxins and hazards, which he is hesitant to assimilate either to "talents" or to traits that should be irrelevant if fair equality of opportunity obtains. See Daniels, *Just Health Care*, chap. 8, and Daniels, *Just Health*, chap. 7.

[19] Richard Arneson, "Against Rawlsian Equality of Opportunity," *Philosophical Studies* 93 (1999): 77–112.

[20] I am indebted here to J. Paul Kelleher.

Within Rawls's theory, the difference principle (coupled with the restriction to ideal theory) addresses these limitations of fair equality of opportunity. Within "ideal theory," where there is strict compliance with the principles of justice, what counts as a talent will not be biased by racism, sexism, or national or religious animosity, and the rewards attached to talents will be determined by economic institutions structured so as to maximize the primary-goods prospects of the least well-off representative individual. When combined as Rawls proposes, the separate elements reinforce one another and constitute a strongly egalitarian theory.

Even though fair equality of opportunity is only one piece of Rawls's theory of distributive justice, it seems to be the sole principle from which Daniels derives his conclusions concerning justice with respect to health care. Daniels borrows the notion of fair equality of opportunity from Rawls, but expands the scope of "opportunity." As one commentator puts it, "Rawlsian 'opportunity' refers to the individual's socially-determined chance of achieving one of the privileged places in society. Daniels's 'opportunity' refers to the individual's chance of achieving any of the goals contained in any of the life plans that can be reasonably adopted in the society."[21] Daniels needs to expand the scope of opportunities in this way, since no one would trace the relevance of health to justice exclusively to the consequences of health for employment.

The extent of a person's opportunities in the sense Daniels employs is equivalent to the set of life-plans that are open to the person. These depend both on the person—on her talents and health—and on features of the society within which the person lives, including the principles of justice that govern the society and the extent of compliance with the principles. To speak of a person's opportunities in this sense is to make a counterfactual claim about what the person could reasonably have chosen in the particular society. Thus, for example, we might say that I enjoyed the opportunity to choose and pursue many life-plans that I never had any interest in choosing and that are impossible for me to pursue now. Perhaps I once had the opportunity to be a musician, but that opportunity was gone decades ago. The relevant notion of opportunity is not conditional on my past choices or my past or present desires.[22]

---

[21] Laurence Stern, "Opportunity and Health Care: Criticisms and Suggestions," *Journal of Medicine and Philosophy* 8 (1983): 339–61, at 340. As Daniels puts it in *Just Health*, 58–59, "The notion Rawls uses is a narrow one focused on producing fairness in the competition for jobs and careers. We are using opportunity range in a broader—and admittedly vaguer—sense when we think about the impact of health on individual shares of the normal opportunity range, that is, the array of life plans persons can reasonably choose in a given society." See also Daniels, *Just Health Care*, 50. In expanding the meaning of "opportunity," Daniels is severing the historical and conceptual connection between equality of opportunity and the notion of "careers open to talents."
[22] Daniels distinguishes the opportunity in question from what I can currently do, which he calls my "effective opportunities." See Daniels, *Just Health*, 45.

What Daniels calls "the normal opportunity range" for a given society consists of all the life-plans that are possible in that society with any array of talents. The normal opportunity range depends on the economic and technological development of the society, its geography and climate, its culture, its forms of social organization, and so forth. The whole of the normal opportunity range could not be open to any individual, because no one person could have (for example) the talents to be both a ballet dancer and a defensive tackle. In Daniels's view (as in Rawls's), limitations on a person's share of the normal opportunity range that result from the person's "talents" are not unjust,[23] unlike limitations due to social factors such as religious discrimination. Daniels maintains that remediable or compensable bad health also unfairly restricts an individual's share of the normal opportunity range. Daniels stipulates that each person's *fair share* of the normal opportunity range in a particular society S is the share of the normal opportunity range that individuals in full health with the person's talents would have if S were otherwise just. Why are these shares "fair" shares? In Daniels's view, "The special importance we attribute to meeting health needs, then, can be explained by the weight we attach to protecting our shares of the normal opportunity range against departures from normal functioning."[24]

Daniels takes Rawls's theory of justice, when coupled with this reinterpretation of opportunity, to imply a more specific principle governing health care:

Daniels's Principle: Other things being equal, justice with respect to health care requires the prevention or cure of health deficiencies to protect or restore normal species functioning.[25]

Daniels does not explicitly formulate what I have labeled "Daniels's Principle," but it fairly summarizes his central principle governing the distribution of health care and public health measures. "Normal species functioning" is "full" health—the absence of any pathology that limits an individual's share of the normal opportunity range. The normal opportunity range is relative to the society, and an individual's fair share depends on his or her talent level. The "other things being equal" clause is complicated, since there are feasibility constraints, resource limitations, and

[23] Provided that the society treats different "talents" fairly. For example, an affluent society that subjected those without mathematical aptitude to abject poverty would not be just. Daniels briefly notes the need for background justice on p. 41 of *Just Health Care*, though he seems to suppose that fair equality of opportunity can do most of the work.
[24] Daniels, *Just Health*, 44.
[25] "Similarly, institutions meeting health needs have the limited function of maintaining normal functioning" (ibid., 60). In *Just Health,* Daniels also requires that there be a fair distribution of the (nonmedical) socially controllable factors influencing the risks of disease, but this essay is concerned exclusively with his views on health care.

competing moral interests. In the interest of brevity, I shall avoid repeating these important qualifications, but they will later be important to appraising the Lockean case for universal access. As Daniels notes, it is sometimes more efficient to mitigate the effects of ill-health on opportunity than to prevent or cure ill-health.

The conclusion that Daniels draws concerning the special importance of health is controversial, even if one endorses fair equality of opportunity. Like the Lockean liberal, Daniels emphasizes freedom, but unlike the Lockean, he identifies freedom with opportunity rather than with self-determination. Regardless of how freedom should be interpreted, health in fact matters to other things besides freedom. It is both a component and an important cause of well-being, and the way in which a society responds to poor health matters to social solidarity. As others have pointed out, the exclusive focus on opportunity seems exaggerated.[26] Someone suffering from colitis or depression may be more concerned with how miserable they are feeling than with the extent to which their health limits either their opportunity or their self-determination. People with severe dementia lose themselves and their relations to others, not just their ability to direct their own lives. Daniels notes the connection between health and subjective well-being,[27] but he questions whether the importance of health to well-being can ground an account of health *needs,* and he devotes his efforts constructively to developing his opportunity-based alternative to a welfarist view.[28] In emphasizing that the relevance of health to justice lies mainly in its implications for opportunity, Daniels need not (and does not) deny that health is important in other ways. Similarly, even if the Lockean case for government action to guarantee access to basic health care rests on the importance of health to life and self-determination, the Lockean need not deny that health matters in other ways.

Suppose one grants Daniels's view that the relevance of health to justice lies mainly in its effects on opportunity. Does Daniels's principle follow? Whether justice requires that health care be singled out for special treatment or implies a right to health care is controversial. As Daniels recognizes, education, wealth, security, nutrition, and shelter all have significant effects on opportunity, too. Furthermore, even if universal access to health care is a moral imperative, it does not follow that government action is required. Further argument, which Daniels only sketches, is needed. Similarly, the analogous case for the importance of health care to the protection of life and self-determination does not, by itself, imply that there is any need for government to act. A crucial additional premise

[26] See Allen Buchanan, "The Right to a Decent Minimum of Health Care," *Philosophy and Public Affairs* 13 (1984): 55–78, at 63; and Stern "Opportunity and Health Care," 345f.
[27] Daniels, *Just Health,* 35.
[28] For an extended argument against evaluating health states by their bearing on well-being or preferences, see Daniel Hausman, "Valuing Health," *Philosophy and Public Affairs* 34 (2006): 246–74.

is needed to make both Daniels's case and the Lockean argument for government health-care provision. This additional premise is that, unlike nutrition, clothing, and shelter, which individuals can generally secure for themselves, most individuals cannot privately manage and pay for their health care.[29] The high cost and unpredictability of meeting health-care needs, plus the public-goods character of public health measures, make it impossible for individuals to pay for their own health care, and the combination of high costs and problems of adverse selection make it impossible for individuals to insure themselves. Daniels takes the importance of health to opportunity, coupled with the special features of health care needs, to imply that justice demands that everyone have effective access to health care for the prevention and treatment of disease and disability. "[T]he account supports the provision of universal access to appropriate health care. . . . Health care aimed at protecting fair equal opportunity should not be distributed according to ability to pay."[30] Lockeans can make an analogous argument, to which I now turn.

IV. A LOCKEAN-LIBERAL ARGUMENT FOR UNIVERSAL
ACCESS TO HEALTH CARE

Although Lockeans as I have characterized them would not endorse the fair equality of opportunity principle, they can recognize the importance of health to life and freedom (in the relevant sense of self-determination and independence), and the problems individuals face in providing for their own health care or in purchasing private health insurance.[31] Lockeans can then make an argument that to some extent mimics Daniels's argument. Rather than relying on the notion of fair shares of the normal opportunity range, the Lockean liberal can rely on the constructs of (statistically) normal life expectancy and of "normal freedom"—that is, normal prospects for self-determination and independence. Life expectancy is a well-defined and well-measured statistic. Normal freedom, in contrast, is vague and hard to measure, but not obviously any vaguer or harder to measure than Daniels's notion of a fair share of the normal opportunity range. Both normal life expectancy and normal freedom might appear to be averages that are independent of any questions concerning fairness and justice, but this contrast with Daniels is misleading. The statistical averages in a destitute autocracy are irrelevant. *Normal* prospects for self-determination and non-subjugation and *normal* life expectancies are implicitly normative. They are averages in just societies.

---

[29] Daniels does not distinguish health needs from needs such as food, clothing, and shelter in quite this way. He emphasizes, in contrast, the fact that health needs are more unequally distributed. See Daniels, *Just Health*, 61.

[30] Norman Daniels, "Justice, Health, and Health Care," *American Journal of Bioethics* 1, no. 2 (2001): 3–15, at 4.

[31] See Lomasky, "Medical Progress and National Health Care."

Because the Lockean's central goals of government are the protection of life, property, and freedom, government has a role in addressing threats to life, property, and freedom when it is difficult or socially costly for individuals to protect themselves. Unlike those who read Locke as insisting that government only protect rights, I take Locke to be concerned with the whole gamut of threats to life, property, and freedom. Crime, ignorance, malnutrition, tyrannical or bloated government, badly defined or poorly enforced property rights, foreign invasion, *and disease* all limit life expectancy or freedom. Individuals can and should cope with some of these threats themselves. But if individuals cannot protect themselves and government action is not itself a greater threat than the problem it aims to tackle, then government should act. If (1) health care and public health measures are effective ways of addressing the threats that disease poses to lives and freedom, (2) these measures do not themselves threaten freedom, and (3) individuals cannot provide their own health care, then government has a responsibility to insure that health care is available.[32] "That equal right, that every man hath, to his natural freedom"[33] implies that health care should be available to all.

This argument for universal access to health care relies on less controversial moral premises than Daniels makes use of. There is less disagreement about the importance of protecting people's lives and their ability to live independently than there is about promoting fair equality of opportunity. At the same time, the range of health care to which this argument justifies universal access is narrower than the range that Daniels would guarantee. Both would justify access to most health care that saves lives or that cures or prevents disabilities such as blindness, deafness, and paraplegia, which may limit independence and self-determination. But there are many pathologies that limit people's shares of the normal opportunity range without threatening either their lives or their freedom (in the sense of self-determination and independence). Consider, for example, infertility, impotence, mild myopia, neurosis, or moderate back pain.

The argument this section has presented defending universal access to health care that protects life and freedom has many loose ends. In particular, a defender of freedom might argue that government regulation of health care, let alone government provision of health care, diminishes freedom more than the promotion of health increases freedom. This diminution of freedom might come about relatively directly by undermining self-reliance,[34] interfering with the choices of individuals and health-care

---

[32] As Lomasky points out, there are important disanalogies between the case for state provision of national defense and crime prevention, which rests in part on the state's monopoly on the use of force, and the case for state protection of health. See ibid., 73. Crucial to the argument in the text is the empirical claim that individuals cannot provide for themselves, even with the help of an insurance market.

[33] Locke, *Second Treatise*, sec. 54.

[34] One of H. B. Acton's main complaints against government provision of goods to satisfy basic needs is that it undermines individual initiative. See Acton, *The Morals of Markets and*

providers, or increasing the burdens of taxation. By enlarging the scope of government, guaranteed access to health care may also create indirect long-run risks to freedom. With respect to relatively inexpensive public health measures and protection against pandemics or chemical or biological warfare, these qualms are hard to defend. But the connection between health care and health is tenuous, and qualms concerning the consequences for freedom of extensive guarantees of health care are not unreasonable.

To assess and fill in this sketchy case for universal access to health care, it will be instructive to examine whether criticisms of Daniels's account also apply to this Lockean-liberal argument for universal access.

V. Health, Health Care, and Fair Shares of the Normal Opportunity Range

In developing his account of justice with respect to health, Daniels relies on Christopher Boorse's insightful view of health as species-typical functioning.[35] Boorse develops the view of health implicit in physiology and pathology, conceiving of organisms as functionally organized systems whose parts and processes enable them to survive and reproduce. When some part or process is operating at a statistically abnormally low level of efficiency, then there is a pathology, and the organism is in diminished health. Many pathologies are trivial, while the effects of others may be mitigated by redundancy built into the organism. The malfunction of one kidney, for example, is a pathological condition, even though it may have no consequences for an individual's survival or reproduction.

The normal function of parts and processes in human beings differs between men and women and at different ages. The inability of infants to walk or of men to bear children is not pathological. So the reference class with respect to which the functioning of some part or process counts as

Related Essays, ed. David Gordon and Jeremy Shearmur (Indianapolis, IN: Liberty Fund, 1993), esp. 80–98.

[35] In Just Health, Daniels points out correctly that he need not take sides in the dispute between Boorse and Jerome Wakefield, who relies on a different account of functions and adds a requirement that poor health be harmful. The differences between Boorse's and Wakefield's accounts are also not relevant to the argument of this essay. Although Boorse's view of health is, in my view, the best one thus far proposed, it is not unproblematic. For example, it has no good way to characterize pathologies that are statistically typical. It faces a difficult line-drawing problem with respect to separating low but normal function from dysfunction, as argued by Peter Schwartz in "Defining Dysfunction: Natural Selection, Design, and Drawing a Line," Philosophy of Science 74 (2007): 364–85. For a very recent and serious criticism of Boorse's view of health, see Elselijn Kingma, "Paracetamol, Poison, and Polio: Why Boorse's Account of Function Fails to Distinguish Health and Disease," British Journal for the Philosophy of Science 61 (2010): 241–64. Boorse's view of functions is also controversial. For a comprehensive defense, see Christopher Boorse, "A Rebuttal on Functions," in André Ariew, Robert Cummins, and Mark Perlman, eds., Functions: New Essays in the Philosophy of Psychology and Biology (Oxford: Oxford University Press, 2002), 63–112.

normal or pathological should be an age group of a gender. Boorse's original definition of health thus reads as follows:

(1) The *reference class* is a natural class of organisms of uniform functional design; specifically, an age group of a sex of a species.
(2) A *normal function* of a part or process within members of the reference class is a statistically typical contribution by it to their individual survival and reproduction.
(3) A *disease* is a type of internal state which is either an impairment of normal functional ability, i.e., a reduction of one or more functional abilities below typical efficiency, or a limitation on functional ability caused by environmental agents.
(4) *Health* is the absence of disease.[36]

Boorse is using "disease" in a very general sense, in which any pathology or significantly diminished function of a part or process counts as a disease. So a broken leg or a headache counts as a "disease" in this sense. In later work, he substitutes the less misleading term "pathology" for "disease." The second clause in condition 3 is part of an unsuccessful attempt by Boorse to deal with the problem that some pathological states (such as tooth decay or hypertension) may be statistically typical rather than abnormal in some reference classes.[37] What is at issue in Boorse's account of health is the normal function of parts or processes, *not* the normal functioning of the person as a whole. When Daniels speaks of "species-typical functioning" or "normal species functioning," he could mean normal overall functioning or species-typical functioning of component parts and processes. These are not the same. If Daniels is following Boorse, he must mean the latter, but, as the kidney example illustrates, what matters to opportunity is in fact overall functioning rather than the functioning of a part or process.

As Boorse notes and Daniels recognizes, this account of pathology allows for the existence of pathological conditions that do not call for treatment or prevention, and for the existence of conditions that call for medical treatment or prevention that are not pathological. Daniels supports the provision of medical treatment of some nonpathological conditions, such as, notably, pregnancies and unwanted fertility. The existence of nonpathological conditions that call for medical treatment suggests that what matters morally is not literally health, nor even statistically normal overall functioning, but how functioning affects desired opportunities.

[36] Boorse, "Health as a Theoretical Concept," 562, 567.
[37] Boorse's current view is that medicine is mistaken to regard any conditions that are statistically normal within a reference group as diseases. See Boorse, "A Rebuttal on Functions," 103. The existence of such diseases means that the "normal opportunity range" may be exceptional rather than statistically normal within a given reference class within a society.

Given this conception of health, an analogous conclusion follows with respect to the Lockean argument in defense of access to health care. The inability to prevent or terminate unwanted pregnancies can obviously diminish women's independence and self-determination significantly, and arguably has a higher priority than pathologies such as infertility.[38] But if what is at issue is not literally health, but instead desired functioning or functioning that affects life and self-determination, one might wonder why the government should single out access to health care as opposed to access to all resources that individuals cannot provide for themselves that protect opportunity or, for the Lockean, life, property, and freedom.

Consider a hypothetical case Daniels discusses of a pill that would increase reading scores among the bottom 10 percent of readers (whose poor reading scores are not due to any known pathologies). Such a pill would apparently enhance the independence and self-determination as well as the opportunities of these semiliterate individuals. Suppose that an interactive computer game has the same effect as this pill. Daniels maintains that "we have no more reason to call the enhancement health care in the case of the pill than we do in the case of the computer game, even though the pill is a medical technology."[39] In Daniels's view, interventions that help people who are healthy but nevertheless "socially disabled," however worthy those interventions may be, do not constitute health care, and they are not within the purview of a theory of just health care. Rather than concluding that we should broaden the notion of health or shift the focus from health and health care as so narrowly defined, Daniels holds that fair equality of opportunity with respect to health care demands prevention or cure only of diminished health states.[40]

Yet Daniels believes that, other things being equal, society also ought to provide the reading-enhancement drug or computer game.[41] He does not make clear whether he thinks that this obligation has the same urgency or general form of justification as the obligation to provide a treatment for a pathology that would have the same consequences. For if the poor reading skills of the bottom 10 percent could be traced to a pathology, then this drug or computer game would be a treatment rather than an enhancement. If the obligation to provide it were just the same, then the distinction between treatments and enhancements would have only definitional significance.

Daniels's principle requires prevention and treatment of disease or disability, not enhancement of nonpathological traits, even when these

[38] Though possibly not in Locke's own view. The Hippocratic Oath he took forbade abortion, yet he questioned whether embryos have souls (*Second Treatise*, sec. 55). See Bradford Short, "The Healing Philosopher," *Issues in Law and Medicine* 20 (2004–5): 121–31.

[39] Daniels, *Just Health*, 155.

[40] Subject, of course, to the exceptions already mentioned of birth control and abortion. Daniels clearly recognizes that fair equality of opportunity has implications that extend far beyond health policy. See ibid., 96.

[41] Ibid., 155.

traits lead to overall functioning that significantly diminishes opportunity. Daniels defends this implication of his views mainly on two grounds. First, limiting obligations to treatment has administrative advantages. It draws a bright line to hold back the flood of demand for medical benefits. Second, echoing Rawls's argument for the difference principle, Daniels suggests that inequalities in traits or skills that are not the result of pathology are better addressed by making strategic use of the differences among people in order to improve everyone's lot. But Daniels allows for exceptions in "specific instances . . . where we can identify a highly efficient intervention to eliminate [nonpathological] traits that are obviously disadvantaging." [42] Daniels also suggests that, in the case of enhancements, the disadvantages of the health state and the benefits of the assistance are likely to be more subjective and debatable than in the case of treatments,[43] but as he acknowledges, this is not always the case. There are also separate questions I shall not address concerning interventions that provide people with capacities beyond the normal range of variation—the government provision of which the Lockean would certainly not favor.[44]

In addition to the consequences of some condition on the range of life-plans open to an individual and the cost and efficacy of a medical intervention, Daniels maintains that obligations to intervene depend on whether the condition derives from a pathology. Why should it matter? Indeed, distinguishing between a treatment and an equivalent enhancement seems, at first glance, inconsistent with fair equality of opportunity, since the effects on opportunity of the condition and its amelioration appear to be the same.

What purportedly justifies treating apparently similar cases differently is that fair equality of opportunity implies only that those whose "talents" are similar should have the same opportunities. The opportunities of those whose talents are different may differ. Recall that "talents" include

[42] Allen Buchanan, Dan Brock, Norman Daniels, and Daniel Wikler, *From Chance to Choice: Genetics and Justice* (Cambridge: Cambridge University Press, 2000), 129. In citing from this coauthored work, I risk conflating Daniels's views with those of his coauthors. On the one hand, although Daniels paraphrases and quotes in *Just Health* a good deal of material from this coauthored book, he does not repeat the explicit qualifications quoted here. On the other hand, the reading-enhancement example apparently provides an instance of such an exception. Buchanan, Brock, Daniels, and Wikler explore the apparent arbitrariness of treating a short child with a growth-hormone deficiency while refusing to treat another child with the same expected stature and responsiveness to treatment, who has no known pathology. Yet they never make explicit whether the much-discussed and clinically and economically important case of the use of human growth hormone to enhance short stature is one of the exceptions they have in mind. It might not be, because its enormous expense and the "arms race" to which it could lead imply that it is not "highly efficient."
[43] Daniels, *Just Health*, 151.
[44] See Michael Shapiro, "The Technology of Perfection: Performance Enhancement and the Control of Attributes," *Southern California Law Review* 15 (1991–92): 11–113; Michael Sandel, *The Case against Perfection: Ethics in the Age of Genetic Engineering* (Cambridge, MA: Harvard University Press, 2007); and Frances Kamm, "Is There a Problem with Enhancement?" *American Journal of Bioethics* 5 (2005): 5–14.

all those nonpathological traits of individuals that are relevant to their ability to form and execute life-plans. A poor reader who lacks any pathology is in this sense untalented, and, provided that his or her opportunities are no more limited than others who are similarly untalented, there may be no violation of fair equality of opportunity.[45] In contrast, someone who reads just as badly, but whose poor reading can be traced to a pathology, does not enjoy the same opportunities as others who have the same talent but lack the pathology; and, other things being equal, fair equality of opportunity requires prevention or remediation of the deficiency. Talents define the fair share of the normal opportunity range. Pathologies prevent individuals from enjoying their fair share.

This way of distinguishing the cases places a great deal of weight on the distinction between "low talent" and pathology.[46] The parts and processes of human beings function at varying degrees of efficiency. According to Boorse, there is a pathology when the level of functioning or capacity to function is in the lower tail of the distribution of efficiency of part function. Whether one has a case of "low talent" or a pathology will depend, accordingly, on where the line is drawn between, on the one hand, low but normal part functioning and, on the other hand, pathological functioning of the parts and processes that constitute the talent or the health condition. Exactly where to draw the line is, however, in Boorse's view arbitrary. There is nothing in theoretical medicine or biology that tells one whether the bottom 5 percent or 1 percent or .001 percent of liver function among some reference class divides the pathological from the nonpathological. Peter Schwartz argues against Boorse that even though theoretical medicine does not tell us where to draw the line, the choice is not always arbitrary.[47] Schwartz maintains, plausibly, that the location of the line between the pathological and the normal will depend on the consequences of the functional inefficiency. For example, suppose that in some reference class, liver function is highly uniform and only one in a thousand individuals has a degree of inefficiency in liver function that may limit his current or future activities or well-being. In that case, it would be odd to take those in the bottom 1 percent of liver function—

---

[45] As Allen Buchanan has pointed out to me, merely equal opportunity is not enough. Suppose that some people's talents resulted in highly restricted opportunities and that there were some easy intervention that could expand these opportunities. In that case, an egalitarian (or sufficientarian) who was concerned about opportunity would surely demand that the intervention be undertaken. This point harks back to the complaints in Section III about the limitations of the principle of fair equality of opportunity and forward to the central argument of Section VI.

[46] Lesley Jacobs makes a similar point: "Daniels could respond that from the perspective of equality of opportunity, the effects of some natural differences—those originating from differences in talents—are fair, but the effects of other natural differences—those originating from illness and disease—are unfair. The cogency of this response depends on the basis for this distinction." See Jacobs, "Can an Egalitarian Justify Universal Access to Health Care?" *Social Theory and Practice* 22 (1996): 315–48, at 337.

[47] Schwartz, "Defining Dysfunction."

90 percent of whom will never experience any pain or limitations—as suffering from liver disease. The line should be drawn farther into the tail of the distribution. If, in contrast, 30 percent of elderly men suffer from hypertension that places them at serious risk of strokes and kidney disease, then it would be just as misleading to regard as pathological only the 1 percent whose blood pressure is highest. What determines where to draw the line is the point at which the inefficiency of part function has a significant effect on overall functioning.

Whether the distinction between what is normal and what is pathological is largely arbitrary or whether it reflects judgments concerning the importance of the inefficiency of part function, the distinction does not justify Daniels's different treatment of disparities due to poor health and disparities due to low talent. If the differentiation between low talent and poor health is arbitrary, then inequalities deriving from the two sources should be treated alike. In contrast, if the distinction depends on whether part inefficiency has a significant effect on overall functioning (and hence opportunities), then limitations in opportunity due to an individual's physical and mental state would all count as pathologies.

If there is no nonarbitrary way to distinguish between poor health and low talent, then one cannot invoke fair equality of opportunity to condemn inequalities in opportunity due to poor health while condoning inequalities in opportunity due to low talent. Daniels has given no reason why we should regard poor health as unjustly diminishing opportunity, while the diminutions of opportunity that are due to low talent are not regarded as unjust.[48] Indeed, as my colleague J. Paul Kelleher has suggested to me, even if there were a nonarbitrary way of distinguishing low talent from poor health, Daniels has not explained why we should be concerned only with poor health. What is relevant appears to be how a condition affects people and whether health care can prevent or treat the condition, not whether it counts as a disease.

The Lockean argument in defense of universal provision of public health measures and basic health care avoids these difficulties, because it does

---

[48] One might distinguish those features of a person that are part of who the person essentially is and those features of a person that are merely accidental. One could then argue that essential traits would be the "talents" that define the reference class within which opportunity should be equal, while accidental traits would be the pathologies that limit opportunities within these reference classes. Such a line, which resembles part of Ronald Dworkin's view concerning which inequalities call for redress, might also help with the question of whether, in the context of employment law, insensitivities to pathogens should be regarded as "talents." But this proposal does not explain why the pathological is opportunity-limiting, while talents are not, because pathological traits can define people and talents can be accidental to who they are. Dworkin does not draw the line in quite this way. His line is between "those beliefs and attitudes that define what a successful life would be like, which the ideal [which holds that people should be compensated for those things for which they are not responsible] assigns to the person, and those features of body or mind or personality that provide means or impediments to that success, which the ideal assigns to the person's circumstances." See Ronald Dworkin, "What Is Equality? Part 2: Equality of Resources," *Philosophy and Public Affairs* 10 (1981): 283–345, at 303.

not rest on the fair equality of opportunity principle and, consequently, does not require a distinction between low talent and pathology. The Lockean is concerned with the protection of property broadly conceived and with freedom in the sense of independence and self-determination. If there are actions that the government can undertake, which individuals cannot perform for themselves, that protect lives and property and unambiguously enhance freedom, then there is a case for government action, whether or not that action can be characterized plausibly as health care. Apparently nonpathological cognitive and emotional deficiencies can limit independence and self-determination more severely than genuinely pathological deficiencies such as compulsions or the inability to walk without a cane. The match between health and what matters— shares in the normal opportunity range in Daniels's case, or life-expectancy and freedom in the Lockean's case—is imperfect. But the Lockean can simply concede the point and agree that to insist on access to health care, narrowly conceived, is unjustified.

What the Lockean should insist on is access to those things that protect and enhance freedom, which individuals cannot provide for themselves— not access specifically to health care. The problem with this response is that it may open the floodgates to demands on government provision so extensive as to render farcical the claim to have developed a liberal position. But attention to the costs of government action—both direct and indirect—can, I believe, close these floodgates. Daniels's problem in this regard is more serious, since the number of things that government can do to secure an individual's fair share of the normal opportunity range is enormous and growing rapidly, while the range of things that government can do truly to promote both longevity and freedom, which individuals cannot realistically do for themselves, is limited. Even though there are many welfare programs that would arguably increase longevity and in some respects enhance freedom, paying for these programs diminishes the freedoms of taxpayers and often also the choices of beneficiaries. So the Lockean should accept the conclusion that Daniels tries so hard to avoid: What these arguments establish is universal access to a set of property-protecting and freedom-promoting services that intersects with health care, but does not coincide with health care.

VI. Does Daniels's Argument for Universal Access Go Through?

Recall Daniels's principle:

> Other things being equal, justice with respect to health care requires the prevention or cure of health deficiencies to protect or restore normal species functioning.

Anything short of universal access fails to prevent or cure preventable or curable health deficiencies. For that reason, Daniels argues, it fails to provide fair equality of opportunity and is hence unjust.

In Daniels's view, my actual share of the normal opportunity range depends on three classes of causal factors: my talents, my health, and an array of social factors. Among individuals whose talents are the same, their shares of the normal opportunity range depend on their health and on their social circumstances (and their health, in turn, depends in large part on their social circumstances). Fair equality of opportunity (with opportunity interpreted in Daniels's expansive way) implies that my share of the normal opportunity range should be the same as the share of anyone else whose talents are similar. But equal shares of the normal opportunity range for those with similar talents does not imply the protection and restoration of normal species functioning, nor even the equalization of health. The healthy pauper and the sickly prince may have equal shares of the normal opportunity range. Curing the sickly prince may make opportunities less rather than more equal.[49] If there are inequalities in non-health determinants of opportunity among those with similar talents, then fair equality of opportunity requires compensating *inequalities* in health rather than protection and restoration of normal species functioning. (Since the Lockean has no equivalent egalitarian objective, he or she will not face this problem.) Furthermore, even if Daniels could establish that those who are equally talented should have *equal* portions of the non-health determinants of opportunity, fair equality of opportunity requires only equalizing health, not protecting and restoring full species-typical functioning.

Daniels maintains, however, that fair equality of opportunity requires more than equalizing opportunity.[50] He maintains that a hypothetical state of affairs in which everyone has a remediable health deficiency, such as anemia, which causes no inequalities among those with similar talents, violates fair equality of opportunity. Yet the existence of a remediable universal condition such as anemia obviously would not violate the requirement that opportunity "be equal for persons with similar skills and talents." Daniels explains his judgment by asserting, "But the opportunity account still helps us here, for it is not only a principle governing competitive advantage."[51] This assertion does not help much, since he does not explain what more the principle requires.

---

[49] Gopal Sreenivasan makes this point in "Health Care and Equality of Opportunity," *Hastings Center Report* 37, no. 2 (March–April, 2007): 21–31, at 22. Since the existence of a prince and a pauper suggests the existence of other injustices, the example may not be relevant to ideal theory. I will comment below on the problem of applying Daniels's views to non-ideal circumstances.

[50] Sreenivasan ("Health Care and Equality of Opportunity," 22–23) misses this feature of Daniels's account and argues for a purely comparative interpretation of fair equality of opportunity.

[51] Daniels, *Just Health Care*, 55; repeated word for word in a footnote in Daniels, *Just Health*, 146.

When Daniels asserts that fair equality of opportunity "is not only a principle governing competitive advantage," he must have in mind something like the following:

> Fair equality of opportunity obtains if and only if the share of the normal opportunity range possessed by every representative individual is as large as possible consistent with an equal share for everyone who has similar talents.[52]

Let us call this the "maximal equality" principle. Although still recognizably liberal, it is certainly not Lockean, and it is a significant modification of a Rawlsian view, making much stronger and more far-reaching demands on behalf of opportunity. One wonders how it can be justified. This principle would explain why universal anemia would be unjust, and it would complete a semi-Rawlsian argument for Daniels's principle. If one supposes that those with equal talents have equal quantities of the non-health determinants of shares in the normal opportunity range, then the maximal equality principle would imply Daniels's principle: that justice requires that health care should protect and restore everyone's normal species functioning.

There is, of course, no reason to suppose that people with similar talents do in fact have equal quantities of the non-health determinants of shares in the normal opportunity range. But if one assumes that there are no perverse interactions between (1) equalizing the social circumstances that affect opportunity and (2) instituting health policies that secure the normal opportunity range, then the maximal equality principle would ground an argument for why government should equalize the non-health determinants of shares in the normal opportunity range. Thus, by helping himself to the maximal equality principle, Daniels can provide an argument for why government policy should separately equalize the health and non-health determinants of shares of the normal opportunity range and why justice requires that health care protect and restore species-typical functioning. Fair equality of opportunity (as opposed to the maximal equality principle) requires only equal shares of the normal opportunity range for those whose talents are equal; it does not require equal health, let alone undiminished normal species functioning. The maximal equality reinterpretation of fair equality of opportunity demands maximal equal shares of the normal opportunity range for those whose talents are equal, and perhaps equality of social advantages rather than merely compensating inequalities in the health and non-health determinants of opportunity.

---

[52] Qualifications concerning feasibility, resource limits, and competing moral considerations are of course needed.

Even if Daniels can make such a semi-Rawlsian case for his principle in ideal conditions, his defense of government action to secure health care faces objections with respect to non-ideal conditions. As I have already noted, preventing or curing a health deficiency suffered by someone who is favored by social inequalities may make opportunities less equal rather than more. Accordingly, Daniels's principle, even if it were well-grounded in a theory of justice, does not prescribe how to distribute health care in actual societies, in which the non-health determinants of shares in the normal opportunity range are not justly distributed. Daniels's principle provides only an ideal theory of just health and does not justify universal access to health care in actual societies.

The Lockean position is concerned with the protection of life, property, and self-determination rather than equality of anything, and it consequently avoids many of these problems. What is crucial are the ways in which diminished health threatens life and self-determination, not how the threats to different individuals or their life-prospects compare. The fact that the effects of diminished health on self-determination are sensitive to social factors does not threaten the case for universal access, but rather reinforces it. For example, Franklin Roosevelt's paraplegia did not prevent him from shaping his own life (and, indeed, the lives of millions of others), but had he not been a man of means, his condition would have limited his independence and his ability to pursue his own life-plan. Technological and personal assistance to those without FDR's wealth can go a long way toward enhancing their freedom. Public health measures, coupled with guaranteed universal access to basic health care, will expand the independence and self-determination of those whose social situations magnify limitations on freedom that are due to health deficiencies.

Once one recognizes that the effects of poor health on opportunity can be addressed in other ways than by restoring health, one can see further limitations in Daniels's argument and (to a lesser extent) in the Lockean argument. Consider two ways in which health deficiencies can differ from one another.[53] First, some are preventable or treatable (or, to use a single term, "remediable"), while others, such as being born without an optic nerve, are not. Second, some health deficiencies are compensable, while others are not. By "compensable," in this context, I mean that moderate amounts of additional non-health-related resources can secure to an individual a level of self-determination or a share of the normal opportunity range that is equivalent to the level or share he or she would have had if in full health. The distinction is not perfectly sharp. Is the provision of a motorized wheelchair remediation or compensation? But the distinction is nevertheless significant. Some health states are both remediable and compensable, while others are neither. Some, such as a

---

[53] I am borrowing this distinction from my essay "Are Health Inequalities Unjust?" *Journal of Political Philosophy* 15 (2007): 46–66.

diabetic coma, are remediable but not compensable. Others, such as an amputated hand, are compensable but only partially remediable.

The argument for Daniels's principle presented above implicitly supposes that the only way to address the consequences of poor health on an individual's shares of the normal opportunity range is via remediation—that is, preventing or curing pathologies. But fair equality of opportunity—even in its maximal interpretation—can sometimes be achieved more efficiently by compensating for inequalities in health with inequalities in non-health determinants of opportunity, rather than by equalizing the non-health determinants and using remediation of poor health to restore the normal opportunity range. Indeed, in the case of unremediable conditions, the provision of additional non-health-related resources will be the only way to address the limits on opportunity (or freedom) caused by bad health. Except for the case of pathologies that are remediable but not compensable, there is no justification for attempting separately to determine a just provision of health care on the one hand and, on the other hand, a just distribution of non-health-related resources.[54]

The Lockean can readily concede this point, and since the fundamental concerns are life and freedom, compensation rather than remediation will often be an attractive alternative. Providing nonmedical benefits to those whose lives or independence are threatened by factors they cannot control creates moral-hazard and adverse-selection problems as well as heightened risks of fraud. But since the objective is the protection of life and independence rather than normal species functioning, the only reasons why the Lockean case for universal health care would focus on remediation rather than compensation arise from the details of specific medical problems and the practicalities of compensation. For example, since there is no (earthly) compensation for death, remediation is clearly called for in the case of life-threatening illness.

VII. CONCLUSION

The increasing (and increasingly expensive) social capacities to prevent and cure illness and to compensate for the activity limitations caused by disease, coupled with growing knowledge of the extent to which social factors influence susceptibility to disease, pose significant philosophical challenges. If, as I have argued, a Lockean maintains that the role of

[54] I argue for this conclusion at much greater length in "Are Health Inequalities Unjust?" Although Daniels implies that the socially guaranteed tier of health-care services consists of those services "needed to maintain, restore, or compensate for the loss of normal species-typical functioning," he would not in fact deny that the basic tier should include palliative care. He distinguishes four levels of care: prevention, restoration, medical and support services for the chronically ill, and treatment for those whose opportunities cannot be improved. He suggests that provision of the fourth level is mandated by other moral considerations such as benevolence and "may be beyond measures that justice requires." Daniels, *Just Health Care,* 48.

government should include the protection of life, property, independence, and self-determination (with a commitment to treating people as equals), then merely respecting rights to noninterference is as grossly inadequate as is the view that all that adults owe to children as a matter of right is noninterference.

Accordingly, in this essay, I have constructed a Lockean case for universal access to health care. Although some followers of Locke may find it unfaithful to the spirit of his philosophy, I have defended its Lockean ancestry[55] and pointed out that the letter of Locke's text would apparently permit still more activity on the part of government to promote welfare. Although the Lockean case presented here justifies access to a smaller array of health services than Daniels's opportunity argument, the Lockean case for universal access compares quite favorably with Daniels's case. But there are gaps in both arguments. The threats to freedom posed by such a significant expansion of the responsibilities of government may outweigh the contribution health care makes to the protection of life and freedom. It is questionable whether the line between what government should secure for individuals and what it should leave to their own efforts can sensibly be drawn between health care and other sorts of social services.

The arguments in this essay permit different readers to draw different conclusions. Some classical liberals may conclude that there is no good case to be made for universal access to health care. This is probably the conclusion most of those who regard themselves as followers of Locke held before they began reading this long essay. Other sorts of liberals and welfarists can conclude that one must seek elsewhere than in Lockean liberalism for a justification of universal access to a robust set of health-care interventions. Finally, the Lockean argument this essay explores in defense of public health measures and universal access to basic health care may be salvageable. I leave it to the reader to judge.

Philosophy, University of Wisconsin–Madison

---

[55] Although Locke did not participate personally in the efforts organized by the City of London to treat the victims of the 1665 outbreak of the plague, some of his associates did, and there is no record of Locke objecting that the City of London overstepped the boundaries of the actions that are proper for governments to take.

EUVOLUNTARY OR NOT, EXCHANGE IS JUST*

By Michael C. Munger

I. Introduction

There are two paradoxes in the moral and ethical basis of our understanding of exchange. The first, long commented on and analyzed by
philosophers and political economists,[1] is characterized by the question,
"How can many greedy actions, taken as a whole, imply a benefit for the
community?" In other words, can selfishness be moral? This debate, often
focusing on the distinction between intent and consequence, has been
developed over the last two hundred fifty years until the arguments on
both sides are well understood.

The second paradox is the inconsistency between many morally acceptable exchanges and the unequal distributions of wealth that accumulate
as a consequence of those exchanges. In what follows, I discuss the precise nature of the paradox, and I specify the requirements for "voluntary"
exchange. In doing so, I suggest that a new concept, to which I give the
name "euvoluntary exchange," may be useful in discussing disagreements about the ethical acceptability of exchange, because such disagreements often hinge on whether exchanges are "well" and "truly" voluntary.
This suggests that euvoluntary exchange needs to be clearly defined.[2]

Even those who might concede the resolution of the first paradox—that
selfish actions might be moral at the individual level—retain a concern
with so-called "social justice," or the distribution of the benefits or economic surplus created by market institutions. No less a liberal theorist
than John Stuart Mill famously uncoupled exchange and distribution. He
wrote: "The laws and conditions of the production of wealth, partake of

* I acknowledge helpful comments from Geoffrey Brennan, Michael Gillespie, Ruth Grant,
David Henderson, Clemens Kauffmann, Hans-Jörg Sigwart, Bryan Starrette, and John Tomasi.
Most of all I thank Ellen Frankel Paul for pointing out problems ranging from small mis-
takes to wholesale nonsense.
[1] Versions of this apparent paradox have been described variously by Adam Ferguson, *An
Essay on the History of Civil Society* (1767), available on the Web site of the Constitution
Society, http://www.constitution.org/af/civil.htm; Bernard Mandeville, *The Fable of the Bees
or Private Vices, Publick Benefits*, 2 vols., with a commentary by F. B. Kaye (Indianapolis, IN:
Liberty Fund, 1988), http://oll.libertyfund.org/title/1863; and Adam Smith, *An Inquiry into
the Nature and Causes of the Wealth of Nations*, vol. I, ed. R. H. Campbell and A. S. Skinner,
vol. II of the Glasgow Edition of the Works and Correspondence of Adam Smith (Indianapolis, IN: Liberty Fund, 1981), http://oll.libertyfund.org/title/220.
[2] The Greek prefix "eu-" means good, well, true, or pleasing. Thus, "euvoluntary" captures the meaning of being essentially or truly voluntary, as well as being good for or
pleasing to both parties to the transaction.

doi:10.1017/S0265052510000269

the character of physical truths. There is nothing optional, or arbitrary in them . . . [T]his is not so with the distribution of wealth. That is a matter of human institution solely. The things once there, mankind, individually or collectively, can do with them as they like."[3]

This quote illustrates the second paradox quite well: "The things," as Mill puts it, are the revenues resulting from exchanges that made both parties better off, and that were undertaken under conditions in which property rights were private and exclusive. But after a number of exchanges have been made, and some traders have accumulated large surpluses, those private property rights are somehow transfigured into collectively defined common property. Simply put, that which was yours is now ours. And the reason is that if we were to allow private property to remain private, we would have to accept an inequitable distribution of goods, even though there was nothing unjust about any one of the exchanges that led to that distribution.

That seems paradoxical. How can the sum of many positives be negative? How can differences in wealth that result from exchanges that *in every instance leave the other party better off* be a justification for coercive policies designed to redistribute wealth and correct Mill's "optional" maldistributions of wealth?

There are at least two answers in the literature. The first claims that social justice is unrelated to individual actions; the second claims that exchange is not euvoluntary. I will consider each claim in turn.

The social-justice objection is the standard Rawlsian argument that a just liberal system cannot function with profound differences in wealth, regardless of whether the sources of the inequalities were themselves blameworthy.[4] Those who hold this position would concede that the holders of disproportionate wealth may in fact have engaged in no unethical action. But that has nothing to do with social justice, because there is no necessary connection between individually just actions and the justice of the aggregate distribution of wealth and power. Social justice, in this view, is a property of the distribution of wealth, not a property of its creation or acquisition. A number of authors have addressed the social-justice argument and its problems, and I will not consider it further in this essay.[5]

---

[3] John Stuart Mill, *The Collected Works of John Stuart Mill, Volume II—The Principles of Political Economy with Some of Their Applications to Social Philosophy (Books I–II)*, ed. John M. Robson, introduction by V. W. Bladen (Toronto: University of Toronto Press; London: Routledge and Kegan Paul, 1965), http://oll.libertyfund.org/102/9661.

[4] John Rawls, *A Theory of Justice* (Cambridge, MA: Harvard University Press, 1971), 303–5.

[5] Perhaps the earliest modern statement of the consequences of individual decisions for the justice of the overall distribution was John Locke's 1695 "Venditio," reprinted in David Wooten, ed., *John Locke: Political Writings* (Cambridge: Hackett Publishing Company, 2003), 442–46. My own view is probably closest to that argued by F. A. Hayek: "There can be no test by which we can discover what is 'socially unjust' because there is no subject by which such an injustice can be committed, and there are no rules of individual conduct the obser-

The second claim—that exchange is not euvoluntary—is much less clear in the literature, but I believe one can find it by looking carefully. This argument concedes that there *would* be a paradox, if in fact exchanges *were* euvoluntary. One might even concede that if exchanges were euvoluntary, there might be no basis for remedial state action. But exchanges in the real world of markets, in this view, are rarely euvoluntary. The position one has in society, and one's relation to the ownership of the means of production (Karl Marx's conception of "class"),[6] are morally arbitrary, and therefore indefensible as a basis for private property claims.

The aim of this essay is to rebut the second ("not euvoluntary") claim, which has been accepted uncritically. I will state the counterclaim as starkly as possible here, though I will admit to some qualifications later. The counterclaim is this: All objections to the morality and justice of the uses of voluntary market exchange are mistaken, because they are misdirected. Euvoluntary exchanges are always justified, and the consequent distributions of wealth are always just. But even exchanges that are not euvoluntary are beneficial, and they benefit most of all the welfare of those who are least well off. Euvoluntary or not, exchange is just, and restrictions on exchange harm the poor and the weak.

II. Euvoluntary Exchange

The objection to markets that I wish to address is this: Exchange is unjust because it is not euvoluntary. Therefore, it is not only acceptable, but morally required, for the state actively to redistribute wealth, because the current distribution of wealth results from an accumulation of unjust exchanges.

This objection is mistaken. Unjust distributions of wealth do not *result* from exchanges, euvoluntary or otherwise, though unjust distributions might well *precede* them. My conclusion, to foreshadow, is that allowing exchange reduces (rather than increases) the social injustices that most people are concerned about. The first step in making this argument is to

---

vance of which in the market order would secure to the individuals and groups the position which as such (as distinguished from the procedure by which it is determined) would appear just to *us*. It does not belong to the category of error but to that of nonsense, like the term 'a moral stone'." Friedrich A. Hayek, *Law, Legislation, and Liberty, Volume 2: The Mirage of Social Justice* (Chicago: University of Chicago Press, 1978), 78; emphasis in the original. There are clearly problems with this view, and, as John Tomasi points out, it is hard to claim that even Hayek believed it fully. See John Tomasi, "Hayek on Spontaneous Order and the 'Mirage of Social Justice,'" (New York: Hayek Lecture, Manhattan Institute, June 20, 2007). See also William Galston, *Justice and the Human Good* (Chicago: University of Chicago Press, 1980); Gerald F. Gaus, *The Modern Liberal Theory of Man* (New York: St. Martin's Press, 1983); and Gerald F. Gaus, "Property, Rights, and Freedom," *Social Philosophy and Policy* 11, no. 2 (1994): 209–40.
  6 Karl Marx, *Capital: A Critique of Political Economy* (1867), trans. Ben Fowkes (New York: Penguin, 1992). The Marxist conception of class has both objective and subjective elements, the complete treatment of which is well beyond the scope of the present essay.

give a clear definition of euvoluntary exchange, elaborating on what it means to be "truly voluntary."

Euvoluntary exchange requires the following:[7]

(1) The conventional ownership of items, services, or currency by both parties;

(2) The conventional capacity to transfer and assign this ownership to the other party;

(3) The absence of regret, for both parties, after the exchange, in the sense that both receive value at least as great as was anticipated at the time when they agreed to the exchange;

(4) That neither party is coerced, in the sense of being forced to exchange by threat ("If you don't trade, I will shoot you!"); and

(5) That neither party is coerced in the alternative sense of being harmed by failing to exchange ("If I don't trade, I will starve!").

Items (1) through (3) are standard requirements for a valid contract in the common law.[8] Likewise, item (4) could be summarized as "no duress"— also a requirement for valid contracts under the common law.[9] And item (4) is also a routine aspect of "voluntary" acts for political scientists. In the political world, "power" means that a person (group) can impose his (its) will on others through the threat of violence.[10] That is the sense of "coercion" in item (4) above.

In the economic world, power is different. This difference is captured in item (5): harm caused by failure to exchange. Most of us have a sense that monopoly is not only economically inefficient, but immoral. Of course, the decision of a consumer to purchase or not to purchase a product marketed by a monopoly is not coercive in the same sense as political power is coercive. But if the product is desperately needed, the choices of the consumer faced with a monopoly do not seem voluntary, and they are surely not euvoluntary.

---

[7] For exchange to be voluntary, it must also be true that there are no large-scale or dangerous externalities. In a private property regime with small numbers, this assumption is easily met by Coasen bargaining. If property is common and numbers are large, however, state action may be required. But this is more a problem with the property rights regime than with exchange itself. See Ronald Coase, "The Problem of Social Cost," *Journal of Law and Economics* 3 (1960): 1–44. The problem of conceiving of "property" in this context is illustrated by Eric Mack's imaginative article on blackmail. Eric Mack, "In Defense of Blackmail," *Philosophical Studies* 41, no. 2 (1982): 273–84.

[8] Henry C. Black, *A Treatise on the Rescission of Contracts and Cancellation of Written Instruments* (Kansas City, MO: Vernon Law Book Co., 1916), chaps. 2, 4, and 5.

[9] Ibid.

[10] Thomas Hobbes argued that coercion must be relegated to government, not to private bargaining, because "covenants being but words, and breath, have no force to oblige, contain, constrain, or protect any man, but what it has from the public sword. . . ." Thomas Hobbes, *Leviathan* (New York: Penguin Classics, 1982), Part Two, chapter XVIII, p. 44.

Fortunately, there is a way of making this notion of power in an economic setting precise. Imagine Jane and Bill are considering an exchange of a product for a sum of money. Jane has power over Bill if Bill suffers more from a failure to exchange than Jane does, and vice versa. In some sense, each has a voluntary choice to make: Jane can sell or not sell, and Bill can buy or not buy. But if the consequences of failing to consummate the transaction are far more dire for one than for the other, then the exchange is not euvoluntary.

Economists call the state of the individual in the absence of an exchange the "Best Alternative to a Negotiated Agreement," or BATNA for short.[11] One might think of the value of the BATNA as the level of welfare of the person without access to exchange. So, formally, Jane has *power* over Bill, and Bill's exchange decision is *not euvoluntary*, if

$$\text{Value (BATNA}_{\text{JANE}}) - \text{Value (BATNA}_{\text{BILL}}) \geq \text{Disparity Threshold}$$

The exact level of the "disparity threshold"—that is, the point where this difference implies that exchanges are not euvoluntary—is not obvious. But at some level, if Jane is indifferent between exchanging and not exchanging, and Bill must either exchange or suffer great harm, then Jane has power over Bill.

A more extended example is useful at this point. Suppose I am considering buying a bottle of water. If I go to grocery store A, one among many possible grocery stores, and notice that the price at this particular grocery store is $1,000, I laugh and push my cart along, choosing not to buy. This is a voluntary choice, because I know that other groceries offer water at a much lower price. It is quite true that I need water, and in fact I will die without it. But I know that I can buy water somewhere else, or get some from the tap, or choose any one of many alternatives. Potable water is identical, or nearly so, regardless of the source, aside from very slight differences in taste. And since there are many sources of water, I am not obliged to pay the $1,000 price being asked by store A. Still, if I did decide to pay the $1,000 at store A, we can all agree that this would be a euvoluntary action. I had other alternatives, the water is not poisonous, it tastes good, and I will not regret making the purchase on health grounds. It is the presence of alternatives at a much lower price that implies that my decision to buy the water at $1,000 is euvoluntary.[12]

[11] This concept of the "Best Alternative to a Negotiated Agreement," or BATNA, comes from Roger Fisher and William L. Ury, *Getting to Yes: Negotiating Agreement without Giving In* (Boston, MA: Penguin Books, 1981).
[12] This example highlights another feature of markets, one that economists call "consumer surplus." If I am denied water, I will die. But if I am denied one opportunity to purchase water, my welfare is little affected, as long as there are other competing opportunities to purchase water. This idea that competition creates value for the consumer, in ways not

Now, let us suppose instead that I am in the desert and am dying of thirst. I happen to have quite a bit of cash on me, but I can't drink that. A four-wheel-drive taco truck rolls over the hill, and pulls up to me. I see that the sign advertises a special: "Three tacos for $5! Drinks: $1,000. Three drinks for only $2,500."

I argue with the driver. "Have a heart, buddy! I'm dying of thirst!" He asks if I have enough money to pay his price, and I admit that I do. The driver shrugs and says, "Up to you! Have a nice day!" and starts to drive off.

I stop him and buy three bottles of water for the "special" price of $2,500. Was the exchange euvoluntary?

It was not. The exchange violates item (5) in the definition of euvoluntary exchange, which requires that neither party be coerced in the sense of being harmed by failing to exchange (i.e., it requires, in effect, relative equality of the BATNAs of the parties to the exchange. My BATNA was death from thirst. The driver was little affected by whether or not a deal was consummated (though he got a bit richer), while I was enormously affected. Even though, in most important senses, the exchange was voluntary (I could have said no), it was non-euvoluntary. The precise definitional line between almost equal BATNAs (and therefore euvoluntary exchange) and unequal BATNAs (and therefore non-euvoluntary exchange) may be hard to draw, but I hope the distinction is clear enough for analytic purposes.

Let me emphasize this point, because we will come back to it later. Did the driver make me worse off? What if high prices for water were outlawed, by the kind of "anti-gouging" laws common in many U.S. states, and as a result the driver had stayed home? Would anyone seriously argue that having access to a market, even if the exchange was not euvoluntary, made me worse off? Sure, I was in trouble. But my difficulties rested on conditions that *preceded* market exchange, rather than being *caused by* access to the exchange. Allowing market exchange always improves the lot of the least well off participants in the exchange, even if the exchange itself is not euvoluntary. The reason is that the participant with the very bad BATNA is able to improve his or her situation, compared to the BATNA (which is, by definition, the outcome if access to market exchange is denied).

III. Examples

To clarify euvoluntary exchange, and the claims about its justice or injustice, let us consider someone whose entire livelihood is derived from negotiating and consummating exchanges—the "middleman." A middle-

---

reflected in prices, is called the "diamonds and water" paradox. See, e.g., Adam Smith, *The Wealth of Nations*, 31–32.

man is a trader who buys as cheaply as possible, and then sells dear, merely moving the product rather than improving it in some way. Traders on the "Silk Road" were middlemen. So is the Web site eBay, today.

The roots of the English word "monger," a common merchant or seller of items, are quite old. In Saxon writings of the eleventh century, described in Sharon Turner's magisterial *History of the Anglo-Saxons* (1836), we find a very striking passage where a merchant (*mancgere*) defends himself on moral grounds:

> "I say that I am useful to the king, and to ealdormen, and to the rich, and to all people. I ascend my ship with my merchandise, and sail over the sea-like places, and sell my things, and buy dear things which are not produced in this land, and I bring them to you here with great danger over the sea; and sometimes I suffer shipwreck, with the loss of all my things, scarcely escaping myself."
>
> "What things do you bring to us?"
>
> "Skins, silks, costly gems, and gold; various garments, pigment, wine, oil, ivory, and orichalcus [i.e., brass], copper, and tin, silver, glass, and suchlike."
>
> "Will you sell your things here as you brought them here?"
>
> "I will not, because what would my labour benefit me? I will sell them dearer here than I bought them there, that I may get some profit, to feed me, my wife, and children."[13]

This makes quite a story—risk, greed, adventure, and profit. The *mancgere* openly admits that he does not change or improve the product. All he does is transport it and then sell it at a much higher price. In fact, he consciously and unabashedly sets out to sell it at the highest price he can obtain.

Are the exchanges between the *mancgere* and his customers euvoluntary? Probably. Many of the items being resold are luxuries. The buyers may be disappointed that they cannot afford the costly baubles, but their physical situations are not harmed by being unable to consummate an exchange. Moreover, there is no reason to believe that the merchandise itself is shoddy or that the claims for its worth are fraudulent.

Suppose that the *mancgere* is very good at what he does and works very hard. It is easy to imagine (since this happened in many cases in medieval Europe, the Middle East, and Asia) that he and his sons might have built up a great trading empire, with enormous wealth.[14] But isn't it still true

---

[13] Sharon Turner, *The History of the Anglo-Saxons*, 6th ed. (London: Longman, Rees, Orme, Brown, Green, and Longman, 1836), 115–16. Portions of this discussion are adapted from Michael Munger, "Market Makers or Parasites?" (Indianapolis, IN: Liberty Fund, EconLib, 2009), http://www.econlib.org/library/Columns/y2009/Mungermiddlemen.html.

[14] See, e.g., Avner Greif, *Institutions and the Path to the Modern Economy: Lessons from Medieval Trade* (New York: Cambridge University Press, 2006).

that since each separate exchange was (suppose, for the sake of argument) euvoluntary, the result must also be just, and morally defensible.

Obviously, I am paraphrasing, with only a few flourishes, Robert Nozick's argument from *Anarchy, State, and Utopia* (1974). Nozick famously posits that even if each separate exchange were morally justified (in my terms, euvoluntary), one might still expect to see enormous disparities of wealth. He gave the example of Wilt Chamberlain, a basketball player of such talent that people would happily pay a quarter extra, per fan, to watch him play.

These myriad euvoluntary transactions sum to a great fortune. In effect, Nozick is arguing two things. First, if the initial distribution of income and wealth is just, and each transaction is individually just, then any consequent distribution is also just. Second, given disparities in ability, the accumulation of these voluntary transactions would necessarily lead to great income inequality, unless exchange is outlawed. As Nozick put it, "The socialist society would have to forbid capitalist acts between consenting adults."[15]

The Wilt Chamberlain example is useful, but only as an existence proof. That is, Nozick was trying to prove that there might exist, at least in principle, a just society with a morally defensible distribution of income that was nonetheless extremely unequal. Nozick's example allows him to argue that the case for the proposition that "inequality is unjust, and requires redistribution" is not prima facie; it depends on how the money was acquired. One would have to inquire about the justice or injustice of the initial distribution of wealth, before exchange started, and also about the euvoluntary (or not) nature of each of the exchange transactions along the path from one distribution to another.

Nozick's example does not do the work he wants it to do, however. Wilt Chamberlain is *sui generis*. One might set aside a preference for egalitarianism for the narrow case of god-figures, truly unique performers. But what about someone who is in no way unique, but just tries harder? What about the *mancgere*? It will be useful here to consider a famous example of a "middleman" in action, from an account of a prisoner-of-war camp in Germany during World War II.

The British economist R. A. Radford was captured by the German army in 1943 and later wrote about the experience.[16] Radford noticed the universality of exchange in (among other things) the contents of Red Cross packets: tinned milk, jam, carrots, butter, biscuits, tinned beef, chocolate, sugar, treacle [i.e., molasses], and cigarettes.

Exchange, if euvoluntary, always makes both parties to the exchange better off. But the initial endowments, or BATNAs, of the parties are a

---

[15] Robert Nozick, *Anarchy, State, and Utopia* (New York: Basic Books, 1974), 163.

[16] R. A. Radford, "The Economic Organisation of a P.O.W. Camp," *Economica* 12, no. 48 (November 1945): 189–201.

central consideration. The interesting thing about the prison camp setting is that each prisoner had precisely the same endowment or total wealth, before initiating any trades. That is, everyone's BATNA was identical, and was composed of two parts: (1) daily rations from what Radford delicately calls "the detaining power" (the German army); and (2) once a month, the full contents of a Red Cross packet.

Note how naturally exchange would appear in such a setting of pure equality. If I like carrots more than milk, and you like milk more than carrots, we can trade. Because everyone has exactly the same endowment, trading is universally approved, and praiseworthy. There is no increase in the total amount of food in the area as a result of trade, but the total welfare of the group is improved. And people do not have to be told this. They recognize it quickly, on their own. As Radford put it, in the prison camp, "Very soon after capture people realized that it was both undesirable and unnecessary, in view of the limited size and the equality of supplies, to give away or to accept gifts. . . . 'Goodwill' developed into trading as a more equitable means of maximizing individual satisfaction."[17] Opponents of exchange had to answer the powerful claim that trade is more equitable than relying on gifts. And the reason is that voluntary trades always leave both parties better off, whereas gifts rely on sacrifice. An exchange of sacrifices might be mutually beneficial, but it might not. Better to exchange goods directly, so that their values can be compared.

It is important to extend Nozick's argument from an existence proof based on many trades and a unique performer (Chamberlain) to a setting where only the "many trades" aspect is preserved. In the prison camp setting, since each person had precisely the same initial endowment, but different preferences, allowing exchange made everyone better off. But there might be a difference between exchanges predicated on (a) *value in use,* where I exchange something I don't much want for something I want more, and (b) *value in exchange,* where I am exchanging for the sake of accumulating a surplus.[18]

The reason such exchanges might be a problem is easy to see, but harder to explain clearly. If I make one trade, and I am better off, then no one begrudges the improvement, provided my trading partner also benefits. But if I make many trades, as the eleventh-century *mancgere* did, then I appear to be acting badly, even if (as before) each of my trading partners is left better off. That is what the middleman does: buys low and sells high, and profits from having made a large volume of trades. If

---

[17] Ibid., 197.

[18] Aristotle makes this distinction most clearly, in arguing that value in use is different from, and superior to, value in exchange. Aristotle, *Politics,* ed. and trans. Thomas Alan Sinclair and Trevor J. Saunders (New York: Penguin Classics, 1981), Book I. And this is precisely the origin of the "labor theory of value" that finds its way through the neoclassical economists into the work of Marx.

someone is sharp-eyed and energetic, he might make a very large amount of profit, either in currency or goods. How could that be a problem?

The prisoners in Radford's POW camp in Germany thought it was a problem. Radford mentions the story of a priest with a sharp eye for exchanges:

> Stories circulated of a padre who started off round the camp with a tin of cheese and five cigarettes and returned to his bed with a complete [Red Cross] parcel in addition to his original cheese and cigarettes. . . ."
>
> Public opinion on the subject of trading was vocal if confused and changeable, and generalizations as to its direction are difficult and dangerous. A tiny minority held that all trading was undesirable as it engendered an unsavory atmosphere; occasional frauds and sharp practices were cited as proof. . . . But while certain activities were condemned as anti-social, trade itself was practiced, and its utility appreciated, by almost everyone in the camp.
>
> More interesting was opinion on middlemen and prices. Taken as a whole, opinion was hostile to the middleman. His function, and his hard work in bringing buyer and seller together, were ignored; profits were not regarded as a reward for labor, but as the result of sharp practices. Despite the fact that his very existence was proof to the contrary, the middleman was held to be redundant. . . .[19]

The padre never made a fraudulent claim or misrepresented what he was offering to trade. The commodities were standardized and interchangeable (one tin of cheese is just like any other; cigarettes are machine-made and indistinguishable; a tin of jam is always the same). At each and every step, in every transaction, the exchange with the padre made the other party better off. Yet the padre accumulated a "profit" amounting to a full Red Cross parcel, a small fortune in the setting of the camp.

Just like the eleventh-century Saxon *mancgere*, the wandering padre created value. It might seem that he only *took* value—buying cheap, selling dear, and changing or improving none of the products he exchanged. But, in fact, he created value at every step in the process. He did this by finding *A*, who would pay six (or fewer) cigarettes for a tin of beef, and then finding another man *B*, who would sell a tin of beef for three (or more) cigarettes. Admittedly, if these two fellows met each other, they might have exchanged directly and cut out the middleman. But finding just the right person to trade with, in a vast, teeming prison camp, is hard. The padre, by searching across trades, can arbitrage the difference: he sells the beef to *A* for five cigarettes, after buying it from *B* for four cigarettes. *A* is better off by at least one cigarette, and *B* is better off by at

---

[19] Radford, "The Economic Organisation of a POW Camp," 198–99.

least one cigarette, and the padre "profits" one cigarette by finding the exchange opportunity.

The padre, by making many of these trades, was able to end up with everything he started with, plus another full parcel—a large amount of stuff. Yet, if you went back and asked every one of the trading partners in the chain, not one would complain of having been cheated . . . until you mentioned the padre's profit. Then every one of the trading partners would likely be outraged and would demand to be compensated. The question is whether this demand is morally justified. That is really the question that Nozick was asking. My answer, even if we are talking about a trader instead of Wilt Chamberlain, is "no"—so long as the trades were euvoluntary.

A similar argument, it should be pointed out, was made much earlier by the French economist Frédéric Bastiat, in his essay *That Which Is Seen and That Which Is Not Seen* (1850). It is worth quoting at length:

> [The] schools of thought are vehement in their attack on those they call middlemen. They would willingly eliminate the capitalist, the banker, the speculator, the entrepreneur, the businessman, and the merchant, accusing them of interposing themselves between producer and consumer in order to fleece them both, without giving them anything of value. Or rather, the reformers would like to transfer to the state the work of the middlemen, for this work cannot be eliminated. [Regarding the famine of 1847,] "Why," they said, "leave to merchants the task of getting foodstuffs from the United States and the Crimea? Why cannot the state, the departments, and the municipalities organize a provisioning service and set up warehouses for stockpiling? They would sell at net cost, and the people, the poor people, would be relieved of the tribute that they pay to free, i.e., selfish, individualistic, anarchical trade. . . . When the stomach that is hungry is in Paris and the wheat that can satisfy it is in Odessa, the suffering will not cease until the wheat reaches the stomach. There are three ways to accomplish this: the hungry men can go themselves to find the wheat; they can put their trust in those who engage in this kind of business; or they can levy an assessment on themselves and charge public officials with the task.[20]

It may take a moment to realize that the problem here is exactly the same as the problem of the itinerant padre. There are three ways of getting food from farm to market. First, every *consumer* goes off on his own, with a cart. This is inefficient and too slow to answer the needs of the hungry. Second, *middlemen* can buy, transport, and resell the products.

[20] Frédéric Bastiat, *That Which Is Seen, and That Which Is Not Seen* (Paris, 1850); reprinted by Liberty Fund, http://www.econlib.org/library/Bastiat/basEss1.html, chap. 6, sec. 1.99.

Third, *the state* can buy, transport, and resell the products, or give the products away for free.

Those concerned about equality might claim that the state can always perform the function of middlemen more cheaply because the state's motivation is public service, not profit. And the state can always do it more cheaply because the costs of profit are not part of the process. But this is disastrously wrong. First, agents of the state are not, in fact, motivated by the public interest. They are no better than anyone else, and they act first to benefit themselves. Second, without the signals of price and profit provided by middlemen, no one knows what products should be shipped where, or when. In short, without middlemen, the state would act more slowly, less accurately, and at the wrong times.

Further, profit is crucial, and beneficial. It is *because* of profit that middlemen create value. And the seeking of profit by middlemen—buying cheap and selling dear—ensures that, as Bastiat puts it, "the wheat reaches the stomach" faster, more cheaply, and more reliably than any service the state could possibly create. The system of middlemen performs what seems like a miracle:

> Directed by the comparison of prices, [middlemen distribute] food over the whole surface of the country, beginning always at the highest price, that is, where the demand is the greatest. It is impossible to imagine an organization more completely calculated to meet the needs of those who are in want. . . .[21]

The fact is that middlemen do not require perfect markets or the conditions of perfect competition. Instead, middlemen are the means by which markets become "perfect." Arbitrage and bargain-hunting are the disciplines that ensure a single price, providing accurate signals on relative scarcity and engendering enormous flows of resources and labor toward their highest valued use.

One final example is worthwhile, because it reveals something of the depth of the antipathy many people have toward exchange, and also shows us something important about euvoluntary exchange. Hurricane Fran made landfall in North Carolina in September 1996, hitting the state capital of Raleigh around three a.m., dropping ten inches of rain.[22] More than one million people were without power the next morning, and many roads were blocked by large fallen trees. Few residences had any kind of backup power. Within hours, food in refrigerators and freezers started to go bad. Insulin, baby formula, and other necessities immediately began to

---

[21] Ibid., chap. 6.

[22] This example is adapted from Michael Munger, "They Clapped: Can Anti-Gouging Laws Prohibit Scarcity?" (Indianapolis, IN: Liberty Fund, 2007), http://www.econlib.org/library/Columns/y2007/Mungergouging.html.

spoil in the heat. More than a million people needed ice. And they needed it immediately.

The governor declared a state of emergency. One might think that thousands of entrepreneurs in the surrounding areas, little touched by the storm, would load trucks and head to the disaster area. After all, they owned, or could obtain, all the things that the residents of central North Carolina needed so desperately. Ice, chain saws, generators, lumber, tarps for covering gaping holes in roofs—these were just some of the needs.

But no such mass movement of resources to their highest valued use took place. North Carolina had an anti-gouging law, passed in 1992. It was General Statute 75-36,[23] a law whose sole object was, in Nozick's terms, to prohibit capitalist acts between consenting adults. The law had been interpreted to limit price increases to less than 5 percent. Each violation of this law could result in a fine of up to $5,000. So, ice that happened to be in Charlotte *stayed* in Charlotte. Why drive three hours to Raleigh when you can only charge the Charlotte price, plus just enough for gas money to break even?

Several people did try to sell ice. One truck apparently parked in Five Points, near downtown, and another parked a bit west, near wealthy St. Mary's Street, and opened for business. I have not been able to find a definitive claim about price, but it was more than $8 a bag. On reaching the front of the line, some customers were angry that the price was so high, but almost no one refused to pay for the ice. Those who did refuse to pay simply reverted to their BATNA, same as before the trucks arrived.

Before long, Raleigh police arrived and shut down the illicit ice sellers, confiscating the ice. Interestingly, it appears that the prospective buyers standing in line did something surprising: They clapped. They clapped, cheered, and hooted as the vicious ice sellers were handcuffed and arrested. Some of those buyers had been standing in line for five minutes or more and had been ready to pay four times as much as the maximum price the state would allow, and they clapped as the police, at gunpoint, took that opportunity away from them.

This example raises two important questions. First, was the exchange of ice for money euvoluntary, or exploitative, or something else? Second, even if the exchange was not euvoluntary, should it be illegal? In other

---

[23] The text of the law at the time read as follows: "(a) It shall be a violation of G.S. 75-1.1 for any person to sell or rent or offer to sell or rent at retail during a state of disaster, in the area for which the state of disaster has been declared, any merchandise or services which are consumed or used as a direct result of an emergency or which are consumed or used to preserve, protect, or sustain life, health, safety, or comfort of persons or their property with the knowledge and intent to charge a price that is unreasonably excessive under the circumstances." The law was amended in August 2006 to be even more restrictive, outlawing price changes reflecting cost increases up the supply chain. See North Carolina SL2006-245, General Statutes 75-38. A much broader and more careful treatment of these issues can be found in Matt Zwolinski, "The Ethics of Price Gouging," *Business Ethics Quarterly* 18, no. 3 (July 2008): 347–78.

words, do anti-gouging laws have a legitimate purpose? In the next section, I will try to use what we have seen in the foregoing examples to offer answers to these questions.

IV. Preconditions, Not Consequences

If an exchange is not euvoluntary, should it be prohibited? It is true that the taco truck driver in the desert stood to make a lot of money by selling me water. It is likewise true that the *mancgere* expected to make a large profit by selling spices, gems, and silk, and that the itinerant padre was trying hard to accumulate extra cigarettes and food through his trades in the POW camp. Finally, the ice sellers were motivated by greed, not charity, in bringing ice to Raleigh.

In every case, the option to buy made the (potential) buyer better off. Nonetheless, the cases divide into two very different groups, according to whether the exchange was euvoluntary. Buying water in the desert, or buying ice after the hurricane, is not euvoluntary, because both needs are desperate. Buying silk rather than linen, or trading for treacle in the POW camp, are euvoluntary, because the alternative to a negotiated agreement or trade is much more equal.

Should we have anti-gouging laws? If a trade is not euvoluntary, should it be outlawed? Those who would answer "yes" are confusing cause and effect, or so I am claiming. The disparity in conditions is a measure of need. Our emotional reaction is that no one should be in that desperate position in the first place. The man in the desert should not have to pay $1,000 for a bottle of water. The people of Raleigh should not have to pay $8 for a bag of ice.

But what we do next is nonsense, a non sequitur. We go from saying that no one should have to pay such a high price to passing laws saying that no one will be able to. The effect of these laws is to imprison people in the desperate position that made us feel sorry for them in the first place.

Without an incentive to search the desert for the thirsty, the taco truck driver would stay in town at a busy corner. Without access to the chance to buy water, the lost traveler would die of thirst. If there is no incentive for truckers to buy ice and transport it to the disaster zone, then hurricane refugees must accept that the price of ice is infinity, because none is available. Thus, it is in those instances where market exchange is not euvoluntary that access to market exchange is most important. Anti-gouging laws, restrictions on organ sales, and other rules designed to suppress markets are based on the idea that the BATNA for the poor, the needy, and the desperate, is unacceptably low. But those laws then ensure that the unacceptable BATNA is the only possible outcome for those same people. Restrictions on market exchange reify and instantiate precisely the harms they purport to avoid. What is the basis for such confusion?

There are many objections to capitalism and exchange, some of which are complex. I will offer a brief summary, as a way of contrasting the objections with the argument so far. Karl Marx, in Book I of *Capital* especially, makes two distinct arguments—one based on exploitation and another based on the inequality of negotiating positions in market exchange.[24] The exploitation argument rests on the claim that wage labor alienates the product of labor from its true owner, and that no compensation could be sufficient.

The second argument is more interesting, at least for my purposes. In chapter 26 of Book I, Marx asks why some men work but own little capital, and others own large amounts of capital but do little work. His answer, borrowed from the neoclassical economists, is that "primitive accumulation," or differences in wealth in precapitalist society, seem to provide an explanation. This saving of capital is "a primitive accumulation preceding capitalistic accumulation; an accumulation not the result of the capitalist mode of production, but its starting point."[25]

Marx claims that primitive accumulation plays the same role in political economy as original sin plays in Christian theology. The reason that some have to work by the sweat of their brow is that their ancestors were spendthrifts—dissolute and morally loose. Thus, while this generation may be blameless, their poverty can be morally justified, because the pitiless gods of capitalism visit the sins of the fathers upon the children.[26] Marx finds this idea laughable, arguing instead that disparities in wealth are actually the result of theft—theft that is protected by the state through the invention of property rights and justified by fables and myths of ownership.

Marx clearly believes that the wage/labor contract is not (in my terms) euvoluntary. The worker can only choose work or starvation. Where the taco truck driver or ice sellers in my examples could charge arbitrarily high prices, the capitalist in Marx's example can pay arbitrarily low wages. The laborer is coerced to work, at a price that enriches the wealthy and further impoverishes the laborer.

What this suggests, as I have maintained throughout, is that the objection to capitalism is not an objection to the process of exchange itself. Presumably, even Marx would see little that is objectionable in labor exchanges for wages among wealthy capitalists. The problem occurs when exchanges are negotiated among parties with profound differences in wealth and power. To repeat: even this objection is not a rejection of the

[24] Marx, *Capital*, Book I.
[25] Ibid., Book I, chapter 26. Adam Smith used the phrase "previous accumulation" to refer to this phenomenon (*Wealth of Nations*, Book 2, chap. 3).
[26] Euripides, in the Phrixus Fragment 970, said: "The gods visit the sins of the fathers upon the children." Christopher Collard and Martin Cropp, eds. and trans., *Euripides: Volume VIII: Oedipus-Chrysippus, Other Fragments* (Cambridge, MA: Harvard University Press, Loeb Classical Library, 2009), 436.

justice of exchange per se. It is an indictment of inequality, because the exchange is not euvoluntary.

But then I must repeat the second portion of my main argument: If inequality is the real problem, then markets and access to exchange reduces the problem rather than making it worse. When comfortable American college students rally to protest "sweat shops" in developing nations, their clearly stated objection is that workers *should not have to work in those conditions.* But outlawing sweat shops means that those workers will not be able to work at all. The reason for the poor working conditions is inequality, not capitalism. And access to jobs, even sweat-shop jobs, is the way to put the poorest societies on the long, steep path toward widely shared prosperity.

Modern liberal thinkers are the heirs to different versions of Marx's second objection (inequality), though not the first (exploitation), perhaps because Marx embeds the exploitation claim in a cumbersome and unworkable labor theory of value.[27] John Rawls and his followers are the mostly widely cited expositors of the conflicts between liberalism and capitalism. According to Samuel Freeman, one can usefully categorize three different, though mutually reinforcing, problems with capitalism for the Rawlsian liberal.[28]

First, the "social minimum" under capitalism is too small, and the income of the wealthy too large, to satisfy the Rawlsian difference principle, which states that inequalities are to be permitted only when they benefit the worst-off members of society. Of course, for this claim to be persuasive, one has to credit the difference principle as a fundamental moral law. Rawls gives two distinct justifications for the difference principle. (1) Every citizen has an equal claim on society's resources, and thus increased resources for the better off can be justified only if there is some consequent improvement in the welfare of the worst off. (2) In the original position, where the chooser does not know his welfare level, a rational person would choose equality, subject only to the kinds of differences accounted for in (1).

---

[27] The relation between liberalism and Marx's theory of exploitation is rather complex, and beyond my scope in this essay. But see Allen Buchanan, "Exploitation, Alienation, and Injustice," *Canadian Journal of Philosophy* 9, no. 1 (March 1979): 121–39; and Allen Buchanan, *Marx and Justice: The Radical Critique of Liberalism* (London: Methuen, 1982) for an extensive critical review. Finally, a fascinating short story of the industrial revolution and the artistic sensibility, written by Herman Melville, asks whether it is possible for an individual simply to "prefer not" to participate in markets. Melville's character Bartleby repeatedly states that he would just rather not sell his labor, even if the alternative is to be sent to the madhouse. Herman Melville, "Bartleby, the Scrivener: A Story of Wall Street," *Putnam's Magazine*, Part I, November 1853, pp. 546–50; Part II, December 1853, pp. 609–16.

[28] Samuel Freeman, *Rawls* (New York: Routledge, 2007), 262–64. See also John Rawls, *Political Liberalism* (New York: Columbia University Press, 1993); Thomas Spragens, *Civic Liberalism: Reflections on Our Democratic Ideals* (New York: Rowman and Littlefield, 1999); and Loren E. Lomasky, "Liberalism Beyond Borders," *Social Philosophy and Policy* 24, no. 1 (2007): 206–33.

The objection here is that the social minimum has nothing to do with justice, and instead is cynically calculated at just the minimum amount to forestall revolution. Under capitalism, the poor are bought off, with a level of income just slightly greater than the level that would make them indifferent between revolution and quiescence. In the rational choice literature, in fact, this is an explicit assumption in several recent works.[29] Thus, the welfare of the poor is treated as a constraint to be satisfied rather than as part of the objective function to be improved.

But this objection fundamentally misunderstands the nature of exchange. The poor in wealthy countries are, by nearly any material measure, better off than the wealthy in poor countries. The reason is that exchange makes both parties better off. Being denied access to exchange actually harms the poor more than it harms the wealthy, since the wealthy are likely to have other means of satisfying their needs and wants.

The second major Rawlsian objection to capitalism is an aggregate level claim, namely, that inequality is unacceptable as a primitive value. The reason is that the political freedoms on which liberalism depends for its existence are ruled out by gross inequalities of income. These concentrations of economic power inevitably can be translated into concentrated, or at least disproportionate, political power. Therefore, the argument goes, inequality is inconsistent with liberal democracy, and the solution is to reduce inequality.

The problem with this argument is that it assumes a large, powerful, and dangerous government apparatus. It is perfectly true that an aggressive and intrusive government, with few restrictions on its power, is likely to be dominated by the wealthy. But why would this lead us to conclude that we should get rid of the wealthy? Does it not follow at least as directly that the correct answer is to limit and constrain the power of government to damage the rights of citizens?

The debate recalls the humorous "Chicago Marxist" moniker that some have attached to George Stigler and the "Theory of Economic Regulation."[30] A number of passages in Chicago-style literature on regulation sound as if they might have been written by Marx, since they emphasize that regulation will generally be created, or else later transformed, to benefit industry. But the solution of Marx was to get rid of capitalism. The solution of Stigler, Sam Peltzman, et al. is to get rid of regulation, as it will generally make things worse.[31] It makes no sense to say that we are scared of government so we should get rid of the rich. If you are scared of government, then get rid of government.

[29] See, e.g., Daron Acemoglu and James Robinson, *Economic Origins of Dictatorship and Democracy* (New York: Cambridge University Press, 2005).

[30] George Stigler, "The Theory of Economic Regulation," *Bell Journal of Economics and Management Science* 3 (1971): 3–18; Richard A. Posner, "Theories of Economic Regulation," *Bell Journal of Economics and Management Science* 5 (1974): 335–58.

[31] See, e.g., Sam Peltzman, "Constituent Interest and Congressional Voting," *Journal of Law and Economics* 27 (1984): 181–213.

The third and final Rawlsian objection to capitalism is that economic inequality in an unregulated market society is too great to preserve even economic freedom. Contrary to the myth of equal opportunity, citizens do not in fact have any reasonable prospect of bettering themselves or achieving great wealth. The wealthy are born wealthy, and capital is concentrated in a few hands. Most workers have no substantial control over their own working conditions, and, because capitalists control the banking system, those workers have no chance of obtaining the loans they need to compete with existing concentrated industries. Finally, the fact that workers may own stocks in their retirement accounts cannot solve the problem, because their voting rights are too diffuse, and the power of the elite board of directors too concentrated and aloof, to allow workers effective participation or real opportunity.

For some reason, I have encountered many opponents in debates who consider this objection to capitalism to be devastating and, in fact, unanswerable. But the claim is absurd on its face. It is true that a system based on politics, or elitism, or power relations (such as racial domination or class conflict) might have just the sort of effects posited here. But capitalism is based on none of these things. Instead, it is based on self-interest or, more starkly, on greed.

Consider the example of Branch Rickey, who broke the color line in baseball by signing Jackie Robinson to the Dodgers in 1947. He did so not because he was an altruist, but because he was a notorious capitalist who considered every angle and sought out every advantage.[32] The fact was that African American baseball players, beginning with Robinson, had enormous talent and could be signed to contracts at prices much lower than comparable white players. Black players were a bargain. A racist would, indeed, work to suppress black labor. But a capitalist motivated by profit will purchase labor of the highest quality at the lowest price. And in a competitive system, even a racist cannot afford to indulge in racism, because he will go bankrupt.

Any system *other* than capitalism suppresses ambition and constrains social and economic mobility. Perhaps capitalism is the second worst system for fostering economic welfare, but only if all the alternatives are tied for worst. Greedy bankers are happy to loan to small businesses that are likely to succeed; greedy venture capital lenders are happy to sign contracts with unknown inventors from Hicksville, people who lack an Ivy League education, if those lenders think they can profit from loaning money to those inventors.

That is not to say that there is no racism, no discrimination—because there is. But it exists only because our system is not fully capitalist. There are pockets of protection for banks and for prospective employers, which

---

[32] Lee Lowenfish, *Branch Rickey: Baseball's Ferocious Gentleman* (Lincoln: University of Nebraska Press, 2007).

allow them to indulge their preferences for prejudice. Competition and self-interest are the surest way of eliminating discrimination, not the cause of discrimination.

John Maynard Keynes is often used as an authority to bolster liberal critiques of capitalism. But Keynes's critique was subtle, and his understanding of markets quite deep. Consider this passage, where he discusses the consequences of monetary inflations following the First World War:

> In the latter stages of the war all the belligerent governments practised, from necessity or incompetence, what a Bolshevist might have done from design. Even now, when the war is over, most of them continue out of weakness the same malpractices. But further, the governments of Europe, being many of them at this moment reckless in their methods as well as weak, seek to direct on to a class known as "profiteers" the popular indignation against the more obvious consequences of their vicious methods. These "profiteers" are, broadly speaking, the entrepreneur class of capitalists, that is to say, the active and constructive element in the whole capitalist society, who in a period of rapidly rising prices cannot but get rich quick whether they wish it or desire it or not. If prices are continually rising, every trader who has purchased for stock or owns property and plant inevitably makes profits. . . . The profiteers are a consequence and not a cause of rising prices. By combining a popular hatred of the class of entrepreneurs with the blow already given to social security by the violent and arbitrary disturbance of contract and of the established equilibrium of wealth which is the inevitable result of inflation, these governments are fast rendering impossible a continuance of the social and economic order of the nineteenth century. But they have no plan for replacing it.[33]

V. Conclusion

It is useful to reprise the main themes I have tried to advance. First, I inquired about the paradox of the aggregation of exchange: If each exchange is individually mutually praiseworthy, how can the results be blameworthy? More simply, if each exchange is good, how can all exchange be bad?

Next I sought to define a notion of exchange in which any trade or negotiated outcome would be morally acceptable. I called this "euvoluntary," or truly voluntary, exchange. I used this concept to argue that all objections to the morality and justice of the uses of voluntary market

[33] John Maynard Keynes, *The Economic Consequences of the Peace* (1919; London: General Books, 2009), 236.

exchange are category mistakes. In fact, they are really objections to imbalances or excessive inequalities in the distribution of power and wealth.

Thus, I tried to argue two main points, using this apparatus. First, euvoluntary exchanges are always justified, and if consummated are always just. Second, and more important, even exchanges that are not euvoluntary are generally welfare improving, and they improve the welfare of the least well off most of all. The confusion that arises in judging exchanges that are not euvoluntary is understandable but unfortunate. The observer, seeing the degree of inequality between the parties to a potential exchange, or the desperation of one of the parties, is actually perceiving a disparity in levels of welfare of the respective BATNAs or "Best Alternatives to a Negotiated Agreement." This disparity is a consequence of differences that come before exchange is contemplated, and are not caused by the exchange.

But the confused observer seeks to help the less well off party by outlawing the exchange. The observer, believing that the party should not have to exchange on such terms, blunders in and dictates that the party should not be allowed to exchange on such terms. The problem is that this ensures that the less well off party is marooned at his grossly inferior BATNA, an outcome that access to exchange could have avoided. In short, interference with "capitalist acts among consenting adults" has effects that are exactly the opposite of its supposed intent.

Political Science, Duke University

RULE CONSEQUENTIALISM MAKES SENSE AFTER ALL

By Tyler Cowen

I. Introduction

Should we analyze policies by asking how they fit into more-general rules? For instance, maybe a single act of corruption has no harmful effects but corruption in general is harmful and many corrupt acts will destroy a polity. Would we be justified in condemning the single act of corruption?

More generally, does a "rules-based perspective" on policy evaluation possess independent force? Or does the doctrine of "rule consequentialism" collapse into "act consequentialism"? Why not make an exception to the rule when the exception is harmless or possibly even beneficial? Defenders of the rules-based perspective are wary of such questions. They know that if we are not willing to adhere to a rule for the sake of the rule itself, then talk of the rule is no better than a myth, albeit a socially useful myth.

Much is at stake. If rules-based perspectives hold up, it is easier to justify strict moralities and strict policy prescriptions and to make a much tighter, more consistent case for our preferred vision of a liberal order. We need only argue that the rule makes sense as a whole, not that it gives the best result in each and every case. Adopting a rules-based perspective also would make us less pragmatic and more willing to generalize. If the generality were true (e.g., "Don't gamble!"), that would be enough to establish its force, even if it didn't offer the best advice for every particular case. The rules-based approach mimics some of the properties of a rights theory, while allowing the rules to be determined by an empirical examination of what is beneficial to human society. It raises the possibility of true foundations for our vision of the good society.

A single act of weakness may not damage credibility much, but many weak acts will destroy credibility. A single investment in research may not boost science very much, but a broader collection of such investments will make a big difference. A single bad tax may not stifle economic growth, but a large number of bad taxes will. Numerous legal "exceptions" may make sense on an individual basis, but only if we fail to consider the more general consequences of those exceptions; for instance, many arguments for the rule of law depend on expectation and incentive effects. In general, when expectations and incentives matter, a rules-based approach and a case-by-case or act-based approach will offer different normative recommendations.

doi:10.1017/S0265052510000270

Or consider the now-dormant Waxman-Markey cap-and-trade legisla-tion (and related ideas), which would limit carbon emissions in the United States. Under one view, this is a proposal with "some cost and no real benefit"; the policy outlined in the bill will not lower global temperatures very much, in part because so many other countries emit carbon as well. Under another view, the bill is "the first step along a much-needed pro-gram to solve the dire and critical problem of climate change." Which view we accept again depends on whether we view the legislation in stand-alone or in bundled terms. The case for the bill is stronger if we adopt the bundled perspective (and, of course, if we see limiting climate change as a priority). In stand-alone terms, it is hard to justify the bill, as it costs something and achieves virtually no good in terms of its net, stand-alone impact on global climate.

The issue of time consistency also creates differences between act-based and rules-based perspectives. Time consistency logic covers a wide range of practical problems, including taxation, monetary policy, trade policy, patents, copyright, research and development, and foreign policy. To give one example, *ex ante* it is optimal to promise not to break the patent rights for a valuable new drug. *Ex post* it is optimal for the policymaker to confiscate the rights to the new drug once it is made. Pharmaceutical companies, of course, understand this logic, and they are somewhat reluc-tant to invest in new drugs in the first place. We would be better off if a no-confiscation rule could be put in place, but once the rule is in place we are better off if we can break it. That is a classic problem of time consistency.[1]

Some of the relevant examples of bundling are about bundling over time (time consistency), whereas others are about bundling across the actions of many different individuals. But in both cases we have the essential feature of doing normative evaluation while putting "up for grabs" more than the single choice of a lone individual.

As this essay proceeds, I will use the term "bundling" for when we treat choices as a collective package, and I will refer to the "small unit perspective" when we evaluate the choices in terms of their smaller com-ponents, such as the participation of a single additional person in the firing squad. Those are simply more general terms for the more com-monly described notions of rule-based and act-based perspectives. If you wish, you also can substitute the more philosophically familiar terms "rule utilitarianism" and "act utilitarianism." The points here apply to a broader context than utilitarianism alone, but the logic of the issues very much resembles the classic rule utilitarian versus act utilitarian debates, even though bundling is the most fundamental concept to this inquiry.

[1] See Finn Kydland and Edward Prescott, "Rules Rather Than Discretion: The Inconsis-tency of Optimal Plans," *Journal of Political Economy* 85, no. 3 (1977): 473–92, among many others. Amihai Glazer and Lawrence S. Rothenberg outline policy issues involving time consistency issues in *Why Government Succeeds and Why It Fails* (Cambridge, CA: Harvard University Press, 2005).

One of Derek Parfit's "Mistakes in Moral Arithmetic," as presented in his book *Reasons and Persons* (1984), outlines a classic divide between an act-based and a rules-based perspective.[2] If a firing squad of six shooters kills an innocent person, all of them firing accurately at his heart, can we say that any one of the shooters is a murderer? After all, the "marginal product" of any single shooter was zero. Should we punish or invest resources to prevent any one of the potential shooters? Does it matter whose bullet arrived first? Should we refuse to prosecute group murders of this kind? How would we feel about a marksman who participates in a group hit on an innocent man, to earn a few dollars, figuring that the fellow is going to die anyway? This marksman might even donate some of those dollars to charities, or to nonprofits that fight to repeal capital punishment. An act-based perspective may suggest that participation in the shooting is fine, but a rules-based perspective creates room for strong objections.[3]

When our actions have nonlinear consequences, much is at stake when we choose whether to bundle and what to bundle. If we bundle the various marksmen's shots and evaluate the overall package of actions, participation will be understood as heinous and destructive, even if a particular marksman is not decisive with regard to the death of the victim and even if the marksman donates his wages to charity. The action, considered in a broader, bundled perspective, causes the death of an innocent human being. Yet if we stick with the small unit perspective, the marksman is improving social welfare. He is killing no one at the specified margin of choice, and both he and the charity may be better off.[4]

F. A. Hayek, James Buchanan, and Richard Epstein have, to varying degrees and in varying manners, linked the case for a free society to the validity of a rules-oriented perspective.[5] The idea is that we should look for those rules which will best delineate the scope of government, rather than evaluating all government policies on a case-by-case basis. In general, a rules-based perspective makes it easier to advocate or defend relatively extreme positions. Exceptions, by their very nature, are mod-

---

[2] Derek Parfit, *Reasons and Persons*, rev. ed. (Oxford: Clarendon Press, 1987).

[3] Ibid., 67, provides a string of related examples and conundrums.

[4] Some of these dilemmas resemble the Sorites problem, which typically involves nonlinear effects. A classic example of the Sorites problem is to ask how many stones constitute a pile. The contribution of any single stone to the "pileness" of the pile is zero or very small, yet the accretion of successive stones brings a pile into being. The analogy is not perfect, because our definition of "pile" is fuzzy, a complication which does not arise in the firing squad case (the death of the victim is unambiguous). Larry S. Temkin considers how the Sorites problem differs from intransitivity and vagueness as issues in moral philosophy in "A Continuum Argument for Intransitivity," *Philosophy and Public Affairs* 25, no. 3 (1996): 175–210.

[5] An extensive literature covers the practical arguments in favor of rules. See Friedrich A. Hayek, *The Constitution of Liberty* (Chicago: University of Chicago Press, 1960); Geoffrey Brennan and James M. Buchanan, *The Reason of Rules* (Indianapolis, IN: Liberty Fund, 2000); and Richard Epstein, *Simple Rules for a Complex World* (Cambridge, MA: Harvard University Press, 1997).

erating, relative to the alternative stance of following the rule all of the time. For instance, a rule that says "Don't bail out failed automobile companies" might be a good idea to prevent indiscriminate bailouts, but it also might be better to break that rule in particular circumstances. Under these assumptions, we will advocate more bailouts if we abandon the rules-based approach for an act-based perspective.

A rules-based perspective may seem attractive, but it has been on the intellectual defensive. To many observers, rule consequentialism is not persuasive, precisely because the underlying concern with consequences leads us to make many exceptions to the rule. If consequences are what matter, then adherence to the rule—for the rule's sake—is hard to justify. It seems we should break the rule when that would bring better consequences.

The strongest arguments against bundling recur in the debate between act and rule utilitarianism. Although I do not wish to defend the exclusive focus on utility found in many of those debates, I will at times borrow the terminology of that literature for expository purposes.

The act utilitarian typically believes that the rule utilitarian does not offer a coherent point of view. Act utilitarians (and others) apply the following *reduction* to rule utilitarianism: "What we really care about is utility (or some other notion of good consequences), not rules per se. So we should act to maximize utility. Sometimes adhering to rules maximizes utility, and then we adhere to rules, but sometimes breaking the rules maximizes utility. So rule utilitarianism, upon scrutiny, ought to collapse into act utilitarianism." Many philosophers accept this "reduction argument," and thus they do not consider rule utilitarianism (or rule consequentialism) to be an independent alternative to an act-based orientation. In debate, it is hard to beat the simple and immediately forceful reduction argument. After all, why *shouldn't* we make an exception and do something which will improve human welfare? The act-based orientation, of course, corresponds to what I am calling the small unit perspective.[6]

These issues have been debated since at least the eighteenth century, but I will propose a new path forward. I will address the oft-cited but underanalyzed concept of *feasibility*. I will start with the idea of trying to define the "feasible set"—or, alternatively, to define "constraints"—in a

[6] The literature here is enormous. See, for instance, Richard Brandt, "Toward a Credible Theory of Utilitarianism," in Hector-Neri Castaneda and George Nakhnikian, eds., *Morality and the Language of Conduct* (Detroit, MI: Wayne State University Press, 1963): 107–43; David Lyons, *Forms and Limits of Utilitarianism* (Oxford: Clarendon Press, 1965); Donald H. Regan, *Utilitarianism and Cooperation* (Oxford: Oxford University Press, 1980); Michael Slote, *From Morality to Virtue* (Oxford: Oxford University Press, 1992); Brad Hooker, *Ideal Code, Real World: A Rule-Consequentialist Theory of Morality* (Oxford: Clarendon Press, 2000): 93–111; John Leslie Mackie, *Persons and Values: Selected Papers, Vol. II* (Oxford: Oxford University Press, 1985); Geoffrey Scarre, *Utilitarianism* (New York: Routledge, 1996); and Fred Feldman, *Utilitarianism, Hedonism, and Desert* (Cambridge: Cambridge University Press, 1997), among many others. This problem has been present in rule utilitarianism since William Paley in the eighteenth century; see J. B. Schneewind, *Sidgwick's Ethics and Victorian Moral Philosophy* (Oxford: Clarendon Press, 1977), 125-27.

maximization problem in a philosophically coherent way. This will turn out to be a difficult problem, and it also will turn out to have some connections with the differences between bundled and small unit perspectives. This way of posing the question will give us access to some new intuitions. It turns out that our best current understanding of the concept of a "constraint" does not boil down to a simple matter of fact. Rather, it involves the murky waters of modal logic—namely, the philosophical literature on what it means to postulate that things might have been different from what they are or were. As it will turn out, the fuzziness of modal considerations will lead us to a partial license for rules-based thinking, yet without a rules-based perspective collapsing into an act-based perspective.

II. What Is Feasible and What Is Utopian?

If we think of utilitarian or consequentialist doctrine as involving problems of constrained maximization, we might look to economics for clarification on what it means to postulate a constraint. At the textbook level, economists use the idea of a budget constraint to delineate the utopian from the feasible. In this view, "moving along the budget constraint" (reshuffling resources) is feasible, whereas "wanting the budget constraint to shift out" (i.e., wanting more resources for no cost) is considered to be utopian, akin to wishing for the proverbial free lunch.

Here is a simple budget constraint:

Maximize U, subject to p1x1 + p2x2 = Y

When we graph this constraint, we get the familiar picture in figure 1.

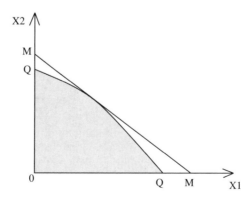

Figure 1. Production possibilities frontier QQ cannot exceed budget constraint MM. The shaded area represents feasible combinations of x1 and x2, given total wealth and resource transformation capabilities.

The diagram in figure 1 appears to indicate that there is a clear difference between "moving outside the constraint" and "moving along the constraint," as illustrated by the lines and descriptions in the diagram. That is typically how economists define what is feasible and what is not.

This distinction, however useful it may be to positive or predictive economics, begs the question as to what is truly feasible at a more fundamental level. A society cannot move from one point along a budget constraint to another point without a cost being incurred somehow, somewhere. The resources expressed and measured by the budget constraint are all owned and controlled by various individuals and, in the absence of interference, agents will allocate these resources one way rather than another. To ask for one allocation rather than another is to stipulate that some existing constraints and incentives be changed. In other words, when moving along the budget constraint, we also are asking for more resources, or for different resources, albeit in disguised fashion. At the very least, we are asking for something to be different, relative to an observed status quo. We are not involved in any straightforward process of choosing among options which "lie before us," like various pairs of socks might be laid out on a bedspread each morning when one is dressing for work. Bringing about other options along the drawn budget constraint requires different facts associated with a different possible world.

Sometimes economists think about this dilemma in terms of transaction costs. When drawing a social budget constraint, we are missing the transaction costs dimension from our measurement of costs. In considering a move along the budget constraint, we are wishing that outcomes could take a different particular form or, in other words, that transactions costs in some manner would be different. We are imagining the involved agents cutting a different set of deals, rather than the status quo. That's another way of wishing for a change, and, on reflection, it is not obviously different from wishing that manna would fall from the sky and wishing to live "beyond" the budget constraint. The specification "Transactions costs change, so we can move along the budget constraint" slides all too easily into "Lower costs would bring a better outcome and push us outside the previous budget constraint."

In any case, the real question is what the social budget constraint looks like in the first place. Once we view it in these terms, we can no longer invoke the budget constraint as an *a priori* circumscription of what is feasible and what is not. Standard economic methods simply assume that we have defined the feasible, rather than providing such a definition.

Milton Friedman, in an essay for the free-market Cato Institute, laid out the dilemma very clearly, albeit unintentionally.[7] He titled his essay "The

---

[7] Milton Friedman, "The Real Free Lunch: Markets and Private Property," in David Boaz, ed., *Toward Liberty: The Idea That Is Changing the World* (Washington DC: Cato Institute, 2002), 55–62.

Real Free Lunch: Markets and Private Property," and he argued that
market economies capture gains from trade and can make virtually everyone better off, if only we would rely on markets more. Whether you agree
with Friedman's positive claim about markets is not the point for this
discussion. Rather, I am interested in how he imagined the feasible set.
Had Friedman not insisted elsewhere that "There Is No Such Thing as a
Free Lunch"? Is not asking for "more markets" another kind of utopianism, no more relevant than the plea for a free lunch?

"What if" we all had more information? What if, to paraphrase James
Madison, men were angels? Would not the world be better off? In each
case the answer is yes, or could be yes if we worded the query to cover
the relevant counterexamples. Yet the real question is what conclusions
we can draw from such simple comparisons. Economists are renowned
for refusing to claim that the absence of a free lunch represents inefficiency per se.[8] Simply listing some states of affairs which would be better
does not establish a meaningful suggestion for political policy or reform.
It also would be better if we didn't have earthquakes.

In denying the normative relevance of the free lunch, economists are
staking out (part of) a position on feasibility, if only implicitly. Let us see
how that position looks if we present it in terms of a simple ordering.
Economists, for instance, might rank some alternatives, in terms of their
degree of feasibility, in the following manner:

Most to least utopian:

(1) Oceans of lemonade
(2) Social state X plus a free lunch
(3) Social state X (with different policies than the status quo)
(4) Status quo

Economists, in denying the relevance of the free lunch, are unwilling to
criticize vision (3) for falling short of vision (2); in other words, vision (2)
is excessively utopian, or (alternatively) it is not sufficiently feasible.

At the same time, many economists do not see it as excessively utopian
to ask for (3) in lieu of (4). In lieu of making pleas for free lunches, many
contemporary economists advocate what they call "comparative institutional analysis." The economist compares one set of (feasible?) institutions to another set of (feasible?) institutions and asks which is better. We
have a relevant imperfection only when an institutional improvement
would bring more benefit than cost.

In other words, many economists consider it normatively interesting to
ask:

[8] Harold Demsetz, "Information and Efficiency: Another Viewpoint," *Journal of Law and Economics* 12, no. 1 (1969): 1–22.

(1) What if we had institution X instead of institution Y?

Those same economists do not consider it normatively interesting to ask:

(2) What if we had a free lunch?

The distinction between these two questions is not easy to defend on the grounds of pure logic. It is difficult to dismiss the free lunch question as utopian while maintaining the normative relevance of the comparative institutional question. If institution X is better than institution Y, then arguably having X is one form of a free lunch. Preferring institution X over institution Y could be, to make a simple comparison, as utopian as wishing the world didn't have major earthquakes or that human beings were more benevolent.[9]

Economists therefore face a "war on two fronts," to borrow Parfit's fruitful concept.[10] It is not easy to reconcile two strong intuitions. The first is that inefficiencies exist and can be pinpointed meaningfully. The second is that there is no free lunch, and it is normatively meaningless to wish for one. Either intuition, taken alone, sounds plausible. But it is hard to put the two intuitions together into a single account of which changes are feasible and which are not.[11]

Moving outside economics to the context of political thought, we can find similar issues in different contexts. A world without scarcity may sound good as an abstract ideal, but we reject the idea as excessively utopian. Fair enough, but now consider some growth-improving policy, such as a revamping of the U.S. tax system. Given all the special interest groups at work, is wishing for a truly good reform much more realistic than Charles Fourier's belief that socialism would bring oceans of lem-

---

[9] This ranked example is drawn from Tyler Cowen, "The Epistemic Problem Does Not Refute Consequentialism," *Utilitas* 18, no. 4 (2006): 383–99. On the concept of utopianism in the economics literature, see Clarence Philbrook, "'Realism' in Policy Espousal," *American Economic Review* 43, no. 5 (1953): 846–59, reprinted in Daniel B. Klein, ed., *What Do Economists Contribute?* (Washington, DC: Cato Institute, 1999), 69–86; Carl J. Dahlman, "The Problem of Externality," *Journal of Law and Economics* 22, no. 1 (1979): 141-62; Pamela J. Brown, *Deadweight Loss: A Nonexistence Theorem* (unpublished manuscript, California State University, Northridge, 1988); and Daniel B. Klein, ed., *What Do Economists Contribute?* (Washington, DC: Cato Institute, 1999).

[10] Parfit, *Reasons and Persons*, Part I, chap. 3.

[11] Alastair Norcross argues that we need to consider the best available action relative to alternatives, and discusses the ambiguities in defining exactly what those alternatives are, in "Good and Bad Actions," *The Philosophical Review* 106, no. 1 (1997): 1–33. On the relevance of related ideas for the free will controversies, see Daniel C. Dennett, *Elbow Room: The Varieties of Free Will Worth Wanting* (Cambridge, MA: MIT Press, 1984). For discussion of the meanings of "if" and "can" in ordinary language philosophy, see J. L. Austin, *Philosophical Papers* (Oxford: Clarendon Press, 1961); and D. F. Pears, "Ifs and Cans," in *Essays on J. L. Austin* (Oxford: Clarendon Press, 1973). Simon Blackburn considers general issues involving morals and modal logic in "Morals and Modals," in Blackburn, *Essays in Quasi-Realism* (Oxford: Oxford University Press, 1993), 52–74.

onade and ship-pulling dolphins?[12] It might be more realistic as a matter of degree, but it is hard to see where a clear line—delineating the feasible from the infeasible—might come from.

The general issue is this. We wish to allow at least *some* scope for normative, big-picture thinking. It is not useful to argue that the world is already as good as it could be. At the same time, we do not wish to think so big that we lose the moorings of common sense and veer off into the excessively utopian. It doesn't make sense to just draw up an ideal wish list and call that an approach to reform.

Many reform advocates wish, at least implicitly, to have it both ways. They require that some degree of utopianism is acceptable. Proposals for change, to some extent, require that we advocate good outcomes for their own sake, without necessarily predicting their adoption. Without this willingness to be at least somewhat "utopian," we cannot elevate a good reform proposal above the status quo. If we advocated only what was already in place, expected, or forthcoming, there would be little point to making policy prescriptions. Nonetheless, for whatever imagined improvement we can cite, there will exist better, yet more utopian, competing proposals. We reject (many of these) proposals by arguing that they are excessively utopian. Yet we again return to the dilemma: Why do we classify some reform proposals as feasible and others as infeasible?[13]

The standard "conservative" critiques of utopianism, as we find in Karl Popper, F. A. Hayek, and evolutionary biology, do not much help in this context. These powerful arguments do tell us that human nature is somewhat fixed or even extremely fixed; they suggest that certain proposals, especially of a totalitarian nature, would be disasters rather than utopias.

---

[12] In fairness to Fourier, he was also an early prophet of the steam locomotive, a view for which he was ridiculed in his time; see Jonathan Beecher, *Charles Fourier: The Visionary and His World* (Berkeley: University of California Press, 1986), 59. On the lemonade idea, see ibid., 125.

[13] The literature on utopias raises related questions, although not usually in a philosophic or rational choice framework. Aurel Kolnai writes: "How exactly can we distinguish between the proper pursuit of the good and its perfectionist aberration?" in Kolnai, *The Utopian Mind and Other Papers: A Critical Study in Moral and Political Philosophy*, ed. Francis Dunlop (London: Athlone, 1995), 17. Frank E. Manuel and Fritzie P. Manuel note that "one man's trivial revision is another man's upheaval" in *Utopian Thought in the Western World* (Cambridge, MA: Belknap Press of Harvard University Press, 1979), 8. Karl Mannheim refers to the "difficulty in defining precisely what, at a given period, is to be regarded as ideology, and what as utopia" in *Ideology and Utopia: An Introduction to the Sociology of Knowledge* (New York: Harcourt, 1936), 203. Since at least Friedrich Engels, this topic has been a staple of socialist debate as well. See Friedrich Engels, *Socialism: Utopian and Scientific* (Peking: Foreign Languages Press, 1975). For a survey of some definitions of utopia, see Ruth Levitas, *The Concept of Utopia* (Syracuse, NY: Syracuse University Press, 1990), 3. See also J. C. Davis, "The History of Utopia: The Chronology of Nowhere," in Peter Alexander and Roger Gill, eds., *Utopias* (London: Duckworth, 1984): 1–18; and Lyman Tower Sargent, "Utopian Themes: Themes and Variations," in Roland Schaer, Gregory Claeys, and Lyman Tower Sargent, eds., *Utopia: The Search for the Ideal Society in the Western World* (New York: The New Public Library/Oxford University Press, 2000), 8–15. Barbara Goodwin and Keith Taylor consider the role that concepts of utopia have played in political debate in *The Politics of Utopia: A Study in Theory and Practice* (New York: St. Martin's Press, 1982).

But these perspectives do not address the utopian dilemma per se, much less resolve it. The key question is not about central planning. Rather, it is about whether, when we consider changes (including a move away from central planning), we should evaluate those changes bit by bit or together as part of a broader bundle. In other words, invoking Popper, Hayek, or conservative thinkers does not settle what is a metaphysical rather than a practical planning question. Indeed, as mentioned above, Hayek himself advocated a high degree of rules-based thinking.

We also cannot look to formal modal logic to resolve these questions about feasibility. Formal modal logic is a well-developed philosophic literature which looks at what it means to analyze or speak of "possible worlds." Nonetheless, without intending any criticism of the broader genre, modal logic is not well-suited to the task at hand. First, the major approaches to modal logic deal with a very broadly conceived notion of what is feasible or possible. For instance, it is frequently accepted that "talking donkeys," however strange the concept may be in common-sense terms, belong to the set of possible worlds. Maybe such donkeys are not impossible in the sense of violating the known laws of physics, but arguably they are still "too impossible" for the more practical and applied purposes of ethics and politics, where far less absurd ideas are dismissed out of hand. Modal logic operates within a broader notion of the feasible than would resolve typical policy debates over the feasible set. I am looking for a concrete and practically useful method of judging feasibility, rather than a purely abstract standard of logical classification based on hard constraints taken from the science of physics.

Second, modal logic itself presents numerous unsolved dilemmas at a quite fundamental level, not the least of which is what the concept of "possible worlds" means in the first place. Some philosophers believe that claims about modal logic make sense only if they refer to real worlds actually out there (modal realism), while other philosophers are suspicious of the concept of modality altogether. I think of the literature on modal logic as reflecting and anticipating the more practical dilemmas discussed above, not as solving them. Ideally, we would like a solution, or at least a means of moving forward, which is independent of any very particular approach to controversial questions of metaphysics and modal logic. In any case, we still must plow forward using stop-gap approaches in the meantime.[14]

[14] On various modal debates, see Michael J. Loux, *The Possible and the Actual: Readings in the Metaphysics of Modality* (Ithaca, NY: Cornell University Press, 1979); Graeme Forbes, *The Metaphysics of Modality* (Oxford: Clarendon Press, 1985); David Lewis, *On the Plurality of Worlds* (New York: Basil Blackwell, 1986); D. M. Armstrong, *A Combinatorial Theory of Possibility* (Cambridge: Cambridge University Press, 1989); William G. Lycan, *Modality and Meaning* (Dordrecht: Kluwer Publishers, 1994); Christopher Hitchcock, "Farewell to Binary Causation," *Canadian Journal of Philosophy* 26, no. 2 (1996): 267–82; Alexander Robert Pruss, "Possible Worlds: What They Are Good For and What They Are Not" (unpublished doctoral dissertation, University of Pittsburgh, 2001); Theodore Sider, "The Ersatz Pluriverse," *The*

III. The Panglossian View as a Stopping Point

Some economists talk as if they believe the extreme claim that all observed outcomes are efficient. Nobel laureate George Stigler and other members of the Chicago School have been associated with this view, although it does not seem that Stigler ever embraced it in print. It may be more of a lunch-room exercise than a view that anyone holds consistently, but I am interested in it nonetheless. Sometimes this claim is presented in a modified form, such as "Everything we observe in markets is efficient," "Democracies are efficient," or "Everything is locally efficient, albeit not always globally efficient." I will consider the most straightforward claim that everything observed is efficient, all of the time. It might seem that I am picking on this attitude by examining its weakest variant, but my purpose is the opposite. I would like to argue that the (ostensibly) weakest version of this view is, in terms of logic, stronger and more plausible than many of the more popular intermediate positions.[15]

Although virtually everyone rejects this Panglossian view, it has a logical consistency which many of its competitors do not. Any beneficial improvement which we do not already have is utopian and thus should be dismissed as a free lunch. In essence, the budget constraint is now a single point, namely the status quo.

One who holds the Panglossian view has a rejoinder to claims of inefficiency: "The current state of affairs *would* be inefficient, if the relevant parties could bargain or trade to bring about a better outcome. But apparently they cannot. Correcting the so-called problem is too costly. The existence of the problem is efficient, once we take *all* constraints and *all* costs, including the costs of bargaining and the costs of change, into account. To claim otherwise is simply to wish that things would be better, a kind of utopian dreaming. We are economists. We do not ask for free lunches."

Of course, the Panglossian view need not be thought of as especially optimistic. We are in the "worst of all possible worlds" as well as in the "best of all possible worlds."

At this point, many individuals will mock the Panglossian view as a tautology or a moral absurdity, more deserving of scorn than an intellectual response. Genocide happens, babies starve, the mail is not always delivered on time, and so on. Surely something is wrong in the world,

---

Journal of Philosophy 99, no. 6 (2002): 279–315; Tamar Szabo Gendler and John Hawthorne, eds., *Conceivability and Possibility* (Oxford: Clarendon Press, 2002); and John Divers, *Possible Worlds* (London: Routledge, 2002).

[15] Parmenides argued that the world could not be any different. The literature on theodicy considers whether God made the "best possible world" and what it means to say that other worlds are possible. See Robert M. Adams, *The Virtue of Faith and Other Essays in Philosophical Ideology* (New York: Oxford University Press, 1987); Robert M. Adams, *Leibniz: Determinist, Theist, Idealist* (New York: Oxford University Press, 1994); and Alvin Plantinga, *The Nature of Necessity* (Oxford: Clarendon Press, 1989).

and it outrages many people to hear that everything is efficient, all things considered. The Panglossian view seems to abuse discourse and our common-sense understanding that real-world improvements are possible.

By the way, the Panglossian view is only one of the available extremes. John Stuart Mill, Marquis de Condorcet, and Herbert Spencer all defended the perfectibility of mankind as a central political vision. Today, tech-savvy advocates of "The Singularity" predict that we will be genetically reengineered for the better or we will become computer uploads. These attitudes, like the Panglossian view, offer a logical consistency of sorts. They tell us to hold out for an extreme utopian vision in which virtually everything is up for grabs and very broad improvements will prove feasible.[16]

Most of us embrace some intermediate view between Panglossianism and extreme utopianism. An intermediate view "feels" right, seems reasonable, and fits with the practice of most of the smart and honest people we know. Yet the intermediate positions, appealing though they may sound, do not have as much logic on their side as we might like to think. Once you push on them, it is hard to defend why we might allow one degree of utopianism yet reject another. The intermediate positions run a high risk of being arbitrary rather than well-grounded and consistent.

The "marginalist" tradition, which in economics stresses looking at incremental changes, might lead many economists to favor the small unit perspective and to lean away from utopianism. Yet the positive analytical successes of economics, using the marginalist method, do not translate into a strong case for the small unit perspective as a means for distinguishing relevant moral comparisons from irrelevant moral comparisons. Once we see feasibility as a matter of degree, the relevant definition of "the margin" is not given immediately or unambiguously by the objective facts of the case.

Furthermore, the economics literature has a lot of well-regarded work which moves away from the small unit perspective. For instance, versions of the bundling problem surface repeatedly in game theory, but in that context the literature has not generally sided with the small unit perspective. One common construct is the "Shapley value," which is used to measure the importance of an individual to a broader coalition. A Shapley value may help measure a worker's contribution to joint production, or a voter's contribution to a political coalition. The details of the Shapley value need not concern us here, but the construct does not refer to an agent's marginal product in the traditional sense; rather, it refers to a metric of bundling. The Shapley value, while it hardly commands universal support, serves as the most popular "rational choice" solution to many bargaining problems. This suggests that economics and rational

---

[16] For a more general survey of utopian thinking, see Manuel and Manuel, *Utopian Thought in the Western World.*

choice approaches do not commit us to the small unit perspective when nonlinear effects are present.[17]

IV. Degrees of Feasibility

In lieu of the Panglossian and pure utopian points of view, we can think of feasibility as a spectrum rather than as an all-or-nothing category. Some specified world-states are more utopian than others, but as a matter of degree rather than of kind.

Most feasibility differences do appear to be differences of degree. For instance, consider the option of inducing more work from a labor force. Probably it is too utopian to expect everyone to work eighteen hours a day and enjoy it; human motivations would have to be "too different" for that to happen. But the judgment of nonfeasibility does not appear to kick in at any particular number of hours, as could be defined by an exact cut-off. Rather, the more extra work is specified, the lower the degree of feasibility that appears to hold. A similar logic holds with regard to many other feasibility judgments, including those in the areas of fiscal restraint, tax reform, changes in the speed of bureaucracy, or, for that matter, declines in the probability of genocide, referring to the world's more violent countries. In most cases, the larger the potential improvement, the more utopian it will appear to be, again without any clear cut-off point as to what is feasible and what is not.

At the very least, when we consider the practical epistemic issues, it is unlikely that we could identify or verify a cut-off point between the feasible and the infeasible, even if such a clear line existed in some rarefied realm of modal logic. Perhaps there is some ultimately true and correct metaphysical theory in which people can work seventeen minutes longer each, but not seventeen minutes and one millisecond longer. But again we are far from having access to such knowledge. For practical purposes, we are left with feasibility as a matter of degree.

We can see degrees of feasibility even in the Fourier vision of a utopian future. Forget about oceans, what if we were told that socialism would bring us a mid-sized lake full of lemonade? A small pond? How about a

---

[17] In formal terms, the Shapley solution looks at all possible differing "coalitions" (combinations of actions or abstentions from action, in the firing squad example) and measures the differing marginal values of an individual unit to the coalition. These marginal values are then averaged across all of the possible combinations of units. In the firing squad example, for instance, the Shapley value averages a single shooter's marginal impact across "all six of us shoot," "only the first five of the six shoot," "only the last five of the six shoot," "only these three of the six shoot," "only I shoot," and so on, across all the possible combinations. We will then find that the Shapley value for a single marksman is positive, but less than the value of an individual life. On the bargaining theory foundations for the Shapley value, see Alvin E. Roth, "Axiomatic Models of Bargaining," *Lecture Notes in Economics and Mathematical Systems,* No. 170 (New York: Springer Verlag, 1979); and Faruk Gul, "Bargaining Foundations of Shapley Value," *Econometrica* 57, no. 1 (1989): 81–95.

glass full of lemonade? (Can you get that in North Korea? I wonder.)
Again, it is difficult to find a distinct cut-off at which the specified world-
states clearly and definitely cross from the realm of the feasible into the
realm of the infeasible.

A spectrum of feasibility might specify a number of dimensions. A
more feasible vision, compared to a less feasible vision, might be "more
like" the world we know in terms of fact, more like the world we know
in terms of adherence to the laws of science, or might stand at the end of
a relatively simple path from "here" to "there." Most likely, the more
feasible world-state possesses some combination of these qualities, relative to the less feasible world-state. For our purposes, the exact number or
nature of the dimensions is not the relevant point; it suffices to note that
some kind of continuum exists.[18]

In some cases physical laws might suggest very definite *limits* to feasibility, but still, along most margins, feasibility will be a matter of degree.
Quantum theory, for instance, might suggest that particles can only become
so small, at which point no further divisibility is possible. Perhaps we can
measure this limit quite exactly in principle, if not always in practice. To
take another example, in Einstein's theory no entities other than tachyons
can travel faster than the speed of light, which again serves as a definite
limit. But the feasibility problems of the social sciences are not so exact or
so amenable to fixed measurement at these kinds of limiting points. We
do not know how to break social science problems down into their quantum elements, and maybe it's not possible at all. We are left again with
feasibility as a sliding scale, at least for the vast majority of our speculations, and our knowledge of physics offers few useful guidelines.[19]

V. In Defense of Rules-Based Thinking

Any plausible normative theory must, to some extent, treat some previously imagined constraints as freely floating parameters of choice. That is
the take-away from the discussion of the Panglossian view. But we do not
have clear guidance for where to stop in delineating the feasible set. In
other words, there is no strong argument—apart from the Panglossian

[18] David Lewis has suggested some standards for ranking worlds in terms of their similarity, and along these lines we might regard the more similar worlds to our own as "more
possible" or "less utopian." See David Lewis, "Counterfactual Dependence and Time's
Arrow," *Noûs* 13, no. 4 (1979): 472. For a treatment of degrees of possibility, see Forbes, *The
Metaphysics of Modality*, chap. 7.
[19] Note that we should not identify feasibility with the notions of probability or likelihood. Feasibility refers in some manner to the "closeness" of some other world to our own,
whether or not we expect that world to occur. Blinking your eyes one more time in a day,
each day, might be quite feasible in the common-sense use of that term, although we do not
necessarily expect such an act to occur with a high probability. Conditional on the number
of blinks changing, the chance that the change is exactly one blink might be quite small. This
example suggests that feasibility and probability are distinct concepts and that a high degree
of feasibility does not have to mean a high degree of probability.

view—for keeping the degree of utopian thinking to a minimum, and such a view does not command much loyalty.

Rather than collapsing into act utilitarianism, rule utilitarianism specifies a differing series of constraints and thus a different maximization problem altogether. For instance, when it comes to bundling across time, we are picking some policy today, under the constraint that a similar policy (or rule) be applied in subsequent time periods. In contrast, act utilitarianism takes the action of one individual at one point in time as a free variable, and asks what that agent should do to maximize utility. Rule utilitarianism takes an entire series of individual actions to be free variables, but it considers them collectively rather than one-by-one. More is "up for grabs" than under act utilitarianism.

More formally, rule utilitarianism looks like this:

(1) Maximize U, subject to Action (t1) = Actions (t2, t3, t3. . .)

In other words, we have to apply a rule consistently over time, and across different persons, when it comes to chosen actions.

Act utilitarianism looks more like this:

(2) Maximize U, allowing for Actions (t1, t2, t3. . .) as different variables and selecting for t1 alone.

Under this understanding, the rules-based perspective is based on the notion of a difference in the constraints. Rule utilitarianism and act utilitarianism postulate different maximization problems, and thus they coexist in some fashion, rather than one subsuming the other or one collapsing into the other. Furthermore, since we do not have a definitive, fact-based way of presenting "the correct constraints," we do not have an in-principle argument for rejecting the rules-based perspective. There is still no argument that the rules-based perspective is better (more on that later), but at the very least it has no longer been knocked out of the running. The thing to be maximized (the maximand) is in both problems the same—some notion of good consequences, with utility as the immediate stand-in—but the relevant constraint is not uniquely determined in any manner which would allow us to adjudicate across the two problems.

For a simple analogy, consider two microeconomic problems. The first asks a business to maximize profit, subject to the constraint that inventories in one particular store never fall below a specified level. The second asks a business to maximize profit, subject to the constraint that inventories in each store in the chain never fall below a specified level. Again the maximand is the same—profit—but we have two differing constraints. It would be wrong to claim that one such problem is "the wrong normative theory," or that one such problem "collapses" into the other. Rule and act utilitarianism/consequentialism hold a similar dual and possibly coexisting status, once we look at both the maximand *and the constraint*.

The reduction argument, as it is used against rules-based perspectives, requires a commitment to a very particular account of feasibility. It requires the implicit claim that thinking of rules or bundled acts as the relevant constraint is incorrect. Supposedly we should look at a smaller unit of choice—the single act—as the relevant constraint. But again, once we see feasibility as a sliding scale and a matter of degree, it is not obvious why this argument should have so much force. Treating "a bundle of choices" as a relevant free variable is no less defensible than treating "a single act" as a relevant free variable. If we can put a single act up for grabs in our normative decision-making, why not treat a larger rule or bundled package as a variable for choice?

The act-utilitarian critique of rule utilitarianism seems plausible because act utilitarianism appears to examine the smallest possible unit of choice, namely, the individual act. But the smallest possible unit of choice is *zero*—namely, no change—not a single act. The logic of the act-utilitarian reduction argument should, taken alone, lead to the Panglossian perspective, not to act utilitarianism. Act utilitarianism "survives," so to speak, only because we allow some utopianism in the door and allow at least one constraint to be loosened. If we can object to taking rules as a free-floating variable, someone who holds the Panglossian view can object to taking individual acts as a free-floating variable. Why stop at one point rather than the other? Once we elevate an "act" perspective over the Panglossian view, we have opened the door for yet additional flexibility in understanding the constraint, and the reduction argument is no longer decisive.

In other words, the act-utilitarian critique fails to win a "war on two fronts," again referring to Parfit's concept. The act-utilitarian perspective might appear strong when faced with either the Panglossian view or rule utilitarianism. But it has a harder time taking them both on at the same time and winning the debate. The logic of act utilitarianism—or, indeed, of normative analysis in the first place—allows for the possibility of moving even further away from the Panglossian view and considering rules-based changes or other bundled approaches to the constraints.

Having covered this ground, I would like to consider two issues which arise commonly in discussions of bundling or rules-based perspectives. One common criticism of the rules-based perspective is that the act-based perspective can embody quite complex instructions, sufficiently complex that rules are not needed. For instance, when coordination problems are present, we might need more complex instructions rather than very simple instructions. A simple instruction might be "Perform action X," whereas the more complex instruction might be "Perform action X, but only if enough other cooperators help make the collective effort worthwhile," or however the instructions might usefully be worded. The underlying claim is that complex instructions are a more useful concept than rules, and that act utilitarianism, combined with sufficiently complex instructions, is robust. One can debate the semantic issue of whether this argument represents a victory for act or rule consequentialism or some other perspective. The important point is that the more complex instructions expand the scope of bundling beyond a single do/don't act. We are still left with narrower and broader notions of the constraints (no one conception of the constraints having a metaphysical priority over the others) and with some license for a broader notion of bundling.

A second common criticism is that a rules-based perspective cannot handle all possible counterexamples. Let us postulate a rule, namely, that everyone should pitch in to achieve some common end, such as moving a car out of the way, to open an important road for passage. It takes ten people to lift the car, and ten are present. We can all agree that all ten should follow the rule and lift the car. At the same time, if it is expected that three people will shirk their duties, and not lift, it makes no sense for the other seven to soil their clothes and strain their bodies, for no useful end. The rules-based perspective would appear to experience trouble with this example, since following a good rule with three noncooperators simply wastes an effort. But the correct conclusion is not that bundled perspectives fail. At best this example shows that there is no single, supreme rule. There still exists a series of imagined constraints—no behavior up for grabs, behavior from one of the agents up for grabs, seven behaviors up for grabs, three up for grabs, all ten up for grabs, and so on. Again, no one of those constraints has a privileged metaphysical position over the other. We might prefer to have "all ten" behaviors up for grabs as the most effective lever for manipulation. But those (hypothetical) practical benefits do not pin down or identify the appropriate level of feasibility or utopianness. To see why not, let's say we had a practical problem which required the tight coordination of billions of agents to be solved. That would not mean we had found "billions" to be an appropriate level of coordinative feasibility; at the same time, it also would not altogether rule out thinking in terms of broader bundles of choice or action.

VI. How Strong Can the Arguments for a Rules-Based Perspective Get?

So far, the argument has established only that the reduction argument, as I have called it, does not defeat a rules-based or bundled perspective. That is progress, but actually the arguments for bundling are stronger than that observation.

Most importantly, the arguments for bundling do not require bundling to be correct with certainty or with a probability of 1. As it stands, we have a set of coexisting perspectives about constraints and modality. One possibility is that one specification of the constraint is shown to be correct and all the others will fall away; that's possible, but at this stage of the game it's not looking likely.

Another option is that all or many of the differing modal perspectives will remain on the table, and for practical choices we will have to add up or aggregate these differing views in some manner. The idea of coexisting moral codes is, in fact, a familiar one, and it appears in the debates on different versions of rule-utilitarian principles. For instance, there are multiple approaches to generating a rules-based code. Should we evaluate the code on the presupposition that it is adopted and internalized by all relevant individuals? Or should we evaluate the code assuming that we must bear significant costs of adoption and internalization? In other words, the code can be treated either as a free variable (to be selected or not), or as an investment in a new custom, including transition costs. Again, we see two maximization problems, each involving a different specification of constraints. Just as one problem does not "reduce" to the other, rules-based approaches do not reduce to the act-based standard. It also can be said that there is no obvious supreme rule, only different methods of thinking about bundling. In this regard, rules-based approaches have to make some very important concessions, and we cannot expect a rules-based approach to support a monolithic approach to moral thinking.[20]

That all said, when we have multiple, coexisting perspectives floating around in our moral theory, it remains true that in the world we must proceed to formulate some view, however provisional or understated. That suggests that we should look to some plausible aggregate or combination of those multiple perspectives, and if we take this approach, bundling has again survived the reduction argument. If we aggregate single-act and bundled perspectives, the overall blend will give some weight to bundling, by the very nature of aggregation. Ultimately that blend is more of a victory for the bundled perspective than for the single-act perspective.

For instance, take a policy that has no effect when applied in small doses but significantly boosts economic growth when it is applied repeatedly. Furthermore, assume that we believe bundling to be correct, applicable, or otherwise relevant or weight-worthy in some manner with, say, a probability of 0.2. In expected value terms, we still ought to pursue the recommendation of the bundled perspective, given how the calculation would proceed. This is a deliberately oversimplified example, but it reflects a more general point. If we combine rules-based and act-based perspectives, the very act of combining means that on net we are left with some form of bundling. More complicated examples will give weight to both

---

[20] On costs of adoption and internalization and rule utilitarianism, see Richard Brandt, "Toward a Credible Theory of Utilitarianism," in Castaneda and Nakhnikian, eds., *Morality and the Language of Conduct*, 107–43; and Hooker, *Ideal Code, Real World*, 78–79. On varieties of rule utilitarianism more generally, see Scarre, *Utilitarianism*, 122–32.

act-based and bundled perspectives, but in net terms some method of bundling, whatever the weights given to the bundled perspectives may be, will be influencing the final decisions.

Aggregation procedures are the friend of bundling, as a general method, not its enemy. In contrast, aggregation procedures move us away from the single-act perspective, which by its nature cannot be combined or weighted with anything else. So again, if we aggregate together bundled and single-act perspectives, the result generally will involve some bundling. That means the relevant question is not whether to bundle but rather which form or method of bundling is the best way to proceed. All of a sudden the debate has been settled in favor of bundling, in some form or another. In future work, currently in progress, I am pursuing the question of whether we can find a focal means of bundling, given the multiplicity of bundling options facing us.

When comparing more or less bundled alternatives, it is also worth asking the practical question: In which direction is our civilization most likely to err? Are we more likely to perish because our decision algorithms involved too much bundling or too little bundling?

In my view, it is unlikely that real-world decision-makers will bundle too much. The nature of politics is more likely to produce too little bundling than too much bundling. Policymakers often make decisions on a day-to-day, case-by-case basis, simply hoping to survive the next election cycle. Politicians typically look at the marginal products of particular actions—if indeed they are that sophisticated, rational, or public-minded in the first place—rather than treating a broader set of actions as a bundled group. That is one reason why we make as many political mistakes as we do.

To be sure, this kind of "noble lie" defense of a rules-based perspective does not get us very far on its own. For instance, plenty of act utilitarians will admit that we are better off for believing in rule utilitarianism, while still insisting that the latter cannot be philosophically justified. But the "noble lie" approach is too cynical a way of viewing the choice between rules-based and act-based perspectives. Calling it a noble lie is assuming that a rules-based perspective is a philosophical weak sister to begin with. I have tried to show it isn't. The notion of rules offers a legitimate and independent perspective which can compete with act consequentialism, or act utilitarianism, on at least equal terms and possibly superior terms.

If that is the case, the practical benefits of believing in a rules-based perspective do not have to be seen as a noble lie. They might just be part of a very important noble truth.

VII. Conclusion

The rules-based perspective deserves another look. The reduction argument, which is often used against a rules-based perspective, is not as strong as it looks. More generally, a lot in moral theory depends on how we think about defining the relevant constraints on our choices. To the extent that a rules-based perspective is defensible, it may be possible to revive a vision of liberal society based on strict constraints and norms.

Economics, George Mason University

LIBERALISM, CAPITALISM, AND "SOCIALIST" PRINCIPLES

By Richard J. Arneson

I. Introduction

After hundreds of years of debate, political theorists are still divided, or
at least ambivalent, as to the moral desirability of the capitalist economic
market. This essay explores some areas of festering disagreement.[1] The
aim is not so much to render verdicts as to what views are correct or
incorrect, but rather to advance the understanding of opposed positions.
In broad terms, liberalism champions individual liberty. We can distinguish (a) political and civil liberties (the right to vote and stand for office
in free elections, the right to freedom of speech and thought, the right to
freedom of association), and (b) personal freedom (the freedom to live
one's own life in one's own way, as one chooses). In this essay, I am going
to set the type (a) liberties to the side. I shall just assume that all the
positions regarding desirable economic arrangements that I am highlighting will agree in defending strong guarantees of political and civil liberties.[2] There is much to say on this topic, but not here.[3]

My aim is to examine some moral principles of social justice that are
invoked to guide the choice of economic systems, and to see where
these principles stand on type (b) personal freedom. A particular focus
will be on clarifying the theoretical options available within a welfarist-
consequentialist tradition of thought, according to which liberal doctrines, or rather, the values that liberal doctrines affirm to be fundamental,
are regarded instrumentally, as helps or hindrances to bringing about
good outcomes.[4]

---

[1] The disagreements are both empirical and normative. Normative disagreement is disagreement about values, about what states of affairs are intrinsically good and bad, and
about what choices of actions and policies are morally forbidden, permissible, or required.

[2] I do not have any profound rationale for dividing the liberties in this way. I mean simply
to set aside political liberties that are not going to be central to the dispute between capitalism and socialism as G. A. Cohen (whose views are the target of this essay) and I
understand that dispute.

[3] I say more about one aspect of political liberty, the right to a democratic say, in Richard
Arneson, "Democracy Is Not Intrinsically Just," in Keith Dowding, Robert E. Goodin, and
Carole Pateman, eds., *Democracy and Justice* (Cambridge: Cambridge University Press, 2004),
40-58 ; and Arneson, "The Supposed Right to a Democratic Say," in Thomas Christiano and
John Christman, eds., *Contemporary Debates in Political Philosophy* (Oxford: Wiley-Blackwell,
2009), 197-212.

[4] Welfarist consequentialism is itself a large tent. It houses many doctrines, including
right-wing views such as those of Richard Epstein, who holds that a capitalist market

doi:10.1017/S0265052510000282

This essay follows a sideways approach to its topic. I begin by considering an evocation of the ideal of socialism, regarded as opposed in principle to private property, market exchange, and a capitalist economic organization. By "capitalism" here I mean an economic system in which economic production is organized through voluntary contracts among owners of resources, in which individuals are free to contract on any mutually agreeable terms so long as these do not generate certain types of harm to third parties, and in which economic production is undertaken for the most part, by business firms that consist of owners of capital who hire nonowners as workers.[5] I examine moral principles that have been proposed[6] as the core principles underlying the socialist ideal, and I suggest revisions that render them more plausible. The revisions move toward a consequentialist standard that might justify various social arrangements depending on the circumstances. From this standpoint, liberal freedoms like ownership rules are means not ends. The upshot is convergence: a new way of supporting the familiar suggestion that capitalist economic institutions might be part of the overall mix of institutions that would best fulfill socialist ideals reasonably interpreted.

II. THE CAMPING TRIP ECONOMY

In his essay "Why Not Socialism?" the late G. A. Cohen describes a likely mode of organization of a camping trip excursion undertaken by some friends.[7] He finds this mode of organization attractive, and tries to

---

economy embedded in a classical liberal framework of laws is an effective and efficient engine for producing human good. It also houses views such as those of the nineteenth-century utilitarian philosopher John Stuart Mill, whose views, though nuanced, all in all place him in the company of left-wing critics of the capitalist market economy. See Richard A. Epstein, *Simple Rules for a Complex World* (Cambridge, MA, and London: Harvard University Press, 1995). See John Stuart Mill, *Utilitarianism; On Liberty; Principles of Political Economy; Autobiography; Chapters on Socialism;* and *The Subjection of Women.* These works by Mill are all available, with details of first publication, at http://www.utilitarianism.net/jsmill/.

[5] The characterization in the text is rough. There is also an important ambiguity here. Recall Mill's hope that as the population becomes more competent and morally minded, superior individuals will be unwilling to work for a boss and will instead form labor-owned cooperative firms. Eventually, the economy mainly contains cooperative firms, and would-be capitalists can only hire the least competent and morally minded workers, and have little real freedom to form and sustain capitalist firms. But in the mainly cooperative economy Mill envisages, full rights of private ownership and free exchange are upheld, so "capitalist acts between consenting adults" are not banned, and no expropriation of private property occurs (or need occur) to bring about this outcome. The legal framework is capitalist, but capitalist firms are few. I disagree with Mill that there need be anything problematic or undesirable about working for a boss, in a privately owned or publicly owned firm, but the distinction between (1) guaranteed legal rights for capitalist activity and (2) actual capitalist activity occurring makes sense. Mill's discussion is in his *Principles of Political Economy,* Book IV, chap. VII, sections 3–4. The phrase "capitalist acts between consenting adults" is taken from Robert Nozick, *Anarchy, State, and Utopia* (New York: Basic Books, 1974), 163.

[6] By G. A. Cohen. See the next section of this essay.

[7] G. A. Cohen, *Why Not Socialism?* (Princeton, NJ: Princeton University Press, 2010). See also Cohen, *Rescuing Justice and Equality* (Cambridge, MA: Harvard University Press, 2008).

distill its principles. He suggests that there is no principled bar to scaling up the camping trip ideal, and affirming it as the ideal way for a society to organize its economy. The camping trip principles oppose the idea of organizing an economy by market exchange, so if after reflection we find we love the camping trip ideal, we hate the market. The camping trip principles encapsulate the socialist ideal.[8] However, it does not follow that we ought to abolish capitalism and establish socialism, because the former, we know, is feasible, whereas the latter might well not be. We should remake the economy on the camping trip model, but only if we should come to discover that this is a feasible project. So urges Cohen.

Cohen asserts that when friends go together on a camping trip, a spirit of camaraderie prevails. For the duration of the trip, items of gear are not treated as private property, but as commonly owned. Everyone is committed to everyone's having fun and, in a rough way, to everyone's having equal fulfillment. Chores are shared, and divided fairly and efficiently, so that the necessary burdens impinge on each member of the party in about the same way and impose similar levels of sacrifice on each. Claims to justified inequality in benefits—on the basis that some have contributed more to the group enterprise even though they have not put forth more sacrifice than others, or on the Lockean basis that some of the resources that emerge in the course of the enterprise were initially unowned resources privately appropriated—would be met properly with derision by the members of the party.

Finding the camping trip ideal ethically attractive, we imagine extending this mode of organization to the economy as a whole, and find the extension ethically attractive. We then are picturing a socialist economy. What would appear to be the case is that the economy is organized as, in effect, one big pot, from which each member of society is free to withdraw goods, and to which each member of society is free to contribute goods or to cooperate with others in the production of goods to be commonly owned.[9] This procedure does not result in the emptying of the common pot, because each

[8] My understanding is that Cohen stipulates that a *socialist economy* is (a) not capitalist (not organized around private ownership of resources and market exchange) and (b) fulfills the egalitarian principles he outlines. According to this usage, it is left an open question what set of institutional arrangements would satisfy (a) and (b); socialism is not then by definition identified with public ownership of the means of production.

[9] The image of the socialist economy as a big pot, with people free to take from the pot and add to it as they choose, comes from Nozick, *Anarchy, State, and Utopia*, chap. 7. Nozick's characterization is pejorative, but I suppose Cohen would have held that a centralized planned economy that imposes slight coercion on those who participate to sustain it would be desirable if feasible. One might query the characterization that says people are free to contribute to the common pot or not, as they choose. Are people in Cohen's imagined socialist society free not to contribute? Answer: yes and no. Yes, it is true that no threat of coercion binds them to contribute, but no, they are morally bound to contribute to the common good and if they are well socialized they will feel pangs of conscience if they do not do what is morally required. Here Cohen and Karl Marx disagree. Marx at least flirted with the thought that a post-capitalist society would be free from moral constraints, so that people would just do what they want and would spontaneously like to do what facilitates

individual's free choices to produce and consume are made in accordance with the slogan, "From each according to his ability, to each according to his needs."[10] Appearances here may be somewhat deceiving, however. Cohen is careful to identify socialism as a noncapitalist economy that fulfills the camping trip ideal, and does not commit to the identification of socialism with any particular set of economic arrangements.

Cohen sees two principles underlying the camping trip ideal: a principle of equal opportunity and a principle of community. The first principle is a strong norm of equal opportunity that Cohen calls "socialist equality of opportunity." This principle is fulfilled when (1) each individual has the opportunity to be as well off as anyone else, and (2) if any individual becomes worse off than others, the worse off individual can reasonably be held responsible for that outcome. Socialist equality of opportunity is contrasted with two weaker versions of equal opportunity. "Formal equality of opportunity" is fulfilled when no one becomes worse off than another as a result of ascriptive caste or class status (e.g., only those born as aristocrats are permitted to enjoy cakes and ale, while commoners must make do with bread and milk), bigotry, or social prejudice. "Bourgeois equality of opportunity" is satisfied when no one who has the same native talent and ambition as another has lesser life prospects than that other.[11]

The second camping trip principle identified by Cohen is community, which has two aspects. Both are forms of caring for one another. One is that each person cares about every other person, and in particular cares that no one be significantly worse off than others in terms of fundamental life prospects. We all want to be in the same boat, so to speak. Communal caring about equality can require compensation to reduce or eliminate inequalities that socialist equality of opportunity tolerates.

The other aspect of community is communal reciprocity. Communal reciprocity obtains in a society when each individual is moved to serve the others with whom she is interacting not in order to gain a benefit for herself but in order to fulfill their needs, and each expects the others to be similarly motivated. Each then values serving others and being served by them.

Communal reciprocity is contrasted with market reciprocity, the disposition to serve others only insofar as that is necessary to induce others to serve oneself. Serving others is valued only as a means, a way of gaining advantages for oneself. This motive can take the form of greed

---

efficient social production. Cohen rejects the freedom-from-morality idea. See G. A. Cohen, *Self-Ownership, Freedom, and Equality* (Cambridge: Cambridge University Press, 1995).

[10] Karl Marx, "Critique of the Gotha Program," in Robert C. Tucker, ed., *The Marx-Engels Reader*, 2d ed. (New York: W. W. Norton and Co., 1978), 531.

[11] Bourgeois equality of opportunity is what John Rawls endorses under the name "fair equality of opportunity." See John Rawls, *A Theory of Justice*, rev. ed. (Cambridge, MA: Harvard University Press, 1999).

(wanting a maximal profit for oneself in exchange) or fear (wanting to avoid losses to oneself that will ensue unless one makes a deal that will prevent the loss). Nothing in the idea of market reciprocity as so far characterized says anything about the ultimate aims of the market agents. In interaction with others, the market agents seek maximal gain for themselves. Behaving this way does not say anything about what these profit-seeking agents might ultimately be seeking. They might be aiming to use their profits in many different ways, such as improving their own lives, improving the lives of those near and dear to them, giving aid to the community, or even giving aid to distant needy strangers.

III. The Camping Trip Model and Coercion

One might object straightaway that if the camping trip Cohen describes sounds attractive, that depends on the voluntariness of the endeavor. Nobody joins who does not agree to come on the terms proposed, and anybody who changes her mind and wants to leave is presumably free to do so. To organize an entire economy as a big camping trip would involve imposing this mode of cooperation on everybody independently of any individual's will. In effect, Cohen is describing a voluntary friendship relationship, and then claiming that it would be great to require everybody in society to be everybody's friend. This would not be great.

This criticism does not inflict damage on Cohen's proposal. In the nature of the case, the form of economic organization of a society cannot be left to the voluntary discretion of each individual. From the individual's standpoint, the basic social arrangements are given, and not up to her to choose. Basic social arrangements are arguably morally acceptable if they are supported by good reasons (and so are rationally endorseable) and are in fact endorsed and accepted by those who live under them.[12] Cohen is not suggesting that the camping trip economy should be imposed on people when they are opposed to it.

Still, one might wonder whether any sensible scaling up of the camping trip model will alter its character. In his "Chapters on Socialism," John Stuart Mill raises a concern that some versions of socialist economic organization might be suitable for small groups of competent and virtuous agents but would be ruined by extension across the entire society, since in that case the entire spectrum of economic agents (including malcontents, cheats, free-riders, exploiters, and other types of scoundrels) would be expected to live up to the high standard of conduct required by socialist ideals.[13] It would be unwise to organize the economy as one big pot from which people may take what they think they need and to which they may

---

[12] This is a sufficient, not a necessary condition for justification.
[13] John Stuart Mill, *Principles of Political Economy and Chapters on Socialism*, ed. Jonathan Riley (Oxford: Oxford University Press, 1994), 423–25.

contribute what they think they ought to contribute according to their own lights, freely and spontaneously. This vision of voluntary, frictionless social cooperation would, with people as they are, swiftly turn into a nightmare. Of course, a socialist organization of economic activity is fully compatible with monitoring and surveillance. The economy might be a big lake with fish, and the social planner determines what level of fishing is socially best and assigns quotas to each individual who makes her living by fishing, so that no one draws too much or too little from the common stock.[14] Socialist inspectors monitor compliance, and the system can work tolerably well if most individuals are disposed to comply with the sensible rules imposed, provided most others are also complying. But in thinking along this line to respond to Mill's worry, we have moved a long way in thought from the idyllic camping trip model.

IV. Does Cohen's Ethical Vision Oppose a Capitalist Market Economy?

Although Cohen says that a one-for-all-and-all-for-one spirit prevails in the camping trip scenario, further opinions he espouses indicate that this is true only up to a point. Cohen is not an act consequentialist; he does not hold that in all one's actions one should be doing what best promotes the common good. According to Cohen, each person has a prerogative to pursue her own projects and aims to a degree, even when other available choices would do more to promote best consequences impartially assessed.[15]

The individual-prerogative idea seems to me to be difficult for the camping trip advocate to resist, but if it is not resisted, then acceptance of something like ordinary market relations seems to follow. Here is what I have in mind. Suppose Bob is a skilled navigator of cross-country terrain; it would be beneficial for us if he accompanies us on our trek to a distant spot. We invite him, but he declines. He would rather stay in camp and rest. There may still be the basis of a mutually profitable exchange: we offer to pay Bob to accompany us, and at that price he is better off than he would be staying behind and we are better off than we would be if we left without him. Bob then is not acting selflessly to serve us, but we have already agreed there is a personal prerogative to favor your own interests; and we can suppose Bob's initial decision not to accompany us falls

---

[14] I borrow this example from John E. Roemer, "A Public Ownership Resolution of the Tragedy of the Commons," *Social Philosophy and Policy* 6, no. 2 (1989): 74–92.

[15] Here Cohen follows a line of thought advanced by Samuel Scheffler. See Scheffler, *The Rejection of Consequentialism* (Oxford: Oxford University Press, 1982). For the record: I myself espouse act consequentialism (one should always do whatever would produce consequences no worse than anything else one might instead have done), so I reject the Scheffler prerogative, at least at the level of first principles. Still, if one accepts a nonconsequentialist morality, something like the prerogative looks very plausible.

within its scope. Bob does not do wrong to follow his own interests here, so what can be wrong with altering his incentives by offering him a deal?

This objection can be pressed further. Economic and social life ought to be arranged so that each person enjoys wide freedom to contribute to the aggregate economic production and make a living in any of a wide variety of significantly different ways. Organizing the economy as a market safeguards this morally important freedom, and organizing the economy as a big socialist camping trip would not. Moreover, since individuals reasonably pursue long-term projects, and require secure access to particular material things in order to carry out some of these long-term projects, private property is morally necessary.

Notice first that two ideas of individual freedom are now in play: (1) the prerogative to choose to favor one's own aims over the common good to some extent; and (2) wide-option freedom, that is, having the real freedom to choose among a wide variety of significantly different options, each of which one has reason to value. I have the real freedom to go to Paris or not if there are some courses of action I can choose, such that if I choose one of those options, I get to Paris, and if I do not so choose, I do not get to Paris.

This line of thought grounds something in the neighborhood of private ownership rights, but not necessarily full private ownership. In principle, a camping-trip mode of organization that eschews full private ownership rights can satisfy the demands for wide individual freedom here affirmed. If the economy is organized as a big pot from which people take and into which they give freely, it need not be the case that one's options are limited. To switch the metaphor slightly, the economy can be organized as a big loose machine, with individuals instructed to interact with it productively, but this might be done in a wide variety of ways, and can be done with a view to minimizing constraint on individual economic choices. To see how this might go, picture an economic plan that takes people's labor and consumption desires and likely spontaneous choices as inputs, and organizes production so that people spontaneously coordinate and work gets done without any onerous compulsion that presses one individual to do one particular task. At this juncture, some might object that any such scheme would prove unimplementable. However, that objection is not in play here. Cohen is urging that the vision of socialism he espouses is ethically attractive and should be implemented if that is feasible. He does not claim that implementation in present or likely circumstances would in fact be feasible. On that issue he is explicitly agnostic.

In a similar way, if people need secure long-term access to particular material things in order to carry out their projects, individuals can be granted rights to keep communally owned items and use them exclusively for long periods of time without having full ownership rights in those things. Compare: the books in a public library, without ceasing to be public property, may be checked out and renewed for indefinitely long periods of time, to accommodate people who want to do things with books that take a long time. One presumes these use-rights will be limited in some way, so that a book you have checked out for a ten-year loan period may, under certain specified conditions, be subject to immediate recall by someone desperate to have that book in short order. Your long-term project may suffer in consequence, and knowing that the communal item you are privately using is subject to recall may make you somewhat anxious, but if the system is working well, your losses will be morally outweighed by others' gains. However, if we imagine people having entrepreneurial projects, the practical case for secure private ownership rights over things is strengthened.

If free use rights (under a system that eschews private ownership) take on the characteristics of property rights, we might as well say we are endorsing limited private ownership rights. We could also arrive at this position by starting with permanent nonoverrideable private ownership rights and seeing that these rights need to be weakened for various reasons (for example, progressive income taxes and estate taxes to keep inequality within bounds). As free use rights under common ownership are adapted to allow secure long-term use by an individual of particular pieces of property, and as full permanent bequeathable Lockean property rights are weakened to allow various forms of taking for the public good, eventually what is being affirmed under the rubric of socialist egalitarianism becomes close to what is being proposed by the private ownership advocate.

V. Responses to the Camping Trip Economy Ideal: Goals and Devices for Implementing the Goals

We should distinguish sharply between a set of principles or goals that specify an ideal of social organization and a set of proposals for implementing that ideal as best one can in given circumstances. In particular, let us focus on possible means for achieving Cohen's socialist goals.

The choice between socialism and capitalism as ordinarily understood involves shifts along several dimensions. The major means of production might be privately owned or owned by the public via its agent, the government. In the latter case, there might be centralization (all workers are employed by one big public bureaucracy) or decentralization. If the latter, many public firms might compete in the market, with the market results determining the remuneration to participants, or there might instead be varying degrees of insulation of individual enterprises from the sting of competition. Going back to the centralization model, there might be more or less coercion to induce individuals to play their assigned roles. Insofar as one gets an idea of Cohen's model of how a camping trip economy would actually be organized, he seems to have in mind centralization plus little or no coercion.[16]

We should note that there is a familiar set of devices that might be employed with a capitalist free-market economy to equalize the distribution of resources and opportunities. Alongside the free market economy with private ownership there might stand a redistributive state that taxes the income of high earners and redistributes it to low earners, compressing the distribution of income and wealth over time. To roughly the same end, one might impose taxes on gifts and bequests.[17] Another device is using the tax system to channel public funds toward subsidizing the education of children of parents who are themselves below average in income, wealth, and educational attainments. The supposition here is that the children targeted for aid are likely to have the bad luck of a worse genetic endowment and a less nurturing childhood social environment than others. Better education is conjectured to improve the lives of the recipients both by improving the marketable skills they will deploy over their adult lives and by improving their personal choice abilities to organize their lives in ways that benefit themselves and others. Both cognitive and noncognitive skills are in play here. Another possibility is to set the tax system to encourage philanthropy, voluntary giving to good causes. Who benefits from philanthropy depends on the tastes of givers, but we might expect some equalizing effect as the level of giving increases, especially if there are in place social norms and a public morality that promote Cohen-type ideals of the good society. (If we happen to know of any reliable means to alter over time the character of social norms and public morality, then add those means to the set of devices available to society for achieving broadly socialist ends by nonsocialist means.)[18]

Finally, note that coercive and noncoercive paternalism is another means by which society might work to improve the lifetime condition of the disadvantaged. Paternalist policies are policies that aim to improve the lives of adult persons and that involve a judgment on the part of the agent that the intended beneficiary of the policy is likely to be making mistakes concerning her own well-being—mistakes which the policy will ameliorate or prevent. Noncoercive paternalistic policies

---

[16] This last point is not a criticism of Cohen. Recall once more that his aim is to elicit the reader's assent to the principles he associates with the socialist ideal, to note that these principles cannot be fulfilled under capitalism, and to urge that if it is feasible to arrange the economy to satisfy these principles, we should do so. Which noncapitalist institutions and practices would best achieve the socialist ideal is a question he sets aside.

[17] A device favored by John Stuart Mill. See his *Principles of Political Economy*, Book II, chap. II, section 3; see also Mill, *Autobiography*.

[18] Sometimes enacting a legal prohibition can help to crystallize a social norm against what is prohibited. Allowing one's dog to defecate in public spaces and oneself not to clean up the mess used to be socially acceptable in the United States but is no longer so in many communities.

include provision of aid to the poor from tax and transfer policies in the form of specific goods and services rather than cash.[19] Coercive paternalistic policies include the use of criminal law penalties to prevent an individual from harming herself. Whether coercive paternalism, if successful in its own terms, specially aids the disadvantaged, depends on the extent to which the mistake-prone segment of the population lies in the advantaged or in the disadvantaged group. Since, in practice, no coercive paternalist measure can be precisely set to constrain only those who would be making self-harming mistakes, such paternalism typically imposes costs, perhaps large costs, on those not prone to such mistakes, who might be concentrated among the more advantaged members of society.

The devices described above are means consistent with capitalism by which a society might seek to achieve socialist equalizing goals. Notice that to the degree that all members of society, including better-off people who are being asked to sacrifice their interests for the sake of those who are worse off, willingly accept and embrace these equalization devices and practices, society exhibits a spirit of reciprocity not captured by Cohen's idea of communal reciprocity, which is a function of how one is motivated with respect to the particular individuals with whom one is interacting. Call this willingness to accept sensible equalizing policies *wide reciprocity* or *solidarity*. A society of people who are market reciprocators, as Cohen defines the term, might also score high on solidarity. In this way, a capitalist society that achieves Cohen-style equalizing aims by the devices described above could also be one in which people's actions toward one another manifest a spirit of caring about each other in the broadest sense—each cares about all of the others. Just as the shift from a racist to a nonracist society is thought to involve a shift not only in institutions but also in the hearts and minds of men and women, a shift from capitalism simpliciter to capitalism reformed to achieve socialist goals also involves a transformation in individual motivations.

VI. Summing Up

The argument we have been examining may be summarized in this way:

1. If organizing a camping trip on socialist principles is feasible, doing so would be ethically desirable (superior to other feasible alternatives).

2. Organizing a camping trip on socialist principles is feasible.

[19] The policies mentioned here are noncoercive with respect to those who are the objects of the paternalism. Of course, they might be coercive with respect to others—for example, those taxed to provide aid in kind, take it or leave it, to people who need help and are not trusted to use cash grants wisely. On this point, thanks to Ellen Paul.

3. Therefore, organizing a camping trip on socialist principles would be ethically desirable.

4. If organizing a camping trip on socialist principles would be ethically desirable, then if organizing an entire economy on socialist principles is feasible, doing so would be ethically desirable.

5. Therefore, if organizing an entire economy on socialist principles is feasible, doing so would be ethically desirable.

6. We don't know whether or not organizing an entire economy on socialist principles would be feasible.

7. Therefore, we don't know whether or not organizing an entire economy on socialist principles would be ethically desirable.

We should add:

8. Organizing an entire economy on socialist principles precludes maintaining capitalist economic institutions.

Our assessment of this argument to this point may be summarized as follows: First, in order to interpret the camping trip ideal as ethically attractive, we have to incorporate within it a guarantee of personal freedom—to some considerable extent, each of us should be left free to live her own life as she chooses. Since each of us wants to pursue her own projects in her own way, requiring each of us always to be devoted heart-and-soul to pursuing the common good is not fair or reasonable even in the context of a small voluntary association. Once we make this concession, we see that we must allow into the camping trip ideal some rights of private ownership of resources and some market freedom to make voluntary contracts with willing others and to cooperate on whatever terms are chosen. If we do this, we have a mixed economy. The upshot of this discussion is an amendment of premise 1, along with denial of premise 8.

Second, it is very much an open question what sorts of institutional arrangements would best promote Cohen's proposed goals of radical equality of opportunity, community solidarity, and communal reciprocity. Organizing the economy as a common enterprise, to which people are free to give and take as they choose—with the announced social norm being that they should do so in such a way that the economy sustainably achieves a high level of productivity and an equal sharing of the products—might generate lots of shirking, greedy grabbing, disgruntlement, and decreasing social productivity. This point challenges premise 8 in the argument above.

Finally, what does feasibility amount to in this discussion? The question calls into doubt the meaning of all of the premises in which feasibility figures. I take it up at the end of Section VII.C.[20]

---

[20] Here is one possibility: organizing an economy to achieve socialist principles is feasible if and only if making the organizational changes does lead to the fulfillment of the principles *and also* promotes people's living genuinely good not squalid lives *and*

VII. Objections to the Principles of the Camping Trip Economy

To this point I have not directly criticized the principles that Cohen finds latent in the characterization of his ideal camping trip and that he identifies as expressing core socialist norms. I turn now to this task. In subsection A below, I challenge the particular version of luck egalitarianism that Cohen espouses. In subsection B, I criticize the principle that Cohen calls "socialist equality of opportunity." Here I challenge the idea that we ought to embrace any principle that affirms that any form of distributive equality as such—everyone having the same or getting the same—is intrinsically morally desirable. Subsection C criticizes the principle of communal solidarity or compassion, and subsection D targets the principle of communal reciprocity.

A. Luck egalitarianism: Choice versus desert

Cohen is an unreconstructed luck egalitarian in his account of distributive justice. (In his view, what justice requires is modified by the nonjustice principle of community or solidarity.) In a just luck-egalitarian regime, institutions and practices are arranged so that each person receives an initial stock of resources such that, if she conducts herself throughout her life as prudently as can reasonably be expected, and obeys moral requirements as far as can reasonably be expected, she will end up with a lifetime advantage at a level no less than anyone else achieves. "As reasonably as can be expected" signals that we should adjust the conduct that we normatively expect from a person depending on how difficult and painful it would be for her to make and execute the right choice. "Advantage" is a measure of individual welfare that amalgamates different independent dimensions of what makes someone's life go better—including, at least, material resources like income and wealth, informed preference satisfaction, and perhaps real freedom to achieve what one has good reason to value. (If equality of opportunity as just specified is unachievable owing to uncompensable differences in the brute luck that befalls people, a fallback luck-egalitarian position would be satisfied if each person has the opportunity to achieve a prospect of lifetime advantage no less than anyone else gets.)

This version of luck egalitarianism is vulnerable to the charge, first leveled by Marc Fleurbaey, that it is too unforgiving.[21] Slight imprudence

---

does all this without running afoul of other moral norms and constraints that we ought to respect.

[21] Marc Fleurbaey, "Equal Opportunity or Equal Social Outcome?" *Economics and Philosophy* 11 (1995): 25–56; Fleurbaey, "Freedom with Forgiveness," *Politics, Philosophy, and Economics* 4 (2005): 29–67; and Fleurbaey, *Fairness, Responsibility, and Welfare* (Oxford: Oxford University Press, 2008), chap. 10.

in youth might send one's lifetime well-being plummeting. According to luck egalitarianism, there is no justice-based case for further compensation to boost the lifetime well-being of the wayward youth. The counterclaim is that there are reasons of justice to favor compensation.

Several possible lines of criticism converge here. One seems especially compelling. This criticism holds that the moral urgency of providing aid to rescue a person from a predicament of poor life prospects varies depending on the degree to which the person's conduct in life is morally deserving.

To see the case for a desert-oriented version of luck egalitarianism, consider that if Mother Teresa has a fair initial set of opportunities and resources, and then voluntarily and freely chooses to devote herself to the poor of Calcutta, then if she ends up heading for low lifetime well-being, there is, according to choice-oriented luck egalitarianism, no case for compensation to boost her well-being. She had her chance. Or consider a spendthrift. Given an initial fair share of resources and opportunities, the spendthrift expends her resources on lesser goods now and, after failing to save for the future, faces a grim future. If the rules of society provide no compensation for people in her position, then her spendthrift ways are viciously imprudent. Suppose instead that the rules of society are set up in a very forgiving spirit, so that if you squander resources early in life, you get more, and if you squander resources again, you get still more, and so on. If faced with this set of rules, the spendthrift is being unfair to others in society if she squanders resources on lesser goods and then keeps taking more from the common pot to which all contribute. To my mind, the spendthrift in the second scenario is exploiting the compassion of her compatriots. In either scenario, the one in which the rules are unforgiving or the one in which they are forgiving, if the spendthrift is fully responsible for her choices, then they render her undeserving. Given that she is undeserving to some degree, the value of bringing it about that she gains extra units of well-being declines to some extent.

Or consider a prudent investor. She makes a wise investment in a venture that has a very good chance of success, but it turns out that the investment turns sour. Let us assume that no moral requirements should inhibit her from making the investment. This was the best deal she could get. In the terminology of luck egalitarianism, she suffers bad option luck. The social rules in effect in her society might dictate that no compensation will be forthcoming to deserving persons (or undeserving persons) who suffer bad option luck, but such rules seem unfair from a desert-oriented perspective.

To my knowledge, Cohen, while affirming choice-oriented luck egalitarianism, does not address the issue of whether that variety of luck egalitarianism is inferior to a desert-oriented egalitarian distributive principle in terms of the fairness of its implications for policy. I submit that once this issue is raised, the desert-oriented version of egalitarianism emerges as more plausible than the choice-oriented version.

B. Rejecting the camping trip principles: Against equality

This section argues that the ideal camping trip as described by Cohen satisfies strong norms of equality that we should judge to be not attractive at all, but rather morally objectionable.

Cohen himself announces two ideals of equality as inherent in the socialist project, properly conceived. One of these is a principle of justice, a socialist ideal of equality of opportunity. This is the doctrine also known as luck egalitarianism: institutions and practices in society are to be arranged so that everyone has the same life prospects except insofar as inequalities in persons' life prospects satisfy a specific condition, namely, that anyone who ends up getting less than others gain could have obtained that greater set of advantages for herself if she had followed a course of conduct that was available to her and would not have been unreasonable for her to pursue. Or, at least, she could have chosen a course of conduct that would have given her just as good a prospect of gaining the better advantages others now have as the prospect that the others had when they chose the conduct that led to their good fortune.

Socialist equality of opportunity does not condemn great inequalities between persons that arise when some persons gain by taking risks that turn out well when those same risky choices were also available to others (and would not have been unreasonable for them to take). But another socialist principle, community, will condemn such inequalities, at least when they become sufficiently large that those whose life prospects are smaller cannot be in a relation of community with those whose life prospects are greater. Fellow members of the same community will help those who are far worse off than others if the better-off people can do so, and they will do this whatever the cause of some people's being far worse off.

Socialist equality of opportunity is a justice principle that permits us to allow people to languish in their bad fortune if they brought it on themselves by their choice or neglect. Socialist community equality is a principle of compassion that requires better offs to improve the lot of worse offs even if the latter are worse off than others through their own fault or choice.

Neither form of equality is morally compelling, so even if these norms militate against acceptance of the capitalist market economy, that does not give us good reason to reject the capitalist market economy. This seems to me the true reason why the description of the camping trip, and of the projected extension of the camping trip into a camping trip economy, does not generate grounds to reject the institutions of the capitalist market economy, on the assumption that capitalist institutions cannot satisfy the camping trip ideals. The ideals, in any case, should not command our allegiance.

Recall that socialist equal opportunity (SEO) requires that no one be disadvantaged by inequality in the distribution of social benefits unless the person could have avoided a lower than average share by some action that he could have taken and that it would have been reasonable for him to have taken. For example, if others now have more income and job satisfaction and I have less, and if I could have undertaken a job that would have afforded me as much as the fortunate ones are now getting, and if taking that job would have been a reasonable choice for me to have made, then the inequality does not violate SEO. If others are in robust good health, because they brushed their teeth daily and submitted to regular dental check-ups, and I could have enjoyed the same robust good health had I reasonably done the same, then, again, this inequality does not violate SEO. In contrast, if you are strong and I am weak, and you are smart and I am dull-witted, by dint of unequal endowments of native talent, and if we work equally assiduously to contribute to economic production, and you produce and earn a lot and I produce and earn a little, and in consequence your life prospects are better and mine worse, then SEO is violated.

What, if anything, is wrong with SEO? My objection is not to the socialist component of the ideal, but to the equality component. A broad objection sweeps away doctrines that hold that it matters morally—intrinsically and for its own sake—how one person's condition compares with the condition of others, and, *a fortiori*, doctrines that hold that it matters that everyone have the same in some respect, or have equal opportunity in some respect.

Think back to the camping trip scenario. Suppose some campers are more naturally fit and athletic than others. There is a fantastic climb to a magnificent view, which some of us can manage, and some cannot. If the more fit and athletic are already enjoying advantages on the trip that others lack, then organizing a climb to the view for the best climbers will improve the condition of the better off and will make the overall distribution of advantages even more unequal, and we can easily imagine that the inequalities are going to the better endowed just in virtue of their unchosen and undeserved special good luck. So equality of outcome and socialist equality of opportunity condemn the climb, unless the pattern of benefits and burdens it generates can be offset by some compensating redistributive mechanism. Suppose any such deliberate redistribution would involve costs that outweigh its advantages. So then we should forgo the climb? I think not. A sensible community of campers will not merely allow the climb, which promises a windfall benefit to some, but will take steps to make it possible. Unfit to participate in the climb myself, I should be willing to undertake some moderate sacrifice to make it possible for others, if the benefits they will get sufficiently outweigh my sacrifices.

If you share my endorsement of the imagined nonegalitarian camping ethos, notice that various rationales might underlie this response. One rationale is straight utilitarianism: In the situation as described, helping to bring about the special climb that boosts the well-being of the already better off yields a net gain in aggregate well-being (well-being summed across all persons), and *that* is why doing so is morally right. I suggest that a more appealing principle is priority: gaining a benefit for a person is morally more valuable, the greater the amount of well-being increase the benefit will yield, and also morally more valuable, the worse off the person would otherwise be in lifetime well-being. The worse off a person would be over the course of her life absent the benefit we might gain for her now, the greater the moral priority that attaches to the project of bringing about this gain. We should maximize, not the aggregate sum of well-being, but priority-weighted well-being.[22] This means that further benefits to people who are already very well off are discounted some-what, the amount of the discount depending on how well off they are, in determining the moral value of generating the further benefits. If there was a limited quantity of mosquito netting available, and if anyone would gain about the same amount of well-being from netting protection, then there is more value to be gained by giving the netting to a person who would otherwise be more worse off, in the absence of this benefit. So it matters to the judgment about the special climb, on this view, that those who can benefit from it would gain a very great benefit, so that it is worth incurring some cost to help them get the benefit, even if they are already better off than anyone else. The same reasoning applies to decisions that involve preventing, lessening, or channeling losses.

From the prioritarian standpoint, equalizing moves are often morally desirable. For example, any time you can bring about a reduction in the well-being of someone who is enjoying an above-average life, and thereby bring about a same-sized gain in the well-being of a person who now is below the average, without reversing their position, and without affecting anyone else's well-being, one should bring about the equalizing transfer, according to the prioritarian.[23] This is so not because it matters how much one person has relative to another, but rather because benefits matter more to a person, the worse off in absolute terms she would otherwise be. Favoring those who are worse off than others is, for the prioritarian, sometimes a shadow cast by what genuinely matters, never something that is morally desirable per se. The same goes for equality of opportunity in any version. More opportunities for people are better than fewer (so long as the opportunities will be used in ways that improve the quality of people's lives), and gaining opportunities for a person is likely to be more

---

[22] On the idea of priority, see Derek Parfit, "Equality or Priority?" reprinted in Matthew Clayton and Andrew Williams, eds., *The Ideal of Equality* (Houndmills, Basingstoke: Palgrave Macmillan, 2002), 81–125. See also the discussion of "extended humanitarianism" in Larry S. Temkin, *Inequality* (Oxford: Oxford University Press, 1993), chap. 9; and Thomas Nagel, *Equality and Partiality* (New York and Oxford: Oxford University Press, 1991).

[23] The condition described in the text is the Pigou-Dalton axiom from welfare economics, which any version of priority satisfies.

valuable, the worse off the person would otherwise be. But equality of opportunity is not a concern for the prioritarian.

Priority conflicts with SEO when achieving or sustaining the latter ideal requires an expenditure of resources that would do more to improve people's lives, in priority-weighted terms, if deployed in some other way. SEO requires eliminating inequalities due to unchosen luck at whatever cost, whereas priority may require letting some such inequalities stand. Another source of conflict between priority and SEO comes into view when people have had the opportunities that SEO demands, and some have squandered these opportunities and now face very grim life prospects, which reasonable action on their part could have avoided. SEO is satisfied in such cases, and is not troubled by inequalities of this sort; but if these people are now very badly off in absolute terms, then priority assigns high weight to benefits that might be secured for them. To revert to the camping trip scenario, suppose some campers recklessly go kayaking without considering the likely dangers, and end up in danger of drowning. They will die unless helped, but if assistance is provided, their life prospects become as good as anyone else's. Given that the inequality of condition here is one for which the threatened kayakers can reasonably be held responsible, the huge looming inequality in life prospects between them and the other campers is not an inequality that violates SEO and calls for correction. In contrast, priority regards it as an especially urgent matter to help them, given the low well-being they will have without help and the great gain in well-being that help can provide (presumably at moderate cost).[24]

SEO is a radical and demanding ideal, one that contemporary wealthy market societies surely are far from satisfying. However, as the example of the imprudent kayakers illustrates, it is also a harsh, unforgiving doctrine in its implications for situations in which individuals bring about very bad outcomes for themselves that they could have avoided by reasonable, prudent choice of conduct.[25] SEO represents an attempt to weld

[24] If priority is yoked to desert, then there may be a consideration that dampens the reason to aid those whose lives are going badly (depending on the degree, if any, to which their conduct has been undeserving) as well as the prioritarian consideration that amplifies the reason to aid. The point in the text still holds. Giving weight to how much benefit to people one's actions would achieve, and giving weight to how badly off they would be absent that benefit, renders priority more prone to recommend extending aid than Cohen-style luck egalitarianism in many circumstances.

[25] There is a large literature debating the merits of socialist equality of opportunity, the doctrine also known as luck egalitarianism. On luck egalitarianism, see Richard Arneson, "Equality and Equal Opportunity for Welfare," *Philosophical Studies* 56 (1989): 77–93; Arneson, "Egalitarianism and the Undeserving Poor," *Journal of Political Philosophy* 5 (1997): 327–50; and G. A. Cohen, "On the Currency of Egalitarian Justice," *Ethics* 99 (1989): 906–44; see also Nagel, *Equality and Partiality*; Ronald Dworkin, "What Is Equality? Part 1: Equality of Welfare; Part 2: Equality of Resources," *Philosophy and Public Affairs* 10 (1981): 185–246, 283–345; and Dworkin, *Sovereign Virtue: The Theory and Practice of Equality* (Cambridge, MA: Harvard University Press, 2000). For criticism, see Fleurbaey, "Equal Opportunity or Equal Social Outcome?"; Jonathan Wolff, "Fairness, Respect, and the Egalitarian Ethos," *Philosophy and*

concern for equality and concern for personal responsibility. Integrating personal responsibility into moral doctrines about what we owe one another is perhaps reasonable, but if construed as a fundamental principle of justice always to be obeyed, rather than as one consideration among many in a pluralist theory, SEO carries out the integration in an excessively rigid way.[26]

C. Rejecting Cohen's principles: Communal compassion

Cohen's statement of socialist principles is responsive to the problem just noted. As I noted previously, he sees two principles as expressing the camping trip ideal: socialist equality of opportunity and a principle of community with two components. Members of an ideal community care about each other and care about belonging to a society whose members care about each other. This caring includes a disposition to help out those who are worse off than others. This component generates principled reasons to equalize people's condition beyond what SEO demands.

My objection is not to a requirement of compassion, which could naturally take the form of a principle of beneficence, but to the requirement that compassion should dispose us to promote equality. Again, if it does not matter morally how one person's condition compares to that of another, it does not matter morally whether or not one person's condition is equal to that of others.

One might suppose that a central animating aim of socialism would be to bring it about that people have good lives, and that the better their lives go, the more the socialist aim is achieved. More exactly, the aim is to bring

Public Affairs 27 (1998): 97–122; Elizabeth S. Anderson, "What Is the Point of Equality?" *Ethics* 109 (1999): 287–337; Samuel Scheffler, "What Is Egalitarianism?" *Philosophy and Public Affairs* 31 (2003): 5–39; and Susan Hurley, *Justice, Luck, and Knowledge* (Cambridge, MA: Harvard University Press, 2003). For responses to criticism, see Richard Arneson, "Equality of Opportunity for Welfare Defended and Recanted," *Journal of Political Philosophy* 7 (1999): 488–97; Arneson, "Luck Egalitarianism and Prioritarianism," *Ethics* 110 (2000): 339–49; Arneson, "Luck Egalitarianism Interpreted and Defended," *Philosophical Topics* 32, nos. 1 and 2 (Spring and Fall 2004): 1–20 (actual date of publication September, 2006); and Carl Knight, *Luck Egalitarianism: Equality, Responsibility, and Justice* (Edinburgh: Edinburgh University Press, 2009). See also Kok-Chor Tan, "A Defense of Luck Egalitarianism," *Journal of Philosophy* 105, no. 11 (2008); and Shlomi Segall, *Health, Luck, and Justice* (Oxford: Oxford University Press, 2009).

[26] If priority by itself swings too far in the other direction, giving no intrinsic weight (just instrumental weight) to factors of responsibility and individual deservingness, one can restore balance by embracing a double priority—priority for the worse off along with priority for the more deserving. Each person earns a deservingness score on an absolute scale, and the individual's score dampens or amplifies the moral value of gaining a benefit or avoiding a loss for that individual. I interpret deservingness subjectively, roughly as conscientious effort, trying to conform to the right and the good—but this is a large issue. See Richard Arneson, "Desert and Equality," in Nils Holtug and Kasper Lippert-Rasmussen, eds., *Egalitarianism: New Essays on the Nature and Value of Equality* (Oxford: Oxford University Press, 2007), 262–93. See also Arneson, "Moral Worth and Moral Luck" (work in progress; essay available from the author).

about good for people, fairly distributed across people. Priority gives one interpretation of the requirement that the aim of achieving more good be balanced appropriately against the further aim of fairly distributing the good. In Cohen's camping trip model of the socialist ideal, the goal of bringing about good lives for people fades into the background, if it can be located within the ideal at all. In the foreground is the aim of equalizing people's condition.

When Cohen adds the qualification that socialism, though desirable, might not be feasible, he evidently does not mean merely to ask whether there is any way his stated ideals might be achieved, at whatever cost to other values. He means to ask whether his ideal can be achieved consistently with adequate fulfillment of other values that he leaves unstated. Clearly a major element of these unstated values is quality of life. Would the attempt to implement socialist equality in given circumstances lead to a malfunction of the economy and a deterioration of the quality of life that people can achieve with the resources and opportunities the economy provides? If the answer is yes, then socialism is not feasible. There is in this way of putting the issue an odd displacement of values. To my mind, what Cohen shoves to the side under the heading of "feasibility" should come front and center. I cannot argue for this claim here, but I would claim that once one gives good for people its due in the formulation of animating principles, one ends up with prioritarian beneficence: choose policies that bring about the best outcome one can achieve, where the best outcome is the one in which moral value is maximized, and where moral value is a function of achieving good for people and priority for the worse off.

D. Rejecting Cohen's principles: Communal reciprocity

Cohen's camping trip model exhibits the fulfillment of yet another norm, besides socialist equality of opportunity and communal equality, that a society whose economic relations are organized around private ownership and market exchange will have no tendency to fulfill. This is community in its second, motivational aspect: communal reciprocity. This is "the anti-market principle according to which I serve you not because of what I can get in return by doing so but because you need my service, and you, for the same reason, serve me."[27] I act for your benefit, and securing an expectation of benefit to myself is not a necessary condition for my choice, but I do, as a matter of fact, expect that some return will

---

[27] Cohen, *Why Not Socialism?* 39. Communal reciprocity is not unconditional provision of service to others; one does not continue to serve others who are able to reciprocate but do not. The communal reciprocator would prefer to cooperate with others who are similarly disposed to cooperate with her, even if she could escape the burdens of cooperation and benefit from the cooperation of others without contributing to the cooperative scheme herself.

be forthcoming, and it is. Cohen contrasts communal reciprocity with market reciprocity, according to which, when interacting, I agree to serve you only because I expect to profit, and you agree to serve me on the same conditional basis. Also, as a market reciprocator, I try to arrange the service so that I benefit as much as I can from the interaction. (My motivation need not be self-interested, but in economic interaction I do not aim to benefit those I interact with except insofar as that is a means to maximizing my profit from the interaction.) In contrast, when motivated by communal reciprocity, each person prefers "I serve you and you serve me" to "You serve me and I don't serve you."

Communal reciprocity has a certain appeal. I doubt that it is morally required. A moral agent should dispose herself to conform her conduct to moral principles, to do what is morally right in whatever circumstances she might face. That might or might not involve actual reciprocity with those with whom one interacts. Perhaps I am disabled and you are able, and morality requires that you steadily serve me without any pay-back from me (if we are disposed to be moral, we are disposed to treat one another well in any possible circumstances in which morality requires doing so). Perhaps you are very talented and I am not, but I can exploit a bargaining advantage and negotiate interaction with you on lopsided terms, in order to help distant needy strangers (as morality, let us say, requires). In this imagined scenario, the spirit in which I ought to interact and negotiate with you is not the spirit of communal reciprocity as Cohen proposes, but rather the spirit of market reciprocity. Does my hard bargaining preclude community between us? If the hard bargaining on my part is justified by moral principles, then in theory you should appreciate this, and endorse what is being done to you in a cool moment (even if you would not voluntarily sacrifice yourself to aid the distant needy strangers if you were given the choice).

One should be motivated to interact with others in ways that are justifiable, and hence justifiable to those with whom one is interacting. But this need not involve being motivated to interact with others only in ways that are of benefit to them. Sometimes A using B as a means to help C is morally acceptable, and hence morally justifiable to B, who is being used as a means in the interaction.

E. Further comment: Promoting socialist reciprocity and rejecting the market

I have been criticizing communal reciprocity as morally undesirable per se. However, suppose one rejects these criticisms, and affirms communal reciprocity as ethically desirable. One cannot will Cohen-style reciprocity into existence, but where it is feasible to try to inculcate it, this is a sensible policy. But so interpreted, a choice for communal reciprocity over market reciprocity does not seem to have much to do with a choice between a private market and a socialist mode of economic organization. A society entirely free of private ownership and market exchange could be populated with market reciprocators, and a capitalist society could be populated with communal reciprocators.

There is no necessary connection between maintaining capitalist institutions and promoting market reciprocity. First, a capitalist market is defined in terms of the rights of property owners and the rules regulating contract and exchange. Nothing is stipulated about motivation. Nothing in the institutional set-up requires that individuals interact on a purely self-interested basis. It is supposed to be a nice feature of the system that it facilitates mutually beneficial cooperation among mutually disinterested agents, but the idea here is not to celebrate selfishness but to note that the system can produce pretty good results when staffed with people pretty much as they are, not as we might wish them to be. Maintaining a capitalist set-up is consistent with instilling an ethos that encourages workers to give a fair day's work for a fair day's pay, encourages sellers to prefer to provide good products rather than shoddy ones to consumers even if the profit from shoddy products would be greater, encourages employers to provide good jobs at good pay to their workers in exchange for good work, and so on.

In a society with a capitalist economy, the legal rules tolerate profit-maximizing within the legal constraints. But this legal toleration of profit-maximizing leaves it entirely open whether or not public morality should condemn certain manifestations of greed and whether social norms should frown on some kinds of behavior that are neither legally nor morally impermissible but nevertheless not done by the best people. If the public morality condemns and the prevalent social norms frown on these kinds of behavior to some degree, the capitalist market economy reflects a wide range of possible compromises between extolling the pursuit of self-interest within broadly tolerant moral constraints and flatly requiring that each person always should behave as an altruistic impartial angel would.

Second, in any event, a capitalist market economy, to function well, requires agents who are not motivated purely by self-interest, but rather disposed to constrain their pursuit of gain by refraining from theft of property, cheating in dealing with those with whom one is bargaining and interacting, fraudulent treatment of others, using the threat of force to induce others to interact with one on favorable terms, and so on.

Cohen urges that in market interaction, participants standardly act from greed or fear or some mix of these unsavory motives. I act from greed insofar as I hope to gather as much as I can of the gains from our cooperation, and from fear insofar as, when acting within a competitive market, I am concerned that unless I behave in whatever way is maximally efficient, the forces of competition will drive me to the wall (and even if I do behave efficiently, the ensemble of others' behavior may bring it about that I lose my job or my business and hence my livelihood). This is a morally bad situation, from which we should extricate ourselves if we can. In Cohen's words: "Every market, even a socialist market, is a system of predation. Our attempt to get beyond predation has thus far failed. I do not think the right conclusion is to give up."[28]

In response I would say that how fearful it is reasonable to be in market interaction depends partly on the likelihood that I will suffer bad luck and partly on how bad the consequences of bad luck would be for me. If the labor market is tight, losing my job leaves me with lots of alternative jobs I can secure. If there is a safety net in place, the consequences of losing my job and being unable to find another will not be too bad. If I now have an especially favorable position, there is the chance of losing it, but presumably this will be true under any mode of economic organization in which there is coordination to keep the economy performing efficiently. Loving my baking job under socialism, I must fear a shift in consumer tastes that would require the bakery I work for to close and me to seek another line of work. Cohen is indulging in purple prose here.

Nothing in the nature of a market requires that anybody be motivated by greedy selfishness. Leaving aside the point already made, that the desire to get as much as I can in interaction with you is compatible with my ultimate goal being the achievement of maximal fair gains for others, it is also true that the rules of market exchange allow me to share the gains of trade with those with whom I interact. Even if the market for babysitting services is competitive, nothing blocks me from paying the babysitter I employ an above-market rate of pay. The "market" does not block people engaged in exchange from softening the terms of exchange in the direction of egalitarian sharing. When I engage in arm's length transactions, as when I purchase books online, I simply pay the going price, but I do not see why the motives of greed or fear must be assumed to be driving the parties on either side of the exchange. Again, I see purple prose in Cohen's texts.

It is possible that, over time, interacting with people through institutions of market exchange tends to cause people to become more greedy and fearful in their underlying motivations, compared to the motivations they would tend to acquire under alternative institutions, but Cohen provides no empirical evidence for a broad causal claim of this sort that would justify the conviction that endorsing his moral vision should press one to reject market institutions.

F. Summing up

Cohen suggests that reflecting on his camping trip story should lead us to embrace the moral principles the camping trip exemplifies: socialist

---

[28] Ibid., 82.

equality of opportunity, communal reciprocity, and communal solidarity. I have criticized these principles. In my view, the ideal that better encapsulates what we should find worthy of endorsement in traditional egalitarian socialist aspirations is desert-oriented priority. This says that we ought to maximize moral value, which resides only in individual well-being or personal good weighted by fair distribution concerns. The moral value of getting a benefit to a person is (1) greater, the greater the well-being gain it would bring to her; (2) greater, the worse off in lifetime well-being she would otherwise be, absent this benefit; and (3) greater, the more morally deserving the person is. (One becomes deserving by conscientiously striving to conform one's behavior to what one takes to be correct moral standards, while conscientiously striving to identify those standards.) I admit that desert-oriented priority is a mouthful, not an inspiring slogan to emblazon on one's banners and bumper stickers. Desert-oriented priority is an abstract principle that, in my view, incorporates the plural goals that a decent society with a sensible orientation to human equality would be dedicated to fulfilling.

Priority appears to be silent on the issues of desirable human motivation that Cohen takes to be at the core of the socialist vision. If we drop the motivational ideals of communal reciprocity and communal solidarity that Cohen affirms, what replaces them? To this question no simple answer is adequate. I say that one is more deserving, the more committed one is to doing what is morally right and the more committed one is to trying to figure out what that is. However, human motives are also tools and impediments to getting good for oneself and others, so we should strive to shape our own motives, our dispositions to act, so that they help us achieve sensible goals. To be a good friend, one needs to develop the motives appropriate to friendship; to be a good soldier or entrepreneur or mechanic or jazz performer, one needs to acquire motives suitable for the chosen role. One size does not fit all in this domain of life. Cohen prescribes that one should engage in economic activities moved by concern to help others and to foster equal shares, and he disparages competitive self-seeking, which he associates with capitalism. To this, my principled reply is evasive: It all depends. What motives will be the best we can acquire will vary with our circumstances, the underlying bent of our personality, and our morally appropriate plan of life.

VIII. THE SUBORDINATION OF LIBERALISM, CAPITALISM, AND SOCIALISM TO PRIORITY

Although the previous section discusses what I have been calling "socialist" moral principles—socialist principles of social justice—we should recall that, so far, it is entirely an open question what sort of economic and social arrangements would be the best means of implementing these principles. Laissez-faire capitalism might be the best institutional arrangement, the one that best promotes the principles in some possible circumstances, and perhaps in likely or actual circumstances. This point holds for Cohen's proposed set of socialist principles as well as for my suggested replacement set, although this point is somewhat obscured by Cohen's highlighting of justice as equality and his sidelining into constraints of feasibility his commitment, implicit but surely real, to the aim of improving people's lives by the measure of the total well-being they achieve. At any rate, although I am happy to present prioritarian consequentialism as a good representation of the animating ideals of the socialist tradition, the doctrine is definitely noncommittal on the choice of economic systems. Priority tilts toward socialism only by ruling out any affirmation of fundamental moral rights that by themselves guarantee capitalist property rights independently of the empirical facts.

How strongly does priority tilt toward equalization of people's prospects on the ground that benefits to a person matter more, the worse off in absolute terms the person otherwise would be over the course of her life? This depends on how much weight is assigned to benefiting the worse off as compared to increasing the size of the well-being boost for the one who is benefited. Priority as characterized so far identifies a family of principles, not a particular position; one gets a determinate principle only by specifying these weights. In other words, priority is a proposed framework for determining what social justice requires, not a proposed specific moral principle. I suppose the objectively correct weights are determined by reflective equilibrium methods—what would an ideally competent judge determine as correct weights after reflectively considering all relevant examples where this trade-off issue arises?

The policy implications of priority, even with determinate weights assigned, depend on what will happen in the long run under various policy choices. Policy choices made now affect the level and substance of resources and opportunities that the economy will make available to future people, so the interests of future well-off and badly-off persons hang in the balance when one decides to what extent social policy should equalize resource holdings to increase the life prospects of people who are currently disadvantaged. The empirical facts here are hard to discern, and left-wingers and right-wingers notoriously disagree as to what they are. For example, we might agree that priority rightly interpreted tells us that if a certain tax cut would reduce the unemployment rate over the next five years to a greater extent than would feasible alternative policies, we ought to implement the tax cut—but we might disagree on the relevant facts. Since the empirical facts are, after all, empirical facts, with improved social science we should eventually tend to agree about what to do insofar as we are in agreement on the norms that should govern our actions.

The reader will have noticed that in the course of the discussion of the camping trip ideal and the principles we should embrace as a result of reflection on it, liberalism in the sense of a fundamental moral commitment to strong guarantees of individual freedom has dropped out of the picture. I have mentioned already that it is implicit in Cohen's discussion that the pursuit of the common good is morally constrained by a prerogative of each individual to pursue her own projects and live as she chooses to some extent. But this idea stays latent in his treatment of socialism-versus-capitalism. My critique of Cohen and my suggested revision of the principles he embraces leaves this fundamental commitment to individual freedom by the wayside. If affirming and implementing rights to individual liberty are part of the best strategy for achieving prioritarian justice, then priority calls for affirming and implementing those rights to liberty, and if not, not. Individual freedom becomes an entirely derivative (and in that sense subordinate) ideal. Both freedom as wide-option freedom and freedom as personal prerogative have only this derivative, subordinate status. Is the proposal then to abandon liberalism?

I do not want to argue about who is entitled to attach the appealing word "liberalism" to his favored doctrine, but I note that the broadly egalitarian consequentialism being proposed here can be associated with a fairly robust contingent commitment to liberal norms. These norms affirm individual rights and freedoms because, and insofar as, they function as core means needed under broad conditions of modern society to implement prioritarian aims as far as that can be done. This is the liberal tradition of which John Stuart Mill is perhaps the foremost theorist. Commitment to liberalism on this basis is not a matter of commitment to liberal rights come what may, but to the goal of good for people fairly distributed, a goal that will be best fulfilled, in certain circumstances, if we adhere to familiar liberal rights. Fundamental principles plus the empirical facts imply liberalism—in certain respects, and to a degree. In the following section, I indicate a further respect in which priority affirms only a conditional, "iffy" commitment to liberal freedoms. The freedom to live as one chooses is prized, roughly speaking, as a means to the good life for oneself and others, not as morally valuable per se. The discussion proceeds once again by criticizing Cohen's position.

IX. AGAINST MULTIDIMENSIONAL "ADVANTAGE"

A surprising aspect of Cohen's critique of free market exchange economies is that he does not criticize the market on the ground that it caters to effective demand—that is, to choices, induced by preferences, backed by dollars. Resource egalitarianism aims to equalize the resources that people command, so that each person has a comparable opportunity to pay for goods and services according to the strength of her preferences for them. Cohen is not a pure resource egalitarian, so he holds that justice should look beyond the distribution of resources in order to see what distribution of opportunities for advantage, for well-being in some sense, is thereby generated. If you are large, and I am small, then equal external resources would not give us equal opportunity for adequate nutrition, and if your nonvoluntary or reasonably formed preferences are expensive to satisfy, and mine cheap, then equal external resources would not, according to Cohen, secure equal opportunity for advantage in the relevant sense, whatever exactly that is.

In fact, a market economy has no necessary tendency to satisfy people's overall preferences over the course of their lives. The market caters to what one wants now. If I want to eat doughnuts, and it is predictable in advance that there will be consumer demand for doughnuts, then the competitive market tends to elicit provision of doughnuts for sale. If I later come to want to stop eating doughnuts and lose weight, the market provides diet aids, and even weight-loss resorts in remote doughnutless settings. If still later I want doughnuts, the market will tend to provide taxi drivers who will take me from the remote resort to the doughnut store, or entrepreneurs who will offer to toss me doughnuts over the resort walls for a fee, and so on.[29]

But suppose the market economy, suitably regulated, provides equal opportunity for equal proportionate satisfaction of everyone's life aims or preferences weighted by their importance (as rated by the individual who has the aims and preferences). An advocate of equal informed desire satisfaction might protest that the market economy as described might not be offering equal opportunity to all to become well informed. Progress on this front could be made by insistence on a fair system of education coupled with requirements that sellers of goods and services must provide potential purchasers full relevant information about them. A socialist might object that an economy organized around market exchange might do a good job satisfying individual preferences but still be unjust in virtue of its failure to provide adequately for fulfillment of everyone's needs. Distinguishing preference satisfaction from need fulfillment in this way involves an appeal to a perfectionist or objective-list account of human well-being—according to which there is a correct list of items that are together constitutive of well-being, and the more one gets of the items on the list, the better one's life goes for one.

Cohen appeals to the idea that the just economy is organized to provide equal opportunity for fulfillment of human needs, but to my knowledge he does not invoke the contrast between preferences and needs to express agreement with a perfectionist or objective-list account of individual well-being.

---

[29] See Robert Sugden, "Why Incoherent Preferences Do Not Justify Paternalism," *Constitutional Political Economy* 19 (2008): 226–46; and Sugden, "Opportunity as Mutual Advantage," *Economics and Philosophy* 26 (2010): 47–68. Sugden is responding to Richard H. Thaler and Cass R. Sunstein, *Nudge: Improving Decisions about Health, Wealth, and Happiness* (New Haven, CT: Yale University Press, 2008). I borrow the example of the individual's changing diet preferences from a lecture presentation by Sugden.

The omission seems consequential for the character of his critique of market exchange. In principle, a market economy could operate under constraints that render it an egalitarian market economy by some measures of equality, while providing almost no human need fulfillment. In this imagined market economy, exchange always has this character: I offer to sell you cotton candy, and you willingly purchase and consume it, thereby satisfying a trivial desire (for now) but fulfilling no significant need. (Notice that Cohen-style communal reciprocity could take the form of my desiring to serve you by doing what satisfies your desires now, in the expectation that you will want to do the same for me.)

Affirming or rejecting an objective-list account of human well-being should have a significant impact on one's position on the desirability of organizing economic life around market exchange. Be that as it may, Cohen surely owes us some account of what is to be equalized under an egalitarian theory such as the one he espouses. If Cohen affirms equality, he must uphold some standard for measuring people's condition, such that, in principle, given any two individuals, we can tell whether their condition is the same, or the condition of one is inferior, or perhaps that the situation is indeterminate in this respect. If there is *equal*, then there is *more* and *less*.

Here is Cohen's account.[30] (1) What is to be equalized is advantage, and there are several dimensions of advantage. (2) There is no exact formula or index for determining, given a person's scores on each of the various dimensions of advantage, what her overall score is. (3) Some overall comparisons can be made, and thus it is sometimes the case that, say, Smith is overall in a more advantageous condition than Jones, and sometimes we can detect that this is so. (4) The dimensions of advantage include resources, welfare (by this Cohen means desire satisfaction or maybe informed desire satisfaction), and need satisfaction (by this Cohen means gaining items on the list of objectively valuable goods). There may be further dimensions; Cohen is noncommittal on this point. (5) The morally right measure of advantage need not correspond to what an individual rationally aims at, when she is trying to make her life go better for her rather than worse. Cohen explicitly denies that "[t]he egalitarian distributor should distribute according to what sensible people care about, as such."[31] For example, perhaps no sensible person cares about desire satisfaction, as such, but because people embrace different conceptions of the good, proper respect for people may require distributing on the basis of desire satisfaction, as a way of maintaining neutrality across people's differing conceptions of their good.

One might worry that if people value resources instrumentally (that is, for what the resources can do to help advance their aims), then if

[30] Cohen, "Expensive Taste Rides Again," in Justine Burley, ed., *Dworkin and His Critics* (Oxford: Blackwell, 2004).
[31] Ibid., 16.

life-aim fulfillment (desire satisfaction) is deemed a determiner of advantage, resources should not be. To count both aim fulfillment and resources as determiners of advantage would be, in effect, to count people better off if they maintain a comfortable body temperature, and also to count, as separate dimensions of how well off they are, the number of blankets and parkas and air-conditioning units they possess (valued only as means to comfortable body temperature maintenance). I believe Cohen's response would be that resources constitute an important kind of freedom, and this counts as a distinct component of advantage or overall good condition of a person's life. Someone with more money in his pocket, in the context of a well-functioning economy, has more choices than someone with less money. Freedom has more than an instrumental value.

As I read Cohen, he is not skeptical concerning the existence of an objective standard of well-being or human need satisfaction. But if one has this standard, the further dimensions of well-being he adds are otiose. If one holds that no such objective standard is available, one should uphold a standard in the family of Ronald Dworkin's "no envy" test, which does not require interpersonal comparisons of welfare or well-being.[32] The middle ground that Cohen tries to occupy is unstable.

Suppose for simplicity that the items on the objective list include pleasurable or happy experience, significant achievement, systematic knowledge, friendship and love, and healthy family ties. Now imagine a person who achieves no desire satisfaction, never gets what he wants for its own sake, over the course of his life. What he aims at he fails to get, but as a by-product of his efforts he gains rich fulfillment in terms of the objective list. (He does not form retrospective desires for the good things he gets; his desires are always forward-looking, itching for what he is not going to get.) He does not experience the continual frustration of desire as deeply frustrating; he is happy. Zero preference satisfaction or desire fulfillment, I submit, is compatible with living an excellent life, rich in fulfillment, high in well-being. This is still compatible with holding that one's life would be still better if, in addition to objective goods, it contained desire fulfillment. But suppose there is a trade-off: to gain any desire satisfaction, one must sacrifice some objective good. If the objective list is correctly conceived, I would maintain that one should regard desires purely as helps or hindrances to

---

[32] On the theory of fairness, see Hal Varian, "Equity, Envy, and Efficiency," *Journal of Economic Theory* 9 (1974): 63–91. The "no envy" test is satisfied with respect to a group of persons, each of whom has a bundle of resources, if and only if no individual would prefer to have the bundle of any other person rather than his own bundle. The idea is deployed in Ronald Dworkin, *Sovereign Virtue: The Theory and Practice of Equality* (Cambridge, MA: Harvard University Press, 2000), chap. 2, pp. 65–119. For a philosophically sophisticated discussion of the family of fairness views (principles of distributive justice that do not rely on any interpersonal comparisons of welfare or well-being or the like), see Marc Fleurbaey, *Fairness, Responsibility, and Welfare*.

getting what matters. (If desire satisfaction did matter, it should be included as a component on the list of objective goods.)

Suppose, in contrast, that a person is fortunate in gaining huge piles of resources throughout his life. However, by some fluke, he fails to satisfy any of his desires or life aims and fails to achieve any items at all on the objective list. Enormous wealth or resource accumulation, I submit, is compatible with a zero score in fulfillment on any dimension that matters. Perhaps I had lots of opportunities and options, but failed to use any of them well, and gained zero fulfillment. In this scenario, I submit that the piles of resources are no consolation.

Freedom in certain respects may be partially constitutive of valuable achievements and valuable human relationships. Freely and voluntarily devoting oneself successfully to scientific achievement is intrinsically superior to coerced equally successful achievement. Acceptance of this point does not require, or support, upholding resource holdings as constituting a separate and distinct dimension of the advantage that makes a person's life go better rather than worse for her.

If the idea of an objectively correct standard of human good is an illusion, then it is disrespectful for an egalitarian society to treat an individual as though there were such a standard that is the appropriate measure of her condition for purposes of determining what we owe to her and she to us. However, if there is an objectively correct standard, I do not see how it is wrongfully disrespectful to me to rely on this standard to measure my condition against others', even if I myself embrace some mistaken standard. Cohen's position on what is to be equalized under an egalitarian theory of distribution mixes and matches elements of opposed views that do not cohere together.

X. CONCLUSION

Cohen argues that the principles that are implemented in the camping trip model cannot be implemented to any great degree in an economy organized around market exchange and private ownership. These principles are ethically attractive, so if we can achieve them to a greater degree by abolishing market exchange and private ownership and organizing the economy on the camping trip model, without sacrificing other values to an extent that morally outweighs any gains we can make by embracing the camping trip ideal, we ought to do so. I have argued that it is not clear to what extent market exchange and private ownership must be hindrances to greater achievement of camping trip ideals, and that in any case those ideals appear to require market exchange and private ownership. Moreover, I have argued that the camping trip principles as interpreted by Cohen are not ethically attractive; they are inferior to rivals. Some of the values Cohen leaves out of his discussion altogether, or at most treats as part of a catch-all category of constraints on feasibility, deserve to be included as an explicit part of the socialist or camping trip ideal suitably amended. Among these occluded values are good lives for people. Cohen's opposition to the market rests partly on a mistaken affirmation of equality as intrinsically morally valuable, and in other respects is more verbal than substantive.

Philosophy, University of California, San Diego

ARE MODERN AMERICAN LIBERALS SOCIALISTS OR SOCIAL DEMOCRATS?

By N. Scott Arnold

I. Modern American Liberals as Socialists

The short answer to the title question of this essay is "Yes, both." The longer answer is given in what follows. The essay is divided into two sections: the first argues that modern American liberals are really socialists; the second argues that they are also social democrats. Along the way, I shall offer some reasons why these commitments might be objectionable. Historically, the relationship between American citizens and the state was Lockean. The main purpose of the state was to give legal expression to natural rights to life, liberty, and the pursuit of happiness. One purpose of this essay is to explain how modern liberal ideas have strayed from those of the American Founding.

As we shall see, there are common historical roots to socialism and social democracy. What about modern liberalism? Not to paint with too broad a brush, but modern liberal politicians comprise the left wing of the Democratic Party. These days they call themselves "progressives"; modern liberal political philosophers include John Rawls,[1] Ronald Dworkin,[2] and Bruce Ackerman.[3] I hesitate to list others because doing so might involve disputes that are not central to the purposes of this essay. Modern American liberalism is the political ideology of the idealized welfare state, and "modern American liberalism," as the term is used here, includes most mainstream left-of-center contemporary American political philosophers, ranging from communitarians to civic republicans to Rawlsians. Of course, there are significant differences among representatives of these different schools of thought, but they all have in common the belief that American society should be more egalitarian than it is. The grounds for that egalitarianism differ, but that belief unites these thinkers and constitutes the essence, if one may speak that way, of modern American liberalism.

What must one believe to be a socialist? All can agree that socialists believe in social or collective ownership of the means of production.

---

[1] John Rawls, *A Theory of Justice* (Cambridge, MA: Belknap Press of Harvard University Press, 1971); John Rawls, *Justice as Fairness: A Restatement*, ed. Erin Kelley (Cambridge, MA: Belknap Press of Harvard University Press, 2001).

[2] See, e.g., Ronald Dworkin, "What is Equality? Part II: Equality of Resources," *Philosophy and Public Affairs* 10, no. 4 (Fall 1981): 283–345.

[3] Bruce A. Ackerman, *Social Justice in the Liberal State* (New Haven, CT: Yale University Press, 1980).

doi:10.1017/S0265052510000294

Social ownership can take a number of different forms; typically, it has been identified with central planning and complete state ownership of the means of production, but there are forms of social ownership compatible with a fully functioning market economy.[4] On October 3, 2008, the U.S. government purchased a significant ownership stake in a number of large banks, and on June 1, 2009, the U.S. government purchased a controlling ownership stake in two major automobile companies, but this cannot be taken as evidence of the socialistic tendencies of modern liberalism. The American economy is very large, and it is doubtful that these ownership stakes even rise to the level of seizing the "commanding heights" of the economy, a typical first step on the path to socialism. Besides, these investments in the banks and in the automobile companies have been defended on pragmatic grounds, accompanied by protestations that these moves are not precursors to any form of socialism. Moreover, these moves were not based on any deeper philosophical principles.

In what follows, I offer two complementary arguments for the claim that modern liberals believe in social or collective ownership and thus are socialists. One of these is based on A. M. Honoré's conception of ownership as a bundle of rights. The fundamental claim of this argument is that the state has effectively taken control of this bundle of rights from private owners. The other argument is adapted from an essay first published in the mid-1980s by Sanford Grossman and Oliver Hart, in which they distinguish specific rights from residual rights.[5] The basic idea behind this argument is that, because of the various regulatory regimes that have been imposed on the private sector without compensation, residual rights of control effectively reside with the state. Let us consider each of these arguments in more detail.

A. The first argument

In his 1961 essay "Ownership," A. M. Honoré observes that ownership—at least full, liberal ownership—is actually a complex of rights, terms, and conditions. They include the items in the following "bundle":

(1) The right to exclusive physical possession;
(2) The right to manage, which includes the right to use or modify, as well as the right to enter into contractual relations with others to use or modify;

---

[4] See N. Scott Arnold, *The Philosophy and Economics of Market Socialism* (New York: Oxford University Press, 1994), for a specification of one form of market socialism that is compatible with a market economy. One of the burdens of the present essay is to argue that modern liberalism is another form of social ownership of the means of production.

[5] Sanford J. Grossman and Oliver D. Hart, "The Costs and Benefits of Ownership: A Theory of Vertical and Lateral Integration," *The Journal of Political Economy* 94, no. 4 (August 1986): 691–719.

(3) The right of disposition, which includes the right to alienate or destroy;

(4) The right to the income and to the capital value;

(5) The right to bequeath;

(6) A prohibition on harmful use;

(7) The right to security, that is, immunity from expropriation;

(8) Absence of term (that is, the other incidents of ownership do not automatically expire at a specified time);

(9) Liability to execution of debt (alternatively, the right to pledge as security for debt).[6]

Let us consider for a moment item (4): the right to the income and to the capital value. What is the nature of the state's claim on the income and wealth of a society in light of its taxing and spending authority? On behalf of modern liberals, it could be argued that the state has a kind of priority of ownership (in a sense to be explicated as this argument unfolds) on an indeterminate portion of citizens' income and wealth. This priority of ownership is based on the fact that the state has wide discretion in how it exercises its taxing and spending authority. Consider, first, taxation. The state can use the tax code for a variety of purposes other than raising revenue, including changing the distribution of wealth and income. In contrast, if private individuals have this priority of ownership, the state is more constrained in what it can legitimately do through its tax policy. Classical liberals, who represent the other side in this debate about the proper role of government, believe that the state must provide something in exchange for the taxes it raises, because they believe that priority of ownership resides with private parties.

Modern liberals believe that it is perfectly appropriate for the state to manipulate the tax code for various social purposes. They believe that the tax code is an important vehicle by which government can achieve a variety of objectives. One of these is the redistribution of after-tax income through a progressive income tax. Some economists have argued, however, that the state is much more limited than one might suppose in its ability to change the distribution of income through progressive taxation on income. Roughly, the idea is that labor markets tend to adjust so as to offset the degree of progressivity of an income tax and to reestablish income differentials that would have existed in the absence of a progressive income tax.[7] In addition, it has long been observed that the estate tax is not a very effective vehicle for changing the dis-

---

[6] A. M. Honoré, "Ownership," in *Oxford Essays in Jurisprudence,* ed. A. G. Guest (Oxford: Oxford University Press, 1961), 107–40. The list to which this note is appended is adapted from Lawrence Becker, *Property Rights* (London: Routledge and Kegan Paul, 1977), 19.

[7] See Richard E. Wagner, *To Promote the General Welfare* (San Francisco: Pacific Research Institute for Public Policy, 1989), 72–88, for an elaboration on this point.

tribution of wealth.[8] For various reasons, taxes on the capital value of assets that are bequeathed to heirs tend to be ineffective. Finally, there is the familiar public choice argument that once the tax code is open to manipulation through the political process, the powerful and the organized will benefit at the expense of the powerless and the unorganized, and that redistribution from the rich to the poor will be, at best, incidental.

Changes in the tax code are also used as a tool of macroeconomic policy. Tax cuts are sometimes instituted in an attempt to stimulate economic activity, as are adjustments in depreciation schedules. Tax increases are used in an attempt to lower government deficits and thereby lower interest rates. Tariffs and "voluntary" import quotas are used to protect jobs from foreign competition. Finally, political leaders change the tax code to encourage behaviors they think should be encouraged and to discourage behaviors they think should be discouraged. For example, "tax shielding" for funds spent on medical care or on higher education are designed to encourage spending on medical care and higher education at the expense of spending on other things.[9] On the other side, increases in taxes on tobacco are seen as a useful vehicle for discouraging smoking, as well as for allocating the alleged social costs of smoking to smokers, though that has turned out to be mostly fiction.[10] The use of the tax code to change the distribution of income, to promote macroeconomic goals, and to encourage or discourage certain forms of spending are reflective of the attitude that a portion of citizens' income fundamentally belongs to society at large, for which the state acts as an (often imperfect) agent.

Further evidence for this conception of ownership can be found in a widely shared attitude among modern liberals toward proposed tax cuts and toward how resources are allocated by the market. Modern liberal politicians and policy analysts label proposed tax cuts as "tax expenditures," which are conceived of as fully equivalent to government subsidies. That is, tax cuts are viewed as subsidies to their beneficiaries, and the question then becomes whether such subsidies are a better use of

---

[8] The argument for this proposition is given in Edward J. McCaffery, "The Uneasy Case for Wealth Transfer Taxation," *Yale Law Journal* 104 (1994): 283–365. See also McCaffery, "The Political Liberal Case Against the Estate Tax," *Philosophy and Public Affairs* 23 (Fall 1994): 281–312. All societies allow for *inter vivos* transfers of wealth (currently in the U.S., the limit on tax-free transfers is $10,000 per year), and indeed it would be hard to prevent such transfers. McCaffery's argument is buttressed by the fact that the main form of inheritance these days concerns human capital formation.

[9] The benefits of tax shielding do not accrue entirely to *consumers* of medical care and education. Providers capture some of the benefits by raising prices. When tax shielding for certain categories of goods or services is instituted, the demand curve shifts to the right, since consumers are paying for these goods or services with cheaper dollars. The public choice analysis is that provider groups are the driving force behind all, or nearly all, forms of tax shielding.

[10] W. Kip Viscusi, *Smoke-Filled Rooms: A Post-Mortem on the Tobacco Deal* (Chicago: University of Chicago Press, 2002), 73, 171.

society's wealth than other things on which these funds might be "spent." For example, in 2001, the U.S. government was trying to determine what to do with actual and projected budget surpluses. For modern liberals, the question was how best to spend this money—society's money. On their view, one way to spend it was to give tax cuts (or welfare payments such as the Earned Income Tax Credit), preferably targeted to those with low incomes (or to some more narrowly delimited segment of the population in order to achieve some other worthy objective).

Negative pronouncements about how society allocates "its" resources abound among those with modern liberal sensibilities, and this provides a further window on modern liberal attitudes about the ownership of income and wealth. Consider the following quotation from Arthur Caplan, in which he reflects on the wisdom of using society's resources to treat infertility:

> [A]ssisted reproduction, unlike sexual reproduction, is a social enterprise. It requires the involvement of many third parties as well as significant amounts of social resources. . . . What level of help society is willing to tolerate, provide or pay for moves assisted reproduction beyond the boundaries of personal choice and individual liberty.[11]

What is especially telling about this example is that infertility treatments are not paid for by the government, and are normally not even covered by private insurance plans, a fact of which Caplan is surely aware. To say that the amount of "social resources" that are allocated to assisted reproduction should be subjected to society's (i.e., the state's) judgment about what it "is willing to . . . pay for" implies pretty clearly that Caplan regards the funds that infertile couples might spend on infertility treatments out of their own pockets as belonging in the first instance to society, in which case society must consider other goods or services on which these funds might be spent; that is, it must consider the opportunity costs. Modern liberals might object that the source of Caplan's observation is the fact that the state directly and indirectly heavily subsidizes medical care. It is not that the state is claiming ownership over the resources private couples would spend on infertility treatments, but that it is simply exercising its ownership rights over the resources it has provided to the medical community. This reply, however, will not do, since it assumes that in any arena in which public and private funds mix, the state should determine how private resources can be spent in the course of deciding how resources controlled by the state can be used. If the state is big enough and ubiquitous enough (as indeed it is in contemporary American society), almost anything a person spends his or her money on will be

---

[11] Arthur Caplan, *Am I My Brother's Keeper?* (Bloomington: Indiana University Press, 1997), 7.

in a place where public and private funds mix. This reduces to the view that the state has an ownership stake in the resources people use to purchase just about anything, which is exactly the view I have been attributing to modern liberals. More precisely, what stands behind the view of Caplan and countless others who question how scarce resources are being allocated in a market society is a conception of ownership in which society has, through the state, a kind of priority claim on an indeterminate portion of all wealth and income.

The priority of society's claim on a portion of social wealth is given further expression in the writings of leading modern liberal political philosophers on the fundamental problem of distributive justice. This is clearest in John Rawls's *A Theory of Justice,* where Rawls defines the problem of distributive justice as the problem of determining how the benefits and burdens of social cooperation should be distributed.[12] Given that it is the state's job to ensure (distributive) justice, this assumes, as Robert Nozick has pointed out, that the state has the right to determine how those benefits and burdens are to be distributed.[13]

Of course, anyone who is not an anarchist, including Nozick, would admit that the state has some legitimate claim on a person's income and wealth; thus, by itself, this proposition cannot be the basis for the claim that modern liberals are socialists. But it should not be taken by itself; it must be considered in light of other propositions about the taxing and spending authority of the modern state. Among those propositions are (1) the claim that it is up to the state to decide, within fairly broad limits, what proportion of people's income to take in taxes, and (2) the claim that the state can expend resources on pretty much whatever programs it believes to be worthwhile.

Rawls is not the only modern liberal theorist who believes that society has some sort of antecedent claim on assets found within a state's borders. Ronald Dworkin, in his exposition of his theory of distributive justice, asks us to consider a hypothetical auction in which all of society's (nonhuman) resources are to be bid upon by people with equal wealth.[14] Bruce Ackerman poses the problem of distributive justice in the context of a story about people in a spaceship trying to decide how to divide up a valuable commodity that they are about to acquire on a planet they are approaching.[15] All of these conceptions of the problem of distributive justice clearly presuppose that the community, for which the state acts as agent, has a prior ownership claim on all natural resources and productive assets, which it then has to decide how to distribute.

To articulate further this view about the modern liberal conception of ownership, more needs to be said about the notion of priority. What does

---

[12] Rawls, *A Theory of Justice,* 4.
[13] Robert Nozick, *Anarchy, State, and Utopia* (New York: Basic Books, 1974), 149.
[14] Dworkin, "What Is Equality? Part II: Equality of Resources," 285–90.
[15] Ackerman, *Social Justice in the Liberal State,* 31–68.

268 N. SCOTT ARNOLD

"priority" mean in this context? I would answer that it consists of two things. First, in the language of social contract theory, it means that society, or the community, would have an enforceable, morally legitimate claim on some of people's income and wealth in a state of nature. This does not mean that the community has full, liberal ownership of all productive assets in a state of nature. That might be one conception of communism. The claim only extends to an indeterminate portion of the income those assets generate or to a portion of the wealth those assets represent, and not to control of the assets themselves. Second, and perhaps more importantly, it means that the extraction of revenue from individuals by the state need not be conceived of as a (forced) exchange for which the state must provide something of comparable value in return, since that revenue did not, at the most fundamental level, belong to individuals in the first place. On this conception of ownership, if the state takes from Peter and gives to Paul, Peter has no legitimate complaint that he does not benefit. The state, acting as an agent for the community at large, is simply taking what antecedently and rightfully belongs to its principal—society—and is using it in ways that it sees fit. Possible foundations for these propositions will be investigated shortly.

The best explanation for this view about ownership is that the state has a claim on the relevant income or on the assets themselves, which it can choose to exercise or not as it sees fit. The question at issue is whether modern liberalism is committed to the view that the state (or society as a whole, for whom the state acts as agent) has a prior ownership claim on some part of the income associated with productive assets. It seems that an affirmative answer to this question cannot be avoided as long as modern liberals maintain that the state has wide discretionary authority both to tax and to spend.

Other considerations support this notion. Notice that private individuals, who also have (partial) income rights in productive assets, are relatively unconstrained in how they can acquire income from employing those assets and what they can spend that income on. The state is similarly unconstrained; it can exercise its income rights in productive assets through myriad forms of taxation and even more multifarious forms of spending. Of course, private individuals, unlike the state, cannot exercise their income rights through coercion. In a corresponding manner, the state faces some modest legal constraints, as well as more substantial political constraints, on its taxing and spending authority, though the political constraints on spending seem to have evaporated in recent years. The only constitutional constraint on private property in the United States is that the state cannot take possession of a parcel of real property, or effectively seize the entire value of someone's property, without compensating the owner.[16]

<hr/>

[16] The takings clause of the Fifth Amendment states: "nor shall private property be taken for public use without just compensation." U.S. Constitution, amend. V. See also *United*

The assumption or presupposition of social ownership best explains the modern liberal attitude that it is up to the state to decide, within fairly broad limits, what proportion of the total wealth and income of a society to take in the form of taxes, how those tax burdens should be allocated, and how the revenues collected should be spent. That spending, on the modern liberal view, can, at least in theory, include selective tax cuts, as well as government spending. In light of these considerations, it is hard to deny that modern liberalism is committed to the view that the state has wealth and income rights in productive assets. What about the other incidents of ownership?

Government regulation is another way in which the state can exercise its ownership rights in productive assets, especially when it effects a regulatory taking for which compensation is typically not owed. Perhaps the most significant Supreme Court case in this regard was *Penn Central Transportation Co. v. New York City* (1978).[17] New York City's Landmarks Preservation Law allowed the Landmarks Preservation Commission to designate buildings and the sites on which they are located as historic landmarks. Among other things, this law required owners of designated properties to get permission before they made major changes to the structure's facade. Penn Central's Grand Central Terminal was designated a landmark. The company wanted to build a multistory office tower in the space above the terminal. The Landmarks Preservation Commission prohibited the proposed development and refused to pay compensation; the company ultimately challenged that refusal in the Supreme Court under the due process clause of the Fourteenth Amendment and the takings clause of the Fifth Amendment, and lost. The denial of compensation is significant, since it shows that the state is under no obligation to pay for development rights it takes from a private party. Of course, if the Penn Central Transportation Company did not own these rights in the first place, then the state took nothing from the company, and indeed, on the modern liberal view, it did not. There is a line of other cases that confirms this ruling.[18]

On what grounds might this presumption of social ownership be based? One might take the view that there is a primordial social obligation to share the fruits of one's labor, land, and capital with the community at large. This might, in turn, depend on deeper principles of moral philosophy, which take a presumption of equal treatment as fundamental to the

---

States v. Causby, 328 U.S. 256 (1946) (military take offs and landings near a farm ruled a taking); and *Loretto v. Teleprompter Manhattan CATV Corp.*, 458 U.S. 419 (1982) (granting an easement to install cable television boxes on the roofs of buildings ruled a taking). In *Lucas v. South Carolina Coastal Council*, 505 U.S. 1003 (1992), the Supreme Court held that depriving a property owner of virtually all economically beneficial uses of his land constituted a taking for which compensation was owed.

[17] *Penn Central Transportation Co. v. New York City*, 438 U.S. 104 (1978).

[18] See *Agins v. Tiburon*, 447 U.S. 255 (1980); *Babbitt v. Sweet Home Chapter of Communities for a Great Oregon*, 515 U.S. 687 (1995); and *Palazzolo v. Rhode Island*, 533 U.S. 606 (2001).

moral point of view.[19] Alternatively, as sociologist L. T. Hobhouse has argued, society contributes in innumerable ways to the value of productive assets and to what entrepreneurs and capitalists are able to earn in a market economy.[20] A more direct argument, also suggested by Hobhouse, drops the presumption that the state acts as an agent for society (its principal). The state itself is responsible for a substantial portion of the value of land, labor, and capital, since it provides a stable framework within which its citizens can use their property to further their own ends.[21] It defines and enforces property rights, which involve expensive and complex criminal and civil justice systems, and it provides for the common defense against external enemies. After all, it is the state that allows us to pass from a state of nature into civil society. It might be argued that the marginal difference the state makes in the value of all forms of property is so substantial that it justifies the partial-ownership claim the state makes on the income and wealth of a society.

B. The second argument

The second argument for the claim that modern liberals are socialists is adapted from an essay by two economists, Sanford Grossman and Oliver Hart, written in the mid-1980s.[22] Their argument begins with the observation, which is foundational for transaction-cost analysis, that complete, costlessly enforceable contracts cannot be written. Also foundational is the proposition that there are asset specificities—that is, some assets are worth considerably more than they otherwise would be when combined with other assets that are fixed as to location, specific use, etc. Finally, transaction-cost analysis presumes that economic actors are inclined to be opportunistic, that is, to take advantage of opportunities to renegotiate contracts to the detriment of other parties when they find that they are able to do so. These conditions combine to create what is called in the literature an "expropriation hazard." That is, some of the value of an asset can be leached away when that asset is tied down to a specific use for which it is particularly valuable.

Part of Grossman and Hart's contribution to this discussion is to distinguish between what they call "specific rights" and "residual rights":

When it is too costly for one party to specify a long list of the particular rights it desires over another party's assets, it may be optimal for [the first] party to purchase all the rights except those specifically

---

[19] Thomas Nagel describes this as the impersonal standpoint. See Thomas Nagel, *Equality and Partiality* (Oxford: Oxford University Press, 1991), 10–20.

[20] L. T. Hobhouse, *Liberalism* (1911; Oxford: Oxford University Press, 1964), 99.

[21] Ibid., 98.

[22] Sanford J. Grossman and Oliver D. Hart, "The Costs and Benefits of Ownership," *The Journal of Political Economy* 94, no. 4 (August 1986): 691–719.

mentioned in the contract [i.e., rights purchased from the seller]. Ownership is the purchase of these residual rights of control.[23]

Grossman and Hart's interest is to explain the determinants of vertical integration. It permits the theorist to discover the factors that determine how far back into the supply chain a firm can profitably go, as well determining how far a firm can profitably go forward into the distribution of the product. Ronald Coase inaugurated this line of research by asking a simple question: "Why are there firms?" Or, alternatively, "Why is it that some transactions take place across markets and others take place internally within a firm?" The general answer that Grossman and Hart offer is that some transactions are best (i.e., most efficiently) organized within the firm and some are most efficiently carried out across markets. The rest of their essay attempts to elucidate the conditions under which the firm or the market does a better job of handling these transactions.

It should be reasonably clear how this distinction between specific rights and residual rights can be adapted to show that modern liberals favor some form of socialism. For modern liberals, residual rights of control reside with the state. The main reason for this is that the state is entitled to impose, without compensation, a variety of regulatory restrictions on private property—restrictions that exactly parallel those placed on income rights and the rights to the capital value of productive assets. These restrictions are so comprehensive that it is fair to say that the state *de facto* possesses residual rights of control, though of course it does not possess them *de jure*. The legal fiction that private parties have ownership rights is maintained, but it is merely a fiction. For example, government restricts management rights by determining the terms and conditions of the employment relation in the form of minimum-wage and antidiscrimination laws; state governments further restrict employment rights by regulating occupations through occupational licensure laws. Health and safety regulations comprehensively regulate the right to dispose of the product. This includes the requirement that most drugs be prescribed by a physician and the requirement that pharmaceutical products be shown to be safe and effective before being put into the stream of commerce. Initially, these restrictions were unilaterally imposed by the Food and Drug Administration (FDA), though they were later codified in the 1951 Humphrey-Durham amendment to the Food, Drug, and Cosmetic Act of 1938. There is also regulation of health and safety conditions in the workplace by the Occupational Safety and Health Administration (OSHA) and the Mine Safety and Health Administration (MSHA). Nonmedical consumer products are regulated by the Consumer Product Safety Commission (CPSC), which is empowered to issue recalls of dangerous products.

[23] Ibid., 692.

Finally, there is environmental regulation, notably the Endangered Species Act of 1973, which prohibits the taking of members of endangered animal (and plant) species, and Section 404 of the Clean Water Act of 1972, which regulates wetlands. Both are designed to protect and enhance biodiversity, and neither requires that compensation be paid. The right to the income and capital value of assets has already been discussed, as has the right to bequeath. As I noted above, prima facie violations of the right to security of possession for which compensation is owed have been limited to physical possession or seizure by the state or to the expropriation of essentially all the value of private property.

    To this argument it might be objected that these regulations are *restrictions* on the associated rights and thus do not imply the reassignment of residual rights of control to the government. The problem with this objection begins with the open-ended character of government regulation. The state can impose on owners of private property pretty much whatever regulatory regime it wants, subject to the exceptions just noted; those exceptions can be conceived of as a residuum of nostalgia for the days when full, liberal ownership rights were more fully respected. Restrictions on any of the other incidents of ownership are permissible—and compensation need not be paid. The state can even impose comprehensive wage and price controls, which it did under President Richard Nixon from 1971 through 1974.[24] Although Nixon is usually thought of as a conservative, this policy is thoroughly consistent with modern liberal principles. Indeed, it is difficult to imagine a more comprehensive regulation of the right of disposition than wage and price controls, and, of course, no compensation was offered when those controls were put in place. Because of the open-ended character of government regulation and because compensation need not be paid in most cases, property rights have effectively been eroded to the point where the state has in fact, though not in law, assumed residual rights of control. It just chooses to exercise those rights across a broader or narrower range of circumstances and conditions.

C. Summary

    The foregoing two arguments establish that modern liberals are socialists who have not yet come out of the closet. To summarize, the first argument is based on the proposition that the state, through its taxing and spending authority, has a kind of priority of ownership on the income and wealth associated with private property. The second argument extends this to government regulation, which typically imposes uncompensated burdens on owners of private property.

[24] See "Wage and Price Controls," *The Columbia Encyclopedia*, 6th ed. (2010). http://www.encyclopedia.com/doc/1E1-wageNpri.html.

In passing, one might ask: What is the harm? What is objectionable about the taxing and spending authority of the state and about all forms of government regulation? Some of these regulatory restrictions, after all, do some good. Nonetheless, taxation and spending, as well as the associated regulatory regimes, fundamentally change the relationship between citizens and the state. The Internal Revenue Service (IRS) is privy to the most intimate details of citizens' lives. Because these regulatory regimes are open-ended, people appear before the various regulatory bureaucracies as supplicants and not as citizens with private property rights and the independence those rights ensure.[25] Regulatory bureaucracies can delay permits, withhold approvals, etc., and suffer no adverse consequences. They do not have to pay, even through the state, for the regulatory restrictions they impose. Moreover, because of the nature of their mission, regulatory bureaucracies must be given broad discretionary power, which will be—indeed must be—exercised in essentially arbitrary ways. The language of the mandates of regulatory agencies such as the Environmental Protection Agency (EPA) and the Fish and Wildlife Service (FWS) is vague and aspirational.[26] It must be filled in through the rule-making process. Of course, there is an opportunity for public comment on any proposed rules, but the various regulatory bureaucracies can proceed in the face of public opposition to proposed rules or rule changes. Finally, the existence of regulatory agencies with broad discretionary power makes property rights relatively ill-defined, and this leads property owners to conceive of their world as one of threats and opportunities. They have an incentive to hire lobbyists to block the threats and seize the opportunities that government regulation and tax policies present. This is a recipe for deadweight welfare losses all the way around.

II. Modern American Liberals as Social Democrats

How can social democracy best be characterized? It is probably most fruitful to characterize it in terms of a set of particular social institutions. These institutions are intended to support people, who, through no fault of their own, are unable to support themselves. Everyone ages; everyone needs health care; some workers get injured on the job and are unable to work; some workers are victims of involuntary unemployment. The institutions of social democracy are designed to deal with these permanent features of the human condition.

The primary historical influence on socialist theorizing is, of course, Karl Marx, and central to Marx's ideas were the claims of historical mate-

---

[25] This is the theme of chapter 1 of Milton Friedman's *Capitalism and Freedom* (Chicago: University of Chicago Press, 1962).
[26] For the EPA, see U.S.C. 42 U.S.C. sec. 7401(b) and sec. 7401(c). For the FWS, see 16 U.S.C. sec. 742a.

rialism, specifically the claims that the relations of production are determined by the extant technology and that the economic base determines
the legal, moral, and political superstructure of a society. The determin-
istic cast of Marx's ideas was reflected in the practice of the SPD (*Sozialdemokratische Partei Deutschlands*, the Social Democratic Party of Germany),
which counseled passivity in light of its belief in the inevitable collapse of
capitalism. Each crisis of capitalism was supposed to involve its death
throes.

Marx's theorizing about the natural history of capitalism eventually
gave rise to an alternative understanding of history and historical change.
Perhaps the central figure—the founding father—of social democratic
thought was Eduard Bernstein (1850–1932). Early in his career, Bernstein
was an orthodox Marxist, but later he came to reject key tenets of Marxism. Fundamentally, the problem for Bernstein was that Marx's predictions did not seem to be coming true, though Marx's followers continued
to plot out the theory's epicycles. There had been an obvious improvement in the workers' standard of living, so Bernstein rejected the claim
that the working class was being progressively impoverished by the capitalist system. He also rejected the propositions that capitalism was becoming dominated by fewer and fewer firms and that the ownership of capital
was becoming more and more concentrated.[27] More generally, a central
element of Bernstein's heresy was the fact that he made room for human
volition, beliefs about morality, and sheer contingency as historical forces.
His cardinal sins were to jettison Marx's determinism to make a place for
moral beliefs and beliefs about social justice as motivators of collective
action. As social democrats rose to power in the first decades of twentieth-
century Germany and elsewhere, the dominant ideas were no longer
those of the ruling class. Bernstein believed that the central problem with
capitalism was the unjust distribution of the social product.[28] This view
undercut the radical character of Marx's critique of capitalism, since it
suggested, especially to trade union leaders, that capitalism could be
reformed by forcing a redistribution of the social product in a more egalitarian direction. This also meant that capitalism was not by its very

---

[27] Eduard Bernstein, *Evolutionary Socialism: A Criticism and Affirmation*, trans. Edith C.
Harvey, introduction by Sidney Hook (New York: Schocken Books, 1964), xxiv–xxv. Bernstein actually did some statistical work on the question of the number of firms under
capitalism at the end of the nineteenth century in Germany, as well as on the diffusion of
ownership of capital. He found that, contrary to Marx's predictions, the number of firms
had actually increased over time, and that the ownership of capital had become more
diffuse. See ibid., 54–73.
[28] This is suggested, though not explicitly stated, in a number of places in Bernstein's
Evolutionary Socialism. See, e.g., p. 139. Perhaps Bernstein was not more explicit about this
because of Marx's criticisms of the Gotha program, which objected to similar ideas offered
by Ferdinand Lassalle. But this is speculative. See Karl Marx, *Critique of the Gotha Programme*
(Moscow: Progress Publishers, 1971). See also Manfred Steger, *The Quest for Evolutionary
Socialism* (Cambridge: Cambridge University Press, 1997), 135; Steger takes this belief of
Bernstein's to be obvious and uncontroversial.

nature an exploitative mode of production, which significantly under-mined Marx's critique of capitalist society.

All this, of course, was heresy from a Marxist perspective. Orthodox Marxism held that the political and legal superstructure of society was largely epiphenomenal (that is, a mere by-product of more fundamental processes). As capitalists pursued "the boundless thirst for surplus value," they substituted capital for labor, which, given the labor theory of value (which Bernstein also rejected), meant that the proletariat would become increasingly impoverished, since capitalists had to squeeze more and more surplus value out of fewer and fewer workers. In the ensuing crises, workers would be laid off and would swell the ranks of the Reserve Army of the Unemployed. But this did not happen. While it is true that capi-talism had periodic crises in the form of the business cycle, it was a genuine cycle, which meant that layoffs did not steadily increase, and hiring ultimately picked up. Other factors that did not fit the Marxist worldview were the passage of factory legislation standardizing working conditions, the democratization of local governments, and the legaliza-tion of trade unions.[29] On the Marxist worldview, it is hard to see how trade unions could be legalized, if the legal structure of a society were genuinely epiphenomenal. The apocalyptic collapse of capitalism had receded into the future.

Bernstein was an SPD member of the German parliament (the Reichstag) beginning in 1902. In April 1917, however, he formed a new party, the antiwar Independent Social Democratic Party of Germany (*Unabhängige Sozialdemokratische Partei Deutschlands*—USPD), though in 1919 he rejoined the SPD. Although he had voted for war credits in 1914, from 1915 onward he opposed German participation in World War I. He served in the Reichstag through the late 1920s, until his retirement from political life in 1928. He died four years later in 1932.

After National Socialist rule in Germany in the 1940s, Bernstein was ultimately vindicated in the dawn of the postwar period in Western Europe. From the mid-1940s to the mid-1970s, social democracy was triumphant, though questions about its sustainability began to arise round the early 1980s. Since that time, unemployment has remained consistently high in Western Europe, and this has put a strain on the welfare systems of the European Union countries. Nevertheless, from the mid-1940s to the mid-1970s, the standard of living rose dramati-cally, unemployment was low, and the inequality of material condition that characterized the American postwar boom was largely absent. West-ern European nations were able to combine democracy and a nomi-nally capitalist system with significant redistribution of income. This was effected by highly progressive personal income taxes and nakedly redistributive social welfare programs.

---

[29] Bernstein, *Evolutionary Socialism*, xxvi.

With this historical background in view, it is possible to identify the central elements of social democracy. The word "elements" is used advisedly, because a choice has to be made about how to characterize social democracy. There are different ways to do this; one way is in terms of its social institutions, but another is in terms of its underlying political philosophy. The latter might well involve some difficulties, however, since there is no guarantee that there is a single political philosophy that underlies social democracy. There is nevertheless a commonality of social institutions, which can serve as the basis for identifying social democracies. More will be said about these institutions shortly.

Which nations can be characterized as social democracies? By any plausible account, the countries of Western Europe should be included in any list of social democratic regimes. Others might also be included (e.g., Canada, Australia, New Zealand), but nearly everyone can agree that social democratic regimes dominate Western Europe. Western European countries include the United Kingdom, Switzerland, France, Ireland, Spain, Italy, the Netherlands, Finland, Belgium, Germany, Austria, Norway, Denmark, and Sweden. One descriptive criterion, which permits identification of the extension of the term "social democracies" is the Gini index. According to the Central Intelligence Agency's *World Factbook,* the Gini

> index is calculated from the Lorenz curve, in which cumulative family income is plotted against the number of families arranged from the poorest to the richest. The index is the ratio of (a) the area between a country's Lorenz curve and the 45 degree helping line to (b) the entire triangular area under the 45 degree line. The more nearly equal a country's income distribution, the closer its Lorenz curve to the 45 degree line and the lower its Gini index. . . . If income were distributed with perfect equality, the Lorenz curve would coincide with the 45 degree line and the index would be zero; if income were distributed with perfect inequality, the Lorenz curve would coincide with the horizontal axis and the right vertical axis and the index would be 100.[30]

The expression "the 45 degree helping line" makes the basic idea harder to understand than it should be. The main idea is given in the sentence following the ellipses: if all families' incomes were equal, the index would be zero; if one family had all the income, the index would be 100. The Gini coefficient, which is also sometimes cited, is just the Gini index with the decimal point moved two places to the left. Table 1 gives the Gini coefficients for the social democratic regimes of Western Europe:

[30] See *CIA World Factbook,* https://www.cia.gov/library/publications/the-world-factbook/rankorder/2172rank.html for the figures given below.

Table 1. *Gini coefficients for selected Western European countries*

Country	Gini coefficient	Year (latest available)
United Kingdom	.34	2005
Switzerland	.337	2008
France	.327	2008
Ireland	.32	2005
Spain	.32	2005
Italy	.32	2006
European Union	.31	2005 (est.)
The Netherlands	.309	2007
Finland	.295	2007
Belgium	.28	2005
Germany	.27	2006
Austria	.26	2007
Norway	.25	2008
Denmark	.24	2005
Sweden	.23	2005

Of 134 countries listed in the CIA's *World Factbook*, Sweden has the lowest Gini coefficient.[31] Notice also the compression among the nations of Western Europe: no Western European nation has a Gini coefficient greater than .34 (the United Kingdom), and Sweden has the lowest at .23. The gap between the lowest and the highest Gini coefficients for the European Union, then, is only .11. By contrast, the United States ranks forty-second out of 134 countries, with a Gini coefficient of .45 (2007), while Namibia has the largest Gini coefficient at .707 (2003).[32] The American ranking more or less accurately reflects the political division in the United States between the left and the right, in the sense that those on the left favor a more progressive income tax while those on the right favor a less progressive income tax. Those on the right have been more successful over the past two decades. If modern American liberals had their way, however, the Gini coefficient of the United States would be much lower than it currently is. That state of affairs would comport best with modern liberal theories of distributive or social justice, which contain a strong egalitarian component.

Marxist theory never had much influence on the Democratic Party in the U.S., or on the theoreticians of the (idealized) American welfare state.[33]

[31] Ibid.
[32] Ibid.
[33] This assumes that the political philosophers of modern liberalism are attempting to justify an idealized version of the modern welfare state. This is not true of John Rawls. Although in *A Theory of Justice* he said that the choice of an economic system was something

N. SCOTT ARNOLD

Modern liberals are, after all, liberals, and liberalism can be broadly characterized in terms of commitments to individual liberty, equal rights, and a more or less free-market economy,[34] which, as the argument of Section I makes clear, is consistent with effective social ownership of the means of production. Contemporary social democrats in Western Europe trace their roots to Bernstein and conceive of themselves as heirs to that tradition, which was first articulated as an alternative to Marx, though it involves Marxist categories to a greater or lesser degree. Although these categories differ systematically from their modern American liberal counterparts, their vision of the institutions of the good society, especially those pertaining to social justice, is essentially the same as that of modern liberalism. This is evident in the tax structure of social democratic regimes and in the American tax code. Both have progressive personal income taxes, though the top marginal rate in America (for married couples) is only 35 percent.[35] The countries listed in table 1 have top marginal rates ranging from 40 percent in the UK and Norway to 59 percent in Denmark.[36] The relatively flatter slope of the progressive tax code in the United States reflects the influence of the conservative or supply-side case against higher marginal tax rates.

What explains the apparent convergence of contemporary welfare states? Though ideology doubtless plays some role, other factors are likely at work. In the mid-1970s, the American organizational sociologist Harold Wilensky argued that this convergence is best explained by the "logic of industrialism."[37] Briefly, Wilensky's view is that, within the framework of a functionalist sociology, the rise of the interventionist state and the blocking of the excesses of liberal capitalism are responses to the new needs implicit in modern industrial societies. On his view, once an economic system reaches a certain gross national product (GNP), it is almost inevitable that the associated social welfare schemes will become pervasive, more elaborate, and better defined. Other researchers, however, have rejected Wilensky's findings. Sociologists Jerald Hage and Robert Han-

---

about which he had nothing to say, toward the end of his life he changed his mind and said that only a "property-owning democracy" or a form of liberal socialism could characterize the economic system of a just society. A "property-owning democracy" is described in J. E. Meade's *Efficiency, Equality, and the Ownership of Property* (Cambridge, MA: Harvard University Press, 1965). Unfortunately, Meade does not specify how property rights would be configured in the system he favors, nor does Rawls. This is an important omission. See Rawls, *Justice as Fairness*, 135–40.

[34] This characterization of liberalism follows John Gray, *Liberalism*, 2d ed. (Minneapolis: University of Minnesota Press, 1995), 45–55.

[35] See http://www.truthandpolitics.org/top-rates.php#table. Rates quoted are as of 2003.

[36] Figures cited are as of 2008. See "Taxation Trends in the European Union: Data from EU Member States and Norway," 2009 edition (Luxembourg: Office for Official Publications of the European Communities, 2009), 81. Available online at http://ec.europa.eu/taxation_customs/resources/documents/taxation/gen_info/economic_analysis/tax_structures/2009/2009_full_text_en.pdf.

[37] Harold L. Wilensky, *The Welfare State and Equality* (Berkeley and Los Angeles: University of California Press, 1975).

neman and historian Edward T. Gargan found that "previous research [i.e., Wilensky's] has overestimated the importance of GNP in welfare state development."[38] Not all social democratic regimes are the same, however. A leading theoretician of social democracies is the sociologist Gøsta Esping-Andersen.[39] He identifies three basic types of social democracies or welfare states. One type is the liberal welfare state, characterized by modest universal social transfer programs, which primarily benefit low-income workers. Here, welfare rights are based on need, and there is a social stigma attached to the receipt of benefits, which are typically relatively meager. Examples include systems in the United States, Canada, and Australia. A second type is the compulsory state social insurance model, which has fairly strong entitlements, though there are elaborate eligibility and benefit rules which depend almost entirely on contributions and thus on labor-market participation. Examples include Austria, Germany, France, and Italy. A third type of system assigns benefits to all citizens or long-term residents, irrespective of need or work performance (though this is subject to a qualification to be explained shortly). In such systems, coverage for health care is universal. Examples of this type include Great Britain, Spain, most of Scandinavia, and New Zealand.[40]

What all these welfare states/social democracies have in common, however, is the same set of social institutions. In particular, all have forms of compulsory social insurance.[41] This is true even of the United States. Participation in Social Security is mandatory, and the benefit formula is mildly progressive. Employer participation in unemployment insurance and workers' compensation insurance are also mandatory, though there is some variation depending on the state in which one lives. As I have noted, the social democracies of Western Europe also have forms of compulsory social insurance. Because of this commonality of social institutions, it is fair to say that modern American liberals are social democrats.

The commitment of modern American liberals to the reduction of inequalities in wealth and income has already been noted, but there are other close parallels between social democracy and modern liberalism that allow us to conclude that they are substantially the same at the level of social institutions. There is a willingness to subordinate the market to

[38] Jerald Hage, Robert Hanneman, and Edward T. Gargan, *State Responsiveness and State Activism* (London: Unwin and Hyman, 1989), 104.

[39] His two most important books are Gøsta Esping-Andersen, *Politics Against Markets: The Social Democratic Road to Power* (Princeton, NJ: Princeton University Press, 1985), and Anderson, *The Three Worlds of Welfare Capitalism* (Princeton, NJ: Princeton University Press, 1990). The typology of welfare states that follows in the text is discussed extensively in *The Three Worlds of Welfare Capitalism.*

[40] In this type of system, health care is financed by the government through tax payments. Most hospitals and clinics are owned by the government, and doctors are generally government employees.

[41] Recent changes in compulsory social insurance programs are discussed in Giuliano Bonoli, Vic George, and Peter Taylor-Gooby, *European Welfare Futures: Towards a Theory of Retrenchment* (Cambridge: Polity Press, 2000), 29–49.

politics in both social democracy and modern liberalism. One might say that according to modern liberalism and social democracy, the market is to be society's servant and not its master. For both viewpoints, this means that the state must correct for various real and perceived failings of the market. These failings involve problems with particular markets for which state action is seen as the proper corrective. Social democrats and modern liberals also believe that an almost irrational adherence to the ideology of laissez-faire is the primary motivation for the opposite preference—that is, a preference for markets over politics. This in part explains why social democrats and modern liberals both have an almost instinctive mistrust of markets.[42] The inequalities that emerge in a free market economy (e.g., inequalities in health care) further explain this mistrust.

For example, in a standard insurance contract, those with preexisting medical conditions would be charged a higher premium or would not be able to get insurance at all. Modern American liberals, as events in 2010 make clear, believe that health care should be heavily regulated to the point where markets have effectively ceased to exist. Underlying this objection to using markets is an egalitarian ideal which holds that the provision of health care should be (1) relatively equal and (2) not based on ability to pay. It would be hard to find a modern liberal or a social democrat who would dissent from either of those propositions. For many years, social democracies have had egalitarian health care systems not based on ability to pay, though there have been variations in the funding mechanisms.

The take-over of health care by the state is part of a larger strategy to immunize workers from the discipline of the market. As Esping-Andersen has written,

> the commodity status of labor in the market was always recognized as an impediment to collectivism. It nurtured competition and uncertainty, and it strenghtened the hand of the employer in bargaining. . . . [S]ocial reform could help free the workers to the extent that it de-commodified their status; i.e. reduced their dependence on market exchange. Guaranteed adequate benefits in the event of sickness, old age, and unemployment would naturally weaken the power of market exchange. . . .[43]

Talk of the commodification of labor—or, to be more exact, of labor power—reflects a Marxist way of thinking that would not occur to modern Amer-

---

[42] I have argued elsewhere that modern liberalism, as well as classical liberalism, should be conceived of as rules of thumb, heuristic devices, or even as expressions of attitudes about the proper role of government. See N. Scott Arnold, *Imposing Values* (New York: Oxford University Press, 2009), 7–8.
[43] Esping-Andersen, *Politics Against Markets*, 148.

ican liberals (unless they had read Marx!), but the basic problems and the social institutions intended to deal with those problems are essentially the same. The U.S. government has taken over the health care system, which has resulted in the further de-commodification of labor power. What would complete the process would be to remove the requirement that welfare benefits be means-tested. In light of the success of the Personal Responsibility and Work Opportunity Reconciliation Act of 1996 in the United States, however, this is not likely to happen. The main components of that act include ending welfare as an entitlement program. An entitlement program is an open-ended commitment on the part of the government to fund that program for all who are eligible. The act also requires welfare recipients to begin working no more than two years after receiving benefits and places a five-year limitation on benefits that one can receive from the federal government. It encourages two-parent families and discourages out-of-wedlock births. Finally, it includes a provision to enhance the enforcement of child support. Esping-Andersen has pointed out that in social democratic regimes,

> every nation has some type of means-tested social assistance or poor-relief arrangement. What counts most heavily in this type of regime are the restrictiveness of the means/incomes tests and the generosity of benefits. . . . [A]lmost all countries dominated by a people's welfare approach have developed earnings- and work-related schemes to complement the usually modest benefits awarded by the flat-rate universal plans. In short, every country today presents a system mix [i.e., a system which is in part means-tested].[44]

Some sort of means-testing, then, is a common feature of what used to be called "poor relief."

Nevertheless, there are new problems for the welfare state to deal with. Professor of social policy Giuliano Bonoli discusses what he calls the "new social risks."[45] In his essay "New Social Risks and the Politics of Post-Industrial Social Policies," he identifies five such risks or emerging social problems: (1) reconciling work and family life; (2) being a single parent; (3) having a frail relative; (4) possessing low or obsolescent skills; and (5) having insufficient social security coverage due to uneven labor-force participation.[46] Notice that Bonoli simply assumes that the government should deal with or address these social problems. The idea that there are some aspects of social life that are off limits to state involvement

---

[44] Esping-Andersen, *The Three Worlds of Welfare Capitalism*, 48, 49.

[45] Giuliano Bonoli, "New Social Risks and the Politics of Post-Industrial Social Policies," in *The Politics of Post-Industrial Welfare States: Adapting Post-War Social Policies to New Social Risks*, ed. Klaus Armingeon and Giuliano Bonoli (London and New York: Taylor and Francis Routledge, 2006), 3–26.

[46] Ibid., 6.

is foreign to the social democratic mind-set. With the rise of the nanny state in the U.S., the idea has become increasingly foreign to the thinking of modern American liberals as well. The U.S. government, however, has not explicitly addressed any of these social problems—but that may be a reflection of the political divisions in this country that have become progressively sharper in recent years. In the end, modern American liberals and European social democrats favor the same social institutions to deal with similar social problems.

III. CONCLUSION

The charge that modern American liberals are really socialists has often been made, but has not been well supported. The basis for this charge is that the incidents of ownership that comprise full liberal ownership have been gradually weakened to the point where they reside only nominally with private parties. When the state can tax and spend with impunity, and when it can impose whatever regulatory regimes it chooses without compensation, this is a clear indication that effective control of the means of production has passed from private hands to the state.

The case for the claim that modern American liberals are also social democrats is only slightly more controversial. This case rests on the fact that the institutions of social democracy are essentially the same as the institutions favored by modern American liberals. These institutions have been created to deal with specific problems of old age, unemployment, occupational health and safety, health care, and the relief of poverty among society's least advantaged members. This institutional agreement is best explained by the hypothesis that the welfare state favored by modern American liberals is, in reality, a form of social democracy.

Philosophy, University of Alabama at Birmingham

INDEX

Abortion, 6, 7
Adams, John, 58
Advantage, 173, 243
Agricultural Adjustment Act (1933), 102
AIG, 159
Amar, Akhil Reed, 8
American Economics Association, 154
American founding, 262
Anarchism, 140
Anti-gouging laws, 204–6
Antislavery movement, 107, 116
Aristotle, 159
Armstrong v. The State of Montana (1999), 6, 7
Arneson, Richard, 232–61
Arnold, N. Scott, 262–82
Atlas Shrugged, 9
Austrian economics, 23 n. 5
Authority: moral, 77–101
Autonomy, 131

Baier, Kurt, 75, 84, 97
Bastiat, Frederic, 13, 202
Bear Stearns, 135, 159, 161
Beattie v Fleet National Bank (2000), 7
Beccaria, Cesare, 2
Becker, Gary, 20 n. 1
Belief: freedom of, 6; moral *versus* religious, 79
Bentham, Jeremy, 2, 9, 38
Bequests (rights of), 33
Best Alternative to a Negotiated Agreement (BATNA), 196–97
Bills of Attainder, 112
Boorse, Christopher, 172, 180
Brennan, Justice William, 104
Brown v. Board of Education (1954), 43 n. 54
Buchanan, Allen, 184
Buchanan, James, 20 n. 1, 214
Bundling, 213–20, 228–29
Bush, George W., 137

California Supreme Court, 104
Campaign spending, 28
Cap-and-trade legislation, 213
Capital, 22
Capitalism, 22, 23, 25, 27, 35, 38, 39, 74, 103, 109, 131, 167, 209; criticism of, 30; definition of, 233

Caplan, Arthur, 266
Careers open to talents, 42–43
Caring, 235
Categorical imperative, 8
Catholicism, 78
Center for American Progress, 56
Centralization, 240
Chamber or Commerce, 30
Chapters on Socialism (1879), 16–17
Charity, 26
Chrysler, 135
Citigroup, 160
Civil Rights Act of 1957, 43 n. 54
Civil Rights Act of 1964, 43 n. 54, 44, 46
Civil War, 104, 107
Class, 194; and economics, 22
Classical liberalism, 26
Clean Water Act (1972), 272
Clinton, Bill, 56
Clinton, Hillary, 56
Coercion, 236
Cohen, G. A., 91–92, 233–61
Communal equality, 250
Communal reciprocity, 235, 250–51
Communism, 15, 74
Community, 235
Competition, 17; economic, 17
Condorcet, Marquis de, 223
Conflict: class, 22
Congress (United States), 104
Conscience: individual, 83
Constitutional amendment: American process of, 67
Constitutionalism: organic, 67
Consumption: owners' abstention from, 39
Contract, 64, 67, 131, 195; freedom of, 20, 43
Contracts, 21; economic, 44–45
Contribution, to productive output: de facto *versus* de jure, 40
Corruption, 212
Covention, 33–34
Cowen, Tyler, 212–231
Crunch of 2008, 136, 148, 153
Cullen v. Auclair (2002), 7
Cummings v. Missouri (1866), 110, 113–15

Daniels's Principle, 176, 186, 190
Daniels, Norman, 166–91
Declaration of Independence, American (1776), 57–73, 105, 116

283

Property equilibrium, 89, 95
Property rights, 29–30, 47, 52–53, 57, 59–60, 63, 66, 69, 71, 72, 85, 89, 90, 92, 97, 100, 109, 117, 122, 127–28, 133, 206; allocation of, 87; and expediency, 68; in American Declaration of Independence, 65; intellectual, 146–50
Property-owning democracy, 51; in Rawls, 41, 49
Protectionism, 15–16
Protestantism, 78
Public good, 24
Public health, 169
Public interest, 128
Public reason, 28
Public-private distinction, 131
Punishment, 118

Rand, Ayn, 9, 20 n. 2, 91
Randolph, Judge A. Raymond, 8
Rational reflection: and justice, 75
Rationing, 171
Rawls, John, 54; as belonging to the high liberal tradition, 27; on distributive justice, 267; on economic justice, 29; on economic liberties, 31; on equality of opportunity, 171; on the social minimum, 208; principles of justice, 48; theory of justice, 74; two principles of justice, 27–28, 173
Raz, Joseph, 75
Reciprocity, 241
Reconstruction Era, 104
Redistribution, 13, 14, 20 n. 2, 241
Reference class, 181
Regulation, 12; right of, 127
Regulatory powers, 161
Rent-seeking, 138
Replicator dynamic, 86
Reputation: and reciprocity, 93–95
Ricardo, David, 20 n. 1, 25
Right of exit, from contracts, 45
Right of inheritance, 15
Right reason, 80
Rights, 8, 271; and alienability, 20–21; and utility, 2; basic, 19; conventional, 143; economic, 20; in John Stuart Mill, 2, 3; individual, 8–9, 57, 62, 74, 80, 116; institutional, 31; nature of, 84; of individuals, 168; of property, 40; of the capitalist, 39–40; of women, 11; to abortion, 6, 7; to life, 123; to refuse medical treatment, 6
Rights, individual, 1, 67
Risk, 152–53
Roemer, John, 41 n. 50
Roosevelt, Franklin D., 63, 64, 73, 102; 68
Roosevelt, Theodore, 62, 67–68, 69, 73
Rothbard, Murray, 20 n. 2

Rousseau, Jean-Jacques, 62, 63; contract theory of, 84
Rule of law, 24
Rules: moral, 98
Rules-based perspective, 212–231

Sanctity of Conscience thesis, 77, 83, 99
Sarkozy, Nicolas, 136
Say, J. B., 20 n. 1
Schumpeter, Joseph, 20 n. 1
Schwartz, Anna, 154
Searle, John, 39
Securities and Exchange Commission, 138
Segregation, 43–44
Self-determination, 169, 178; in Locke, 166
Self-government, 3, 4, 53
Self-interest, 89, 140, 238
Self-ownership, 20 n. 2, 79
Sixteenth Amendment to U.S. Constitution, 73
Slaughterhouse Cases (1873), 103, 107, 120–25
Slavery, 9, 10
Small business, 22
Smith, Adam, 20 n. 1, 23–24, 42, 148, 166–67; and utilitarianism, 25; influence on judicial liberalism, 105; on property, 35, 122; on publicly funded education, 46; on the invisible hand, 139; on the market
Social Authority of Private Conscience thesis, 77, 82–3, 98
Social contract theory, 57–58, 61–63; of Locke, 66, 79, 82, 100, 122, 268
Social Darwinism, 105
Social democracy, 140, 273–74
Social minimum, 207
Socialism, 15, 16–17, 41, 140, 234, 249; definition of, 262–63
Socialization: of financial loss, 160
Solidarity, 241
Sovereign: as voice of public reason, 81
Sovereignty: individual, 3, 8, 10, 12
Special interest, 70
Spencer, Herbert, 13, 104–05, 223
Square Deal, the, 72
Stalin, 8
Stanford, Leland, 105
State: authority of, 83
State of nature: in Hobbes, 142
States, 99
Steiner, 21 n. 2
Stigler, George, 208, 222
Subsistence needs, 25–26
Substantive due process, 102, 103, 108
Surplus, 40

Talents, 174, 188
Tax, 241

Taxation, 129, 180
Taxes, 219, 240, 264, 265
Test oath cases, 110–120, 118, 119
Time consistency logic, 213–14
Tocqueville, Alexis de, 4, 42
Trade, 200
Transaction costs, 217
Troubled Asset Relief Program (TARP), 156
Tyranny, 4

United States, 42, 43
United States Constitution, 103
United States Supreme Court, 7, 28, 43
n. 54, 102, 103, 108
Utilitarianism, 2, 8, 23, 216, 226; and liberalism, 25; in liberal traditions, 52
Utility, 8–9, 10, 11, 72, 91; and individual rights, 2; in John Stuart Mill, 3; principle of, 30–31
Utopianism, 216–231

Vallentyne, Peter, 21 n. 2
Value, 200–01
Value at Risk (VaR) models, 158
Van Donselaar, Gijs, 90
Vertical integration, 271
Virginia Declaration of Rights (1776), 58

Voluntary marketplace, 12
Voluntary society, 9
Voting Rights Act of 1965, 43 n. 54

Wage relationship, 50
Wall, Steven, 77
Warren Courtism, 103
Wealth, 13–14, 17, 30; distributions of, 192
Wealth of Nations, 24–25
Weitzman, Martin, 41 n. 50
Welfare, 25, 52, 72, 91, 169
Welfare rights, 279
Welfare state, 25, 167
Welfare-state capitalism, 49
Well-being, 9, 10, 177, 247–50; objective-list accounts, 258–60
Wilson, Woodrow, 61, 63, 65, 66, 67, 69
Wilt Chamberlain example, 199–200
Work, 17
Workers, 22
Workers' Associations, 51
Workers' compensation, 68
Working class, 17
Working classes, 54

Zoning, 21
Zuckert, Michael, 59, 102–34